# HENRY WELLCOME

OTHER WORKS BY ROBERT RHODES JAMES

*Lord Randolph Churchill* (1959)

*An Introduction to the House of Commons* (1961)

*Rosebery* (1963)

*Gallipoli* (1965)

(Edited) *Chips – The Diaries of Sir Henry Channon* (1967)

*Memoirs of a Conservative: J. C. C. Davidson* (1968)

*Churchill – A Study In Failure, 1900–39* (1970)

*Ambitions and Realities: British Politics 1964–70* (1972)

(Edited) *The Complete Speeches of Sir Winston Churchill* (eight volumes; 1974)

*Victor Cazalet: A Portrait* (1975)

*The British Revolution, 1880–1939* (two volumes, 1976 and 1977)

*Albert, Prince Consort* (1983)

*Anthony Eden* (1986)

*Bob Boothby: A Portrait* (1991)

FRONTISPIECE Henry Wellcome. Etching by Max Schulz after H. van der Weyde, 1890 (*Wellcome Institute Library, London*)

# HENRY WELLCOME

Robert Rhodes James

*A John Curtis Book*
Hodder & Stoughton

First published in 1994
by Hodder and Stoughton
A division of Hodder Headline PLC



10 9 8 7 6 5 4 3 2 1



**British Library Cataloguing in Publication Data**

James, Robert Rhodes
Henry Wellcome. – (John Curtis Books)
I. Title II. Series
338.4361072092

ISBN 0-340-60617-7

Photoset in Linotron Ehrhardt by
Rowland Phototypesetting Ltd, Bury St Edmunds, Suffolk

Printed and bound in Great Britain by
Mackays of Chatham plc, Chatham, Kent

Hodder and Stoughton Ltd
A Division of Hodder Headline PLC
338 Euston Road
London NW1 3BH

FOR MEGAN

*from Sweet Aleck*

*and her Grandfather*

# Contents

# Illustrations

Henry Wellcome on horseback and J. Baiz 'on the hurricane deck of a mule, our trip through Central and South America', 1878 (*Wellcome Centre Medical Photographic Library*)

Silas Mainville Burroughs (1846–95) (*Wellcome Group Archives, London*)

Henry Wellcome in 1880 at the inauguration of his partnership with Burroughs (*Wellcome Centre Medical Photographic Library*)

Snow Hill Buildings on the corner of Snow Hill and Holborn Viaduct, London, which served as the head office of Burroughs Wellcome & Co. from 1883 until destroyed by bombing in 1941 (*Wellcome Centre Medical Photographic Library*)

Pharmaceutical samples offered for sale by Henry Wellcome when a salesman for McKesson & Robbins (*Wellcome Centre Medical Photographic Library*)

Burroughs Wellcome products on display at the International Medical and Sanitary Exhibition, London, 1881 (*Wellcome Centre Medical Photographic Library*)

The interior of the head office of Burroughs Wellcome & Co. at Snow Hill, designed by Henry Wellcome with Moorish motifs and the Statue of Liberty (*Wellcome Institute Library, London*)

The Wandsworth factory of Burroughs Wellcome & Co., 1883–9 (*Wellcome Centre Medical Photographic Library*)

The opening of the Dartford factory of Burroughs Wellcome & Co. in 1889, with a firework display, organised by Burroughs, forming the words 'Welcome to Henry George'. Wood engraving published in *The Pictorial World*, 11 July 1889 (*Wellcome Centre Medical Photographic Library*)

Speeches at the opening of the Dartford factory of Burroughs Wellcome & Co. in 1889. Wood engraving published in *The Pictorial World*, 11 July 1889 (*Wellcome Centre Medical Photographic Library*)

Transport of raw materials by Thames barge on to the site of the Dartford factory, 1895 (*Wellcome Group Archives, London*)

The Tabloid compressing machine designed and made between 1900 and 1910 at the Wellcome Chemical Works, Dartford (*Wellcome Centre Medical Photographic Library*)

BETWEEN PAGES 140 AND 141

'Ozozo brightens pale complexions', 1927 (*Wellcome Group Archives, London*)

'Wellcome Toilet Lanoline for petal smooth skin' (*Wellcome Group Archives, London*)

'Beautiful hands kept beautiful by using Wellcome Toilet Lanoline', 1929 (*Wellcome Group Archives, London*)

'Kepler Cod Liver Oil with malt extract' (*Wellcome Group Archives, London*)

'Kepler Solution' (*Wellcome Group Archives, London*)

'Kepler Solution' (*Wellcome Group Archives, London*)

'Chinese-style' calendar for 1887 printed on one of Burroughs Wellcome & Co.'s own products, paper-fibre lint, used as a promotional gift (*Wellcome Group Archives, London*)

BETWEEN PAGES 268 AND 269

Syrie Wellcome *née* Barnardo (1879–1955). Drypoint by Paul-César Helleu (*Wellcome Institute Library, London*)

Henry and Syrie Wellcome (*Wellcome Institute Library, London*)

Syrie Wellcome with Henry Mounteney Wellcome (*Wellcome Institute Library, London*)

Wellcome on a collecting tour in Spain and Portugal in 1908. The photograph of the car was probably taken by Wellcome; inside is his courier and interpreter John Ferreira (*Wellcome Centre Medical Photographic Library*)

Syrie Wellcome entertaining General Adolphus Washington Greely (1844–1935) and guests at The Nest (*Wellcome Centre Medical Photographic Library*)

Walter Dowson, Director of the Wellcome Physiological Research Laboratories from 1899 to 1906 (*Wellcome Institute Library, London*)

Scientific staff of the Wellcome Physiological Research Laboratories, 1906: C. T. Symons, Henry Hallett Dale, Walter Dowson, H. J. Sudmersen, George Barger (*Wellcome Institute Library, London*)

General William Crawford Gorgas (*Wellcome Institute Library, London*)

The Wellcome Bureau of Scientific Research in Gordon Street, on the site of the later Wellcome Research Institution (Wellcome Building), with gardens to right along Euston Road (*Wellcome Institute Library, London*)

The stonework for the Wellcome Research Institution (Wellcome Building) at Trollope and Colls's yard, with Henry Wellcome and the architect Septimus Warwick, 1931 (*Wellcome Institute Library, London*)

The Wellcome Research Institution's building, Euston Road, London (the present Wellcome Building), constructed 1931–2 (*Wellcome Centre Medical Photographic Library*)

Entrance Hall of the Wellcome Research Institution (Wellcome Building), 1932 (*Wellcome Centre Medical Photographic Library*)

The Pocahontas portrait presented by Henry Wellcome to the Senate of the United States in 1899 (*Wellcome Centre Medical Photographic Library*)

Father William Duncan (1832–1918), founder of the Metlakahtla Mission (*Wellcome Centre Medical Photographic Library*)

Sir Henry Wellcome with Captain Peter Johnston-Saint (1886–1974), Conservator of the Wellcome Historical Medical Museum, at St Augustine, Florida, 1935 (*Wellcome Centre Medical Photographic Library*)

Dr Paira Mall (1874–1957), collector of Indian manuscripts and paintings for Sir Henry Wellcome, 1910–25 (*Wellcome Institute Library, London*)

Ada Misner (later Reed), Sir Henry Wellcome's secretary (*Wellcome Institute Library, London*)

Sir Henry Wellcome. Photograph by Clarence Sterns, 1932 (*Wellcome Institute Library, London*)

BETWEEN PAGES 332 AND 333

A miraculous surgical operation by Saints Cosmas and Damian. Oil painting on panel by Alonso de Sedano, Burgos, *c.* 1495. Bought for Wellcome by Peter Johnston-Saint in Spain in 1930, and now no. CC 8164 in the Iconographic Collections of the Wellcome Institute Library (*Wellcome Institute Library, London*)

*The Wellcome Apocalypse*, a German manuscript of the early fifteenth century containing sacred, medical and allegorical texts, richly illustrated. Bought by

Wellcome at Sotheby's in December 1931 for £2,300 and now Western Manuscript no. 49 in the Wellcome Institute Library (*Wellcome Institute Library, London*)

The *Horoscope of Iskandar Sultan*, Shiraz, AD 1411. Formerly in the collection of the orientalist John Herbert Harington (d. 1828). Bought by Wellcome at Sotheby's in 1923 for £6 15s, now Persian Manuscript no. 474 in the Wellcome Institute Library (*Wellcome Institute Library, London*)

Saint Catherine of Siena, *The orcharde of Syon . . . with ghostly fruytes & precyous plantes for the helthe of mannes soule*, London, printed by Wynkyn de Worde, 1519. Bought at Sotheby's for £151 in December 1898, this is one of many books which Wellcome acquired from the library of William Morris. Now Early Printed Book no. 1377 in the Wellcome Institute Library (*Wellcome Institute Library, London*)

A Chinese acupuncture figure, seventeenth century (?), bought by Wellcome in 1917. Wellcome Museum of the History of Medicine, the Science Museum, London, no. A 604024 (*Science and Society Picture Library*)

An iron manikin following the forms of the human body as published by Fabricius ab Aquapendente in 1614. Bought by Wellcome at Stevens's auction house in London in 1928. Wellcome Museum of the History of Medicine, the Science Museum, London, no. A 73318 (*Science and Society Picture Library*)

The Giustiniani medicine chest. Named after Vincenzo Giustiniani, *podestà* of Chios 1562–6, who is believed to have been its first owner. Acquired by Wellcome in Rome in 1924. Wellcome Museum of the History of Medicine, the Science Museum, London, no. A 651515 (*Science and Society Picture Library*)

Three Italian pharmacy jars from the many (some original, some replicas) in the Wellcome Museum of the History of Medicine. Wellcome Museum of the History of Medicine, the Science Museum, London, nos. A 43087–8 (*Science and Society Picture Library*)

John Bell and Co. pharmacy, 225 (formerly 338) Oxford Street. John Bell's pharmacy was open on this site from 1798 to 1908, after which the firm merged with Croyden and Co. of 55 Wigmore Street to form the firm of John Bell and Croyden Ltd. Wellcome acquired the old shop for his museum in 1908 when it was rescued from demolition by his museum curator C. J. S. Thompson. Wellcome Museum of the History of Medicine, the Science Museum, London. (*Wellcome Centre Medical Photographic Library*)

An English wing-fronted medicine cabinet from Richard Reece's Medical Hall, 171 Piccadilly, 1813. Wellcome Museum of the History of Medicine, the Science Museum, London, no. A 630142 (*Science and Society Picture Library*)

French etching with gouache satirising vaccination, 1800. Bought for Wellcome by Peter Johnston-Saint on one of his collecting trips in Paris and now in the Iconographic Collections, Wellcome Institute Library (catalogue no. 16129) (*Wellcome Institute Library, London*)

Physiognomical heads of terracotta for diagnosis of human character traits, nineteenth century. Wellcome Museum of the History of Medicine, the Science Museum, London, no. A 642804 (*Science and Society Picture Library*)

A gallery in the Wellcome Museum of the History of Medicine at the Science Museum, 1994, showing some of the museum objects collected by Wellcome. In the foreground, a statue of St Sebastian, patron saint of plague-sufferers (*Science and Society Picture Library*)

The Reading Room of the Wellcome Institute Library in the Wellcome Building, 1994. The Library holds the printed books, manuscripts, paintings, prints and other documents collected by Wellcome (*Wellcome Centre Medical Photographic Library*)

LINE ILLUSTRATIONS IN THE TEXT

# *Preface*

Biography is perhaps one of the most difficult of all historical and literary ventures, because it involves not only the compilation of material and its understanding, but also the attempt, which can never be wholly satisfactory, to enter the soul of the subject and to create an honest account of a life as well as to present a portrait. In this laborious and sensitive process the biographer is, as has been rightly said, 'an artist upon oath'.

All my endeavours at writing biography have been undertaken about men who were well known and distinguished in their lifetimes, but whose existing biographies seemed to me to be capable of revision in the light of later knowledge and a longer perspective, and whose fame has endured. The sole exception was Victor Cazalet, whose biography I wrote at the request of his sister; but although he was killed relatively young, he was a well-known Member of Parliament in the 1930s and early 1940s.

Henry Wellcome, eminent, if enigmatic, in his lifetime, is today virtually unknown, although his company and creations continue his name, not only in the Wellcome Foundation, his pharmaceutical company, but also in the Trust and Institute for the History of Medicine that he founded. The Trust's role in modern contemporary British medical research and funding has become one of major importance, as Wellcome had hoped and intended. He was, in his life and after his death in 1936, the most generous benefactor ever to British medical science, eventually on a scale far greater than even he could have envisaged.

But the man himself is now forgotten, both in America and in Britain. There are few alive now who had even met him, and then only in his old age, when he was withdrawn and reclusive. His Trustees commissioned a biography of him in 1939 by Mr A. W. J. Haggis, of the Wellcome Historical Medical Museum, whose first draft was delivered in 1942. It was a worthy and very lengthy production, but the Trustees were dissatisfied and decided against publication. However, his typescript has been made available to authors and historians. The Wellcome Foundation and the Wellcome Trust have published two brief factual biographies of Wellcome, and other studies of real merit and interest, but with a limited readership.

Some of Wellcome's personal papers were destroyed after his death by his Trustees, and others, both personal and relating to the company, were lost when the company's offices at Snow Hill, Holborn, in London, were bombed in 1941. But a remarkable quantity have survived, and have been brought together and catalogued with great skill and dedication. Other archives, in the United States as well as in this country, have also provided material relating to Wellcome's life and career. Also, Haggis did not strive in vain, as he saw and quoted from papers and letters that were lost in the destruction of the Snow Hill offices, and which I have found valuable. Haggis had the further advantage, obviously denied to me, of having known Wellcome – admittedly in the later period of his life – and several of his insights into his character I have found shrewd and sensitive. I understand why the Wellcome Trustees decided not to publish his book, but it has been far more useful to me than I had expected when I first read it.

When the Wellcome Trustees, at the suggestion of my friend Philip Ziegler, approached me to ask if I would write Wellcome's full biography, my own knowledge of him was limited to the outlines of his life and achievements. However, I was greatly attracted by the idea of embarking on a field of biography that was totally new to me, and was intrigued by the prospect of working on the life of a man about whom so little is known. All biographies are journeys of discovery, but few more than this one.

I was particularly struck by a comment made by Mr Leslie Matthews, who is one of the few people alive who knew Wellcome, at the beginning of my researches:

> I was wondering which Wellcome you are writing about – there were lots of Wellcomes: Wellcome, the Man about Town; Wellcome, the Collector; Wellcome, the Businessman; Wellcome, the introspective man after his wife had been taken from him; Wellcome, the man disappointed with his son; Wellcome, the Archaeologist.

Indeed, this list could have been even longer.

Sir Henry Dale, one of Wellcome's most inspired appointments, and later one of his first Trustees and a subsequent Chairman of the Trustees, in a moment of exasperation added 'Wellcome, the poseur', which he knew was unfair, but was interesting because it reflected another view of Wellcome, held by many.

The Wellcome Trustees promised me full support and assistance, and have given me both. I owe particular debts of gratitude to Mr John Davies, the Wellcome Foundation's archivist, and Miss Julia Sheppard of the Contemporary Medical Archives Centre, and their colleagues, including Mr William Schupbach and Mr John Symons of the Wellcome Institute of the History of Medicine, who have been immensely helpful throughout my researches; and my special gratitude is for Miss Nicola Perrin – herself the granddaughter of a distinguished Chairman of the Wellcome Foundation, Sir Michael Perrin – who spent several months with me going through the Wellcome and other papers copying and collating them, and conducting other research. As I was for part of that time still an active Member of Parliament, her work was even more important and helpful.

In the United States, I am particularly grateful to my kind friends and hosts in Madison, Wisconsin, James and Mary Alice Wimmer; Dr Nicholas Muller, the Director of the Wisconsin State Historical Society, with whose invaluable help I was able to find the original

Wellcome Wisconsin farm, and Mr Michael Stevens; Dr Gregory Higby of the American Institute of the History of Pharmacy in Madison, and Mrs Doreen Nemec for her assistance with the papers of Frederick B. Power; Mr John Benz, the County Clerk at Waushara County Court House in Wautoma, and Mrs Janet Schumacher, the Deputy Registrar of Deeds, who were also very much involved in the quest for the Wellcome farm; Dr Timothy Glines and the staff of the superb new Minnesota Historical Center in St Paul; Dr Edward D. Henderson, the Chairman of the Mayo Historical Committee; Dr Caroline Beck of the Mayo Foundation; the Principal and staff of the Wellcome Memorial School in Garden City, and Mr Ernest Hanson, who showed me around Garden City; and the members of the Historical Association of Blue Earth County, Mankato, who were able to provide me with valuable original material on the early history of Garden City.

I am also very grateful to Dr E. M. Tansey for permitting me to read, and quote from, her admirable and very detailed unpublished University of London thesis on the early scientific career of Sir Henry Dale; to my friend and former Cambridge constituent, Lord Butterfield, for his careful analysis of Wellcome's illnesses between 1885 and 1898, which was of considerable value; to Mrs Diana Magee of the Griffith Institute of the Ashmolean Museum, Oxford, for her assistance on the Sudan archaeological archives; to the Librarian of the Royal Geographical Society for access to the papers of H. M. Stanley; to the Librarian of the University of Durham for access to the Wingate papers and the Sudan Archive; and to Lady Wagner, the biographer of Thomas Barnardo, and the University of Liverpool for access to the Barnardo papers.

Again, I am indebted to my secretary and dear family friend, Polly Andrews, who, like me, flits happily between current political events and historical biography, for endless typing and retyping; and to John Curtis, the wisest of editors and advisers. Once again I am profoundly grateful to Linda Osband for her meticulous editing of the final typescript and much good advice.

# PREFACE

What began as a somewhat daunting task, as Henry Wellcome's papers were considerably more voluminous, and his character more complex, than I had expected, became a pleasure, and I am very grateful to everyone in the Wellcome 'family' for their friendliness and interest in the project, especially Sir Roger Gibbs, the Chairman of the Governors of the Wellcome Trust, the Governors themselves, Dr Peter Williams, the former Director of the Trust, and Dr Bridget Ogilvie, his successor.

*

Wellcome became an elusive personality to his contemporaries and staff in his later years, and has certainly been one to his biographer, who laments the destruction of so many of his personal papers. But although the full story of the tragedy of his marriage has suffered from this, enough material remains to correct other versions that have seriously misled writers interested in the life of Syrie Wellcome, better known to posterity as Syrie Maugham. I am especially grateful to her daughter, Lady Glendevon, for her assistance in dealing with a particularly painful episode in her mother's life.

The lives of successful entrepreneurs are not often interesting. This one was extraordinary, and I am deeply grateful to have been given the opportunity of exploring it.

*Robert Rhodes James*
The Stone House
Great Gransden
Near Sandy, Bedfordshire

# I

# An American Upbringing

There is a considerable frustration in researching the histories of most families, and their antecedents, as too often we have only bare outlines. We have, if we explore dutifully, the simple facts of birth, marriage, offspring and death. But that is all. We ask, vainly, who *were* they? What did they *do*? What work did they undertake? What did they *feel*, or *think*, or *suffer*, or be *joyous* about? And what did they even *look* like? Even with the well known and famous there are alarmingly large gaps in our knowledge and understanding, but with the vast mass of humanity the search is difficult and the results are unsatisfactory. Thus, the historian is confronted with a daunting multitude of The Unknown.

Family legend, firmly believed by Henry Wellcome, was that a French family called Bienvenue emigrated to England at the end of the sixteenth century and, understandably, changed its name to Wellcome, although why with two lls is unclear. In the last decades of the sixteenth century Europe was convulsed with bitter religious hatreds, from which England was beginning to emerge, and which were especially virulent in France. The actual expulsion of the Protestant Huguenots took place after the Bienvenues took refuge in Protestant England, but the reason for their decision was clearly religious. The persecution, and eventual expulsion, of one of the most talented and significant parts of the French nation was an act of immense and enduring folly, and not least because one of the principal beneficiaries was France's rival and long-standing enemy, England.

We know little about the Wellcomes. Nor do we know why one member of this family, Richard Wellcome, decided to take the perilous voyage to America in the 1640s and to settle in the Isles of Shoals off the east coast of New England,* although we can assume that, again, the reasons were principally religious, as was the case in the majority of the English emigrants to New England at that time. We do know that in 1664 he married Eleanor Urin, the widow of 'a fisheries master of Star Island', had issue, and established his family as farmers and fishermen in Maine. They had a son, also named Richard, born in 1690, who married Elizabeth Hodgskin. They too had a son, Zaccheus, who was born in June 1722 and who married Alice McCarty, whose son Michael Wellcome was born in Gloucester, Massachusetts, on 20 December 1746. He was to live until 1825, and is the first Wellcome of whom we have any real knowledge.

In 1770 Michael Wellcome married Judith Ball (1752–1825), and they had eleven children, six girls and five boys, most of whom died young. But Timothy, who was born in 1780 and who married Mary Cummings of Paris, Maine, on 3 February 1814, after he had served in the American army in the war of 1812 against the British, gives us the first clear evidence of a Wellcome that is not simply a name on an elaborate family tree.

In Maine the Wellcomes had been farmers owning smallholdings rather than farms, making modest livings and remaining strongly religious. Their sagas were quite typical. The land was poor and the climate was severely inhospitable, but their needs were simple, and if they did not prosper greatly, nor did they suffer too much. New England farming was difficult, but, until the prairies of the West were conquered in the 1850s, it provided a reasonable living.

* The speciality of the Isles of Shoals was dun-fish; in Maine this was originally split cod cured in a manure pile, and thereby 'dunned', but in the Isles, where manure was in short supply, the split fish were piled in a dark building and covered with grass and salt hay. It was a great delicacy, much favoured by the Kings of Spain in the eighteenth century for their Good Friday repast. See Samuel Eliot Morison, *The European Discovery of America, The Northern Voyages* (Oxford University Press, 1971), p. 491.

Mary Cummings Wellcome has been described somewhat bleakly by a contemporary as 'a woman of strong moral and religious principles, and her impress was left upon her posterity'. Her husband Timothy left little 'impress' upon anyone, but he comes down to us as a good, kindly and ineffectual man, dominated by his wife and her Quaker family and beliefs.

On 29 August 1813 Timothy Wellcome wrote to his future wife:

> My dear and affectionate girl, the time has been but short since I saw you although to me it hath seemed verry long I calculate to be at Monot by the third Sunday of September we have progressed verry well in selling crops my health has been verry good since I came from home and I hope yours has been the same I persume you have enjoyed yourself verry well since I left Monot I send you these lines for you know that I sometimes think of you. I remain your lover, Timothy Wellcome.*

In another letter to her written on 27 July 1817, he said:

> You must be careful of the Children and goods and bring as many goods as you think we shall want and fail not of starting by Monday Next as I am impatiently waiting to se you. Your ever loving husband, Timothy Wellcome.

Timothy Wellcome's limited grasp of grammar and spelling was not surprising, because there is a letter from his father, Michael:

> We have none to depend upon but 1 bushel and half of weat are our milk buter and cheas our beef is spitt as to money I cant git a cent one head one doler I let Mr Whitehouse have it to go down east and he got none. From your most obedient Parent Michael Wellcome.

From all the letters to her it is very clear that Mary Cummings Wellcome was a formidable woman. She was respected, but apparently

* This and subsequent letters are reproduced exactly as they were written.

not loved, by her friends and relatives; however, the kind and simple Timothy was. One friend wrote to her before her marriage that,

> when a person has nothing to do he is almost always tempted to do wrong. You need not urge Timothy to do good; he loves to do it. A young man so learned and virtuous as Timothy is I think promising to be a very useful member of society. Therefore I think you will not do better [than to marry him].

Timothy and Mary Wellcome had eight children, two of whom died in childhood.* Of the others, the most remarkable was Jacob, born in 1825; two years later Solomon was born, in Freeman, Maine.

It was in Maine that they were brought up and educated, in a poor farming family, sincere and God-fearing. But for both Jacob and Solomon the life that the Wellcomes had endured for two centuries was stultifying and inadequate. Their father's farm made a poor living, and Solomon's surviving records show that he worked not only for his father, but also for other farmers. His education had been a fair one, but not as good as that given to his elder brother, Jacob; whereas Solomon left school early to work on the farm, Jacob graduated from the high school at Hallowell at the age of twenty-one and studied medicine, becoming a qualified physician and surgeon. But there are no indications of jealousy on Solomon's part; he was by all accounts a gentle young man, somewhat physically frail and without Jacob's intellectual abilities, with a mild and unambitious temperament, yet with a desire to move and travel.

There is a curious silence in their papers about their parents, and especially their mother. They were respectful of both, but there is a conspicuous lack of reference in their letters – and those of their grandchildren – to Mary Cummings Wellcome. Her death in 1881 aroused remarkably little emotion in her family, whereas Timothy

* Michael (1815–93); Isaac Cummings (1816–17); Isaac Cummings (1818–95); Louisa (1822–3); Jacob (1825–1906); Solomon Cummings (1827–76); Mary Elizabeth (1829–1921); and Cyrus (1834–70).

was deeply loved, and his death in Garden City, Minnesota, in 1872 was genuinely mourned.

In the late 1840s Jacob and Solomon read of vast new opportunities opening up as the great movement to the West began. Both had a restless disposition and, as prospects in Maine were poor and getting poorer, like so many Easterners they looked to the West for what was thought to be a glittering new life.

Thus, in 1849, twenty-one-year-old Solomon Wellcome and a group of others made the long and difficult journey of over a thousand miles from Freeman, Maine, to Wisconsin. As he had little money, he could not buy his own land in Wisconsin, but worked for others until he met and married Mary Curtis in 1850. Among her many attractions was the fact that she owned some thirteen acres of land just south of Almond, in Portage County. Solomon was authorised by Power of Attorney by his wife

> to do all the work on the farm, or lease it as he sees fit, take care of the crops and dispose of them when raised at any time he thinks best, and to do all or any business on the said premises that needs to be done.

Solomon urged his parents to join them, and between them they farmed some forty acres.

The Curtis family was considerably more distinguished than the Wellcomes. According to family legend, although there are no facts to prove it, one of Mary Curtis's ancestors was John Eliot – a particularly interesting man for Henry Wellcome's biographer.

Eliot was an assistant teacher at the grammar school of Little Baddow in Essex. He became a strict Puritan and, unable to fulfil the tests imposed by the English Church, was deprived of his licence to act as a schoolmaster. Eliot, who had long desired to enter the ministry, now decided to seek freedom of conscience in the New World, and in 1631 he sailed from Kent for Boston, accompanied by his wife, Mary Curteis, or Curtis, of Appledore in Kent, and a party of sixty emigrants.

Eliot became a Presbyterian minister within a year of his arrival and, while engaged in ministering to his fellow colonists, he was moved with sympathy towards the native Americans, whose wigwams were scattered around. He had probably no intention of becoming a missionary pioneer when first he parted from his mother country, but when he saw the miserable conditions under which the Indians lived he conceived a plan by which they might be collected in settlements of their own. Having, by the aid of a native, learned the language of the Iroquois, and with much skill and patience constructed a grammar of the language, he commenced in 1646, that 'Great work among the aborigines which is indelibly associated with his name'.

He convened a meeting of Indians and whites, and after a conference of about three hours he returned home highly pleased with the success of his first visit. As a result, he repeated this convocation. At the Indians' request, he then acquired from the Government some land on which they built themselves a town. This was the beginning of several settlements. Helped by funds from England, Eliot built a college and taught the Indians trades. In 1651 he laid the foundations of the town of Natick on the Charles River, and by dividing the Indians into hundreds and tens, caused them to elect rulers for each division on a plan similar to that then employed in Britain. Governor Endicott, visiting the town, said, 'I count this one of the best journeys I have made for many years.' In 1652 a book entitled *Tears of Repentance*, being confessions of a number of Indians at their belief in Christianity, was published and sent to England, dedicated to Oliver Cromwell, a more congenial national leader to Eliot than those he had left.

The enormous task which Eliot undertook of giving the Indians the Bible in their own tongue was completed between 1662 and 1663, and a copy of this literary masterpiece is treasured in Yale University. He also published an Indian grammar.

Tragically, the endeavours of this remarkable man failed when the Indians turned against the white men. Eliot, now seventy-one years of age, had to endure the agony of seeing the town he had founded entirely ruined. 'Broken in health, and spent with labour, Eliot was gradually obliged to relinquish his work, and to hand over his duties to an assistant.' He died on 20 May 1699 at the great age of eighty-seven.

However, other Curtises came to America to join Eliot's widow, in Maine. They became farmers and brickmakers, traders and missionaries. In 1818 Ebenezer Curtis (1793–1877) married Sarah Dingley (1794–1893). They first lived and farmed in Bowderham, Maine, and then moved to Kenneboc County; in 1843 they moved again, to Newburgh, in Penobscot County. They had nine children, of whom the second was Mary, born on 10 January 1821, at Bowderham.

The Curtis family, like the Wellcomes, took the long and arduous trail by waggon to the empty, but allegedly lush, pastures of Wisconsin. And there, in Almond, Mary met Solomon Wellcome and married him on 12 April 1850.

*

The Wellcome and Curtis families had one thing in common: they were deeply religious; indeed, three of Timothy's sons were to become ordained ministers. Solomon and Mary Wellcome became members of the Second Adventists, which devoutly believed in the speedy and personal return of Christ. They embodied all the virtues of the new migrants – modest living, hard work, good neighbourliness, civic concern and an unquestioning Faith. But it was in many respects a hard life, and not a great improvement upon Maine.

Mary Wellcome gave birth to her first son, George Theodore, on 31 July 1851; her second, Henry Solomon, the subject of this biography, was born on 21 August 1853. Like his brother, Henry was actually born in his grandfather's home, a large log house, in which were also living several of Timothy Wellcome's sons and a daughter. 'I have two as fine boys as you can scare up in Maine,' Mary wrote somewhat quaintly to her sister, Ellen. 'My babe is very good-natured.'

The Solomon Wellcome house was not completed when Henry was born. Although small, it was sturdily built of stone and stands to this day on precisely the same thirteen acres as in 1853.* It is poor land, in marked contrast with the rich soils to the south, which can even now only be effectively farmed by the help of modern irrigation machinery. The land is flat and uninteresting. In 1850 Almond was a tiny settlement of a few houses, a store, a small school and a cemetery. It is not much larger today. The combination of long, hard winters and short, torrid summers does not enhance the attractiveness of the area as a habitation, and certainly made farming arduous and hazardous in times long before the advent of quicker growing seeds. Potatoes were a staple crop in the area (now 'The Christmas Tree Capital of the World'), although the Wellcomes also tried to grow wheat and sorghum. It was a lonely and unproductive life, which, understandably, the Wellcome boys did not remember with pleasure, although, romantically, one of the last actions of Henry's life was to buy back the little farm and to make plans for rebuilding the log house in which he had been born.

Even today, the emptiness of the area is depressing, especially during the winter, and it is not difficult to realise how dispiriting it must have been to try to make a living and have some pleasure in the 1850s. The fact that Solomon had poor health did not help. But he and his wife were loving parents, and their sons grew up as strong, high-spirited, little boys in their simple home.

Henry's later memories of his childhood at Almond were vague, the most vivid being his discovery at the age of four of a paleolithic arrowhead, which he said first aroused his interest in history, and especially very early history. His father told him that this improvement had been, to primitive warriors, relatively a greater achievement than the invention of the electric telegraph. This, he later recorded,

* Although contemporary records are not conclusive, they indicate strongly that the Solomon Wellcome house was not completed until the autumn of 1853, when its existence was recorded. The fact that both the Wellcome sons were born in their grandfather's house seems to point to this fact. It is not clear how much of the original house, apart from the stone basement, is in the present one, but it would appear to be a substantial amount; the eagerness of Wellcome in his old age to buy it is strong confirmation of this.

'stimulated a babyish interest [in history] that lasted through my life'. He also remembered when, again at the age of four, he and his mother made a family visit to the East and crossed Lake Michigan on their way to Maine. At one point they bought apples from a Red Indian squaw, which, significantly, he did not forget. He also recalled his early schooling in the log-built Almond schoolhouse with George and other local children.

It was not surprising that Solomon Wellcome's wanderlust began to manifest itself again. Two factors then assisted it: the failure of the precious potato crop in 1861, and the excited reports he received from his brother Jacob about the opportunities in the West in the new State of Minnesota.

Solomon's health had begun to suffer severely from the exertion of not only running his own small farm with little help, but also assisting his ageing father to manage his. It is not clear whether the double burden strained his heart or whether he had heart disease, but it became obvious that he could not continue with farming. At the age of thirty-four, with a young family to support, and his only financial asset his tiny farm, the situation was not promising. When the potato crop was totally lost in 1861, this disaster persuaded seventeen families in the Almond area, including the Wellcomes, to move West.

Meanwhile, Jacob had established himself and his growing family* in the newly created State of Minnesota, in a small village inappropriately called Garden City in Blue Earth County. This was located between the Sioux and Winnebago Indian tribes, 'in the Land of Hiawatha', close to 'The Falls of Minnehaha, the Merry Laughing Water,' and the sacred Red Pipestone Quarry where the tribal Pipes of Peace were made. The Winnebago chiefs were friendly to the white settlers and kind to the Wellcomes; they loved children, and the family's first experiences of the Indians were happy ones. From

* Jacob had married Abigail Starbird in 1846; after her death in 1856, he married Sarah Houser, who lived until 1888.

here Jacob sent his brother accounts of a land of majestic beauty and immense prospects. So Solomon and Mary sold their farm and, with their children and Solomon's parents, set off for Garden City in a covered waggon drawn by oxen, in the company of other families for protection. Although it appeared that the Indians were quiescent, it could be a dangerous as well as an arduous journey.

Unsurprisingly, there appear to have been very few regrets at leaving Almond. The trek, which took nearly a month, was an adventure, Henry and George being given the task of 'forking' rattlesnakes and removing the rattles. There were no railways, and not many roads, in that area in 1861. 'The Prairie Schooners' travelled only by day, and halted, coralled and camped at night.

*

The first accounts of Garden City Township appear in 1854, when a Mr S. D. Mills moved his family from Lake County, Illinois, in a covered waggon drawn by two yokes of oxen to Blue Earth County. He reached Mankato on 1 June, whereupon he proceeded to buy Section 13, a claim which was located on the east side of what became known as Mills Lake. Mills built a log cabin and moved his family to their new home, thus becoming the first white settlers in the area.

The site for Garden City was not acquired until July 1854, when 'a colony headed by Edson Gerry concluded that their travels were at an end and their future homes had been found'. Gerry made a claim of 400 acres on the banks of the Watowan River, because one of the first things that he had noticed was the advantage of the excellent water supply located within his claim, and he immediately conceived the idea of establishing a town site using this power to run grist mills. This he called Watonwan. He also acquired other land in the area, 'platting'* another settlement nearby which he called Fremont. For reasons which have defied research, the name was changed to Garden City, when in fact it was, and remains, a modest village. Ironically, Watonwan itself with its mills and houses, the

* 'Platting' was an amalgam of 'planning' and 'plotting'.

source of Garden City's existence, was to become derelict and is no more.

The builder and owner of the mill was C. F. Butterfield. The power of the river was controlled by man-made dams, and the large iron wheel operated the grinding-stones, on the classic English pattern. As the colony grew, and farming prospered, the mills became the crucial factor in the rise of Watonwan and its tiny satellite, Garden City.

In 1946 the aged son of a local farmer, Peter Kraus, recalled the scene at the Butterfield Mill in the early 1860s:

> In the early days the people were not blessed with the ready cash, so part of the grist of wheat went to the miller in payment of his work of grinding the grain. The exchange was on this method: for every bushel of grain brought to the mill the farmer received 38 lbs of flour, 8 lbs of bran, and 6 lbs of shorts. The miller's toll for the grinding was 12 lbs. You ask me if that flour was good. You can bet your life it was. I can remember the fine loaves of bread my mother used to make from it. We never heard of vitamins, but the wheat of those days had the quality of building strong, healthy men and women.
>
> On one trip to the mill with my father I counted at least twenty ox-drawn wagons loaded with grain standing in line to have their grain ground. Sometimes when the water was low, this wait extended into days. The drivers, however, fared well while waiting. Game was very plentiful, and fishing was excellent. Each driver brought along his trusty old muzzle-loader, and fish-hooks. In the light of camp fires it was indeed a neighbourly and jolly throng of men, who ate their evening meal of fried fish and partridge. About 1874 a school house was built near the mill.

Butterfield entered into partnership with Samuel M. Folsom, who provided the necessary capital, and the small village began to expand. Mr E. P. Evans built a store and got himself appointed postmaster. There was then a bitter dispute between Folsom and Evans about their property rights, 'which sometimes involved the whole community on one side or the other'. There was an eventual settlement, whereby

Evans got ownership of the town site by the river, and Folsom the higher land south of the river. Evans turned out to be the winner, although Folsom opened his own store, in a tent at first, selling 'coffee, and sugar, and in small quantities'. Gerry then sold his Garden City land to a Baptist minister, Anthony Case, who had joined the settlement with his family in 1858 'and became active in the matter of village business'. The first 'plat' of Garden City was filed by Gerry in March 1858 and expanded in October. Garden City had been formally 'platted' and surveyed, and its building faithfully followed the original plans.

The year 1856 had seen the completion of a saw mill, a flour mill and several houses. Unclaimed land in Garden City township was selling for about $1.25 an acre until after 1861, when Indian land could be had for the asking. The chief product was wheat – even as late as 1870 the area of southern and central Minnesota was outranked only by central California in the production of wheat – but there were other crops as well, and the area rapidly developed to the point when, in 1857, Evans built the first hotel in Garden City, which became known as Evans's Hotel. The first census of population in Garden City Township took place in 1860, when the total population was 394.

Another feature of Garden City was the early construction of a school. The first schoolhouse was built of logs in the late summer of 1857 and had an enrolment of fifty-eight students. 'It had no pretensions to beauty, and but little to comfort or convenience,' one of its early pupils later recorded.

> In winter it was very cold, and too small for convenience. We had no uniformity of textbooks; people had emigrated from the States East of us and brought their school books with them. School books could not be got this side of St Paul. Times were hard and known to the old settlers as Johnny Crake times. People were content to get the necessities of life with few luxuries. The teachers boarded around with their patrons and took their chances of being caught in a blizzard two or three miles from the school house next morning, yet notwithstanding all these difficult times the pupils made good progress with their studies.

The later, self-appointed historian of Garden City, Mrs Lucie Phillipson, whose surviving handwritten memories are an invaluable source, recorded of the school that

> nearly all the settlers took a hand in the furnishing of logs and other material, and in its erection. The old school house was probably 26 feet long by 18 wide, had two windows on each side and a door in the north end. The shingles were handmade. The chimney was partly stone and bricks.

It was in this school that George and Henry Wellcome continued their education. The log cabin was replaced by a frame building in 1867, and a graded school started the following year. 'For many years the Garden City schools ranked among the highest in the County,' its historian proudly recorded.

Out of this tiny school there emerged ten boys who were each in his own way to achieve remarkable eminence. In addition to Wellcome, these were Charles J. Rockwood, George M. Palmer (Wellcome's particularly close friend), Elsworth C. Warner, Eli S. Warner, Amos L. Warner, Adoniram Judson Rockwood, Carlos Boynton, Wellcome's cousin Frank (Isaac's son), and George F. Piper.

Charles Rockwood became a judge and was a highly esteemed lawyer; Palmer became a wealthy miller and banker; Elsworth Warner became a prosperous Minneapolis linseed oil miller; his brother, Eli, after making a substantial fortune, went into State politics; Amos Warner became a highly profitable real-estate operator and served in the State legislature; Adoniram Rockwood became a wealthy farmer and legislator in Idaho; Boynton went to St Paul and his eventual estate was estimated at $7 million; Frank Wellcome became a very substantial banker, President of the Union Investment Company and also a millionaire; and Piper became one of the wealthiest capitalists in Minneapolis. In contrast with the circumstances of the Wellcome family, which was one of the poorest of all the families in the little township, Carlos Boynton's father was described as 'the Croesus of Garden City', being the proprietor of the general store. Carlos went to the nearby village of Madela and launched into the real-estate business in St Paul. His chief operation was in farm lands, but he also invested in the railway boom to very considerable advantage. In some respects Wellcome's great friend, George Palmer, with whom he kept in touch for the whole of Palmer's life, was the most remarkable. Charles Rockwood remembered distinctly the day 'when George Palmer returned to Garden City from Mankato – he had walked both ways – it is 17 miles from Garden City to Mankato – and told the crowd at Boynton's store that he had got a job with [the] Hubbard and Hubble mill in Mankato'. He subsequently became President of the Hubbard Mill Company, President of the First National Bank of Mankato, and millionaire owner of a line of coal and lumber yards.

Almond, Wisconsin, had been a charmless place, but Garden City was set in lovely countryside, a site well chosen, and a settlement well 'platted' and built by the settlers out of the abundant timber. The soil was rich and fertile, and the climate infinitely more kind. Mankato, on the Minnesota River, was a rapidly growing town, the river being as vital then to its prosperity as the railroad was to be later. The Garden City settlers were almost wholly of English stock, whereas New Ulm, thirty miles to the west of Garden City, was an almost totally German settlement, soon famous for its beer. In short, this was a completely different economic and social climate from bleak northern Wisconsin, and it was in this beautiful little place, which in Britain would be described as a small village, that Henry and his brother not only grew, but also blossomed.

The houses were principally built of wood, until the first cement-brick building in Minnesota, the First Baptist Church, was completed in 1868. In 1859 the first County Fair was held in Garden City, a tradition that lasts to this day. In 1861 The Garden City Bank opened; it eventually failed, but, honourably, none of its customers losing their money. In 1859 the citizens began an American Congress; there was only one House, and that was the Senate. Senatorships were given by lot, every State in the Union being represented, and there was also a President and a Cabinet. The debates were vehement, one

'Senator' later recalling that 'People came from miles for this really brilliant entertainment. Eloquence flowed like a river.'

*

The Wellcomes moved into a small, recently built, wooden house, which Jacob Wellcome had bought on their behalf. He also gave his brother employment in his drugstore, which was an important part of his growing practice; indeed, it was so successful that Jacob made Solomon the store's part-owner. His sons helped in the shop, Henry being considerably more enthusiastic and interested than his brother.

If Solomon Wellcome, through no fault of his own, was, in career and financial terms, unsuccessful, his brother Jacob had laid the foundations of a remarkable reputation, recorded by a younger Minnesotan doctor, J. W. Andrews, in 1902:

> When he located at Garden City the broad sparsely settled prairie south to the Iowa line, and south west to Spirit Lake, was a part of his undisputed field. So busy and varied was his practice, and so great was the territory, that it required most of the time six horses to do the business, and he practically lived in his buggy and at the bedside of the sick.

Although the Solomon Wellcome family, which had just arrived, escaped the diphtheria epidemic that ravaged southern Minnesota, it was a constant fear, which Henry never forgot. It was then only curable with skilful nursing and a large element of luck; the possibility of immunisation, of course, did not yet exist. As in so many ailments and diseases, drugs were non-existent except as sedatives. The doctor did his best, and hoped that the patient was resilient enough to survive the crisis; too many did not. But, if life expectancy in Minnesota was not high, nor was it in other American or considerably more sophisticated European cities. The records of the time grimly demonstrate how common an occurrence was death, especially among children, and how helpless were the best of doctors and surgeons.

That Jacob was very definitely among the best was widely recognised. The weapons at his disposal in the battle against illness and disease may now appear to us to be painfully limited – and, in the cases of too many, did not exist at all – but those he had, he employed vigorously and with a remarkable degree of success. As a surgeon, he had wonderful dexterity, with an artist's hand and eye, and his willingness to travel long distances, and his phenomenal energy, made him a legendary figure.

He also had style and was long remembered as one of the first settlers, and as

> a tall, stripling young man, who wore the first stovepipe hat ever seen in the valley, and the mosquitoes were so bad that year that it left his nose fearfully exposed. He drove a white horse, too, but the doctor did not kill many [people], and no one was ever sick, or if sick, had sufficient power of endurance to beat the doctor.

Jacob Wellcome was Henry's first hero. His uncle loved his father – the brothers were devoted to each other – and Jacob treated Henry and George as though they were his sons. He was the first major influence upon Henry, who was fascinated by his uncle's work, constantly asked him questions about it and was eager to emulate him. For his part, Jacob saw his nephew from an early age as having exceptional potential for a career in medicine, in spite of his relatively basic education.

Garden City was a prosperous and happy community; it was, Wellcome later recorded, 'the home of my boyhood, the scene of happy days'. He learned the excitement and contentment of canoeing from the friendly Winnebago Indians, in their birch bark canoes, whose beautiful lines and sturdiness made them supreme craft, on river or lake. He learned to ride and to shoot – two vital necessities – and was to become a good horseman and an outstanding shot. But he was also a voracious reader and learnt much from the tales of the older settlers. Although Garden City was a very religious community, it enjoyed itself. When it decided to have 'a grand party' in the home of Charles Thurston, one of the original settlers, one of Henry's schoolfriends related how he was sent to Mankato 'to buy good things for the party' with $1.50; he bought nuts and candles, 'and with good pumpkin pie the party danced until broad daylight. Those were glorious days, and the men and women were as noble a set of people as ever laid the foundations of a State.'

However, the Minnesota idyll was quickly, and brutally, interrupted within a year of the Wellcomes' arrival.

*

The history of the State of Minnesota began in 1846 after the American Congress for the third time reduced the area that 'the eternal compact' in the Ordnance of 1787 had assigned to the last State to be constructed in the old North-West. Wisconsin was now cut short of the Mississippi River, which had been designed as its western limit, and instead offered statehood only if it would accept the St Croix River as its boundary. This curtailing of Iowa and Wisconsin made room for an additional Mississippi Valley state, Minnesota.

As early as 1837 the Sioux Indians of this region had ceded to the United States all their lands east of the Mississippi and Fort Snelling at the junction of St Peters, and the Mississippi was the only haunt of white men among them. But when Iowa and Wisconsin became States, some five thousand white settlers moved into Indian territory. In March 1849 the Bill to create a territory of Minnesota became law, but Minnesota was entirely within unceded Sioux lands, and had no room for a swelling population except in the angle between the St Croix and Mississippi Rivers, which had once belonged to the North-West territory.*

In 1851 Governor Alexander Ramsey conducted treaty councils with the Sioux, in which they agreed to cede all their claims to territory east of the Red River in the north and the Big Sioux River. The compensation promised to the tribes was considerable, but its

* This section is largely based on Frederic L. Paxson, *History of the American Frontier 1763–1893* (1924), and from contemporary accounts of the Sioux Rising in the records of the Minnesota Historical Association, and Henry Wellcome's subsequent accounts.

payment was diverted, because at the time of the signing sessions the tribes were persuaded to sign an agreement that the claims of the traders against individual Indians should be satisfied out of the fund before the proceeds were divided. The traders saw to it that their claims were greater than the whole purchase price, with the result that the tribes had the mortification of seeing their lands disappear without receiving an equivalent in any form that they could understand.

To make matters worse, the encroaching settlers moved upon the lands as soon as the treaty was signed and before the Senate had ratified or Congress had appropriated the purchase price in 1853.

'I used all my efforts to prevent this state of things and to induce the white population not to occupy the land until it could be done lawfully,' declared the local Indian agent. 'I called on the military at Fort Snelling to assist in removing improper persons; but they refused to act. The current of emigration became irresistible, and the country is virtually in the possession of the white population.'

Frederic Paxson comments:

> The treatment of the Minnesota Indians was tragically unfair as the agricultural frontier swept over them and left a train of grievances to drench the Minnesota farms with blood before they were forgotten. Further west on the open plains the other tribes of Sioux and their relatives were brought into the negotiations the same summer, and only less unfairly dealt with.*

No serious evidence has yet emerged to confirm the Union view in the Civil War that the Confederacy had fostered the Indian uprisings, which began on 18 August 1862, when the Santee Sioux of Minnesota led by Chief Little Crow ravaged the valley of the Minnesota River and slaughtered hundreds of its unsuspecting inhabitants. There is controversy about how many were killed, the figures varying between 490 and 737.

This came at a desperate moment in the Civil War in the fortunes

* Paxson, *op. cit.*, p. 425.

of the Union, when John Pope had succeeded George McClellan only to be decisively out-generalled by Robert E. Lee at the second battle of Bull Run. As Paxson has written, it was

> hard to avoid the suspicion that the desolate frontier above New Ulm and the exiled survivors who rushed in panic to their village in Fort Ridgely were consequences of the military measures of the Confederacy. The Secretary of the Interior thought so; and whether they were or not the whole Minnesota frontier west of St Paul and extending to the Yellow Medicine River was aflame with murder.*

In reality, the uprising had nothing whatever to do with the state of the Civil War. For years the white Indian agents in Minnesota had been protesting against the abuse of the Sioux by Congress, Senate and the United States Government. As they repeatedly warned, the manner in which the ceded lands had been seized by the settlers from the Sioux, and the absence of any payment for these lands, fomented a strong sense of resentment; in Paxson's words, 'the agents saw trouble coming for many years before it arrived. The sense of grievance soaked in, and it called for no more than a chance accident to provoke an outbreak.'**

The Sioux chief, Little Crow, had attempted negotiations, without success. As a recent history of the episode has rightly emphasised,† both sides were playing for high stakes. When the explosion occurred, the conflict was conducted on both sides with a desperate brutality. What then happened brought out the worst in both. The Sioux seemed to gain positive pleasure in torturing and killing white infants and children, and were especially cruel to white women; the settlers responded in kind. There was a deep savagery in Minnesota in 1862.

The murder, on 17 August 1862, of five white settlers in Meeker County began the uprising. This was not premeditated, but once it was done the Sioux recognised that white retribution was almost

* *Ibid.*

** *Ibid.*, p. 487.

† Duane Schultz, *Over the Earth I Come.*

certain to follow and would hit them without discrimination; they therefore struck first.

Within three days the war had reached Garden City. On the morning of 20 August, two German settlers from New Ulm rode into Garden City with the alarm that the Sioux were massacring settlers nearby and were within a short distance of New Ulm. Messengers had been sent to all settlements in the Minnesota River Valley east of New Ulm and up the Blue Earth Valley, warning them and appealing to them to hasten to the relief of New Ulm, then the largest and most important town in the Indian country west of Mankato.

Wellcome later wrote an account of the uprising in which he recalled:

> Word was received that New Ulm was surrounded. Dr William Mayo took his rifle and medicine kit and manoeuvred his way through Indian lines to give medical aid in New Ulm. Dr Piper, a very tall man, was scouting, and was chased by Indians, but he hid in the tall grass and escaped. While Dr Mayo was away the Indians surrounded his home. Mrs Mayo organised the women – they all put on men's clothing – beat tin pans and anvils and walked about. The Indians, hearing the commotion, and mistaking the masquerading women for men, departed.

When the Sioux threatened Garden City, Wellcome's father and uncle were among the volunteers to defend the town, and Henry, not yet nine, not only became the captain of the boys casting bullets, but also assisted his uncle in treating the wounded, holding bowls of hot water while Jacob operated.

The people of Garden City received assistance from Chief Good Thunder of the Winnebago tribe, while they watched the burning of haystacks and barns by the Sioux. Sentinels were sent out constantly and Evans's Hotel, where they sought refuge, was fortified. 'Hardships were great, the village lacked food,' says the official account of the siege.

The Government's response to the war was swift and brutal, led by the discredited General Pope. In September its forces caught up with the Sioux and defeated them in battle, and Little Crow and the other guilty leaders fled from the field and took refuge in Dakota territory. Pope declared that 'The Sioux War is at an end.' But when the accounts of the ferocity of the Indian massacres were broadcast, there was a loud and bitter demand for retribution. Several hundred captured Sioux were tried by military commission at Fort Snelling and 303 were found guilty of murder, rape and arson, and sentenced to death after a travesty of a trial. Mobs of citizens from St Paul tried to take the matter into their own hands and for some days maintained a state of siege around the Fort. President Lincoln pardoned all but thirty-eight, 'the more guilty and influential of the culprits' – although two were clearly innocent – who were hanged on a single scaffold at Mankato on 26 December 1862, walking to their deaths in Indian file, in warpaint and with their feathers, and singing on the scaffold. The other Sioux prisoners were transported to a Dakota reservation and the fugitives pursued and scattered by Pope's troops.

Even the Santee Sioux who had played no part whatever in the uprising, and many of whom had protected the whites, were cruelly banished to a new reservation, at Crow Creek on the Missouri River. 'The soil was barren, rainfall scanty, wild game scarce, and the alkaline water unfit for drinking. Soon the surrounding hills were covered with graves; of the 1,300 Santees brought there in 1863, less than a thousand survived their first winter.' When the first shipment left St Paul by steamboat on 4 May 1863, 'white Minnesotans lined the river landing to see them off with shouts of derision and showers of hurled stones'.*

It might have been expected that this traumatic experience of war and bloodshed would have embittered the boy Wellcome against the Indians; in fact, exactly the reverse happened. He considered the treatment of the Sioux, and of all the North American Indians, as brutal, disgraceful and shameful to America. He was never to change this view and was to describe the North American Indians as 'the

* Dee Brown, *Bury My Heart at Wounded Knee* (Holt, Rinehart & Winston, 1970), p. 65.

noblemen of God's primitive peoples'. He certainly agreed with the opinion of one of his uncle's medical colleagues, Dr Asa Daniels, who subsequently wrote in his account of the conflict:

> In closing this paper the writer, who was so long intimately associated with the Indians as a government official, desires to say that he found this people possessed of many of the virtues common to the human family and that socially and morally their standards were quite as high as among many of the civilised races. The outbreak was induced by long continued violation of treaty obligations on the part of the government, inflicting upon these unfortunate wards untold want and suffering. Like violent acts of mobs among civilised communities the massacre was a barbarous and unreasoning act against injustice. Had the government faithfully carried out the treaty obligations and dealt with the Sioux justly and humanely, the outbreak would not have occurred.*

In 1865 there was to be another alarm when some Indians, led by a half-breed Sioux named Campbell, murdered the whole of the Jewett family at Rapidan, with the exception of William Jewett, then a baby, who was struck on the head and left for dead. Fortunately, thanks to Wellcome's uncle, he survived.** Jacob Wellcome had himself had a very narrow escape. He had visited the Jewett farm that night for a sick call and had remained until four o'clock in the morning, when he had left to attend another patient, only hours before the Campbell attack. Campbell was caught and condemned to death. On his way to gaol in a waggon belonging to Solomon Wellcome, he was stopped by an angry crowd, who dragged him from the waggon and hanged him from the limb of a tree. Henry was not present at this lynching, nor at the Mankato mass execution; he always strongly resented the claim that Campbell had been officially executed from his father's waggon, a fable that long endured in Blue Earth County.

The experience of the Sioux rising was a deeply unpleasant one

* *Collections of the Minnesota Historical Society*, vol. XV (1915).

** He lived until 1908.

for a young boy – although Wellcome later described it as 'the most interesting experience of my life' – but he never forgot that the Winnebago tribe had protected him and his family. The Sioux had behaved barbarously, but although he was subsequently contemptuous of attempts to glorify them and to condone their brutality, he recognised that their savage bitterness had had strong justification. But, like his ancestor, John Eliot, he had learnt a lesson that he never forgot.

*

Garden City and the area around it continued to prosper after the profound shock of the Sioux uprising. The Civil War hardly affected it at all. More houses were built, and Jacob Wellcome's widespread practice continued to develop. He became the first surgeon at the new hospital at Mankato, while his continuing country practice required him now to own over twenty horses. But his brother's fortunes did not prosper. Solomon Wellcome was an inadequate businessman, and although the small drugstore did reasonable business, Solomon turned to a religious vocation and became an ill-rewarded minister of the Adventist Church. His family was probably the poorest one in Garden City. Henry Wellcome's parents were untroubled by this fact, but he was not. None of his exceptionally ambitious schoolfriends in the log-cabin school saw Garden City as their limit; nor did he.

His cousin Frank later recorded that

> Henry's childhood was spent in an environment which, perhaps unconsciously, curbed too much an eager, restless desire to get out and do something worthwhile. Anyway, that is what he did. From then on [after leaving Garden City] he paddled his own canoe and sat on his own bottom – something that I do know that he thought that every person should do.

Frank shared Henry's keen dislike of Adventism, which he described as 'that fanatical doctrine', and from which he, also, escaped at the first opportunity.

Henry's interest in medical matters really began during the Sioux war, and notably when he had assisted his uncle. But it was an English chemist from Leeds, H. J. Barton, who had come to Garden City and established a small pharmacy, who encouraged Wellcome's evident interest and instructed him in chemistry. It was Barton who first revealed to the young Wellcome the glories of England, and not least its educational and scientific institutions. He gave him a copy of Attfield's *Chemistry*, and Wellcome's usually disastrously explosive experiments were vividly remembered by his contemporaries, particularly one with ammonium nitrate which could easily have had very serious results. Even less popular was his enjoyment of practical jokes, which shocked his father when the complaints came in. In the summer he reluctantly pitched hay for five cents a day, which his mother kept in a red purse as a memento of his first wages. He grew watermelons on their small allotment of land and sold them for a dollar each. He loved firecrackers, which others did not. He was a high-spirited, cheerful and normally popular boy, unusual in his fascination for pharmacy, medicine and history.

Solomon Wellcome now became so often absent on his religious missions that his sons saw little of him. Even if they had, Solomon's personality was so mild that it would have had little impact. The boys went dutifully to church, but although it was a religious household and family, there are few indications, later confirmed, that Henry himself was greatly imbued with genuine fervour.

Although Henry remembered his Minnesota childhood with pleasure, and was grateful for what was a good basic education for the West, by the time he was a teenager he was oppressed by the limited opportunities that Garden City offered. The Sioux war may have been a frightening experience, but it had at least been exciting. When Garden City returned to its humdrum daily existence, heavily based upon the Church, there was little flavour to it. Also, as he later wrote after he had fled, he was depressed by the fact that, for all their religious appearances, so many Garden City people were blatantly materialistic, selfish and unreliable. His family's poverty was an ad-

Advertisement for Wellcome's magic ink, 1869

ditional discouragement. He left school at thirteen and worked at the Wellcome store, which, although he did it diligently, was unexciting and ill-rewarded.

He emphatically did not want to be a farmer, nor, despite Uncle Jacob's urging, a doctor, even if his family could have afforded his training, which it could not. He amused himself by 'inventing' a form of invisible ink, which he proceeded to advertise in the town's newspaper. It has an historic character, as the very first of the myriad Wellcome advertisements, but it also demonstrated an interesting aspect of his developing personality, in which an element of cheek was present.

The most important formative influences upon Henry Wellcome, after Jacob, were English. As well as Barton, there was now William Worrall* Mayo, a personal friend and professional colleague of Jacob

* The Mayo family in America spelt the middle name 'Worrell' until the Mayo sons went to England in 1929 to dedicate a stained-glass window in memory of their father in Eccles Parish Church, when they discovered that the name was spelt 'Worrall' in their father's birthplace. Henceforth, the family used the original spelling.

Wellcome during the Indian war, whose sons were younger contemporaries of Henry and George.*

Mayo had been born in Manchester in 1819 and had studied medicine at Owens College, later the University of Manchester. In 1845 he had sailed to New York to become an instructor in chemistry and physics at the Bellevue Medical College, subsequently graduating at the University of Missouri. He was a rarity, especially in the West, of being a scientist as well as a practising doctor. Jacob Wellcome was a particularly good doctor, but totally without the sophistication and scholarship of Mayo, and his drugstore was more a general merchant's shop that also sold medicines rather than the specialised houses now being established in Philadelphia, New York and Rochester, Minnesota. Mayo's experience and outlook opened up a new and exciting world for the young Wellcome, who became Mayo's enthusiastic student. Mayo took an immense liking to this eager youth, showed him many kindnesses and encouraged him in his studies. Wellcome, many years later, spoke of Mayo with gratitude and reverence as 'the one who, in my youth, inspired and guided me in my studies, and insisted on my qualifying myself for a career in a field of science'. Mayo also inspired his own sons, who were to rise to the top of the medical profession and found the Mayo Clinic in Rochester.

Little inspiration came at home. Solomon Wellcome was frequently away and George, a singularly unambitious boy, eventually drifted into the same ill-paid occupation as his father. 'You are a very fortunate boy, did you know it,' he was to write to Henry in March 1871. 'It is as I have told you, you were born with a silver spoon in your mouth and mine must have been pewter for it isn't worth a cent.' Christian semi-poverty had no appeal to Henry, and the placid routine of little Garden City was as claustrophobic for someone of his intellectual energy and ambition as it was for his schoolfriends.

* Mayo married Louise Abigail Wright, also a doctor. Their first son, William James, was born at Le Sueur, north of Mankato, on 29 June 1861; the second, Charles Hovis, in Rochester on 11 July 1865.

Now, encouraged by the two Englishmen who had, almost miraculously, entered his life and changed it for ever, he made his decision to leave Garden City.

The Mayos had moved from Le Sueur to Rochester, so it was to Rochester that Henry Wellcome decided to go at the age of seventeen, taking with him a letter of reference signed by the leading physicians, druggists, lawyers and merchants of Garden City. It was prepared and written by a general merchant, Albert T. Williams, and read:

> *Garden City, Minnesota*
> August 17th, 1870
>
> To all whom it may concern be it known that Henry S. Wellcome a young and worthy young man is about to leave our town for the East, and we would further say that he is trustworthy in every respect. And is well qualified to be a clerk. As respects business ability and Honesty. Honest as the day is long, and no Bad habits of Character about him.

Armed with this testimonial, and with little money, Henry Wellcome began his long journey to the East by moving to Rochester to find employment, and his destiny.

# 2

# An American Education

Wellcome had successfully applied for a position with Poole and Geisinger, a firm of pharmaceutical chemists in Rochester recommended by Mayo. His pay was modest and his hours long, but he had the kindness of the Mayo family, and was soon well thought of by his employers as a diligent young man.

Wellcome's job was as a prescription clerk, and his place of work was immediately below Mayo's office. In the next room to Mayo on the first floor was another young man who was working as an office boy to a dentist. Mayo was impressed by him and told him that he was far too able to be an office boy in Rochester; the young man became a successful dental surgeon in Paris. Mayo told Wellcome that he too should go to college and acquire professional qualifications so that he could achieve greater things. He also mentioned to the young man Pasteur's statement that 'men without laboratories are as soldiers without arms', which Wellcome never forgot.

Mayo was a difficult man, but his wife was considered by many to be even more formidable. But they, and their sons Charles and William, became what Wellcome later sentimentally called 'my barefoot friends on the Prairie'. In the last weeks of Wellcome's life, on his final visit to Rochester, Will was to say of him that 'he has the love and esteem of the medical profession in the United States, Great Britain and Europe'; in reply, a moved Wellcome said that he owed everything to the inspiration, kindness, teaching and advice of Will and Charlie's father.

Separated for the first time, Henry and George began what was to be for them both a lifelong correspondence. George wrote to Henry on 23 October 1870 from Newburgh:

> O Henry I wish I could be with you today. I have plenty of company but it seems lonesome without you but we must not give up to our feelings altogether we must use a little self control. . . . God knows I love you as a brother can but we must be separated sometime and we must submit if we are not permitted to meet on Earth we have the promise of it in the world to come if we are faithful let us try. I wish I could step in and enjoy a few games with you. I never play a game but that I think of you.

Henry now found that he had become the breadwinner of the family, a position he was destined to retain for the whole of his life.

The financial situation for the Wellcome family in Garden City was bad. The Curtis family – itself hard-pressed – helped with gifts, mainly clothes and shoes, which were gratefully received. The Wellcomes had to take in lodgers, and Wellcome's mother undertook not only all the housework, but also repairs and decoration, as well as making rugs and clothes for her husband and sons. When Henry enquired from George how much money was in the house, George wrote back: 'Mother has got $5.40, I think, and I have now $1.80 and three postage stamps.' He added that his own income for over five months was $5. On 12 February 1871 George wrote in gratitude for a loan of $2 'to pay my tuition at writing school. Henry I am ever so much obliged to you for your accommodation & will repay you as soon as I can get anything to do [to] get any money.'

This was to become a recurrent theme; even in April 1893 George was writing: 'Oh Henry I cannot thank God too much or do too much for him for giving me such a brother as you are & I think of more when I see the hardness & selfishness &c many times between brothers.'

In a letter to his mother and George on 18 November 1870, Henry wrote:

I asked you Mother in one of my letters how you was off for curency now please let me know in your answer to this.

Now I will tell you of myself I am enjoying myself first rate everything looks bright before and now I often think how fortunate I was to git this situation I find that if I had been one day later that I should not of have gotten the place for others applied within that time afterword that would otherwise of have taken it there are others now that are standing ready and would be verry glad to get the place from me (but I guess this they wont) if I had not of have got it what would I of have done this winter I dread to think of it but now I am as cosy as you please enjoying life as well as one can posibly that has no home the people here seem to take an interest in me that I never experienced elsewhere you know how it was at Garden City every one for themselves (unfortunately).

I think that I never enjoyed society as well as I do here and a verry moral class of young people I have not seen as much rowdy and roughness amoung the young men here as there is in G.C. their mind seems to run the other way I have seen but one man drunk since I have been here and then saw the marshal march him and the one that sold it to him to the lock up (how is that for justice).

Dear Mother I did not treasure my good home nor does any one until they are without I miss that mothers watch over me but feel that God watches over me and guides me for I put my whole life in his hands and am striving to live a truly christian life and Dear Bro George I feel as rejoiced to think that we as a family are all trying to live to the honor and glory of our maker and may he be with and bless each of us daily is my prayer each night as I retire to couch Your ever true and affectionate son and brother Henry.

His mother wrote to him on the same day:

My Dear Son as I have not the privelege of speaking to you face to face I will try the virtue of pen and paper you seem to be so grateful for the little favours that I bestow upon you and that is all that I can do at present but hope the day will come once more that I shall have the privelege of doing for you as in gone by days if we live and the Lord prospers and the time will soon come. I am so glad you are so pleasantly situated and we will contented hope you will continue so and be faithful to your heavenly father and he will never leave nor for-sake you. . . .

Solomon Wellcome's letters to his son were primarily on the religious aspects of his life, but then on 31 April 1871 there is a rebuke:

I told you long ago to leave off some of your little tricks or jokes but you did not heed it and I find a number of cases where you put Campsicum or other articles in your letters and in the doctor's family caused a regular fuss, Jackie got hold of the letter and got the Campsicum in his eyes and it came near putting them out, and while I say this in all kindness I must say that I consider practical joking very wrong, almost always bringing forth evil fruit. Will you heed what I say & may God bless you and help you to shun every evil way & turn near to him.

The Wellcome family was so dependent upon Henry's contributions that when one failed to arrive in August 1871, Solomon wrote to his son accusing him of extravagance, 'worldly notions', and living above not only his means, but also his station, no doubt because he was ashamed of his family's humble circumstances. Henry replied on 15 August:

My dear Father

Your very kind affectionate and instructive letter was so very gladly received yesterday am so very very sorry to hear that you feel so sad about me for dear father I fear that you have not taken the thing as it realy is but as it apears to you for, dear Father, you must know that I could not do such a thing as to spend money thriftlessly. So far from it since April I have bought my 2 white shirts they cost me 60 cents and Board $75.00 and washing $2 month Shirts socks, travelling bag $2.25 and the bal. I have spent in collars neck ties & other things except a little that I sent mother & Geo the amt. earned is $16. and 15.00 on back wages. . . . These two suits will wear me one year, or I mean the business suit and the dress suit will last me several years I only go in respectable society but no style make no pretentions of such but go into the society of leading people where I could not feel at home if dressed very shabyly I acknowledge that I have some pride and have always had a small degree but dear Father I have not indulged in any fancy notions and fashionable society and dress that other boys and young men do for I cannot afford it and have no desire to go beyond my means I am now fitted out and shall expect to let you and mother have what I get over and above current expenses I needed a good dress suit and am very careful of it, I could not very well wear one in the store for you know that one gets clothes perfumed by the drugs and not very agreable to residence it is the best suit I ever had and do not in my own consience reflect upon it.

I have not represented that I was wealthy or a pauper but alowed them to judge for themselves and dear father you think that I am ashamed of you, why what can you be thinking me capable of ashamed of my Father why it realy makes me feel hurt for it is so far from it I have requested you not to make remarks that could let people know that you was poor thinking that it would be to your good as well as mine not to have the real truth known as have heard you remark that it should not at all times, and Father I have always tried to make you comfortable and if you think or know of any thing to the contrary please let me know it and if I have done any thing that was improper or have left undone any thing that I should have done I beg your forgiveness and for the forgiveness of God.

My mind is not on the fashionable society or dress but on God and my daily labours I spend most all leisure hours in study to increase my knowledge of my business I never neglect my duties to God but ask his blessing upon us as a family and individualy. . . .

But dear Father your claim that the world is blinding my eyes is a great error for I larn each day more of it and how to shun it I have always had personal courage (if I may be alowed the personal remark) to refuse what my conscience has told me was wrong I have changed associates several times not for the worse but as you must know one going into a new place must look before he jumps I went where some methodists recommended me and found not as agreable and moral persons as it was my desire to asociate with and droped them immediately I shun altogether rowdey and drinking boys. . . .

I thank God for the good and kind parents that he has given me to teach me his way in the days of my youth I attend church & S.S. [Sunday School] regularly and Sunday morning & evening prayer meetings always try to do my duty. . . .

To be sure it is not as easy for one to live a humble christian among every class of persons as one finds in a town like this as it is in the country where he does not mingle with everybody. But others have lived good christian lives in cities and I can as well.

Wellcome's letters to his mother, however, had a different tone:

My dear Mother

Your real good kind and instructive letter I received over a week since and have been so very busy that have not felt at all like writing and do not this morning but will try to have a little conversation with you, but seems rather dull to do all the talking and keep my mouth closed too. Well, dear Mother I am enjoying myself first rate although have considerable to do I enjoy it, I like business, it drives dull care away I want something to do that there is life about. I have almost the whole charge of the prescriptions, or wholly while I am in. I have a room by myself, just a cosy one too. I think that I could not have found another as good place in this state for as I have often told you the city is so good and not of a class that will try to pull one down but help him on, and this is the means by which I have become as contented and made to enjoy the society place etc and makes it feel like home to me.

Yes mother, I try to live devoted to God and try to pass over the trials and temptations, and when anything comes up that I cannot help myself I ask His help and blessing. . . .

Your ever true and affectionate son Henry S. Wellcome.

*

Although Wellcome enjoyed his work in Rochester, and earned the respect and trust of his employers, his ambitions went considerably further. It was Mayo who impressed upon him the importance of obtaining academic qualifications in either of the two outstanding Colleges of Pharmacy, Chicago or Philadelphia. He chose the former, which was to prove an unhappy error.

As his family was quite unable to pay his fees, it was necessary for him to obtain employment, and a Rochester friend of Mayo, Dr L. H. Aiken, commended him to Dr Thomas Whitfield, an experienced Chicago pharmacist. This new move troubled his family, Solomon Wellcome writing to his son on 15 March 1872:

> I cant help feeling sad to think you are going to leave Rochester as I think it is one of the best places in the West. I have been worrying about you for two weeks I dont know why but I have felt as though something was going to happen to you. Now put your trust in God & dont move out without consulting me.

Henry did move out, and without consulting his father.

Whitfield had agreed to take Wellcome on so that he could attend lectures at the College of Pharmacy three evenings each week, and to

> provide him a place to sleep as is customary, & pay him $30 a month for the first year. His board will cost him $4.50 or $5 a week, just as he pleases & think he can get along very nicely and possibly save something on that salary. I will make room for him by May 1st, or if he prefers will hold the place until June 1st, but think the earliest time the best.

Wellcome replied to Whitfield on 12 April to say that, 'Your offer will be very satisfactory to me, I will accept it to commence May 1st. I am very much pleased with the advantages that the place will afford me.'

Wellcome arrived in Chicago at the end of April, immediately after the Great Fire had devastated a large part of the city, killing over 250 and leaving thousands homeless. This was disconcerting enough. What was even more troubling was that Dr Whitfield turned out to be an unreasonable employer, expecting Wellcome to work seventeen hours a day in his pharmacy, and denying him free afternoons. 'Our hours are very long, 18,' he wrote to his mother on 24 May; 'I am now writing in job late as I have to stop to wait on customers as I am in the store. I do get a wee bit lonesome sometime but business is business and I attend to it.' This burden, on top of his studies, was too much, and he decided that he must move. This was particularly serious as Whitfield was a senior member of the College of Pharmacy – a fact that makes his actions even worse – and was to become its President a year later.

Solomon Wellcome was deeply concerned about his son's situation in Chicago and wrote to him on 20 June 1872:

> I was sorry to hear about you having so much trouble about your place as I had supposed you would be all right, but somehow I felt very anxious about you & I do now. I hope you have a good place, but I am afraid that if you have anything to do or say about the man's iniquity that he may get revenge on you, he is a prominent man in Chicago & you are a lone boy, among strangers & dont know whom to trust. You must be very careful about what you say about anyone. It is better to suffer wrong than to do wrong. Say your case before the Lord & ask for wisdom to direct you. I pray much & God will bless and direct you.

Wellcome found a new appointment with J. H. Byrne, 'a thorough Druggist', in Henry's description, which only lasted until November, but was a quite different experience. Byrne was not only an able pharmacist, but was also kind-hearted, encouraging and was himself studying for a medical degree. Wellcome always remembered him with special affection and gratitude. Byrne's judgment of Wellcome was that, 'I found him very industrious and studious, and in every way worthy of confidence. I have seldom met a young man better adapted to the business or who was more desirous of mastering it.' Wellcome then joined an apothecary called Arend, where, according to his approving leaving testimonial, Wellcome 'was both occupied in manufacturing and dispensing'. But Arend then questioned Wellcome's honesty, having testified to it in his letter of recommendation. Wellcome, for the first time in his life, took legal advice, and Arend hurriedly withdrew his allegations. Wellcome was becoming hardened to bad employers, another lesson learnt and not forgotten.

This was an unhappy and frustrating period of Henry Wellcome's life. He seems to have made few friends, and was poor and lonely in a city only gradually recovering from the havoc of the Fire. His parents became worried, Solomon writing on 21 August:

> My dear Boy Henry I will write especially to you this morning as it is your 19th birthday how glad we should be to see you & George & be all together but as this cannot be we will talk with you a little with pen and ink. It has been but a little while since you was a nice little baby tossed on your mothers knee, but time has flown, & you are man grown & out in the world for yourself seeking your fortune. Well our prayers are that God will help you that you may be successful in business and never forget that man may plan as he will yet God watches over us is ever willing to give us wisdom & we should never lean on our own strength for it is but a weakness. Oh may you so number your days that you may apply your heart with wisdom, you & George are now together and can be a help to each other, you can assist each other in giving & taking advice, & I do hope & pray that you may both be wise enough to keep clear of bad company of both sexes. You are both fond of female society & this is well enough in itself, but do not depend upon such society for true happiness, be independant of it if you think too much of this society it will lead you to the fickle minded, & when you are about your business your mind will be away here & there where the girls are, remember they are fickle as the wind as a general thing, and many a young man has been ruined by being led away by flirts, but enough of this, I hope you will both be firm & described to be men in every sense of the word, do not be in haste to get rich but be content with doing well. He that maketh haste to be rich shall not be innocent says the wise man, and it is often so.

His mother wrote on the same day:

> My dear boy Henry as your father has been writing to you and it is your 19th birthday I take my hands out of the wash tub, where you have seen them so many times, and write a few lines. It has been very warm the past week and the heat overcome me very much but when it is cool I feel quite comfortable when I do not have to work and get heat up.
>
> It is time to get dinner.
>
> Goodbye from your mother Mary Wellcome.

In February 1873 Jacob Wellcome continued his endeavours to persuade his favourite nephew to become a qualified medical practitioner:

> I am much pleased with the idea of your going through College. I would recommend that you study Medicine and Surgery: you would make one of the best in the country. If you will do this and graduate I will take you in as partner and go into business in any City you wish, and I have means to set up in good shape.

He repeated this advice on 8 July, saying, 'I feel anxious to have you go through College. Go through and graduate as a physician, and then you will be all right in any City or Town.'

Jacob was now, by Wellcome standards, financially assured and could have assisted his nephew towards acquiring medical qualifications, but Wellcome, under the influence of Mayo, had definitely made up his mind to concentrate upon pharmacy. He had developed a keen dislike of being poor, and although he respected his father as a man, he had no intention of emulating him; also, although Uncle Jacob had been professionally and financially successful, the life of a rural doctor was a hard one and the financial rewards were not lavish. By contrast, the rapidly expanding pharmaceutical industry was lucrative and, therefore, enticing. Furthermore, Wellcome had received a firm offer of employment from the successful and innovative pharmacist, John Wyeth of Philadelphia. The salary offered was $200 for the first year and $300 for the second, but there was a stipulation that he must stay for at least two years, which Wellcome felt that he could not accept. However, he had had another offer, which would begin his real education as a pharmacist.

*

By far the most important thing that happened during Wellcome's otherwise unhappy time in Chicago was that he had begun the greatest friendship of his life. Frederick Belding Power was also working in a pharmaceutical store to earn enough to finance his future studies.

How they met is unknown, but when they did, they found an immediate and, as it happened, lifelong affinity, although they were in many respects very different personalities. They had at least in common the fact that they were both poor – Wellcome even more so than Power – and wished to achieve distinction in pharmacy. It was when Power moved to the Philadelphia College of Pharmacy, and wrote to Wellcome to suggest that he should do so as well, that the Chicago period ended.

Chicago had been a severe disappointment, but the lure of Philadelphia was intense. At the beginning of July 1873 Wellcome arrived there to take up employment with Mr Heisher, apothecary, of 994 Fifth Street, and to enrol as a student in the Philadelphia College of Pharmacy.

In 1821 the druggists and apothecaries of Philadelphia had met to establish the first college of pharmacy on the American continent. Philadelphia was then the largest city in the United States, and by far the most cultured and influential. Stimulated by the leadership of Benjamin Franklin, Philadelphia had been the pioneer of the former Colonies and boasted the first American hospital, the first college of medicine, the first law school of the New World and the first botanical garden. In this city of great beauty and charm, the continental Congress had met to begin the processes that had led to the Declaration of Independence and the birth of a free American nation. Although the District of Columbia was to be the new national capital, for many years the main business of government was conducted in Philadelphia, and most embassies and consulates remained there rather than move to the mainly unbuilt and deeply unhealthy Washington. As has been written, with merited pride:

> With a famous bar, famous physicians and surgeons, famous publishing houses, a prosperous trade on the river with Europe, the West Indies and all the rest of the world, which brought every kind of merchandise to her wharves and established fortunes for many of her citizens,

Philadelphia had come to be regarded as the most distinguished of American communities.*

The condition of medicine in America was then significantly worse than in Europe. There were relatively few qualified physicians outside the large towns, a fact that made Jacob Wellcome and Mayo unusual, even by the early 1860s, but in 1821 their type was virtually unknown. Preachers often combined medical with religious duties, but the principal medicines and 'cures' were based on old superstitions, family remedies and the products of charlatans. As the historian of the College wrote:

> What men would believe about the value of some recommended remedy was almost without limit. This or that foolish method of healing the sick, the halt and blind, of relieving physical distress of whatever nature, of saving life, would be eagerly tried. Rubbing wens with dead toads, warding off disease by burying a piece of flitch under the eaves of a house, treatment with the thighbone of a man who had been hanged, vipers' tongues, urine, dung, calculi, the brains of this and that animal, the head of a coal black cat burnt to ashes in a new pot which was to be blown into the eye for cataract, rattlesnake poison mixed with cheese formed into pills for palsy and rheumatism, spider's web for fever and ague, and sixty things as senseless as these taken together and mixed into some mess. . . . At the very moment the College was being formed in Philadelphia, an 'Indian Physician' was stationed at Center Square where he advertised that he would cure all diseases which are curable in their nature and state. 'Three years' practice in the city', he declared, 'had furnished ample testimonials of the superiority of the real Indian practice over all other medical practice in this country'. . . . Another practitioner of the same school established himself in South Street, where he flattered himself that he would be enabled 'under Providence to effect cures by means of herbs and roots for all diseases incident to humanity'.**

* Joseph W. Ingrams (ed.), *The First Century of the Philadelphia College of Pharmacy 1821–1921* (Philadelphia College of Pharmacy Society, 1922).

** *Ibid.*

If the records of the quacks and crooks of so-called medicine at that time in the United States make comical reading today, the alarm of serious doctors and druggists was understandable. For one thing, they were losing much business to cynical rogues; for another, their professional status was being grievously undermined, and people were dying, too often in agony, from these alleged nostrums, who might have been saved even by the still primitive medical facilities that were available.

Philadelphia was the birthplace of American pharmacy, founded, appropriately enough, in the Carpenters' Hall, where the Congress of the American Colonies had met. The College developed rapidly, founding its own journal in 1825, investigating patent medicine abuses, exposing quackery and espousing new standards of quality and originality. For many years it had relatively few students – by 1850 only 146 had qualified as 'graduates in pharmacy' – but its publications, and the interest shown in its lectures, had given it a unique reputation. The first *Pharmacopoeia of the United States of America* had been published in Boston in 1820, but by 1830 it had had to be substantially rewritten, almost entirely by members of the new Philadelphia College.

Physically, the College expanded; intellectually, its status was recognised nationally when its journal became in 1835 the *American Journal of Pharmacy*. Philadelphia had become 'The Mecca of American Pharmacy', drawing international interest and respect; and its commercial stores selling and manufacturing drugs were of exceptional quality. A not at all untypical example was Frederick Brown (1796–1864), who had opened his own business in 1822. He was an excellent pharmacist as well as a banker and was one of the founders of the College. He was not a scientist, but one of the first of the new breed of pure pharmacists engaged in the serious business of high quality. William R. Warner graduated from the College in 1856, opened his own store in Philadelphia and was the first manufacturer in America of sugar-coated pills, a French process developed in America.

In 1874 the chair of pharmacy was occupied by Joseph P.

Remington, by which time the College had new premises, designed specifically for practicality rather than for beauty.

Courses of instruction were still given only in the evenings, on three days a week, from October until the end of February. The matriculation fee was $2, that for each course of lectures $10, and the graduation fee was $5. Diplomas were only given to persons of 'good moral character'; they must have attended two courses of each of the lectures given in the College, and completed an apprenticeship of at least four years with 'a person or persons qualified to conduct the drug or apothecary business'. An examination and the presentation of an 'original dissertation or thesis upon some subject of the materia medica, pharmacy, chemistry or one of the branches of science immediately connected therewith, which shall be written with neatness and accuracy', were required before a diploma was granted.

The dominating personality at the College was Remington, described as 'the foremost figure of American Pharmacy'. Born in 1847, of Quaker ancestry, he had graduated from the College in 1866. After working in the business of the eminent manufacturing pharmacist, Dr Edward R. Squibb of Brooklyn, he returned to Philadelphia to open his own business and to be a teaching assistant at the College. In 1874 he became a Professor; like his predecessors, William Procter and Edward Parrish, he continued to run his own drug business as well, giving to the students that mixture of theoretical scholarship and research with practical experience of business that gave the College its particular quality, and which so appealed to Henry Wellcome.

*

'We are sorry to have you go any further way from us,' his father wrote, 'but hope it will all turn for your good. You are dear to our hearts and we are sorry that you can't be near us while we live.' By this time the financial condition of the Wellcomes had become grievous. Solomon had had to sell his house in Garden City and had taken his wife to live in Monticello, on the banks of the Mississippi, but he remained in debt to the extent of $150.

In 1872 he carefully recorded in his diary that he had preached 222 times and had travelled a total of 5,351 miles, of which 100 miles had been on foot, 2,575 by horse and coach, 2,530 on the railway and 146 by boat. He had baptised twenty-two infants, had preached in houses thirty-nine times and had visited twenty-six towns. His income consisted of $275 for preaching and his travel expenses had been $110, so the profit he received above expenses was $165 with another $30 promised. 'Closed the year in prayer after a glorious meeting and ushered in the New Year. God bless our cause this year is my prayer.' In 1873 he preached 170 times, but his financial circumstances did not improve, and he turned to Henry for support, seeking a loan of $50, which, with considerable difficulty, his son was able to arrange.

If Chicago had been a deep disappointment to Wellcome, Philadelphia was to be another major step forward. His start was inauspicious, when he failed to secure the Qualified Assistant's Certificate of the Philadelphia Pharmaceutical Examining Board in August. But his attempt had been premature, and by October he was an enrolled student at the College and attending lectures. His spirits were high and his first letters to his parents from Philadelphia were in striking contrast to those from Chicago:

> Dear Parents
>
> My first week in College has closed with bright prospects for the future.
>
> I have not the least reason to regret my change, except the financial embarrassment which causes me a great deal of uncomfortable feeling beside the trouble it may have caused you. I hope to meet my obligations to you at the time I told you in my last letter.
>
> Beside the lectures and so forth we have a society which is composed of second course students; it has a quiz master and is intended to prepare students for the examinations and to promote a friendly feeling among the students and a general hearty cooperation and also have a course of instruction in itself.

It was at Philadelphia that Wellcome continued his friendship with

Frederick Power. 'My friend Fred Power', he wrote home, 'is the best student in the College, and is bound to excel all others. . . . He has been similarly situated to myself in life, and am rejoiced to see him stand as he does: he is a natural chemist.'

Power was his exact contemporary, having been born in Hudson, New York State, on 4 March 1853. Like Wellcome, he had to finance his way through College by working by day at the pharmacy of Professor Parrish, and by studying in the evenings. Unlike Wellcome, he was a true scholar, his graduating thesis receiving the highest honours in 1874. His academic ambitions were to take him to the German University of Strasbourg specifically to study under the famous Swiss pharmaceutical scientist, Friedrich Flückiger. He returned to Philadelphia in 1880 to a Professorship specially created for him by the College of Pharmacy. It was to be written of him that 'He not only brought home his learning, and the results of his several investigations, but also that love for truth, that ardour for scientific investigation and that high regard for his profession which has become characteristic of him.' He was to become the first Director of the Department of Pharmacy at the University of Wisconsin in 1883, where his achievements became legendary; he had students of poor background and education, including Edward Kremers, his successor, whose own achievements were to be remarkable, building brilliantly on the foundations laid by Power.

Wellcome deeply admired Power's intellect, which he recognised was far greater than his; Power admired Wellcome's ambition and practical approach to medicine. In the course of their many discussions they agreed that they would make an ideal partnership. Wellcome reported developments to his parents on 28 February 1875:

> Spent Sat eve and Sunday [in Philadelphia] at Mr Luce's & the store with Fred Power (Mr Luce is Fred's preceptor in German and an old acquaintance & friend, it is a pleasant home). We had a good visit and talked over our plans for the future and recalled some of our struggles in the past but only to feel thankful for our success.
>
> I went down to Prof. Maisch's residence . . . the Prof. soon came

> out and welcomed me in a very cordial manner, we talked over old associations, then reviewed the developments in Pharmacy for the past year, then the prospects of the Colleges & comparatively. Then I had many questions to ask him in regard to some investigations which I have been making and expect to make all of which he cleared up, then I told him of Power & my plans for the future and he seemed delighted and said that it was just such a team as he wanted to see get together and said he could aid Power while abroad in associating himself with the leading Chemists and scientific men of Europe and putting him in a place when he could best learn what he will go specially for &c &c.

When Wellcome decided in 1880 to join with Silas Mainville Burroughs, he travelled specially to Strasbourg to tell Power, apprehensive that his friend would be affronted. He was not; if anything their friendship deepened, and was to extend to Power's children, on whom Wellcome doted, especially after the tragic early death of their mother. Their letters to 'Uncle Henry' are among the warmest and most charming in his papers. And Wellcome never abandoned his youthful suggestion of a partnership between himself and his friend, with momentous consequences for them both.

It often happens that the best and most permanent friendships are formed at college or university, and the attraction of opposites certainly worked in the case of the young Wellcome and Power. Both were serious, but their ambitions were totally different, Power aspiring to academic distinction, Wellcome to a profitable career in pharmacy. Power's rise to eminence gave Wellcome immense pleasure; his own success brought letters of delight from Madison, Wisconsin, especially from the devoted Power children.

The fact that Wellcome was so attracted to a true scholar was interesting in itself. Although not entirely a theoretical medical academic, as his later career was to prove, Power's approach to scholarship was wholly different to that of the pragmatic and practical Wellcome. But the latter's almost hero-worship of better minds than his own, and his fascination with ideas and intellect, although manifested at an early age, matured at Philadelphia and was particularly demonstrated in his close friendship with Power. His eye for great potential academic talent developed early.

Power was the first of Wellcome's contemporary friends, and was the most enduring, especially when his paths and those of the Mayo brothers separated. Although Power's circumstances were almost as straitened as his, he was far better educated than Wellcome had been and, academically, had a better mind. He later told his daughter, Louise, that in Wellcome's early days in Philadelphia, he

> noticed that he seemed unusually depressed. Upon asking the reason, my father learned that Henry needed books, but had no money with which to purchase them. He was told that 'Fred' would furnish them, although his own resources were decidedly limited. Henry felt that he could not apply to his home for help. They both worked and studied at the same time, and on more than one winter night the two dear friends sat closely together in a poorly heated room, clad in overcoats and covered with all available blankets for warmth, while they pored over their books.

Power invited Wellcome to his home for Christmas 1874, when Wellcome drew from his pocket a worn-out, dilapidated wallet and said to Power's mother: '"You see *this*, Mrs Power? A pretty poor showing; only a few cents in it now; some day it will be bulging."' This incident was characteristic of the difference between them – Power, the serious and unworldly scholar; Wellcome, the entrepreneur, to whom pharmacy was the means for him to escape poverty and to become rich.

Before the College examinations took place at the end of February 1874 each candidate had to produce and submit an original dissertation. It was significant that Power's was a scientific examination of the properties of *Resina Podophyllii*, and was highly regarded by the academic scientific Professors, whereas Wellcome's was on urethral suppositories. He not only demonstrated that the standard ones then supplied were poorly manufactured, were usually brittle and painful, and were a source of irritation and even inflammation, but were also, because of their shape, more likely to be ejected. The fact that they were made by hand was another objection. Wellcome proposed a quite different shape and content:

> The writer has devised a mould forming a suppository two and a quarter inches in length, and three sixteenths of an inch in diameter at the base, and tapering to two sixteenths of an inch, with a conical point, and weighing ten grams. The moulds are refrigerated in a tray, made of zinc instead of tin; the objection to tin is that it rusts out soon if not thoroughly dried each time after using.
>
> By having the mould well chilled and the substance melted to a proper consistence when it is poured in, and when they have become thoroughly cooled, they are easily removed by inverting and striking the mould on the counter.
>
> This form possesses advantages over all others, being more easily inserted and perfectly smooth. The mould is more conveniently and rapidly refrigerated than any other, and costs about the same as the ordinary rectum suppository mould.

Wellcome's researches and proposals were based on those of others, and not least those of Professor Parrish, but it was the practical approach that so struck his examiners. He also had recommendations for the improved composition of the suppositories, and detailed suggestions for their storage and presentation in cotton-lined boxes: 'The observance of these points should be carried out by all those who appreciate the reputation of neat dispenses of pharmaceutical preparations.'

Wellcome subsequently wondered whether he should not have patented his invention as it was, in its small way, almost revolutionary. As the examiners realised, and as did others, his mould system worked, was totally reliable and cheap. When it became widely emulated, Wellcome wisely declared with ostentatious magnanimity to the American Pharmaceutical Association that he had not patented it as it was his personal contribution to the development of good pharmacy and the relieving of pain.

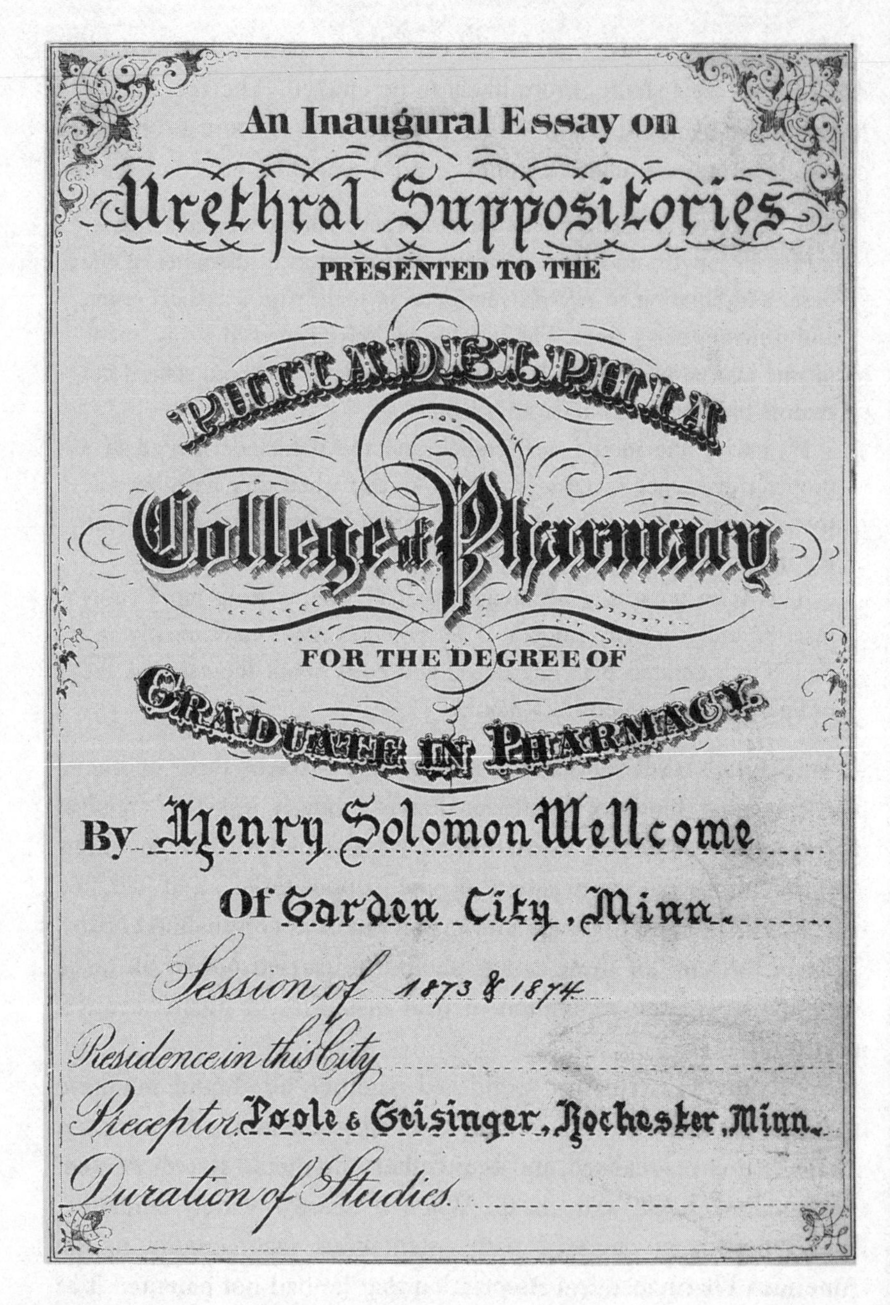
An Inaugural Essay on
Urethral Suppositories
PRESENTED TO THE
PHILADELPHIA
College of Pharmacy
FOR THE DEGREE OF
GRADUATE IN PHARMACY.
By Henry Solomon Wellcome
Of Garden City, Minn.
Session of 1873 & 1874
Residence in this City
Preceptor Poole & Geisinger, Rochester, Minn.
Duration of Studies

Wellcome's essay on urethral suppositories for his degree at the Philadelphia College of Pharmacy, 1874

In retrospect, we can see that this was pure Wellcome in every respect, and not least in the importance of packaging and presentation for sale. He almost certainly took the advice of others on the new chemical content, but he designed several types of mould before he found the right one, and the shape was certainly his idea. The experience also introduced him to the importance of patenting pharmaceutical advances and inventions, a lesson that he learnt well.

There is another particularly interesting fact. Wellcome himself designed and drew the plans for his moulds, but there is no surviving record of him having had any teaching in design or art. What is the case is that he was to become a designer not only of imagination and utility, but also of considerable artistry and style. From where, and from whom, did he develop these skills? It is one thing to have an artist's eye; it is another to learn technique. He could only have acquired these either in Garden City, which seems unlikely, or in Rochester. His drawings of plants were exceptionally accomplished and give clear evidence of professional advice, and probably training. These were part of the necessary skills at Philadelphia, but obviously were acquired before. But who taught him remains unknown, although it is very probable that, once again, the influence of Mayo can be discerned. It certainly gave the young Henry Wellcome's character another dimension. Here was not only an ambitious young pharmacist, but also one fascinated by history, a keen reader in non-medical subjects, and an already talented designer and artist. These talents were to develop greatly, but can already be seen at the age of twenty-one. It is not surprising that Remington and his other professors regarded him as one of their most industrious and determined students, as well as one of the most interesting. One can already glimpse the many-faceted older man, with his myriad of interests, in the young one, while the sensitivity of his drawings tells us something more about his developing character, of which there seem to be no clues in any of his ancestors, on either side. But, then, there are none about where his ambition derived. It remains, as with so much of Henry Wellcome's personality, a mystery, but the fact that he had this talent, which is born rather than acquired only by diligence, was to be of considerable significance in his subsequent rise.

He enjoyed the theatre, when he could afford the price of entry or the time, which would have horrified his parents. He was to develop an exceptional sense of theatre, and to appreciate the importance of the dramatic and unexpected in presentation and exhibition, first of goods, and then in his hospitality and style when he matured in London. He saw the theatre rather more as an artist than as a dramatist, appreciating the value and excitement of visual drama, although he was later to cultivate the friendship of writers, actors and actresses when he had the opportunity to do so.

At the beginning of his course Wellcome had had to borrow $20 from his parents to help with the expenses of his lectures and tuition, and in a letter home he was curious to know how they managed to provide the money. His mother explained in a letter of 17 August 1873 that she had just received $55 for boarding two schoolteachers for eleven weeks, all of which she had decided to lend to her husband who was negotiating for the purchase of their house. Instead, when Henry's request was received, she sent him the $20 and Solomon had borrowed the rest. She had asked Henry to repay it as soon as convenient, remarking that she 'was very glad we could accommodate you which is a pleasure always – to do my children a favour'. Remembering when Henry's gift of spectacles had afforded her such pleasure, she added, 'I shall never forget the favour you did me when you gave me the glasses, that I am now enabled to see to write to you.'

Apart from this loan he had succeeded by his own endeavours, but not without a struggle. His financial circumstances remained difficult, as he reported to his mother on 8 March 1874:

> You know the new clothes I bought in Christmas – two pairs of cheap pants, and I have been doubly careful but am now completely cleared out in that line so you will forgive me for delaying the payment until the date given on the post card but you know that I will pay it as soon as I can. I think Phila. life has learned me to be economical. I never

was so hard up at any time. I dont see how I could have got along if the Profs had not been so kind to me.

I will settle that as soon as I possibly can but as a fact I have not bought a rag of clothes since I came in the city and have not a whole pair of pants or boots to my name, and am pretty shabby generaly – have had to wear rubbers over my boots. I want to get a suit of clothes and then I shall settle honorable debts. Dont think I am complaining of my lot, for though I have had many such trials I feel the better for it.

He had awaited the results of his exams with considerable trepidation, but in his letter of 8 March was able to report triumphantly to his family:

My dear Parents Bro & Cozs

You cant picture the joy that I had last night when I rec'd the answer or notice from Profs, for I was down to the college anxiously waiting (and there I wrote the words with a lead pensil on that p. card) Hoping; fearing; trusting; doubting; anxiously waiting. I was the second one he spoke to when he came from the final meeting of the Profs and trustees which decide the standing of each. He said 'We wellcome you.' I almost fainted for fear but when the words you have passed satisfactory passed his lips I fairly leaped with joy.

One examination lasted four days, commencing in the afternoon and lasting until about 11 o'clock at night. We had divisions of questions although they contain from 2 to ten questions some of these questions take at least one to 2 pages of foolscap paper to write out, and oh, didnt our arms and brains get tired. Oh dear, I would not go through such a siege again for money (though if I had not passed I should try it next year). Six young men gave up during the examination as they could not pass and knew it. Have just learned that 20 were thrown (thrown that is ejected), there are between 90 and 100 graduates. Our graduating exercises will be held in the Academy of Music March 12th (Thursday eve.). The class will be on the stage and will be 3 or 4000 people present many from N.Y. accnd Boston, Baltimore, Washington etc. I do wish you could be present. Why have a rule that none shall graduate under the age of 21 years? But they passed me (20) but my aged appearance had much to do with it I think. There are many who had all their time studying and had no cause and passed below me. This is a grand success for me and I appreciate it.

*

Wellcome had contemplated either staying in Philadelphia or going to Washington, but on 14 April 1874 he wrote to his parents: 'I think that maybe I will go to New York if nothing turns up here that is encouraging'. Ten days later he wrote letters of application for employment to McKesson & Robbins and Caswell Hazard & Co., two of the most important pharmaceutical firms in New York. McKesson & Robbins replied that they had no vacancy, but said that they would place his name on their register. But Caswell Hazard & Co. replied immediately. 'If in New York in a few days please call at our 24th Street store, we anticipate engaging another assistant.'

Wellcome went, secured the position, and moved to New York on 1 May 1874. Three days later he commenced work with his new employers. The pay was not high, and his father told him when he learnt of his son's move, 'It seems that you have gone to New York, well, perhaps it is all for the best, but cannot see it . . . it seems hard work for small wages when you get much more in Western towns but I do not know what is best.' His mother was more alarmed about the possible perils of New York. 'In this evil day, there are few you can trust, but I thank God there are some, and we only know them when we prove them. I expect you have had considerable experience, but you must be on your guard.' Henry replied:

> My stay in New York is not for the purpose of making money, but for cultivating my knowledge of business as can only be learned by practical business in such a house as this. This firm stands above all others in the United States, and no other firm has as fine a class of people to deal with . . . in fact this [is] the store of the city and any production from the house is relied upon everywhere. I could make more money now by going to Chicago.

On his twenty-first birthday he wrote to his parents to inform them that '*life now becomes a reality!*' He reminded them that they had stressed to him that 'he that hasteth to be rich is not wise', but responded with the quotation that 'He that striveth not for earthly blessings is not wise'. He also added that,

> There are far more people who want God to raise their crops, thresh and grind the grain, and almost put it in their bellies. I do believe that God helps those who help themselves. I know I used to think a great deal about when I should be able to lay up wealth. I have always had a desire for wealth, and still have . . . but I want to live a life devoted to the true God and to mankind.

The emphasis of his priorities was very clear, and the last sentence rings only partly true; certainly, Henry Wellcome had never been a convinced, let alone a sincere, Adventist, and none of his friends, then or later, commented on him being deeply religious. He had his Faith, but saw no contradiction between God and Mammon, and he was determined to succeed in the latter pursuit. What was to be interesting was what he did with his wealth once he had acquired it, but his material ambitions dominated him then, and for several years to come. The contrast to the academic and scientific ambitions of Fred Power could not have been more starkly expressed, and disconcerted his pious parents. Ambition had never been a Wellcome characteristic – perhaps it came with his Curtis blood – but Ambition is an inexplicable phenomenon.

Wellcome's service with Caswell Hazard & Co. lasted for two years, and it was another important formative period in his life; for the first time he was involved in a major international, as well as national, pharmaceutical company. Until then he had only worked for local druggists, or at the most provincial ones, but he was now with a firm whose products were known throughout the United States and were developing abroad. With this company he learned the business value of selling products of good quality, and in quantity. But, apart from his letters home, his detailed accounts of his travels throughout the United States, and the frequent praise from his employers, few details are known about Wellcome's life in his first two years in New York.

None the less, the essential elements have come down to us. He had now matured physically. He was not very tall – five foot eight inches – had ginger hair and moustache, with striking blue eyes; he was slim, always well dressed, smart and alert. He was a handsome young man, but not greatly interested in women, recognised not only as exceptionally intelligent and hard-working, but also, as Fred Power and his Philadelphia teachers had noticed, formidably ambitious. To his employers he was almost the perfect assistant and traveller, courteous, charming, able and dedicated to his profession. At this stage he seems to have devoted himself virtually exclusively to his work and to the acquiring of more knowledge, especially of plants, on which of course all drugs were then based, the era of synthetic drugs being far in the future.

One feature of Wellcome's work particularly struck his new employers. It was the firm's policy that their travellers should stay at the best hotels and charge the bills to them. Wellcome invariably stayed in cheap boarding-houses, so that his expenses were remarkably low. His cousin Frank would relate that when Wellcome was in Portland, Maine, on business, 'he stopped at a cheap boarding-house on India Street. That ramshackle old wooden building is still standing [in 1939] and I often see it.' The combination of Wellcome's frugality and his considerable talents as a salesman deeply impressed his employers, who had become used to a very different type of commercial traveller.

But the fact was that Henry Wellcome, then or later, was not interested in luxuries, whether at his own or others' expense. 'He regarded both wealth and prestige as necessary tools with which to build permanent benefits to all peoples,' Frank wrote. 'He cared nothing for either as factors of personal importance. He was a modest and exceedingly humble personality.' This was written after his cousin had risen to fame and wealth, but it was true of the young Henry Wellcome, except that his personal modesty and reticence concealed a very powerful personal ambition. Such men tend to be underestimated.

Solomon Wellcome's health began to deteriorate badly in 1874. Henry, in response to sad appeals from his mother, wrote strongly against them moving from Monticello. She had a total faith in him: 'I have that confidence in you to believe that you will succeed.' Also, 'you are more comfort to me than a fortune, or what some call a fortune. I think I have a fortune in having true and faithful boys.'

Wellcome's tribute to his parents written to them on his twenty-first birthday emphasises his devotion to them:

> I can look back and see your patience, and love, and watchful care: the lessons which you taught us in our younger days, and [how you] always strove to lead us in the true path. You have nothing to regret in any way, unless it was that you didn't whip us when we deserved. You have always manifested towards us that true parental love and affection which shall endear you to us, and to our memories throughout our lives. May God bless you both my dear parents, and may you be near and dear to each other, and be a blessing to each other, in every way. You are no longer bound to the government of your children but we do assure you again that the bond of influence can only be broken by death.

His father lingered unhappily, at Monticello, where he eventually died on 17 May 1876. Wellcome returned to Monticello for the funeral and also discussed his future career with his mother and brother; on 30 May he wrote to them:

> I told you of a contemplated change which has now matured into an engagement with Messrs McKesson & Robbins, the largest drug house in America, I shall do some travelling for them. . . . I feel some reluctance in leaving such good friends . . . my employers I regard very highly – while they express themselves as sorry to lose me, yet they saw it to be for my best interest.

The principals of his new firm, John McKesson, Daniel C. Robbins and W. H. Wickham, were all active members of the American Pharmaceutical Association, and they had been impressed by Wellcome's growing reputation. When he made an application to them, they replied on 29 May 1876: 'We have decided to give you a trial if you can start immediately, as it is important to lose no time.' He was offered a salary of $16 a week with travelling expenses.

It was as a travelling salesman that Wellcome made his reputation with McKesson & Robbins, to the point that his salary was to rise to $2,500 a year. His principal task was to introduce and sell its new gelatine-coated pills to the medical profession and to druggists.

McKesson & Robbins regarded itself as 'the greatest drug house in the world', a claim challenged by several houses in Philadelphia and Chicago, but its reputation was justifiably high. John McKesson had opened his first shop in New York in 1833, and was joined two years later by Daniel Robbins. Positioned close to the harbour, the business flourished in the supply of medicines to ships. But it was a time of rapid growth for the expanding city, and one of McKesson's friends was Samuel Morse, experimenting with the possibility of sending messages over wires by the use of electrical impulses, transformed into a code of dots and dashes. He was by trade a portrait painter, and a not very successful one, and McKesson helped to finance him until, in 1844, the first Morse telegraph appeared.

As the United States expanded westwards, so did the business of McKesson & Robbins. By 1851 the firm had business in most States and territories and had established a large export trade. The key to this remarkable success was that McKesson & Robbins manufactured drugs and medicines to new standards of purity and quality at generally low prices. It built its own laboratories at Bridgeport, Connecticut, and put great emphasis on effective distribution, which became rapidly more easy as the railways opened up vast new areas, and access to potential customers.

McKesson & Robbins quickly realised that in Wellcome it had a young man of exceptional energy and enthusiasm, and a natural commercial traveller. 'Your success in Buffalo is splendid,' McKesson & Robbins wrote to him on 14 October, after Wellcome had secured large orders from doctors and pharmacies. He even tried to sell to Dr Whitfield in Chicago, but his old master's terms were unacceptable. In Chicago he had also received an offer from another major druggist;

McKesson & Robbins's building in New York City, 1880

when he told McKesson & Robbins, it replied at once that, 'We note your offer in Chicago and can only say that we hope that you will continue your connection with us for several years to come. We have perfect confidence in you & know it is not misplaced.'

One of the great attractions to Wellcome of his new job was the opportunity it gave him to travel throughout the United States, and which he described in considerable – and sometimes rather excessive – details in long letters to his family. Mary Wellcome's replies were often rather sad. One began: 'Dear Henry as George and the girls [Wellcome's cousins] have gone to meeting tonight and I am left alone for I felt more like talking with you than going to the meeting or talking with any one else'; and in another she wrote:

> . . . almost 2 years have rolled around since I last saw you my dear boy but your mother['s] affection does not lessen, time cannot erase the love I have for my dear children. . . . We have yours and George's picture hung up one on each side of the picture you sent last Christmas in our sitting room and we are daily reminded of your goodselves.

Wellcome wrote to her from Los Angeles on 3 January 1879 with a characteristic account of his travels:

> My dear Mother
>
> Your good letters have all been received and I am much ashamed of my neglect it is too bad but dear mother do not think it is carelessness for I think of you every silent moment & often when active at my business. No other love comes between us and you have not been neglected for other social correspondence.
>
> I have been very hard at work & meeting strong competition & have stood ahead & still do but it has required every energy and the closest attention I get tired, but my health is excellent, and courage good. . . .
>
> I sent you a Christmas present a fur muff & cape which I hope you received in time.
>
> I worked all day Christmas & New Years & enjoyed them my mind went back though (during those days) to my dear mother & brother &

to thoughts of the merry Christmas days at our own home and our 'Happy New Years' gone with time.

I do enjoy your good letters so much dear mother please write often if I do neglect you.

How are you prepared with money?

I will send you a draft from San Francisco for 50$ which you can get cashed in Bangor by signing your name on the back.

I shall start from S.F. on Jan'y 20th for the lower coast & will visit Guynas Mozattan, Colina, Acupulco, Mexico and may go to City of Mexico.

You must not worry about me for I shall not be rash and get into danger. You know I have been in just as bad places. Much depends upon a mans behaviour & habits about his getting into trouble. Most men who get harmed in that country, do so on account of whiskey or Women, and you know neither will have the opportunity with me. . . .

Wellcome was eager that his mother should also benefit from his travels, at his expense, and wrote to her from Toronto on 10 September 1877, ungrammatically as usual:

I have anxiously looked for answer to my last letter. I have been attending meeting of Am. Pharm. Ass. here for past week. . . .

Mother please write to me all about your going east & when you want to start, Do you know of any one else going. I want you to have company the folks expect you to remain in Maine for several years at least, and this is what I plan for and in coming you had better plan for permanent change. You will come by Mil & St Paul or St Paul Head & Chi. to Chicago & by Mich. Southern & chng Central to Albourg, Boston & Albany from Albany to Boston & Eastern R.R. to Bangor. You will take a pullman car at St Paul change in Chicago & take pullman car for Boston, 1 change & take pullman car for Bangor. You will buy ticket through to Bangor which costs the same as to Hermon and as you can use the company time, you can buy what is now known as limited ticket as that is for a continuous passage and so a few dollars less.

You make but two changes & have to recheck your baggage twice & once in Boston. The Pullman cars will cost you about $7.00 or $9.00 and I would not consent to have you come in any other way.

> If you travel with any one else & they do not take pullman car you can have one companion in your seat during the day as your car ticket allows a full seat. If you take other cars you will have to make several other changes & much annoyance which this prevents. In these cars you will always take the lower berth. Please let me know all about your plans & I may be able to meet you in Chicago.
>
> Let me hear from you very soon.

But in this happy reunion, Mary Wellcome made it plain that she had no desire to move to Maine.

*

Although Wellcome did not claim to be a medical scientist, he had a deeply enquiring mind and began to attract considerable attention by his regular contributions to the *American Journal of Pharmacy* and *The Pharmacist*, the first appearing in the *Journal* in July 1874, on 'Chlorinated Alkalies as a test for morphia and other proximate principles'. Another denounced in scathing terms the selling of liquor in pharmacies:

> We believe that the greater number of druggists confine their sales to its legitimate requirements [for strictly medicinal purposes]; but there are still a large number who do disgrace the profession by using their titles as a cover under which they carry on an extensive liquor traffic, and in some cases so remunerative that many saloon keepers might envy it. Some druggists make no secret of this department, and sell without restrictions; but this is rarely the case; usually there is a back room, where the right customer can get whatever he wants, but a good watch is kept that they don't let the wrong men into their secrets. Some sell it to their customers in bottles, and allow them to be concealed in a convenient place about the back room, so that customers with their friends can have easy access and resort to it *ad libitum*. A very popular custom, for several years past, is that of selling liquors from the soda fountain, so that the favoured customer can get his drinks without calling for them as he would at an ordinary bar. There are many other devices resorted to by which they manage to escape the tangles of the law and just censure of the public. It seems unreasonable that cham-

> pagnes and other fancy liquors should be included in the stock of the legitimate pharmacist, but we frequently find them there. Not only are such pharmacists a disgrace to the profession, but they are casting an atmosphere of suspicion about it so that not infrequently we see the name coupled with that of the saloon-keeper. . . . This class of druggists are frequently troubled with dissipated and unreliable clerks, and is it to be wondered at?

This article was not only strongly worded, but also well researched. Wellcome had observed what was indeed a scandal, and had found and published a circular from the Chicago liquor dealers to druggists seeking their support against proposed more stringent liquor laws. It is difficult to calculate its general effect; its immediate one was to arouse a great deal of interest in the profession about this twenty-one-year-old graduate. Its themes were also of interest. The first was his concern for the good name of the profession; the second was his strong feelings about drink. Both were to be lifelong.

On learning that his paper had been reproduced in *The New York Weekly Witness*, Wellcome wrote to his parents that,

> I was surprised but really pleased to know that it had received attention for it is a subject which I feel deeply upon and have resolved to use my continued influence (be it ever so little) against The Evil. There are three great evils which we as Christians must fight without ceasing. viz. sensuality, Liquor drinking, and The Use of Tobacco. . . .

His former Philadelphia Professor, Albert E. Ebert, was so impressed that he suggested to Wellcome that he should become the editor of *The Pharmacist*, but Wellcome declined the honour, probably because of the time that would be involved. But it was a remarkable tribute to such a young man who had only recently qualified.

When Wellcome visited Garden City in 1877, he was invited to speak in the Baptist Church. He wrote to his mother that 'taking one distinct matter in particular I touched on the matter of temperance and the temptations of young people in the larger cities'. He also reported with much pleasure that 'Garden City has no saloon'.

It is not at all clear when and why the young Wellcome became alarmed about the liquor question, but his letters from Rochester and Chicago often assure his parents that he was very careful to keep away from 'drinking people', which he was. It may be that at that time he was a teetotaller; he certainly was not later, and was to be a generous host. But he was a keen advocate of total sobriety at work, and urged abstinence before the age of twenty-six – why this age is not at all clear – and at least before the evening meal. He was not himself to keep these stern rules, devised for his employees, although he was to be a very moderate drinker. But he must have had experiences in Rochester, and Chicago and Philadelphia, that had clearly shocked him, and his tirade against pharmacists being in the liquor business was totally sincere. Furthermore, he was absolutely right.

In November 1875 the *Journal* published a paper by Wellcome on damiana, delivered in October to the New York Alumni of the Philadelphia College. Damiana was claimed to be an aphrodisiac, and Wellcome's paper examined leaves obtained from San Francisco, Washington and New York. He had found substantial differences in the products, but could not determine 'which is the true damiana'.

Wellcome published nine papers between 1874 and 1880, of which the most celebrated was his account of his exploration of the native Cinchona forests of Ecuador. He set out on this expedition in 1878 to find the increasingly rare Cinchona trees, whose bark was the prime source of pure quinine. His subsequent account, published at length in both the American and British *Pharmaceutical Journals*, created something of a sensation in those circles, and brought the name of Henry Wellcome for the first time to the attention of English pharmacists and medical practitioners. With one paper, at the age of twenty-six, he became, if not famous, a seriously considered figure.

Wellcome's education had not included much attention to either grammar, spelling or punctuation, which made his letters, although lively and arresting, hardly literary models, and these early deficiencies were not wholly eradicated for many years. But in conversation, as well as in his letters, he had a real eloquence and enthusiasm, and his increasingly wide reading had had its influence. Writing never came easily to him, which makes this, his first important contribution to medical literature, so impressive. It is too long and detailed to quote in full, but deserves to be included at some length as an Appendix, as the product of a young man engaged in an important adventure.* It also made his name, most importantly in England, where sources of quinine were eagerly sought for British soldiers and administrators in malaria-plagued parts of the Empire. The regimen of a daily dose had had almost magical effects, particularly in West Africa, and then seemed to be the definitive preventive of a disease whose cause was as yet unknown, but whose results – before quinine – had been devastating.

What Wellcome did not state in his paper was that this, his first major expedition and adventure, had been highly dangerous. On his return to America he related his experiences to Power, who subsequently told his daughter, Louise, about them, and she recorded them in her unpublished Reminiscences:

> Being a foreigner of position, his life was in danger at every step, and he realised that in some way he must get into the good graces of the natives. Hearing of an old woman, who was supposed to be sick unto death, Mr Wellcome went to see her, administering some stele quinine pills, which he knew could do her no harm – and probably no good. Strange to say, the old woman revived, and word was soon passed around that an angel from Heaven had appeared and was working miracles. One woman fell upon her knees before his mule, saying in Spanish – 'If I ever marry, it shall be a handsome man like you, with a ginger colored moustache.'
>
> It was Mr Wellcome's desire, while in Peru, to stand upon the very spot where the artist Frederick E. Church painted his famous picture 'The Heart Of The Andes'. This desire was realised, but to his great physical discomfort, for, as he brought his mule to a standstill, the animal lost footing, slipped, and fell over the embankment. Mr Wellcome

* See Appendix 1 on pages 387–93.

> was painfully injured. As soon as the fact was made known, people of high and low degree rushed to the rescue. The ruling official of the city insisted upon having Mr Wellcome taken to his palace, where he was cared for. He was detained there for several weeks, and when he came again to visit the Power home in Hudson, New York, he was still limping and walking with the aid of a cane.
>
> He brought with him many unset jewels of great value, which had been given to him as tokens of friendship. He himself made quite a collection of opals, which he never had set, but frequently took out and admired for the fiery brilliance and beauty.

Wellcome also brought as a gift to the Powers some live parakeets from Peru, in a cage, as a memento to them of their young friend's first foreign exploration.

As a result of his paper people began making enquiries about who he was. And then one day, while Wellcome was serving at the counter at McKesson & Robbins, a small, darkly tanned man with noticeably bright, almost feverish eyes walked in to place an order. Wellcome recognised him at once and introduced himself to the explorer and journalist who had found David Livingstone. It was his first meeting with Henry Morton Stanley.

By now the young Wellcome had acquired not only a reputation, but also an appetite for travel, adventure, history and collecting, but his immediate ambition was for financial security and responsibility. The opportunity for achieving these now came from an unexpected quarter.

# 3

# Burroughs and Wellcome

Wellcome had first met Silas Mainville Burroughs, who was seven years older than him, in Philadelphia, where Burroughs was working for John Wyeth. When he went to the Philadelphia College after Wellcome, he had specialised, significantly, in the new compressed medicines, the first tablet drugs, which were the subject of his graduation thesis in 1877. The earliest surviving letter of their subsequent large correspondence was from Burroughs to Wellcome on 31 October 1877, in which he recommended friends of his on whom Wellcome might call on his commercial travels, and suggested a joint holiday for the next summer. The jocular, friendly and personal tone of the letter implies that they had known each other for some time.

On leaving the Philadelphia College, where he was regarded as an outstanding student, and an immensely popular one, Burroughs rejoined John Wyeth as a salesman. An admirer wrote of him after his death that he was

> the most original, the most attractive, and the most widely known personality in the ranks of pharmacy. His circle of acquaintance was marvellous. He had friends, intimate friends, in every part of the world. Wherever he went – and he went everywhere – he attracted around him numbers of people who never forgot him, and very many who loved him.

Burroughs was not tall, but he was handsome, vivacious and charming. He was an enthusiast, but also an ambitious man of business who had seen the immense international potential of the new compressed medicines. Wyeth was so impressed with him that, in 1878, it sent him to London as its representative; it is not clear whether this was on its initiative or his, but there is no reference to his move in his letters to Wellcome, which were of an entirely personal and bantering nature, before he arrived in London early that year. He had some personal capital and decided to found his own company, S. M. Burroughs & Co., with the approval of Wyeth.

Burroughs opened his small business in June 1878, renting part of an office building in Southampton Street, just off the Strand, as an agent for Wyeth's goods. This was inadequate, and he then moved to two rooms in Great Russell Street, with a rented basement at 1, Cock Lane, in the City, as a warehouse and packing department. In November he moved again, to 8 Snow Hill, Holborn, retaining the Cock Lane building. His total premises consisted of an office for himself, another for his very small staff, and a small printing machine.

Burroughs's agreement with Wyeth was that he had the right to sell its goods worldwide, excluding the United States, and Burroughs took this literally. His first venture was to attempt to enter the French market through an American friend, Edward Lindewald, who was based in the American Bureau at the Exposition Universelle, where Burroughs wanted to exhibit Wyeth products. Pricing was a problem, but there were to be more.

Characteristically, Burroughs opened on a note of high optimism, informing Lindewald that 'you can take orders for the goods and we will fix your commission as agreed upon all sales. . . . Please give the lint to the hospitals in Paris also give them a pound or so each of the Dialysed Iron, one pound of Lint to each is enough.' Burroughs was so active in pushing Wyeth products in Britain that he could not get to Paris until September 1878. It was then that he discovered a problem that had not occurred to him, and which was to cause him, and later Wellcome, considerable difficulties.

The British Customs had been difficult about giving permission to import American drugs. This was partly overcome by the simple expedient of changing the labels by substituting the name of Wyeth to that of S. M. Burroughs & Co., but stamp duty was still payable. The French authorities, encouraged by their own pharmaceutical interests, flatly refused to allow the importation of foreign drugs and medicines, and so, for the time being, Burroughs's grandiose plans for flooding France with Wyeth products were frustrated before they could even be translated into orders.

He was determined to expand the business abroad, none the less, but the burdens of establishing it in Britain were heavy enough, and it was at this point that he realised that he needed a partner who could run the British side while he travelled in search of business in countries that did not protect their own firms in the way that the French – and, as later transpired, the Germans – did. Also, the success of the rather dubious ruse of making American products appear to be English could be applied elsewhere if the conditions were right, but it was already evident that protectionist Europe was a problem. Free Trade may have been the British talisman, but its practice had not been universal.

This episode demonstrated the scale of Burroughs's ambitions for his little company, but it also demonstrated his limitations. Wyeth had, reasonably, expected him to build up the potentially lucrative British market first, but before he had really begun to do this effectively, he was trying to push into other markets. This caused the first strains in a relationship that was to become very strained indeed, until it sundered acrimoniously six years later.

One of Burroughs's first appointments, and his best of all, was Robert Clay Sudlow, who joined as a clerk, aged thirty-three. Born in Liverpool, his family had moved to London, and he had worked as a clerk in several city firms before he joined Burroughs in February 1879. He quickly proved himself exceptionally capable and diligent, and had capacities far beyond those of a clerk; he was destined to play a key role in the expansion of the little company he had joined.

The recollections of one of the first employees of S. M. Burroughs & Co. demonstrate how small an operation it was. Miss Hunt was engaged in January 1880 'for correspondence & circular addressing' with one other lady, who stayed for only a few months. The staff was as small as their premises, and soon Miss Hunt found herself the only woman employee in the office: 'We were all fairly busy until the middle of the Summer [of 1880] when we had hardly anything to do & I remember my ever kind friend Mr Sudlow sending me out for walks.' Subsequently, the workload increased, and the staff numbers grew dramatically, particularly among women employees. Some of the family atmosphere of this early period is captured in Miss Hunt's concluding words: 'At the end of the year 1887 I left to be married, & although with the prospect of a happy future, it caused me very keen regret to part with my work & from those who had been such kind friends as well as employers.'

Burroughs's choice of principal assistant, T. Y. Kelly, however, was far less happy. As Kelly knew next to nothing about medicine, pharmacy or the medical profession, his appointment remains a mystery, and it was not long before Wyeth was expressing dissatisfaction. But Wyeth's disappointment went beyond the incompetent Kelly, and reflected poorly upon Burroughs himself. Although Burroughs does not appear to have realised it, there was a real possibility that Wyeth might withdraw its business from him, which would have been disastrous; indeed, it would probably have been the end of S. M. Burroughs & Co. shortly after its birth.

Burroughs's excessive self-confidence became rapidly apparent to John Wyeth. Burroughs wrote to the company on 13 July 1878:

> I am happy to inform you of my continued and uniform success with the medical profession here. I have yet to meet with the first rebuff or coldness. They all treat me first-rate, and all like the goods. Are now trying the samples & have begun to prescribe them some. I am showing the Lint to several of the leading surgeons who take to it readily and will give it a good trial in the hospitals. They say 'Leave some at such and such a hospital with my name on it & I will be sure to have it tested & call the attention of the other surgeons to it.' I have not visited the hospitals much yet but I am now going to pay them especial attention afternoons as I can find medical men in their offices but during the

forenoons. Messrs Squire & Co. gave me a good order today and I had a long conversation with young Mr Squire. Like everybody else they treat me very well, and have a good deal to say to me about business, our country, etc. . . . Mr Kelly has just returned from a trip to Hull where he got a good reception from the trade & profession. The goods promise to sell there. Mr Kelly takes well with the trade. . . .

Since I have observed the manner of doing business here I have found that it will require the investment of a much larger capital on my part than I had anticipated in order to conduct this business properly. This is owing to the long credits. . . .

Kindly bear in mind that I am furnishing the capital to start and run the business here which I am perfectly willing to continue to do. I have investments in the States which as you know are paying me large returns in dividends, but upon which I cannot realise at present without considerable sacrifice that I cannot afford to make. I have now my spare cash in deposit with you for the present & likely some time to come I shall wish to leave it at the rate of int. [erest] you have been paying [six per cent]. I also propose to make it to your interest to take my acceptances instead of this cash for goods by agreeing in this event to charge you nothing for the fine set of office furniture that I have purchased, neither for the substantial shelving & fixtures I put into the store and which are large enough to accommodate three times my present stock of goods. . . .

The start was indeed modest. The accountant reported on 1 October 1878 that 'The sales for September amount to £158.15.9d, more than double last month's. That's a decided progress and I hope will continue on the same ratio.' Wyeth was not impressed.

Burroughs's technique was certainly unusual, both in England and in Scotland. On 6 May 1879 he was writing to Messrs Lowe and Co. of Dumfries: 'Not having received the promised list of clergymen, lawyers, public speakers, & singers of your neighbourhood, we conclude you must have forgotten it, & beg again to call your attention to it, as a matter of importance to yourselves as much as to us.' To one dilatory salesman, Mr G. Evanovitch, came this reprimand on 24 August 1879:

> If you don't attend to your business, nor take any interest in it, we don't propose to pay you for neglecting it. You have a very mistaken idea in thinking that we are stuck with you and that by reason of friendship we are willing for you to impose upon us. Your pursuance of this policy will certainly show you that you are greatly mistaken.

Another feature of Burroughs's approach to the business was to supply British hospitals, particularly in London, with modest amounts of Wyeth goods and medicines – especially Chlorate of Potash and Borax, as well as his own Kepler Malt Extract and Cod Liver Oil – as presents and to suggest that they might be interested in placing some orders. The compressed drugs were also pushed and advertised, and a characteristic letter to an eminent surgeon (17 October 1879) reads: 'We feel much complimented in reading your article in *The Medical Times and Gazette* that you should speak so kindly of the compressed drugs, and beg to thank you for remembering to do them justice.'

It was Burroughs who prepared the standard hospital donation letter, which was circulated widely in 1881. It read:

> Dear Sir, We have much pleasure in donating for the benefit of your hospital [blank] medicines guineas worth of acknowledged value by the medical profession. If properly utilised we have no doubt they will be of greater service to the hospital than a similar present of money.
>
> We beg you will place this donation at the disposal of your entire medical staff that they may each have the opportunity of prescribing them.
>
> Please let us know when this supply is exhausted as we may desire to make a further donation sufficient for a thorough trial. After which should you wish to purchase for hospital use, we shall quote such special terms as will place them within easy reach of any charitable institution. We do not consider that this donation places you under any obligation to us, but shall be glad to know if any reports upon them are published in the medical journals or if your physicians are pleased with them.

One of Burroughs's first successes was when he became interested in acquiring and producing what seemed to him a promising and

ABOVE Henry Solomon Wellcome, 1864

RIGHT Henry Wellcome (right) with his brother George (left) and their parents

BELOW The original log cabin school at Garden City, Minnesota, early 1860s

ABOVE Solomon Wellcome
RIGHT Dr Jacob Wellcome

BELOW The Wellcome Home,
Garden City, Minnesota

The Young Pharmacist – Wellcome in Chicago

ABOVE William Worrall Mayo (1819–1911)
RIGHT John Michael Maisch (1831–93), Professor at Philadelphia College of Pharmacy 1866–93

Phila. March th 1874

Dear Folks at Home
I have graduated and
am happy
yes — I am Happy
So rejoice with me and
be exceeding glad
With much affection

Postcard from Henry Wellcome to his parents telling them of his graduation at the Philadelphia College of Pharmacy, March 1874

LEFT Frederick Belding Power (1853–1927) as a young man

BELOW Henry Wellcome on horseback (left) and J. Baiz, 'on the hurricane deck of a mule, our trip through Central and South America', 1878

ABOVE Henry Wellcome in 1880, at the inauguration of his partnership with Burroughs

OPPOSITE Silas Mainville Burroughs (1846–95)

ABOVE Pharmaceutical samples offered for sale by Henry Wellcome when a salesman for McKesson & Robbins

LEFT Snow Hill Buildings on the corner of Snow Hill and Holborn Viaduct, London, which served as the head office of Burroughs Wellcome & Co. from 1883 until destroyed by bombing in 1941

BELOW Burroughs Wellcome products on display at the International Medical and Sanitary Exhibition, London 1881

ABOVE The interior of the head office of Burroughs Wellcome & Co. at Snow Hill, designed by Henry Wellcome with Moorish motifs and the Statue of Liberty
BELOW The Wandsworth factory of Burroughs Wellcome & Co., 1883–9

LEFT The opening of the Dartford factory of Burroughs Wellcome & Co. in 1889, with a firework display, organised by Burroughs, forming the words 'Welcome to Henry George'

BELOW Speeches at the opening of the Dartford factory of Burroughs Wellcome & Co. in 1889

Transport of raw materials by Thames barge on to the site of the Dartford factory, 1895

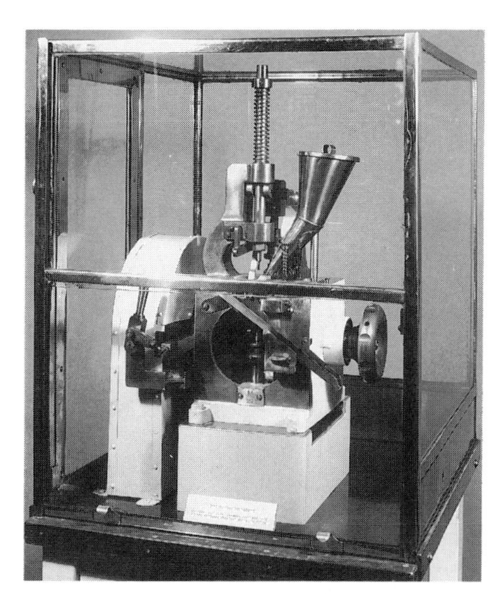

ABOVE The Tabloid compressing machine designed and made between 1900 and 1910 at the Wellcome Chemical Works, Dartford

ABOVE RIGHT
R. Clay Sudlow

RIGHT Henry Wellcome in fancy dress as a penitent renouncing earthly pleasures and contemplating mortality, *c.* 1890

May Sheldon (Mrs French Sheldon)

Sir Henry Morton Stanley (1841–1904)

Henry Wellcome in 1902

lucrative commodity, a good malt and cod liver oil preparation. He became associated with Philip Emery Lockwood, who held some patents, and on 17 January 1879 he formed the Kepler Malt Extract Co. with a capital of £3,000 and himself as managing director. This did not please Wyeth's when it learnt of it.

Burroughs's dynamism and the quality of his American products, to which Kepler Malt was the first British addition, brought him swiftly to the attention of other pharmacists and the medical profession. His little company initially made very modest profits, but business increased rapidly. Burroughs then added the Nubian Blacking Co., of which he became a director, to his increasing list of interests. Again, Wyeth's was displeased and concerned.

The key to Burroughs's hopes of success in Britain and Europe, and worldwide, lay in the compressed medicine tablets in which he had specialised at Philadelphia, and which were Wyeth's principal original products.

The revolution in pharmacy that was to have a crucial role in the early careers of Burroughs and Wellcome was, in fact, an English invention by William Brockedon, who took out a patent in 1843, under the title of 'Shaping Pills, Lozenges and Black Lead by Pressure in Dies'. The purpose was 'by causing the proper materials when in a state of granulation dust or powder to be made into form and solidified by pressure in dies'. But the method, and the product, were crude, his pills being made by a small hand-punch struck with a mallet; the results were unimpressive, but some Americans saw the potential. Compressed tablets were first imported into the United States in 1854, and the first production of American pills by Brockedon's method was begun by Jacob Dunton, a wholesale druggist in Philadelphia and a graduate of the College of Pharmacy, who began his experiments in 1863, built his machine a year later, but did not market his products until 1869; his machine was not patented until 1876. The results were an improvement on the Brockedon method and opened up the possibilities of mass production, but the problems of maintaining the precise quantities and quality were formidable. Dunton's machine was improved upon by Henry Bower and John Wyeth, with a rotary production machine in 1872, whose sale in America of their 'Compressed powders and pills' originated compressed hypodermic tablets, triturates and medicinal lozenges. McKesson & Robbins had countered with gelatine-coated preparations, which were also very popular. Neither was known in England or Germany until Burroughs introduced Wyeth's products in 1878.

They were limited in composition and variety, but the era of the mass-produced pill to replace medicines delivered either in liquid or powdered form had arrived, although the difficulties of exact measurements and uniform quality, and their preservation in bottles over time and in varying conditions of heat and cold, had not yet been fully surmounted. Wyeth's machines, although in many respects revolutionary for their time, could not produce certain categories of tablet; these still had to be made by hand. Wyeth jealously guarded its patented machines, which were the foundation of the fortunes of S. M. Burroughs & Co., and then Burroughs Wellcome & Co., until, as will be related, the latter produced an even better machine that could produce 600 tablets of high quality a minute by 1887. However, this was not anticipated in 1879. Also, the deeply conservative English doctors, druggists and chemists had yet to be persuaded that this foreign innovation was in any way an improvement on their long-standing methods. Suspicion of change was to prove the greatest challenge in England to these Yankee novelties, few realising that the originator had in fact been English. But by 1880 their popularity had begun to be established on both sides of the Atlantic.

*

Burroughs was essentially a superb salesman, not an innovator, who loved travelling. He was at his best with people, but the necessary chores of running a business did not attract him, nor was he particularly good at them, a deficiency he frankly recognised. He began to look for a congenial partner who could run the business in London while he travelled abroad for the company.

Indeed, the idea of Wellcome filling this role had occurred to him very early in the life of S. M. Burroughs & Co. The first letter actually opening the possibility of a partnership is dated 6 January 1879, but this may well not have been the first occasion on which he had raised the idea:

> I hope I shall have the great pleasure of welcoming you to these hospitable shores, at an early day, as soon as your engagement will allow you to come. You need not say to McKesson and Robbins that you certainly will never come back, but rather that you are coming over here to spy out the country or prospect it, and my opinion is that you will report so favourably that you will decide to unite your fortunes with mine. I think we would make a pretty lively team in the pharmaceutical line. . . . Just you take your vacation in a little trip over here and I haven't much doubt of your staying a while.

Although Wellcome did not like Burroughs's somewhat cavalier attitude to his employers, and was cautious, he was interested, but no more. He was doing well with McKesson & Robbins, and had to think of his family in Minnesota; also, he had no capital at all, which would make it a somewhat one-sided 'partnership'. But Burroughs was persistent, writing in August 1879:

> You can join me or not, just as you like, in my business on Wyeth's goods and in Malt Extract, and I will let you in at a just cost to me, charging nothing on personal account, time, etc.
>
> We are now making money on Wyeth's goods above expenses, and the Kepler malt goods are selling more than all the rest together, I think. It is a limited Co. of which I own ⅓ the shares. . . .
>
> If you prefer, I will go in with you – partners on new things, manufactured or not, and you need not go into any of my other things unless you want to. If you would like to travel and prospect, will give expenses and fair salary according somewhat to what you do. Think there is a big show for manufacturing Pharmaceutical preparations and if we go into it, will be about the first in the field. Our house is the only one in the Kingdom making a business of calling on doctors with samples of new things.

In fact, Burroughs's team of salesmen were a mixed lot, whose dilatoriness and excessive expenses caused frequent angry letters of explanation from Snow Hill and from Wyeth, but it was, inevitably, a scratch team operating in what was to most of them a wholly novel field. Moreover, although Burroughs himself was a poor administrator and businessman, he was an enthusiast, and if the overall success of his sales team was considerable, it is due to the fact that they had virtually no competition.

As Burroughs had quickly realised, the state of British pharmacy, both in the quality of products and in attitudes towards selling them, left the market wide open for someone with better products and a zeal for salesmanship. The new American compressed medicines were the key. They were to be the foundation of the fortunes of Burroughs and Wellcome, and it was Burroughs who had seen the possibilities. Like all strokes of commercial genius it seems obvious enough in retrospect, but less so at the time.

If Burroughs had no doubt about the glittering promise of his company's future in England and Europe, Wellcome remained cautious. He was only twenty-six and was making a considerable name for himself in American pharmaceutical circles while earning the plaudits of his employers as an exceptional salesman. He was earning a good income from his salary and commission, a significant part of which went regularly to his family in Minnesota, whose dependence upon him remained considerable. His mother and uncle had lamented his departure to the East Coast; he knew, rightly, what would be their reaction if he went to work and live in Europe. But he was ambitious for fame, wealth and adventure, and was as compulsive a traveller as Burroughs himself. There was also the discouraging fact that the American academic community heaped odium on pharmacists who went into trade. The American pharmaceutical market was becoming fiercely competitive; according to Burroughs, in England there was almost no competition at all, and there was also the alluring prospect of living at the heart of not only an enormous Empire, but also a vast and available world market.

Burroughs persisted, urging Wellcome on 20 October 1879:

> Take a short vacation at least and come over. You will not regret it, and if you do I will agree to pay your passage. . . . If you get [agency for] McKesson and Robbins' pills I will offset Wyeth's business to them, and we can go in both equally. I have no partners here. You are the man I want to pull with, and we have confidence in each other's ability and straightforwardness.

Wellcome replied that he had discussed the matter of going to England on a European prospecting visit with his employers, who had agreed willingly, but he deliberately made no reference to any partnership. However, the fact that he was definitely attracted either to join Burroughs or to establish his own agency in London for McKesson & Robbins's products was demonstrated by his obtaining letters of recommendation from his medical friends to prominent European physicians. Notwithstanding Wellcome's professed caution, Burroughs wrote back enthusiastically: 'I expect to see you over here soon. Don't you fail to come. I'm sure if you do and see the prospects here, and look over our books you will stay, either on salary or for an interest in the business.' Burroughs's very eagerness to have him as his partner convinced Wellcome, as he later admitted, that his apparent reluctance would ensure him much better terms if a partnership did take place.

Wellcome's character had already demonstrated an unusual admixture of cool calculation and impulsiveness, a contradiction that was to become much more apparent later; a man of sharp ambition, but with high standards, he could also make rapid decisions based on careful calculation of the advantages or otherwise. However, on this, the most momentous decision of his life so far, he moved slowly.

At the end of 1879 he travelled to Yarmouth, Maine, to discuss with his uncle Isaac, also an Adventist minister, the possibility of his migration to England. Isaac's advice to his nephew was to stick with McKesson & Robbins and stay in America. This was, naturally, the opinion of his family, but Wellcome chose to ignore it. Isaac wrote to him on 13 March 1880:

After a long and anxious waiting your letter, [of] the 10th is received. We are truly glad to receive it and to learn you are well. I am however quite sad in consequence of the news you give of resigning your situation, and planning to go to Europe. It may be a good movement; I am no prophet. But your place was an extra one. The reputation you have earned is of much value to introduce you to business in the most important places in this country. The salary you had was larger than one could reasonably expect in any other legitimate business. I cannot expect you can do so well in Europe. Perhaps you may. If you wished to change your business, I believe you would have found better business in America. If you have an ambition to see the chief parts of Europe, then you must go there. But when you have seen those you will wish to visit Asia. It is however your business and I ought not to complain. I cannot reasonably expect ever to see you again. . . . I suspect you will be disappointed in Europe and meet with difficulties you do not look for. If Europe is not in a blaze of war during the present year it cannot avert it much beyond. England must have nearly filled her cup as a nation. The other nations are not far behind. God's wrath is impending.

Although Isaac's gloomy view of the future of mankind, especially in Europe, was discouraging, although not without prescience, he had realised that Wellcome intended no casual visit, but one destined to be permanent. To his mother and Uncle Jacob, Wellcome stressed that no definite decision had been taken, although in his own mind it had.

McKesson & Robbins accepted Wellcome's resignation with much regret, offering to increase his salary from $2,500 to $3,500, plus expenses and commissions if he would remain with them. When he gratefully declined, he also offered them a contract, to which they agreed, drawn up by him, giving him personally the exclusive agency for their products 'for Europe, Asia, Africa, East Indies and Australia'. The agreement, for five years, also stated that 'H. S. Wellcome may associate himself with partners in handling said pills, in which case this agreement will apply to such firm while Mr Wellcome is with it.' This was Wellcome's trump card in his future negotiations with

Burroughs. His former employers had in effect given him the sole personal agency for their products throughout the world, excepting the United States, an extraordinary achievement for a young man of twenty-six, and a notable tribute from shrewd businessmen of his worth. They deduced that they had made a bargain; they had. For his part, Wellcome had in his possession something even more important than the capital he lacked.

This was the calculating Wellcome. Burroughs's letters to him have survived, but not many of those from him to Burroughs. But it is plain that it was Burroughs who was the ardent suitor. 'I am not the sort of chap to flatter anyone,' he wrote to Wellcome on 7 February 1880, in delight at the news that he was coming to England, 'but I would rather have you for a business partner than anyone I know.' He did not know about the McKesson & Robbins agreement with his future partner, then in negotiation and concluded on 2 April.

Wellcome's handling of the whole affair provokes the suspicion that there was more than natural caution involved – in short, that he did not wholly trust Burroughs. Burroughs was a hearty East Coast extrovert, with booming self-confidence, an independent income and significant private capital, the talented son of a United States Congressman; Wellcome came from a totally different background and had a very different temperament, which, for all its complexities, was considerably more stable than Burroughs's. All that they had in common was that they were ambitious young Americans who already knew much about pharmacy and salesmanship. It was also already plain that Burroughs's idea of a partnership was one in which Wellcome would run the business in England while he set off on his travels as the firm's chief salesman. This was exactly what Burroughs had in mind, and although it was not a wholly exciting prospect for Wellcome, it was one that he decided to accept.

It is not only the benefit of hindsight that makes Wellcome's care to cross the Atlantic with a powerful weapon with which to negotiate with Burroughs so significant. Burroughs's casual advice to him in effect to deceive his employers as to his intentions had concerned him, as had the fact that Burroughs had not told Wyeth of his plans. Wellcome knew the Wyeth brothers both personally and professionally, and although there is no conclusive documentary evidence, it is inconceivable that he would have contemplated such a major adventure without consulting them, and their correspondence clearly reveals that the Wyeths informed Wellcome of their concerns about Burroughs. These did not deter Wellcome, but made him justifiably wary.

Wellcome sailed to England at the beginning of April 1880 on *The City of Berlin.* On board he wrote to his mother:

– *Mid Ocean* –

My dear Mother

It was my fullest intention to write you from New York the morning our ship sailed – but the few hours were so crowded with business that I barely had time to get ready and on board before she cleared. . . .

Our passengers are rather cosmopolitan and none of a very interesting character. It has been a time of quiet and repose for me. Have not for many a day had so much time to look back over the past and study the changes that have occurred since early boyhood and when we were a happy family in a happy home, but it is all in the voyage of life, and God our great Captain.

I received your good letter a day or two before leaving N.Y. and presume you have ere this rec'd the money order. Always let me know when you are short or want more. I rec'd a good long letter from Uncle I.C. in which he deprecated my change very much. . . . Uncle's advice is always good and I always like to receive it but of course he cannot judge of my projects as well as I can myself, and yet I do not claim to be beyond making errors – but a motto which has helped me is 'God helps those who help themselves' and too, I believe in what someone has said that 'We often lose the goods we might gain, by fearing an attempt.'

In my new departure I shall bend every nerve to make a success, and with God's help and good health and strength I do not expect to fail. I have never accomplished anything without severe efforts and it is only such things as are not worth an effort that fall into the hands

> as bits of luck. I have known all say that hard work from the hoe to the use of the pen and am in good trim to repeat any portion of it. I am now at the age when most people begin life in its realities. Do not worry about it – just trust in me in the hands of our Good Father in Heaven and I will work manfully to gain success.

Wellcome's plan was to stay briefly in London and then to travel to Paris and Strasbourg to see Frederick Power, who was completing his thesis for his doctorate at the university, to explain why the proposed Wellcome–Power commercial partnership would not take place. Afterwards, he would visit the principal cities of Germany, Austria, Switzerland and France, 'then back to London and settle down to hard work'.

Wellcome's misgivings about Burroughs were increased when they met in London. He found that Burroughs had already grandly informed *The Chemist and Druggist* that Henry S. Wellcome 'is now, we believe, in London with Messrs Burroughs & Co., and is likely to stay among us'.

Their reunion meeting was not satisfactory. When Wellcome realised that Burroughs had not told Wyeth of his plans for a partnership, he insisted that Burroughs should go at once to Philadelphia to arrange matters while Wellcome continued with his planned trip to Europe. This Burroughs agreed to do. On his return to England Wellcome wrote to McKesson & Robbins on 18 August:

> . . . Some of the most eminent Drs here have already expressed their highest appreciation of the goods & will lend us their support and I have not a shadow of a doubt about the success in the introduction but of course it means an abundance of <u>hard positive work</u>.
>
> My trip on the Continent has been a most valuable school for me and was highly enjoyable throughout.
>
> I was taken quite ill with nervous prostration in Milan due to over exertion & excessive heat & while in Rome & Naples, but I hastened into Switzerland and with good care soon regained strength & have returned much improved in health. Am now in the best of spirits for active work.

On one matter there was total agreement. Burroughs's principal assistant, Kelly, had proved virtually useless. As Wyeth wrote to Wellcome, 'he lacked the ability to talk intelligently in regard to medicinal preparations and their therapeutic effect: also their mode of manufacture. This holds good with physicians as with Druggists.' But Wyeth was also disappointed with Burroughs's sales of its products and blamed him as much as Kelly, as a result of 'in some degree to his trying to do too much. He has wasted his energies and his time upon agencies or upon preparations that pay but little profit.' Wyeth, who had a high opinion of Wellcome, warmly welcomed the proposed union and wrote that, 'We have advised Mr Burroughs that your co-operation would be most advantageous to him.' Kelly's services were dispensed with and the Wyeth contract saved. This and the McKesson & Robbins contract were Wellcome's first, and crucial, contributions to the new partnership.

This was formalised when Burroughs returned from Philadelphia. Wellcome brought substantial business with him, but no money. The agreed Deed of Partnership fixed the capital of the firm at £2,000, of which Burroughs held £1,200 and Wellcome £800. In fact, Wellcome could only contribute £400 in cash and had to borrow £550 from Burroughs, at interest of ten per cent per annum, to enable him to establish himself in London.

Wellcome had his own misunderstandings with McKesson & Robbins, which were soon resolved, Wellcome writing to them on 18 August:

> Your letter of June 22 after some delay reached me in Rome and would have been answered earlier but I desired to confer with Mr Burroughs before doing so. In regard to your reference to the fact that our contract was drawn up by myself & copied from my own hand writing (based upon our brief discussion & memorandum of the matter) I would say that as a rebuke for my stupidity I accept it as well deserved, and in my former letter I endeavoured to make due acknowledgement of my own folly in treating the matter with such slight consideration.
>
> I have not doubted your desire to make a perfectly equitable arrange-

ment. I understood that you proposed giving me favourable terms & I did not construe that such terms implied any gratuity. I want our transactions to prove to your profit and I should never enjoy any arrangement that would be a burden to you.

I was not in a position to know what the actual expenses & requirements would be here until I came over and made a careful investigation, which showed clearly the facts that I have written you, proving beyond question that a continual net loss must result from an attempt to work the goods on the basis of our arrangement, considering these facts I felt perfectly justified in asking you for more liberal terms, and the requests were based upon a careful study of necessary expenses, and a desire to ask for nothing more than sufficient to insure us against loss.

Wellcome's priority was to establish Burroughs Wellcome & Co. virtually single-handedly during Burroughs's proposed world tour early in October 1881. He had already greatly increased the company's stock of products with the McKesson & Robbins contract. He had also come to London armed with a list of important British doctors and surgeons and with imposing letters of recommendation from well-known Americans in the medical profession. He not only took great trouble in meeting them and impressing them, but he also made a detailed study of the leading dispensing chemists in the country by travelling to them, principally to discover their requirements rather than to sell his products. They were flattered that they were being visited not by a salesman but by a partner, which was highly unusual.

Within a short time of Wellcome's arrival the company had outgrown its modest premises, and at the end of 1881 moved to somewhat larger ones at 7 Snow Hill.

The Deed of Partnership, on which so much later depended, provided for profits and losses to be divided in strict ratio to the partners' investment, but it also provided that at any time during the partnership after two years Wellcome could increase his capital holding to equal Burroughs's, so that the profits could be divided equally. The Deed stated that the agreement was for ten years, but at the end of five years either partner, by giving the other six months' notice in writing, could end the partnership.

Burroughs continued his interest in Nubian and Kepler, the output of the latter taken over by the new company of Burroughs Wellcome & Co., so titled as of 30 September 1880.

*

At an early stage in their partnership there was an unwritten agreement that Wellcome would in effect run the British and to some extent the European market, while Burroughs would seek custom from further abroad. Wellcome had already demonstrated that he was an able administrator as well as a salesman, whereas Burroughs, while fertile in imagination and ideas, was far less interested in the business side. Wellcome greeted Burroughs's proposal that he should set out for a world tour lasting at least two years with an enthusiasm that confirmed that at even this early stage there were personality tensions. Wellcome was very much aware that he was not only the junior partner but was also financially beholden to Burroughs, a situation that he was determined to change.

In Sudlow, who by now had experience of Burroughs's ways, Wellcome found he had an ideal assistant. He was efficient, hard-working, serious and an active Mason, who was to introduce Wellcome to Masonry in 1885. They quickly formed a good working relationship that developed into real friendship and mutual admiration, as Burroughs was later to discover to his cost.

Sudlow was one of the most important figures in the history of Burroughs Wellcome & Co. By 1881 he was in effect the company's General Manager, and one who inspired exceptional affection and loyalty; he was also noted as an after-dinner speaker of wit and eloquence, and as a keen musician. Seven years older than Wellcome, he befriended the young American with a warmth that Wellcome never forgot. Years later, when the company had over a thousand employees, Sudlow could recall with truth that he could count the paid staff of S. M. Burroughs and Co. on the fingers of one hand. The profits had been equally modest, as he well knew.

Sudlow, although unqualified, was deeply interested in medical and pharmaceutical matters, but was essentially a businessman; in Henry Wellcome he found a kindred spirit. Although both admired Burroughs's drive and energy, they were concerned about the more practical aspects of the company, about which Burroughs took an approach that was more cavalier than either appreciated. The fact that the futures of both were totally dependent upon the success of the firm was another bond. They both had everything to lose – and gain.

Initially, all seemed well between Burroughs and Wellcome, the latter assuring McKesson & Robbins that 'there is a perfect union of feeling between Mr Burroughs and myself'. He also secured from them better prices than in their original agreement and an increased allowance for travelling salesmen. In agreeing to these terms, McKesson & Robbins gave him exclusive rights to their products for five years.

But it was at the annual meeting of the British Medical Association (BMA) in Cambridge in August 1880 that Wellcome made his first British coup.

The simple fact that Burroughs and Wellcome were Americans, brought up on the dictum that 'it always pays to advertise', can hardly be emphasised enough. Both had experience of the quality and originality of pharmaceutical exhibitions at medical conferences in the United States; the BMA had not, and the Burroughs Wellcome exhibition caused a sensation. The design of the exhibit, its location and its dramatic impact were entirely Wellcome's work, undertaken in a remarkably short time. It was the result of his American experience, his energy, imagination and dramatist's eye. He had planned and organised it while Burroughs was in America, and before the partnership had been legally confirmed.

In ten varieties of Wyeth's compressed tablets and eighteen of its hypodermic tablets, sixty-three items of McKesson & Robbins's capsuled pills, and Kepler Malt and Cod Liver Oil, they had goods to sell that were far superior to the competition, such as it was ('Pharmacy in England is not advancing, and shows little prospect of early improvement', as Wellcome reported to Flückiger as late as 1885), but it was the display itself that caught the eye and the attention. There was a special reference to it in the *British Medical Journal*, and Wellcome reported that it 'received the most flattering attention'. There was another Burroughs Wellcome display shortly after at the Antwerp International Exhibition, where it received a Diploma of Honour – destined to be the first of many. *The Lancet*, in an analytical report, declared that the new tablets were 'the one form of pill that is a real advance on anything previously manufactured'. Sales began to rise dramatically, to the delight of the two American producers, who noted how quickly matters had improved since Wellcome's arrival.

This was a good beginning, but Wellcome was dissatisfied, particularly with the variable quality of the malt extract supplied by Kepler, to a formula devised by Mr Lockwood. Wellcome also discovered that although Burroughs had an agreement with the Kepler Co., he had never got round to actually signing it, which was another disconcerting example of Burroughs's somewhat slapdash approach to tedious business details. The uneven quality of Kepler Malt was getting Burroughs Wellcome a bad name, and Wellcome's business correspondence was filled with justifiably angry complaints from dispensers and customers. He had some shares in Kepler himself, and resolved that the only solution was to buy Lockwood out. This was not easy, nor was it effected without some acrimony and legal complications, but eventually Burroughs Wellcome bought Lockwood's shares and all the company's patents, rights and interests for £2,500. It was to prove another excellent bargain, as Burroughs recognised. Of greater importance to Wellcome was that Burroughs Wellcome was now responsible for production and quality control. It also retained all the profits, which, when the reputation of the product was eventually restored, were to be considerable.

Wellcome's confidence in Sudlow was such that he had appointed him the Manager of the company and made him a director of the Kepler Co., which was not wound up as a separate entity – although it had been wholly merged into Burroughs Wellcome – until 1910.

The Burroughs Wellcome Goods List of December 1881 emphasised the severe limitations of their products, and how few could be legitimately described as drugs.

Kepler Malt
Kepler Oil & Malt
Burroughs' Beef & Iron Wine
Burroughs' Hazeline
Burroughs' Coca-Beef
Burroughs' Inhaler
Fellows' Syrup
Florida Water
Wyeth's Chlorate Potash
Wyeth's Potash & Borax
Wyeth's Chl:L Ammonia
Wyeth's Soda Mint
Wyeth's Peptonic Tablets
Wyeth's Dialysed Iron
Bishop's Citrate Caffeine
Lawton's Cotton (absorbent)
Enterprise Tinct Press
Plasters
McK & R Pills
    Salicylic acid
    Arsenious acid
    Calc Sulphide
    Calomel
    Monobrom Camph.
    Digitalin
    Ergotin
    Pepsin
    Red Zinc
    Phospos
    Quinine
Pine Tar Soap
Nubian Blacking

Morphia and cocaine were to be added soon, but the original Burroughs Wellcome goods on offer were primarily cosmetic rather than curative. 'Hazeline', made from Witch Hazel, was entirely a cosmetic; the value of Kepler Oil and Malt was debatable; and 'Ergotin' was a totally unknown, and untested, element. On these very slender foundations was their business to be created.

*

On 8 May 1881, Wellcome wrote to his mother:

Dear Mother

I received your kind and affectionate letter several days since, and now take the first quiet moment to write to you. You are very charitable and kind to overlook my long and often repeated neglect.

Yes: Mr Burroughs – my partner, is an American – and a real live energetic one too. We are making rapid progress and every prospect of a successful future shines upon us. The only thing which troubles me at all is the fact that I am in debt, and I shall never feel really comfortable until all my obligations are cancelled – however, I do not fear at all my ability to pay every cent I owe if health and strength are allowed by our heavenly father.

I confess I have been very negligent of my duties to God to whom I am in reality indebted more than to any earthly friend. In the earnest endeavors to prosper in business one is very prone to overlook the guiding hand of God from whom all our successes come. I have endeavored to do my duty so far as my personal acts in life are concerned and towards my associates & employees but so far as letting my light shine before others I fear that it is very dull and would do very little toward guiding the footsteps of others.

I am very anxious that you should enjoy an opportunity of visiting all of your old friends and early day acquaintances. I think too that travelling about will benefit your health, and you should not attempt to work for it will wear upon your strength. I shall send you 50$ very soon and I want you to live with comfort and enjoy yourself in every way possible. Do not fear that you are inconveniencing me in the least as I can easily spare all that you will require. Always write me when you are getting short of money and I will immediately forward more to you. . . .

Please write me often as you can, and forgive and allow for my many shortcomings.

By this point the paths of Wellcome and Burroughs had literally diverged, when the latter set out in October 1881 for a long and extensive global tour on behalf of the partnership, leaving Wellcome responsible for the business in London. From this separation, of over two-and-a-half years, much was to result, and not wholly positively. But Henry Wellcome, at the age of twenty-eight, was now master of his own destiny. His rise had begun.

# 4

# The New Pharmacy

It is not easy to draw a clear picture of Wellcome's first two years in London. Initially, thanks to Burroughs's loan, he was able to rent rooms near St James's Square in Bury Street, an imposing address and area, but at a modest rent. Servants' wages were very low, and even on his straitened circumstances he was able to afford a cook-housekeeper and a general assistant male servant, who also served as valet and waiter. He dressed as well as he could afford to, began to entertain and became interested in London club life, something new in his experience. He found that London had the best entertainment, at very reasonable prices, that he had known. He came to enjoy Smoking Concerts, a particular vogue of the time. He was quickly enraptured by the bustle and sophistication of London, and was fascinated by the ritual of The Season and by the culture of a nation in which Parliament adjourned for Ascot Week. He was to become a familiar figure at the Henley Rowing Regatta and at Cowes Yachting Week; for a time he was a keen sailor on the largely undiscovered Norfolk Broads and in the Channel; and he had his own canoe on the Thames – frivolities for which Burroughs was later to castigate him. He also came to enjoy the company of actors and actresses – especially the latter, which was noticed. However, all the evidence is that the young Wellcome greatly preferred male company, and particularly male clubs. He was by no means the first or last American to feel far more at home and happier in England than in his native country, and especially more so than in the vibrant but raw New York of the time.

Those who met Wellcome later in life found him somewhat intimidating and, although courteous, sometimes abrupt; he was not an easy person to have a conversation with. Some doubted whether he had a sense of humour. All this would have astonished those who had known the younger and more ebullient Wellcome. Although serious and ambitious, he was excellent company, and greatly enjoyed listening to, and being with, his American friend, the comic and humorist Frank Lincoln, considered by many, including George Grossmith and Oscar Wilde, as one of the funniest men of the time. Wellcome's youthful delight in practical jokes blessedly faded, but his sense of humour and pleasure in life only declined later after misfortunes had saddened him. But his blue eyes often twinkled even then.

Despite their contrasting temperaments, Burroughs shared Wellcome's enthusiasm for the English way of life, although for very different reasons. Burroughs was to become not only a British citizen in 1900, but also an ardent advocate of radical political change in his adopted country; Wellcome cultivated politicians for personal and financial benefit, but had a horror of political involvement by himself or his company; however, his father had not served in the US Congress. Burroughs, although it was not so clearly evident at the time, was a political animal; Wellcome was not, but he rapidly became a social one.

By the summer of 1881 Wellcome had moved into a larger house, reporting to Burroughs:

> The house I occupy is one of those in Marylebone Road, about two blocks above Baker Street (second door from the Tussauds' private residence). This house was formerly occupied by an Indian rajah and is rather elaborately, in fact barbarously, decorated inside – but as barbaric decoration is now the rage it is in perfect accord with high art of the day. I fitted up the house to correspond in general style and quaintness. My collection of curiosities, [American] Indian relics, etc., tally admirably with the house, and so everybody seems rather fascinated with the effect, and in fact I rather like it myself. Some call it 'Aesthetic',

some say, 'Heathenish', some 'Bohemian', 'Ideal', 'Artistic', etc., etc.

All in all it is very cheerful. I bought my library and museum from America last Winter. The house I get for the very nominal rent of 28/- per week including attendance. I think that I have been the better for following your advice in regard to social matters and shorter business hours, and this little home has been a restful harbor for me to seek for quiet moments and deliberate thinking, which has been very necessary in the important transactions of the past few months.

This is the first reference in Wellcome's papers to his collections of books – primarily medical, although not exclusively so – and what he called his 'curios'. These were at the time a mixture of American Indian artefacts and old medical instruments, some bought in America and others in London. He later said that he had been a collector 'for the whole of my adult life', but it was not until the company was very successful that he had the means to be one on a major scale. But the bug had bitten him early. Only years later did Wellcome reveal that he spent 'many, many hours', indeed 'years', studying in the British Museum Library and its collections. It was there that he read the works of E. B. Tylor, whom he was to quote at length, and whose most famous message was that 'the science of culture is essentially a reformer's science'.

It is not at all clear who introduced Wellcome into London Society, but within a year he was evidently a close friend of William Baskcomb, the Chief Clerk to the Household of the Prince of Wales. He also met and knew a number of older and much more eminent people, including W. S. Gilbert, Arthur Sullivan, Henry Irving and Oscar Wilde.

Burroughs's subsequent caricature of Wellcome as a lazy playboy inattentive to business is utterly disproved by his achievements during Burroughs's long absence abroad in the early years of their partnership, but it was a fact that he rarely appeared at Snow Hill's pokey little offices before ten o'clock in the morning, had a long lunch, usually for business reasons, and left the office shortly after four. Wellcome took the view that this was quite long enough for formal business matters, and that making the name of Wellcome known socially was equally important. He considered, perhaps induced by the London atmosphere, that the quality of one's work was more important than the hours devoted to it, which Burroughs found incomprehensible.

One of Burroughs's later complaints against Wellcome, that he spent too much time with actresses, was specifically directed against another American, Genevieve Ward. Originally a promising opera singer, her singing voice suffered severely after she had diphtheria, so she turned to the stage, with considerable success. She was sixteen years older than Wellcome when they first met in the early 1880s and they became close friends. Wellcome was a regular visitor to her house in Hampstead, but their correspondence, although warm and affectionate on both sides, and which was to remain so until her death in 1922, when he called her 'the most loved woman in the world', reveals no evidence of anything more than close and sincere friendship. Like Stanley, she was famous long before Wellcome was noted, and her kindness to the young, ambitious fellow-American alone in London was never forgotten. Nor did he ever forget her birthday, 27 March. On that day in 1921, her eighty-fourth, he wrote to 'My very dear friend, Sweet Genevieve!' but signed himself 'Ever your affectionate friend of many years, Henry S. Wellcome'. In her last days, in August 1922, by which time she was Dame Genevieve Ward, he was constantly with her and, with her other close friend, the actor-manager Sir Frank Benson, was a pallbearer at her funeral.

However, as his staff knew, and his papers demonstrate, he was working immensely hard in his home, often very late into the night and through weekends. He took personal responsibility for every decision, kept a very close eye on the firm's accounts and the quality of its products, and was particularly concerned that the reputation of Burroughs Wellcome was enhanced in every way. But he was also enjoying himself, more completely than he had ever done before, and, although he was not to realise it then, more than he was ever to do again after 1884, when Burroughs returned and shadows fell.

By the end of 1881 he was in command of a developing company in the forefront of 'the New Pharmacy'. But his interests and ambitions went beyond this, and as his circle of acquaintances grew so did his friendships, which extended far beyond the medical profession, although this was his first priority. When others later marvelled at Wellcome's extraordinary ability to find and appoint young men of outstanding potential and subsequent eminence, they did not realise that they were recommended to him by men like Joseph Lister, Cooper Perry and Patrick Manson – among many others – whom Wellcome had cultivated, flattered and entertained in his early period. At a time when there was justified suspicion among serious medical men about the pharmaceutical industry, Wellcome earned their respect, friendship and trust. The long-term dividends were to be incalculable.

Wellcome's cheery accounts to Burroughs of his active social life clearly subsequently grated upon the latter, although not at the time. Wellcome wrote to him in September 1882:

> At the end of the Season we held a rather special musical afternoon and evening – had the front garden entirely covered with a tent, thus giving us ample room for our guests. . . . We had some magnificent singing and instrumental music, recitations, etc. Among our friends present were many eminent in literature, music, drama and art, but what would have most pleased your fancy – so many really handsome girls. Bright, charming ones full of sparkle and wit, girls who had something to say for themselves, and for someone else as well. I thought many times that day what a delight it would be for you. Your photo, the one with the rose, was framed and on the piano. It was much discussed by the charmers – one in particular who fell in love with it and quoted 'and there are times when even a photograph will not satisfy'.

Wellcome was to become even more ambitious. In May 1884 he booked the large Princes' Hall in honour of Frank Lincoln; when, rather late, Lincoln had to cancel, Wellcome starred William Winch, a rising American tenor, instead, and invited 600 guests for a late evening buffet, with wine and entertainment, which included George

Grossmith. It was not surprising that one newspaper report of this lavish event referred to Wellcome as a millionaire; this he certainly was not, but he took no steps to deny it.

Wellcome genuinely enjoyed entertaining, and was a courteous and attentive host, but the real purpose was self-promotion, at which he was becoming rather too successful, in Burroughs's opinion. Rather more important, he felt, was Wellcome's work on the firm's travelling medicine chests, of which Henry M. Stanley was the first recipient. Stanley returned the favour with a glowing tribute to the 'nine beautiful Chests replete with every medicament necessary to combat the epidemic diseases peculiar to Africa' in his *Through the Dark Continent*:

> Every compartment was well stocked with essentials for the Doctor and Surgeon. Nothing was omitted, and we all owe a deep debt of gratitude to these gentlemen, not only for the intrinsic value of these Chests and excellent medicines but also for the personal selection of the best that London could furnish.

This was a remarkable coup, to be followed by many more. The Burroughs Wellcome medicine chests were to become part of the standard equipment of explorers during a period in which exploration became an international preoccupation, with a huge and fascinated public following. The fame of the explorers was now shared by Burroughs Wellcome, who succeeded in totally dominating this unique market. Stanley, Theodore Roosevelt and later Byrd, Nansen, Peary, Shackleton and Scott praised their Burroughs Wellcome medicines and chests, frequently donated by Wellcome, who took particular care over their composition, packaging and presentation. The results in terms of publicity were beyond estimation, to the point when an expedition *without* Burroughs Wellcome products and medicine chests was a rarity.

Thus, the somewhat earnest and dedicated devotee of work, money and ambition had quickly matured into something different and more attractive. Wellcome was happy in his work, his life and his surroundings. His little staff became devoted to him; his initial tiny circle of English and American friends began to expand rapidly; and New York, Chicago, Philadelphia and, most of all, Almond and Garden City had been put emphatically behind him. If money remained a problem, he was determined to remedy that defect.

*

Wellcome always believed in employing the best staff, at every level, and at the beginning of the partnership sought another American, a Mr Powell, who had been one of his most able colleagues at McKesson & Robbins; they shared Wellcome's high opinion of Powell and flatly refused to release him. 'Although we can get energetic and well-educated men here,' Wellcome wrote to them on 18 August 1880, 'they all seem to lack in the more practical points. I would prefer a live American of Mr Powell's qualifications.' This second request was also rejected, with some acerbity, by his former employers, indignant that Wellcome should so soon be trying to poach one of their best men. But he was more successful in luring another American friend, William Shepperson, across the Atlantic. After two years as an energetic and highly successful traveller in Britain, Shepperson was sent by Wellcome to India to supervise the characteristically ambitious Burroughs Wellcome stand at the Calcutta Exhibition in 1883, and to be the firm's representative during it; he then undertook a long and fruitful tour of India, before going to Australia to become the first Manager of the newly established Melbourne branch.

Wellcome nearly lost Shepperson's services at the outset of what was to be a long association. Miss Hunt, virtually the only woman employee in the firm at the time, later related that,

> He arrived in a fairly bad fog & observed to me how fearfully we must feel such an occurrence, to which I replied, I am afraid rather mischievously, 'Oh, we are used to fogs, this is nothing to what we have sometimes.' I shall never forget the look of horror on his face & the next thing I heard was that he had booked his return passage to America as he did not think our climate would agree with him!

But he was persuaded to remain.

Wellcome's first priority was to cover the British market. His strategy was two-pronged: personal canvassing by representatives of a far higher quality and knowledge than the departed and unlamented Kelly; and publicity. By October 1883 he could report to Burroughs: 'We have had every town in this country with two or more medical men visited by our traveller and samples distributed: also sent to medical men in isolated hamlets – so that we have covered the ground more thoroughly than ever before.'

This, in itself, was unprecedented in the somewhat languid approach of British pharmacy. But one thing Wellcome and Burroughs had in common was their near-obsession with publicity, and some of their strongest arguments were over this, right down to the quality of labels.

Wellcome's target was the medical profession and the medical and pharmaceutical press and journals, on which he concentrated exclusively. He would have nothing to do with other newspapers or journals, 'on account of the prejudice which the medical profession have to such a course'. When one of his staff in the publicity office suggested advertising in *Harpers Magazine* – a perfectly respectable journal – he rejected the idea with the withering comment that 'we might as well advertise the Pharmaceutical preparations in the *Daily Telegraph*'. His fear was that Burroughs Wellcome might

> be classed as patent medicine vendors and lose ground with the medical profession. The profession have given us the greatest encouragement and will stand by us so long as we follow a legitimate course – we could not in any circumstances afford to risk giving them offence.

Wellcome's 'advertisements' went far beyond the full-page ones he designed, with great care, for the professional journals; some of his announcements ran for pages, and one in particular, in *The Lancet* for 31 March 1883, was twenty-seven pages long, consisting of authentic medical reports on the firm's products and clinical notes. Wellcome took immense trouble over this side of the business and over the firm's public exhibits, whose standards and imagination had already achieved a remarkable impact.

Advertisement for Lanoline toilet soap

# BURROUGHS, WELLCOME & CO's. MEDICAL PRICE LIST.

*TERMS: CASH WITH ORDER.*

| | | Retail s. | Retail d. | | s. | d. |
|---|---|---|---|---|---|---|
| Burroughs Beef & Iron Wine ... | ½lb. bot. | 2 | 6 | per doz. | 24 | 0 |
| ,, ,, ,, ,, ... | 1lb. ,, | 4 | 6 | ,, | 40 | 0 |
| ,, ,, ,, ,, with Quinine | ½lb. bot. | 3 | 0 | ,, | 27 | 0 |
| ,, ,, ,, ,, ,, | 1lb. ,, | 5 | 6 | ,, | 50 | 0 |
| ,, Hazeline ... ... | ¼lb. ,, | 1 | 6 | ,, | 14 | 0 |
| ,, ,, ... ... | 1lb. ,, | 4 | 6 | ,, | 40 | 0 |
| ,, Ammonia Inhaler ... | ... each | 12 | 0 | each | 10 | 0 |
| Bishop's Citrate of Caffeine (*Effervescing*) | per bot. | 2 | 6 | per doz. | 20 | 0 |
| ,, Ext. Nux. Vomica ,, ... | ... ,, | 1 | 6 | ,, | 12 | 0 |
| Enterprise Drug Mill | { *Plain* 40s. 60s. 100s. / *Ornamented* 50s. 70s. 110s. } each | | | | | |
| ,, Tincture Press ... | ... | | | each | 15 | 0 |

Fellows Syr. Hypophos. (*Stamped*) Large — Retail 7s.; 1 doz. to 8 doz. 66s. Small — Retail 4s.; 1 doz. to 8 doz. 38s.

*Special Prices for Unstamped in Ireland only.*

| | | | | s. | d. |
|---|---|---|---|---|---|
| Lawton's Absorbent Cotton ... ... | 2 oz. | pkts. | per doz. | 8 | 0 |
| ,, ,, ,, ... ... | 4 oz. | ,, | ,, | 12 | 0 |
| ,, ,, ,, ... ... | 16 oz. | ,, | ,, | 36 | 0 |

## The "McK. & R." (Ovoid) CAPSULED PILLS.

*According to Formulæ of the British Pharmacopœia and other Standard Authorities.*

Per Bottle of 100.

| | | s. | d. |
|---|---|---|---|
| **A** | | | |
| Aloes Barb. B.P. - - - - | 5 gr. | 1 | 8 |
| Aloes Dilute - - - - - - | 4 gr. | 1 | 8 |
| (*Dr. Hall's Dinner Pill*) | | | |
| Aloes Socotrine, B.P. - - | 5 gr. | 1 | 8 |
| Aloes & Assafœtida, B.P. - | 5 gr. | 1 | 8 |
| Aloes & Iron, B.P. - - - | 5 gr. | 1 | 8 |
| Aloes & Myrrh, B.P. - - | 3 gr. | 1 | 10 |
| ,, ,, ,, - - | 5 gr. | 2 | 2 |
| Arsenious Acid, ,, - - - | 1-50 gr. | 1 | 8 |
| ,, ,, - - - | 1-20 gr. | 1 | 8 |
| Assafœtida Comp. B.P. - - | 5 gr. | 1 | 8 |
| **B** | | | |
| Blauds (*see Ferruginous*) | | | |
| **C** | | | |
| Calcii Sulphid. - - - - | 1-10 gr. | 2 | 6 |
| ,, ,, - - - - - | 1-4 gr. | 2 | 6 |
| ,, ,, - - - - - | 1-2 gr. | 3 | 0 |
| Calomel Colocynth & Hyoscyamus. | | 3 | 4 |
| Calomel Comp., B.P. - - | 5 gr. | 1 | 10 |
| (*Plummer's*) | | | |
| Calomel & Opium. | | 2 | 8 |
| Camphor Monobromide | 2 gr. | 4 | 6 |
| Cathartic Comp., U.S.P. (*Purgative*) | | 2 | 0 |
| Colocynth Comp., B.P. - - | 4 gr. | 3 | 0 |
| ,, ,, ,, - - | 5 gr. | 3 | 4 |
| Colocynth Comp. & Calomel. | 5 gr. | 3 | 4 |
| Colocynth Comp. & Hydrarg | 5 gr. | 3 | 4 |
| Colocynth & Hyoscyamus, B.P. | 5 gr. | 3 | 0 |
| Conii Comp., B.P. - - - | 5 gr. | 1 | 8 |
| Copaiba & Cubebs. - - - | 5 gr. | 4 | 6 |
| **D** | | | |
| Digitalin Pure, Crystal - | 1-60 gr. | 2 | 6 |
| Dover's Powder (*see Ipecac Comp.*) | | | |
| **E** | | | |
| Ext. Colocynth. Comp., B.P. | 5 gr. | 2 | 6 |
| Ergotin - - - - - - - | 3 gr. | 7 | 0 |
| **F** | | | |
| Ferri Carb., B. P. - - - | 5 gr. | 1 | 8 |
| Ferri et Quiniæ Cit., B.P. - | 2 gr. | 4 | 8 |
| Ferruginous - - - - - | 3 gr. | 3 | 6 |
| ,, - | 5 gr. | 3 | 6 |
| Ferrum Redactum - - | 1 gr. | 1 | 8 |
| **H** | | | |
| Hydrarg., B.P. (*Blue Mass*) | 1 gr. | 1 | 8 |
| ,, ,, - - - - - | 2 gr. | 1 | 8 |
| ,, ,, - - - - - | 3 gr. | 1 | 8 |
| ,, ,, - - - - - | 5 gr. | 2 | 0 |
| Hydrarg. Coloc. et Hyoscy. | | 3 | 4 |
| Hydrarg. Iod. Rub. - - | 1-16 gr. | 1 | 10 |
| Hydrarg. Iod. Vir - - - | 1-4 gr. | 1 | 10 |
| Hydrastia (*White Alkaloid*,) | 1-2 gr. | 8 | 6 |

Per Bottle of 100

| | | s. | d. |
|---|---|---|---|
| **I** | | | |
| Ipecac. Comp. Pulv. - - | 5 gr. | 3 | 4 |
| (*Ipecac and Opium.*) | | | |
| Ipecac & Squills. B.P. - - | 5 gr. | 1 | 8 |
| Iodoform - - - - - - - | 1 gr. | 4 | 6 |
| **L** | | | |
| Laxative Vegetable (*Imp. Cathartic*) | | 2 | 0 |
| **M** | | | |
| Morphia Hydrochlor. - - | 1-8 gr. | 2 | 6 |
| ,, ,, - - | 1-4 gr. | 3 | 4 |
| **O** | | | |
| Opium - - - - - - - - | 1 gr. | 3 | 6 |
| **P** | | | |
| Pepsin Pure Concentrated | 1 gr. | 3 | 6 |
| Phosphorus - - - - - | 1-100 gr. | 3 | 6 |
| ,, - - - - - - | 1-50 gr. | 3 | 6 |
| ,, - - - - - - | 1-30 gr. | 3 | 6 |
| Phosphorus & Iron. | | 4 | 6 |
| Phosphorus & Nux Vomica. | | 4 | 6 |
| Phosphorus Nux Vomica & Iron. | | 4 | 6 |
| Phosphorus & Quinine. | | 8 | 0 |
| Phosphorus & Valer. Zinc. | | 4 | 6 |
| Plumbum et Opium, B.P. - | 5 gr. | 2 | 6 |
| Podophyllin - - - - - - | 1-4 gr. | 1 | 8 |
| ,, - - - - - - | 1-2 gr. | 2 | 0 |
| Podophyllin Comp. | | 3 | 6 |
| **Q** | | | |
| Quinia Bi-Sulph, (*Sol. Sulph*) | 1-4 gr | | |
| ,, ,, ,, - | 1-2 gr. | | |
| ,, ,, ,, - | 1 gr. | | |
| ,, ,, ,, - | 2 gr. | | |
| ,, ,, ,, - | 3 gr. | | |
| ,, ,, ,, - | 4 gr. | | |
| ,, ,, ,, - | 5 gr. | | |
| Quinia Comp (*Anti-Malarial.*) | | 8 | 0 |
| **R** | | | |
| Rhei Comp. B.P. - - - - | 5 gr. | 2 | 6 |
| Rhei Comp. et Hydrarg. | | 2 | 6 |
| **S** | | | |
| Salicylic Acid - - - - - | 2 gr. | 2 | 0 |
| ,, ,, - - - - - | 5 gr. | 4 | 6 |
| Salicylic Acid, Comp. (*Rheumatic.*) | | 5 | 10 |
| Saponis Comp. B.P. (*Pil. Opii.*) | 5 gr. | 3 | 0 |
| Squills Comp. B P. - - - | 5 gr. | 1 | 8 |
| Strychnia - - - - - - | 1-50 gr. | 1 | 10 |
| **Z** | | | |
| Zinc Valerianate - - - - | 1 gr. | 3 | 3 |
| Zinc Phosphide - - - | 1-4 gr. | 2 | 6 |
| ,, ,, - - - - | 1-2 gr. | 3 | 6 |

*NOTE.—Subject to changes in Market Prices of Quinine.*

"*For Composition see Formulæ List.*

Private Formulæ of 3,000 or more Pills prepared to order.

| | | Retail s. | Retail d. | | s. | d. |
|---|---|---|---|---|---|---|
| Kepler Extract of Malt ... ... | per ¾ lb. bot. | 2 | 9 | per doz. | 24 | 0 |
| ,, ,, ,, ... ... | ,, 1½ lb. ,, | 4 | 6 | ,, | 42 | 0 |
| Kepler Extract of Malt with Hypophosphites | per 1½lb. bot. | 6 | 6 | per doz. | 54 | 0 |
| ,, ,, ,, Pepsine | ,, ,, | 6 | 6 | ,, | 54 | 0 |
| ,, ,, ,, Phos Comp (*Chem Food*) | ,, ,, | 5 | 0 | ,, | 42 | 0 |
| ,, ,, ,, ,, Citrate Iron and Quinine | ,, ,, | 7 | 0 | ,, | 54 | 0 |
| ,, ,, ,, ,, Hops .. | ,, ,, | 4 | 6 | ,, | 42 | 0 |
| ,, ,, ,, ,, Beef and Iron | ,, ,, | 7 | 0 | ,, | 54 | 0 |
| ,, ,, ,, ,, Cod-liver Oil & Phosphor. | ,, ,, | 5 | 0 | ,, | 42 | 0 |
| ,, ,, ,, ,, ,, ,, Iod. of Iron | ,, ,, | 6 | 6 | ,, | 54 | 0 |
| Murray & Lanman's Florida Water ... ... | | 3 | 6 | per doz. | 36 | 0 |
| Symes' Lac Bismuthi ... ... ... | 8 oz. bots. | | | per doz. | 24 | 0 |
| ,, ,, ,, ... ... ... | 16 oz. ,, | | | ,, | 48 | 0 |
| ,, ,, ,, et Cerii ... ... | 8 oz. ,, | | | ,, | 30 | 0 |
| ,, ,, ,, ,, ... ... | 16 oz. ,, | | | ,, | 60 | 0 |
| ,, Ol. Lavand. Rect. ... ... ... | | | | per lb. | 21 | 0 |
| ,, ,, ,, ... ... ... | | | | per ½ lb. | 10 | 6 |
| ,, Urethral Irrigator (*Harrison's*) ... ... | | | | each | 6 | 6 |

## WYETH'S COMPRESSED TABLETS.

| | | Retail s. | Retail d. | | s. | d. |
|---|---|---|---|---|---|---|
| ,, ,, Ammon. Chloride 3 grs. | 25 in box | 1 | 0 | per doz. | 8 | 6 |
| ,, ,, ,, ,, 3 grs. | 50 in box | 2 | 0 | ,, | 16 | 6 |
| ,, ,, ,, ,, 3 grs. | 100 in bot. | 3 | 0 | ,, | 27 | 0 |
| ,, ,, Bismuth. Subnit. 5 grs. | ,, ,, | 3 | 6 | ,, | 42 | 0 |
| ,, ,, Cinchonidia Salicylate 2½ grs. | 100 in bot. | | | each | 10 | 0 |
| ,, ,, Lithii Carb. 2 grs. | 100 in bot. | 3 | 9 | per doz. | 45 | 0 |
| ,, ,, Potass. Chlorate 5 grs. | 30 in box | 1 | 0 | ,, | 8 | 6 |
| ,, ,, ,, ,, 5 grs. | 65 in box | 2 | 0 | ,, | 16 | 6 |
| ,, ,, ,, ,, 5 grs. | 100 in bot. | 3 | 0 | ,, | 27 | 0 |
| ,, ,, Potass. Chlor with Ammon. Chloride | 30 in box | 1 | 0 | ,, | 8 | 6 |
| ,, ,, ,, ,, | 65 in box | 2 | 0 | ,, | 16 | 6 |
| ,, ,, ,, ,, | 100 in box | 3 | 0 | ,, | 27 | 0 |
| ,, ,, Pot. Chlor. with Borax | 30 in box | 1 | 0 | ,, | 8 | 6 |
| ,, ,, ,, ,, ,, | 65 in box | 2 | 0 | ,, | 16 | 6 |
| ,, ,, ,, ,, ,, | 100 in bot. | 3 | 0 | ,, | 27 | 0 |
| ,, ,, Peptonic | 25 ,, | 2 | 6 | ,, | 21 | 0 |
| ,, ,, ,, | 50 ,, | 4 | 6 | ,, | 40 | 0 |
| ,, ,, ,, | 100 ,, | 7 | 6 | ,, | 78 | 0 |
| ,, ,, Potass. Bromidi 5 grs. | 100 ,, | 4 | 3 | each | 3 | 6 |
| ,, ,, ,, ,, 10 grs. | 100 ,, | 5 | 0 | ,, | 4 | 0 |
| ,, ,, Potass. Iodidi 5 grs. | 100 ,, | 5 | 3 | ,, | 4 | 6 |
| ,, ,, Potass. Bicarb. ,, | 25 ,, | 1 | 0 | per doz. | 8 | 6 |
| ,, ,, ,, ,, ,, | 50 ,, | 2 | 0 | ,, | 16 | 6 |
| ,, ,, ,, ,, ,, | 100 ,, | 3 | 0 | ,, | 27 | 0 |
| ,, ,, Sodii ,, ,, | 25 ,, | 1 | 0 | ,, | 8 | 6 |
| ,, ,, ,, ,, ,, | 50 ,, | 2 | 0 | ,, | 16 | 6 |
| ,, ,, ,, ,, ,, | 100 ,, | 3 | 0 | ,, | 27 | 0 |
| ,, ,, Soda Mint | 25 ,, | 1 | 0 | ,, | 8 | 6 |
| ,, ,, ,, ,, | 75 ,, | 2 | 0 | ,, | 16 | 6 |
| ,, ,, ,, ,, | 100 ,, | 3 | 0 | ,, | 27 | 0 |
| ,, ,, Sodii Salicylate 3 grs. | 100 ,, | 3 | 6 | ,, | 42 | 0 |
| ,, ,, ,, ,, 5 grs. | 100 ,, | 4 | 6 | ,, | 54 | 0 |

## WYETH'S HYPODERMIC TABLETS.

| | | | | | |
|---|---|---|---|---|---|
| Morphiæ Sulphas | 1-4 gr. | Morphiæ Sulphas | 1-3 gr. | Atropiæ Sulphas | 1-60 gr. |
| Sodæ Sulphas | 1-4 gr. | Atropiæ Sulphas | 1-120 gr. | Sodæ Sulphas | 1-4 gr. |
| | | Sodæ Sulphas | 1-4 gr. | | |
| Morphiæ Sulphas | 1-6 gr. | Morphiæ Sulphas | 1-4 gr. | Atropiæ Sulphas | 1-100 gr. |
| Sodæ Sulphas | 1-4 gr. | Atropiæ Sulphas | 1-150 gr. | Sodæ Sulphas | 1-4 gr. |
| | | Sodæ Sulphas | 1-4 gr. | | |
| Morphiæ Sulphas | 1-8 gr. | Morphiæ Sulphas | 1-6 gr. | Atropiæ Sulphas | 1-150 gr. |
| Sodæ Sulphas | 1-4 gr. | Atropiæ Sulphas | 1-180 gr. | Sodæ Sulphas | 1-4 gr. |
| | | Sodæ Sulphas | 1-4 gr. | | |
| Morphiæ Sulphas | 1-12 gr. | Morphiæ Sulphas | 1-8 gr. | Strychniæ Sulphas | 1-60 gr. |
| Sodæ Sulphas | 1-4 gr. | Atropiæ Sulphas | 1-200 gr. | Sodæ Sulphas | 1-4 gr. |
| | | Sodæ Sulphas | 1-4 gr. | Strychniæ Sulphas | 1-100 gr. |
| | | | | Sodæ Sulphas | 1-4 gr. |
| Morphiæ Sulphas | 1-2 gr. | Morphiæ Sulphas | 1-12 gr. | Strychniæ Sulphas | 1-150 gr. |
| Atropiæ Sulphas | 1-100 gr. | Atropiæ Sulphas | 1-250 gr. | Sodæ Sulphas | 1-4 gr. |
| Sodæ Sulphas | 1-4 gr. | Sodæ Sulphas | 1-4 gr. | | |

(Additional Formulæ will soon be added to this List.)

*2s. PER TUBE CONTAINING 20 TABLETS.*

| | | | | s. | d. |
|---|---|---|---|---|---|
| Wyeth's Pepsin Concentrated in 1 oz. bottles | | ... | per oz. | 10 | 0 |
| ,, ,, Saccharated | in 1 oz. bottles | ... | per doz. | 30 | 0 |
| ,, Podophyllin ... | in 1 oz ,, | Retail. | ,, | 24 | 0 |

Burroughs Wellcome & Co. medical price list 1882

However, the growing business brought the firm into increasing difficulties with the Inland Revenue authorities in Somerset House, who interpreted an Act of 1812, which had been intended to prevent the importation of quack drugs, to apply to all imported drugs and make them liable to stamp duty. The result was much tedious litigation and endless correspondence with Somerset House, and an eventually successful national campaign waged by Wellcome for the repeal of the Act. But the real consequences were far more important.

The true long-term answer to the problem, Wellcome was convinced, was that the firm should manufacture its products in England. The first step was to buy the compressed medicine machines from Wyeth and the rights for the products for all countries except America. At the time, from Wyeth's point of view, this seemed an excellent arrangement. It was one that it came deeply to regret. The machines arrived from Philadelphia at the end of 1882, and on Burroughs's recommendation Wellcome appointed Dr Otto Witte, a German chemist, to take charge of the manufacturing side. Witte was immediately sent to America to inspect the latest machinery, under strict instructions not to reveal anything about Wellcome's plans except that the firm contemplated building its own manufacturing factory. Wellcome's private attitude to Wyeth would have worried the latter if it had known of it. 'I know full well', he wrote in October 1882, 'that they [Wyeth] need us far more than we need them.' This was not absolutely true at that time, but Wellcome's early determination to become independent, and much more than an agent for foreign products, had been sharpened by his disputes with Somerset House.

Another factor was that the British competition had woken up to the success of Burroughs Wellcome products. Some were behind the Somerset House campaign to compel Burroughs Wellcome to pay stamp duty, and thereby to increase the price of most Burroughs Wellcome products; others imitated their products and even their titles. In September 1882 Wellcome took one to court for selling its product under the name Haseline in order to steal some of the market from the highly successful 'Hazeline'. 'Our competitors', Wellcome reported to Burroughs in January 1883, 'have never been so aggressive, or so enterprising and active.'

Wellcome had been careful from the outset of the partnership to register the firm's trademarks for each of its products, and he and his agents kept a careful watch on the competition's attempts to circumvent them. Whenever a breach was discovered, the perpetrator was firmly asked to desist; if he did not, legal proceedings were immediately instituted, at 'a matter of considerable expense and not a small amount of care and anxiety', as Wellcome reported to Burroughs. One, 'Cleaver the Perfumer', stole the Burroughs Wellcome trademark 'Edenia' for one of its own products and was compelled to pay Burroughs Wellcome its gross profits on sales, to pass on to Burroughs Wellcome all orders it received, and to publish a public apology in all the daily papers in London, Edinburgh and Dublin, and selected American ones.

But this did not deter others. 'We have never had such severe competition before,' Wellcome wrote to Burroughs in October 1883. 'The feeling of jealousy at our success has taken a more practical turn than before. Others are imitating our goods and packaging vigorously. Compressed goods in bulk are reaping the benefit of our expenditure and cutting into our sales badly.' Burroughs by now had also become convinced that,

> Unless we shortly begin making the goods in England, we will soon see the trade we have worked so hard to build up all tumble into the hands of such houses as Wyley's of Coventry, Richardson & Co. and others. . . . If McKesson and Robbins are unwilling to set up a factory in England, had we not better seek to throw up our contract with them and begin to manufacture on our own account, before all the trade has fallen into the hands of our English competitors who are just now very zealous and enterprising?

An additional problem was that some of the competition was of high quality. Wyley's produced a range of ovoid capsuled pills, which, Wellcome wrote to Burroughs,

> I acknowledge that they were very well made and would pass for the McK and R without difficulty. . . . I can see no hope of preventing the sales of McK and R pills gradually dwindle down to nothing unless prompt steps are taken to manufacture the goods in this country, and do away with the stamp. . . . Messrs Squire have imported a machine for making ovoid capsuled pills and there will be many more besides them.

The actual manufacturing resources of Burroughs Wellcome were initially extremely modest and were limited to a few preparations in small premises close to Snow Hill. Wellcome now began a search for much larger ones.

Wellcome envisaged a factory that could undertake all the firm's work, and went out of London, as, he explained to Burroughs, 'it is desirable to have the factory in the country where we can have a clear atmosphere, as in the compressing of the tablets, and in the making of fine products, the soot and smoke of London is very likely to contaminate the goods'. He also looked for an abundant supply of fresh water – 50,000 gallons a day – and good communications.

All these he found on the south bank of the Thames, at Bell Lane Wharf, Wandsworth. It consisted of three reasonably large buildings, outbuildings and a cottage. It had a private dock for barges and excellent fresh water from the River Wandle. The fact that a site located on the south side of the Thames between Wandsworth and Putney bridges was considered in 1882 to be 'in the country' demonstrates the then comparatively small size of London. It was ideal for Wellcome's purposes, and he took a six-year lease, as from 25 March 1883.

This was a gigantic step forward. Wellcome insisted that all the machinery and equipment should be installed before 25 March, so that actual production could begin on that date. Also, new staff had to be recruited and, in many cases, trained, and the buildings cleaned and painted up to Wellcome's high standards. All this had to be done – and was done – in less than three months, with Wellcome supervising the entire operation.

The first Burroughs Wellcome factory contained the machinery and facilities for producing Kepler Malt Extract, including equipment for analysis and experimentation – which was to cause severe trouble later; this occupied a considerable space. The production of the famous compressed tablets was separate, with the Wyeth machines capable of producing 200,000 a day. Here, the presence of drugs and chemicals had a considerable potential danger, of which Wellcome was acutely aware, and safety and security were impressed upon everyone from the beginning. The buildings also had a large space for bottling and packing products – another process closely monitored by a professional scientific chemist – and storage. If the first Burroughs Wellcome factory was not under one roof, it was at least on one site.

The Snow Hill premises were also by now hopelessly inadequate, and Burroughs had set his heart on acquiring the whole of a new building at the corner of Snow Hill and Holborn Viaduct, as 'we shall need larger premises, as large as Wyeth's in Philadelphia, some day'. Although Wellcome agreed in principle, it was his opinion that that day had not arrived. 'What splendid windows to cover with gilt-edged advertisements,' Burroughs wrote excitedly from Auckland on 16 December 1882. 'What a noble building to command respect for the business to be carried on within it.' He also wanted 'an elegant Retail and Dispensing Drug Store, that would take the shine out of everything in all London', laboratories and 'a modern elevator worked by steam', so that Burroughs Wellcome 'would have the "Boss" premises of the Drug business in London'.

This was carrying ambitious enthusiasm rather too far. By January 1883 Wellcome was working immensely hard over the new Wandsworth factory and devoting particular attention to its soaring costs, and the owners of the new Snow Hill building were asking for a rent of £1,800 a year; they then reduced this to £1,350, which Wellcome also considered beyond the means of Burroughs Wellcome. Moreover, the building was much larger than the firm then really needed, and the lease offered was a short one. But he, too, coveted the building, as much as Burroughs did, and had the advantage of knowing how depressed business was in London. Five days after the Wandsworth factory started production on 30 March 1883, he informed Burroughs that he had acquired the Snow Hill building for a rent of £900 for the first year and £1,245 per annum for the remainder of the twenty-one-year lease. 'It is perhaps a little in advance of our actual requirements', he wrote, 'and the heavy rent will make a large addition to our general expenses. . . . The expenses for fitting up the Factory and the Snow Hill Building have been vastly beyond what we expected, and figured upon, this is the cause of our little pinch.'

Both ventures involved huge risks. The prudence of Wellcome and Sudlow in watching the profits, and making every effort to maximise them in the face of mounting competition, had meant that Burroughs Wellcome was in a position to make short-term commitments for the future of the firm, but these undertakings were of a far greater scale. If they did not succeed by increasing business and profits, the gamble – for such it was – would end in disaster and, as far as Wellcome was concerned, a return to penury. This, he was totally resolved, must not happen.

*

Furnishing and equipping the Snow Hill building caused difficulties because of its awkward shape. 'There is not a single right-angle in the whole building,' Wellcome wrote to his partner, but he took great trouble over it. The most radical of his actions was to have 'the Edison Electric Light' installed, making use of the first public supply station that had begun to operate in the basement of a house in Holborn Viaduct in March 1882. By the end of 1883 the work was completed, and Burroughs Wellcome had achieved its 'Boss Drug' headquarters and showplace.

There is unfortunately no extant contemporary description of it beyond Wellcome's correspondence and instructions, but one in *The Chemist and Druggist* five years later describes it well:

The interior arrangements were all designed by Mr Wellcome and executed under the direction of Dr Christopher Dresser, the eminent art decorator of Sutton, by English workmen. The wood used is all American walnut. The floor of the vestibule is made of mosaic work, with pictorial insertions representing Commerce and Industry. The vestibule is very wide . . . but this has enabled the designer to throw across it an imposing screen of unpolished plate-glass, the door is similarly treated, and its furnishings are made of hammered copper. The windows, of which there are four, each contain three walnut wood screens, quaintly carved on the lower part, and composed above of intricate Moorish or Baghdad spindle-work. The centre of each screen is filled in with a small plate of hammered copper bearing the name of one of the firm's specialities. Everything about the exterior of the building has a solidarity which seems to say 'We come to stay', and this is no less apparent in the interior.

The premises . . . are in the form of a half-circle, but the commonplaceness of this form is counteracted by a screen with half-moon galleries, which divides it into two parts, the greater being coupled as a general office accommodating a dozen clerks, half of whom are ladies. But there is little of the office tone about the apartment; there is neither the polished mahogany, nor the spider-legged desks and stools; were it not, indeed, for the presence of a huge American safe, timed to be opened at a set hour each morning, and messengers coming and going, the office would not impress one as being connected with trade. The screen, like all the furnishings of the street floor, is made of walnut wood, with heavy mouldings relieved by carving in straw-plait style. The lower part of it is formed into a book-case for bound volumes of periodical medical and pharmaceutical literature. The half-moon gallery is curtained with art shades of plush which harmonise beautifully with the dark unpolished walnut. The office furniture, chiefly consisting of writing tables and a large enquiry table, are uniform in design with the screen and with chairs and settees, which are upholstered in alligator hide. . . . The gangway is controlled by a ponderous gate of hammered copper, a material . . . also used for paper-weights, twine boxes, and other office utensils. The whole appearance of the office is rich and artistic. It strikes one that it has been fitted regardless of cost, but there is not a pennyworth about it, even the Statue of Liberty (modelled we are told by Bartholdi's own hand),* nor the American Eagle standing on the safe, which could be spared. . . .

All the floors are connected by means of a spiral staircase, and a 'lift' for heavy goods. Ascending the staircase we first reach the half-moon gallery, which we find utilised as a room for lady clerks. . . . The first floor is divided into three apartments which are used by the principals and their amanuenses. . . . The rooms are *en suite*, the first of them is fitted up as a library and writing room, the furniture being in richly carved English oak. . . . In this room is placed for the use of employees after business hours a magnificent grand pianoforte, and near by is an American organ. Mr Sudlow, the general manager, is an accomplished musician, and under his guidance a good deal of excellent harmony is produced. The next room is used by Mr Burroughs and is triangular in shape. There is little pretension in the furnishing of this room; an ordinary writing cabinet stands in one corner, and beside it a revolving book-stand containing the most modern medical and pharmaceutical text and reference books. . . . The presence of a chemical test cabinet in this room shows that experimentation is part of the work done in it.

The third room of the suite is used by Mr Wellcome and is furnished as a library, although hunting trophies, works of art from other countries visited by the occupant, a striking statuette of Henry Ward Beecher, and a varied selection of general literature, give it less the look of a commercial room and more the appearance of a bachelor's den. The decoration of this suite of rooms and their furnishings are of a highly artistic character, but quiet in tone.

The second floor is a stock-room, as is also the floor above it. . . .

* One of Burroughs's more remarkable contributions, in which Wellcome was also involved, was the donation of a bronze replica of the Statue of Liberty presented by Americans to the French nation. This reproduction of the original model of Monsieur Auguste Bartholdi's mammoth Statue of Liberty enlightening the world was presented to France in 1885, the year the French gift arrived in New York for construction. It stands nine metres high on a twelve-metres-high tower. The statue in New York towers fifty metres-high. The scale of Burroughs's contribution is not revealed in the certificate which was presented to him as one of the major contributors.

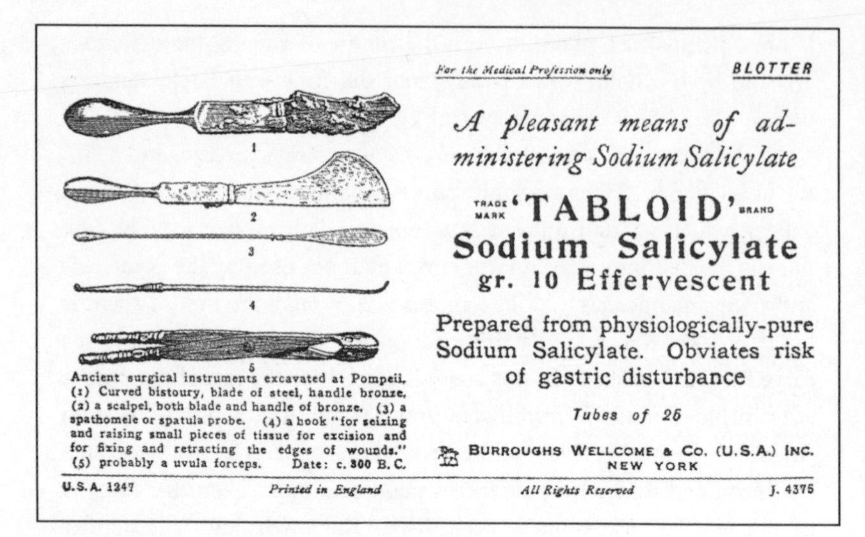


Advertisement for Tabloid Sodium Salicylate

> The top floor is occupied by a staff of seven printers and compositors, who execute a large part of the printing work required by the firm. . . .

The problem of the trademarks remained. 'Imitations of the tablets', Wellcome wrote to Burroughs on 19 October 1883, 'are coming out so rapidly that although I have made most of them withdraw, they are becoming so numerous that I fear we shall be swamped.' For months he had tried to discover a comprehensive name for Burroughs Wellcome products, and especially its compressed medicines, that could be patented internationally. '"Equivalents" is good, but too cumbersome,' he informed Burroughs. '"Equaloids" or "Equoids" or "Equivaloids" have each suggested themselves, but not to my satisfaction. It is important that we get a good pat name.' Eventually, he chose 'Valoid', which was registered on 14 March 1884; but also registered on the same day was his true inspiration, 'Tabloid'.

This extraordinary word, together with his other inventions, including the word 'Soloid', was Wellcome's own. He later said:

> In 1884 we thought of having a new name. To find this I passed through my mind all the letters and syllables I could think of. I wanted to coin

> some word that would be euphonious – that is something that would be pleasing to the ear, that would be easy to remember. The result was the word 'Tabloid'! It was an entirely new word. I have never found the word in any shape or form before the date of my invention or registration of it.

Burroughs played no part whatever in this development, but must have approved, as before the end of the year Burroughs Wellcome was advertising 'Pepsin Tabloids'. The word rapidly entered the language of pharmacy and medicine, and then into the English language and dictionary, as the registered trademark of the compressed medicines of Burroughs Wellcome & Co.; it was not until many years later that it was also used to describe a cheap newspaper of a particular format.

The word was, of course, a mixture of 'Tablets' and 'Ovoids', but it was more than an advertising name, important though that was; it gave to their compressed medicines a unique and patented title that their competitors used at their peril. As will be related, one did, to his immense cost, in 1903, when the word 'Tabloid' was definitely established as belonging only to the products of Burroughs Wellcome & Co. Wellcome had not only added a new word to the English language, but had also thrown the Burroughs Wellcome competitors into confusion.

The secret of the success of Burroughs Wellcome was later well described in *The Pharmaceutical Era*:

> First, they had something to sell, something that was wanted. English medicine was labouring in the slough of big bottles, big doses, and nauseous drugs. A revolution had already taken place in favour of the elegancies of Hahnemann, but homeopathic medicines had proved useless for people with anything the matter with them. 'Tabloids' hit the happy mean. They provided an allopathic dose in a convenient and palatable form. They, and the other preparations introduced by the firm, were backed by novel and continuous advertising, and in a few years the Newer Pharmacy, of which Burroughs Wellcome & Co. were the British pioneers, had revolutionized medical preparations in this country.

In the summer of 1882 there came the first seriously discordant episode in relations between Wellcome and Burroughs. Under the Deed of Partnership Wellcome was entitled to increase his capital holding in the company to equal Burroughs's in September 1882, and this he was fully determined to do. However, Burroughs was equally determined to continue the situation that gave him the dominant position in the partnership.

What followed created a pattern with which Wellcome was to become only too familiar. Burroughs wrote, apparently early in August 1882 (the letter has not been found), to propose, obviously somewhat sharply and abruptly, that Wellcome should waive this right for another two years. He replied to Burroughs on 25 August in what were, for him, unusually strong terms:

> I must express my very serious regret and chagrin at your proposal – in the first place that you request me to put off my claim to equal share in the business until four years from the date that our partnership began.
>
> You know as positively and clearly as man can know any fact, that I have worked sincerely and devotedly for the success of this business, and have spared no effort to gain that end.
>
> You know that when the management fell into my hands the business was in such an entangled snarl that had you gone on in the old way you would have been ruined.
>
> You know that as a result of my care and hard work the whole snarl has been cleared away.
>
> You know that the policy which was adopted by the firm under my management (though such policy was strongly opposed by you) has been thoroughly successful – while if the course urged by you had been carried out we should have been ruined, and I have proved such to you in figures.
>
> You have worked hard and done your share in your department – but in the conduct and management of the business, and in the consequent cares and responsibilities, you have shared very little.
>
> The management and success of a business does not depend upon

sales alone. There is a necessary care which you have never known – the thinking and judgement which are essential do not come in hasty flashes of impulse. Careful judgement in the government of a business is the result of hard brain work, and what I have accomplished for our firm has been the result of much work, and I am willing to stand by the results as an evidence.

I do not for an instant reflect upon you or belittle your own good qualities and abilities, although your request to me to put off the equal partnership until the end of four years is a most stinging reflection upon me – and one which I most positively resent.

Every man who knows anything about our business knows that the value of my services has been as great as yours, and I claim the full right under the partnership agreement to an equal partnership on the first of Sept. 1882.

He then quoted verbatim the clauses of The Articles of Partnership which had a bearing upon his rights to equality. 'I consider the request you make,' he continued, 'a very unhandsome one, and one that you should feel very heartily ashamed of.'

Wellcome then dealt at considerable length with the proposed purchase of the outstanding shares in the Kepler Malt Extract Co. by Burroughs Wellcome. On this point Burroughs seems to have offered to sell all his shares in the Kepler Malt Extract Co. to Burroughs Wellcome, 'without any remuneration . . . on a/c of interest in royalties, commissions &c . . . if you [Wellcome] agree not to demand a half interest in the whole business of BW & Co.'.

It is difficult to see what inducement Burroughs thought this proposal held for Wellcome to sacrifice his right, and Wellcome proceeded to point out to his partner that the offer he made was invalidated by the fact that Burroughs's agreement with the Kepler Co., on which he had been receiving five per cent commission or royalty, had never been signed. In any case the term of this unsigned agreement had already expired and, in the opinion of Queen's Counsel, Burroughs had no right of claim under its provisions.

Wellcome's letter went on:

I do not bring these things up to taunt you with your mistakes, but simply to remind you that the burden of correcting the complications which you had brought upon us has fallen mainly upon my shoulders. I should never complain of this nor recall it to your memory were you not as ungrateful as to offer me such unjust reflection as is contained in your proposal.

You know that from the first I have worked as faithfully for the promotion of your personal interests as for my own.

I know full well the value of your work, and applaud you in your accomplishments, but you must not entertain the fallacious idea that you alone have made the success of BW & Co.

I hope you will read, and re-read, this letter very carefully and thoughtfully, as it deals with important facts which are carefully weighed after deliberate consideration, and every word of it I am prepared to sustain in full.

Had you written to me that owing to your absence it might be agreeable to me to delay the equal partnership until your return, or something of that sort, I might have entertained the idea, but your proposal as I understand it is very improper.

At the best such differences are not pleasant and with a view of preventing any further discussion from arising on this subject I will without prejudice make the following offer of concession and compromise if you will sign the enclosed agreement which provides that I shall be entitled to equal partnership with yourself on Sept 1st 1883 (instead of 1882) on my making my share of the capital equal to yours, and without submitting the matter to arbitration, I will grant the one year specified. If you do not sign this or agree to this proposal I shall maintain my claim to equal partnership from Sept. 1st 1882, and I shall have no difficulty in clearly defending my right to it.

I am very sorry that such a matter should arise between us for our relations have been unmarred by any serious misunderstanding, but I cannot, with any self respect, permit my rights in this matter to be treated as lightly as you seem to treat them.

I am willing to meet you halfway in the matter as evidenced by my offer in which I concede you one year, providing you make the matter definite then, so that no further discussion could ever again arise upon the subject, and also avoid arbitration which would expose our private business pattern to outsiders which would not be pleasant for either of us.

I have spoken very plainly and earnestly in this letter, and have entered into much detail in order to show you how very mistaken you are in the view you seem to entertain.

I have not written this with any ill feeling, on the contrary you will observe the concession I propose; but I prefer to sacrifice a certain part of my rights rather than endanger our kind relations by allowing differences to arise between us.

Trusting that this will end the matter.

Burroughs evidently took this rebuke to heart, for by 30 November 1882 the capital holding of Wellcome was equal to that of Burroughs.

Wellcome was anxious to maintain reasonably cordial relations with his partner, writing emolliently on 6 September that,

I know very well your impulsive and often too hasty disposition, and although you have written some very severe and cutting criticisms I have made allowances for impulse, and not allowed them to annoy or anger me. You ought to be well enough acquainted with me to know that if I had been angered I should have very frankly told you of it in the plainest English I could command. . . . In our relations you have most always found me patient (at least trying to be) and yet not hesitating to speak plainly when it seemed the proper occasion. You know that I am not a fellow to harbour ill feeling, and that I can hold strongly different opinions from my friends and yet not lose my most sincere feeling of heart friendship. I have looked upon you with the warm-hearted friendship that I could upon a brother, and I have enjoyed what I always believed to be a full reciprocity with you.

Burroughs wrote back with fulsome expressions of friendship.

But this first trial of strength had left its mark on both. Wellcome, with some justification, believed that he had, almost single-handedly, saved the firm from an early collapse, so chaotic had been Burroughs's operations and methods of work, and that he was entitled to equality. Burroughs, while admitting, somewhat grudgingly, that Wellcome had certainly achieved much, reiterated that he was, after all, the founder of the company and its senior partner. Both were ambitious, but Burroughs had never experienced the near-poverty Wellcome had, and it was this that gave the latter the harder approach. His ambitions went beyond wealth, but wealth was essential to them. He had come to England to make his fortune and, as the company developed under his leadership and began to prosper, he was not going to have that jeopardised. This had been the first shot in the battle between two strong egos for the control of Burroughs Wellcome. Burroughs had had to concede on this occasion, but was to regroup his forces for another assault. It was an ominous but instructive episode.

*

Burroughs, excitable and passionate, was quick to criticise Wellcome, too often in personally offensive language. When Wellcome, whose self-control was remarkable, wrote back stiffly and with bleak anger to deny the charges, Burroughs would then write long letters of apology – and then, sometimes within days, would fire off another letter or telegram accusing Snow Hill and his partner of incompetence in fulfilling the orders he had secured on his travels, neglecting the business and ignoring his precise instructions. Wellcome would reply indignantly; Burroughs would then climb down again with lavish apologies. These often harsh exchanges made Wellcome increasingly concerned about their relationship.

By August 1882 Burroughs had reached Australia. Here, he had another of his fits of remorse:

> August 8, 1882 Adelaide
>
> Now my dear friend I have meant to treat you kindly but I have felt so sure of your loving friendship that I fear I have treated you carelessly and coldly without meaning it. Forgive me dear Wellcome. I am very sorry. I will be more genuine in future, more true to myself.

The next day he was writing again:

Your long letter of May 26th is just to hand upon my return from Port Adelaide this evg. You may be sure I am glad to hear from you after your letter has been so long on the way, and I am more glad to see that you bear me no ill will for the unkind and ungenerous letters I have written to criticise your management. Well that this disturbance caused by my own stupidity, carelessness and obstinacy is over I think we shall have smooth sailing together the rest of our lives. You are the last one in the world I could wish to quarrel with (though I don't want to quarrel with anyone) because your friendship is too dear for me. You will get no more ugly words from me and you dear patient kind-hearted old fellow have never given me any at all.

And on 10 August he repeated his call for forgiveness:

By God's grace I hope this business I have shown towards you and others may be thoroughly purged from my being and that I may, though late, learn to appreciate and love as I have been loved, and that I may grieve dear friends and companions with ingratitude no more.

I am sure you will forgive me and that you have suffered more than I do now thinking of injustice I have done myself and you in disregarding your dear friendship and affectionate counsel.

In future we will be as brothers and you will know that one of the best ways you can strengthen the warm regard of your brother will be to renew the counsel from your heart which in time past I ungratefully rejected and forfeited what I should most highly prize in all the World the loving regard of a sincere friend. Let me hear soon of your forgiveness and the renewed confidence and dear friendship of the old days.

The respite was very brief. Matters deteriorated again between the partners in October 1882. Burroughs wrote apologetically from New York to say that 'I have probably misunderstood your views and motives in those matters with which I have found fault. When we see each other again everything will be mutually understood and satisfactory to both of us.' Wellcome was very doubtful, replying that,

> For your own happiness as well as for the happiness of your friends, you must think more carefully before you speak – wait and consider both sides and see if you are doing your friends full justice. When you condemn them without a hearing, consider for a moment and see if the judgment and opinions of others are not of sufficient importance to deserve weighing. While you are excessively sensitive yourself, you unintentionally but very often do say things which cause others a good deal of pain.

He added that he wrote 'as a friend to a friend whom I love with all my heart and with a hope that you may give it more than a passing thought', but he also said that 'I have sometimes wondered if you ever carefully read my letters'.

One of Wellcome's most serious problems was over the calibre – or lack of it, in too many instances – of the Burroughs Wellcome staff. Burroughs's outstanding appointments were Robert Sudlow and William Henry Kirby, who joined in February and March 1879. Sudlow was to serve the company for his entire working life, and Kirby until his death in September 1895 as a result of a tragic accident in his home. But others were as unsatisfactory as Kelly, as Wellcome soon discovered. The company's first personnel register contains entries for men for whom Burroughs had acted as referee or personally appointed; it also includes a dismal record of dismissals for being 'valueless as traveller', 'very bad man, thief, liar &c', 'incompetency', 'altogether undesirable' and 'worthless'. The worst of all was Dr Otto Witte, appointed on Burroughs's reference as factory manager in 1883, and whose betrayal of company secrets to competitors brought his downfall in 1887. In general, Burroughs was a poor judge of character, whereas Wellcome had a quite exceptional capacity for spotting talent from a remarkably early age; as he developed more self-confidence, this quality became even more notable. As the circle of his friends and acquaintances in the medical profession widened, he could call upon advice from the most prominent specialists in the profession, and often did so.

In this, the role of his personal doctor and close friend, Chune

Fletcher, was incalculable. In addition to being a professional doctor, Fletcher was also an expert in medical-legal matters, on which Wellcome increasingly sought his guidance. Fletcher became perhaps Wellcome's closest friend in London as well as his most trusted adviser, and Henry Dale was right when he later remarked that Fletcher knew Wellcome better than anyone. His failure to make a correct diagnosis of the chronic illnesses that plagued Wellcome from 1885 until 1898 was to have unfortunate results, but Wellcome's trust in him as a doctor and shrewd adviser never faltered.

Fletcher was two years younger than Wellcome, and when they first met in 1881 he had just qualified from St Bartholomew's Hospital and set up his practice in Charterhouse Square. He was the medical officer of Charterhouse and the Sutton Foundation, and was to serve in the same capacity to Merchant Taylors' School and Company and a considerable number of City firms and insurance companies. It is not clear where and when they met, but it was not long after Wellcome had established himself in London and their mutual attraction was immediate and lasting. As in the case of his other real friends, Wellcome's friendship extended to Fletcher's wife and daughter. With the exception of Power and his family, Wellcome's closest friendship was with the Fletchers. He never forgot those he had known at the beginning of his career, and with whom his relationship had been more than professional. In all the professional and personal crises of his life Wellcome invariably turned to Fletcher for his advice and assistance, until the latter's relatively early death in 1913, at the age of fifty-eight.

Burroughs's most serious and outrageous action so far was to offer a partnership in Burroughs Wellcome to a young American, John Van Schaack, without consulting Wellcome. Wellcome knew the family, and the young man, very well. As he wrote to Burroughs:

> He is a clever, active, fellow and good-hearted, but he is in no way suited for our business, his brusque, cheeky, demonstrative, 'harum-scarum' manner would never be accepted in this country. He possesses the faculty of saying the wrong things at the wrong time so often as to get

> himself seriously disliked by people who do not have the patience to excuse the disagreeable peculiarities of others, or do not have the opportunity of becoming acquainted with his better qualities. . . . In short I would not want him in connection with our business in any capacity, even if he would pay us $2,000 a year for the privilege.

Wellcome realised what Burroughs's game was – to bring in a young partner beholden to him, which would give him back his dominant position in the company. The fact that Wellcome was a friend of Van Schaack's parents made the situation even more embarrassing, as Burroughs's offer of partnership depended upon Wellcome's consent, and, as he wrote, 'I positively decline, and they [the Van Schaacks] will never forgive me for it.' Burroughs then arranged for the young man to travel to London at the firm's expense, where Wellcome offered him an appointment as a representative, but made clear that a partnership was out of the question. Van Schaack did not stay long with Burroughs Wellcome.

Burroughs tried again within months to bring in a third partner; again, Wellcome refused. Burroughs then proposed in October 1884 that Burroughs Wellcome should become a limited liability company; the object of this, also, was that Burroughs and his associates would have a predominant shareholding. Wellcome, again on solid legal ground, rebuffed this equally transparent attempt to put him into a subordinate position, and even to force him out. But he had no doubts that Burroughs would try again; foolishly, and uncharacteristically, he was to give Burroughs his opportunity. But, for the time being, he was secure.

*

The potentialities of the Australian and New Zealand markets fired Burroughs's imagination, even though their populations were small. He wrote in a different vein to Wellcome from Sydney on 19 October 1882:

> I am anticipating a jolly big sale for nearly all our goods here & hope I can get the wholesale houses to supply the demand.
>
> Both Elliott's & Prosser's people are very nice folks. Mr Prosser took

me out to Botany Bay for a ride last Saturday and afterwards to his house. He has got one of the prettiest anywhere round here.

The doctors treat me first-rate & like our stuff. If we keep it before them constantly we are in for a fine trade here. I think we should have a traveller or salesman constantly here in Australia looking after our interests. . . . I can get a good man here – a thorough young gentleman, thoroughly honest, reliable & competent for a very reasonable compensation, say £750 the first year and expenses to a very less than £1 a day, what would you think of my engaging such a one? He could begin by canvassing the small up-country towns which I have not had time to visit now, nor the samples to spare – good towns through which it would pay well to work.

All such a man would have to do would be to go to doctors & turn over his orders to the chemists to the wholesale trade here. He could spend in each year three to four months advantageously in Victoria, three to four months in New South Wales, the same in New Zealand and two months in South Australia and Western Australia. I really believe that Australia is the best field we shall find anywhere for our goods and that the Australian [market] will be worth more than the English trade.

Burroughs eventually established a Burroughs Wellcome agency in Melbourne, which was to prove one of the best investments made by a foreign company in Australia.

One of the key differences in the approach of Wellcome and Burroughs to their business was that the former was far more interested in scientific and medical research, and the creation of new drugs, than in merely selling existing products and perfecting their preparation and production; even at this stage he was contemplating Burroughs Wellcome having its own research laboratories. Burroughs thought differently and, although he entirely agreed that Burroughs Wellcome should expand its drugs list, believed that this could best be achieved by the purchase of the patents and rights of those produced by other companies. The eventual establishment of the Wellcome Physiological Laboratories in 1894 was to owe everything to Wellcome and very little to Burroughs.

This is in no sense to disparage the latter. His energy, zeal for business and exceptional skills as a salesman were crucial to the early success of Burroughs Wellcome, but he simply was not a scholar *manqué*, which Wellcome was. Wellcome attended the conferences of the Pharmaceutical Society, the BMA and other institutions involved in medical research, and was an avid reader of learned journals, not only as a businessman, but also as someone genuinely fascinated by the subject. He was already collecting old medical instruments, books and artefacts. He knew, through his own experience and his constant contacts with doctors and surgeons, that the remarkable advances, inspired principally by Lister and Pasteur, had not been accompanied by a comparable one in drugs. Ailments today either unknown, or easily curable, or immunised against, were then often lethal, especially for children, and diphtheria was one of the most common and feared of all. If the Victorians are now considered to have been obsessed by death, the fact was that it was a very common occurrence in almost every family. These tragedies were not confined to the poor, although Andrew Mearns's *The Bitter Cry of Outcast London*, published in 1883, and the later works of Seebohm Rowntree, demonstrated that poverty and destitution greatly increased the odds. This was also one of the themes of the American Henry George, whose *Progress and Poverty* (1879) made an impact in Britain and America far greater than any Socialist, or Karl Marx.

George was a superb orator and polemicist. His thesis was that the ownership of land was the root cause of the ailments of society; he therefore called for a single tax on land. Burroughs first read George's writings on his voyage from Australia and espoused them ardently. He became one of George's most passionate supporters and advocates, in England as well as in the United States. Wellcome, who believed with equal fervour that business and politics did not mix, and should not mix, found George's arguments both absurd and dangerous, and considered Burroughs's zealotry in this cause incomprehensible and unsettling. What he particularly resented was the implication that whereas Burroughs was considered to have a social conscience, he was not.

Wellcome was more concerned with medical and business matters. In his quest for new drugs he became intrigued by the research undertaken by Sir Thomas Fraser at Edinburgh University on the medical possibilities of the African arrow poison *Strophanthus*. The pods of the plant from which it was obtained were first brought to England from Zanzibar in 1865, and research confirmed that they had a strong effect on the action of the heart. Fraser's work was to harness this power for beneficial results for cardiac patients. After a long talk with him at a BMA conference, Wellcome at once ordered a consignment of pods from Zanzibar, which arrived adulterated. On Fraser's advice, Wellcome tried to discover another variant; those available in Britain were unsatisfactory, so he instructed a special agent to go to Africa to find them. This expedition, very reminiscent of Wellcome's in the Cinchona forests, was wholly successful – although extremely expensive. The supply cost Burroughs Wellcome over £20 a pound to procure, but the firm had a complete monopoly, which was maintained by buying up all supplies when they came on to the market.

Guided by Fraser's pioneering work, the first samples of the new drug were circulated to doctors and hospitals for evaluation and further research, Burroughs Wellcome not having the facilities or expertise to conduct this itself. The results were so satisfactory in the relief of heart disease, both in Britain and America, that within a year 'Strophanthine' was introduced in the United States, and later in Britain. It was the first original drug introduced by Burroughs Wellcome and has it place in the history of the firm, but it also emphasised again to Wellcome the necessity of having his own research laboratories and team.

*

In February 1883 Burroughs informed Wellcome that he proposed to become engaged to Miss Olive Chase, of New York State. Wellcome's insufferable reply of 13 March will be given almost in full, as it caused understandable offence:

Now about your 'Olive branch'. . . . As you say in your letter you are very impressionable and have fallen in love many times – yes listen! And in falling in love you have not looked deep into the soul of the object of your admiration, in fact you know you don't try to study human nature either among men or women. You judge too liberally and too readily accept compliments gusto and flattery as sincere expressions, while you resent criticisms which are really sincere and honestly beneficial in guarding you against error. I mean to say that the complimenting acquaintance wins your heart while you repel the frank critic. I have seen this repeatedly when you trusted those who flattered you . . . while their sole object was to use you or gain some selfish end.

I have always feared that you would marry a woman whom you did not know, and that you would sadly repent it at your leisure, or that your polite attentions would allow some woman to fasten herself on to you with the plea that you had encouraged her into the belief that you meant to marry, and would finally marry her out of charity.

I quite approve of conditional engagements for a few years with the undertaking that either can quit if agreeable.

Your personal acquaintance and association with Miss Chase seems very slight for an engagement, and especially that you have not seen her for more than four years – occasional correspondence is not association, nor does it mean acquaintance. In fact it counts for very little, especially when of the formal sort of letters that you have shown me from Miss Chase.

I am taking a very plain and matter-of-fact view of this subject and express to you the feelings that would guide me in such matters.

When a man marries and begins the new life, the second half, it means either a little Paradise, or a big Hell for the rest of his and her days – there are seldom any half-way forms, except perhaps for people who are not sensitive and only marry for convenience and by mutual consent there is no love lost between the contracting parties.

A man must marry a woman who loves him in response to his own love for her. A woman who can sympathize with him in his social life, in his business cares, and can fill his home with sunshine. The taste and ideas of both must harmonize to secure harmony and happiness.

A woman who is simply pure and even as good as an angel may be as cold and frigid as an *iceberg*. Ice may be an emblem of purity and very good in its place, but no man wants to place ice in his bosom to chill his own warmth and vitality if he has any. . . .

Above all things I wish you a happy home with a true loving wife – I know no woman too good for you. Regarding Miss Chase I will only add that I hope you will become associated with her and she with you *before* marriage; it is better for both to become acquainted before than after. You are absolutely strangers to each other and you do Miss Chase as *great* a wrong as you do yourself by even encouraging her and especially by marrying until you are familiar with the disposition of each other. . . .

I don't urge 'Punch's' recommendation* but I would say '*Caution* the ice is thin.'

There is certainly no hurry for either of us to get married, and there are several very good reasons why neither of us should marry for several years to come and I hope you will not hasten yours too quickly – at any rate I want to be present, even if it is in Borneo.

As regards my prospects of matrimony I have *none*, and am not at all anxious, I expect to meet *the* one some day; until then I am a contented bachelor.

On 20 October Burroughs wrote to Wellcome:

Now my dear old fellow I want you to let me know by return mail if our business prospects are sufficient to warrant my taking a life partner to share them with me. I should exceedingly like to be married this fall or winter and to bring my wife with me to London.

To which Wellcome replied on 5 November:

Now about the subject of matrimony, you ask me if the state of our business is such as to warrant your marrying *Fall* or *Winter*. In reply I can only say *no*! and I would strongly urge you to postpone the marriage until next summer or the Autumn, when our footing will, I hope, be more certain, and the heavy burden we are now labouring under will be lightened and things generally more easy with us. I sincerely hope you will trust my judgement in this recommendation.

* 'Advice to those about to marry – Don't.'

I would like to enjoy the privilege of being present on the occasion of your marriage, my dear friend, as I shall feel that your wife is akin to me. Would it not be far better for you to first prepare a nice comfortable home to which you could bring a wife, so that her first experience would not be in the wretched cheerless London Boarding or Apartment house. I would strongly urge this course. . . .

I think you could set the tune as next September, and then I shall be glad to wish you all joy and happiness.

Please write me fully upon this subject as I feel almost as much interested as if I was going to be married myself, a circumstance which is not very likely to occur within an early date.

I have never met one to whom I was sufficiently attracted, to invite her to share my life – not but what I have met many ladies whom I regard as more than worthy of me, but somehow I have never become acquainted with one whose life and inclinations seemed to tally exactly with my own fancies. It is more than likely that I shall become a sordid old bachelor and then look upon your happy fireside with envy. You ought to be able to select an ideal for me from among the great numbers upon whom you have been sweet.

Wellcome's own views on love and matrimony had not changed greatly since 1876, when, on the engagement of his brother George, he had written to his mother:

My own destiny in love's course is unknown. It is as much hidden from my knowledge as at the day of my birth. My life's work may be complete without the association of one who shall confide in me and I in her, but I don't think it will harm me, for though the wedded life brings joys it too brings cares.

Unsurprisingly, Burroughs took no notice whatever and married Miss Chase in the following February, bringing her to England in March. Wellcome tried to retrieve his position by writing a letter of congratulations (5 February 1884):

I want now at the first quiet moment to express to you my most sincere and hearty congratulations on your winning a wife of such a true and noble character. I wish you and yours all of God's blessings.

I presume that I am getting too much fossilized, and drifting away from romance and sentiment. You have now left me in the vast sea of bachelorhood in which we have so long drifted together, and I am afraid that this candidate will continue at sea for a long time to come unless you graciously persuade some heart hungry maiden to have pity on me.

I want you to convey to Mrs Burroughs my most cordial greetings and to it I must add congratulations . . . say that a wedding present awaits her in London which shall be a token of my respect and friendship.

Burroughs may well have shown his wife Wellcome's letters, because her relations with him were not good from the beginning, and were rapidly to become considerably worse. Hers was a harder personality than Burroughs's, and although it is impossible to cite evidence, Wellcome's belief that she played a considerable part in cooling relations between the two partners, and then in precipitating a crisis, seems fully justified, particularly in view of later events. Quite unnecessarily, Wellcome had made a formidable enemy.

*

Also, the strain of Wellcome's hectic life, both business and social, was now beginning to show, and his health became a matter of concern to Sudlow and Kirby, who alerted Burroughs when he reached New York at the end of September. At this time their relations remained good, and Burroughs wrote solicitously:

October 5th 1883

Dear Wellcome

I am extremely sorry to learn of your illness and hope you are by this time restored to your usual health and strength.

Let me caution you again not to work too hard nor to deprive yourself of necessary rest and recreation.

Mr Kirby writes me that he thinks your illness was brought about solely by your close attention to the work of getting the new Factory and warehouse in proper working business shape.

Perhaps I should have come over sooner to relieve you of some of all this extra work for a while and give you an opportunity of visiting this country on a vacation.

However, Burroughs, with his wedding plans, did not return to London until the end of March 1884. In the meantime, Wellcome continued to carry the full burden of the business, which included a long tour of Spain at the end of 1883 and beginning of 1884.*

When Burroughs eventually returned to London, he was delighted by the condition of the firm's finances, which were beginning to look impressive. 'The fact is', he wrote, 'our business never was in such a promising and profitable condition as at the present time. If I was out of business and you owned the whole of this business, I would think $100,000 very cheap for one half of it, saying nothing of the value of the Goodwill.' This, and other similar tributes, were to be very useful when Burroughs's attitude towards Wellcome later changed.

*

Although Wellcome was a devoted son and brother, and made himself entirely responsible for his family's financial well-being, the pressures of business and pleasure had prevented him from visiting them until the late summer of 1884. The speed and comfort of the transatlantic ships had vastly improved, and were to improve even more dramatically, and the railway connections between New York and Minnesota were now excellent, so it is somewhat puzzling that Wellcome had allowed nearly five years to elapse before he visited his mother in Monticello. He wrote regularly, and saw to it that her financial circumstances were good, but even when she became obviously very seriously ill in 1893, he did not hasten over to see her.

Even Mary Wellcome was quietly protesting, writing to her son on 20 July 1884 that,

* Spain had not proved to be the lucrative market that Burroughs had anticipated, and a severe outbreak of cholera persuaded Wellcome that his representative Christie was too valuable to lose. It was on his initiative that Christie was sent to be the firm's representative in South America late in 1885, by which time the cholera epidemic was sweeping Spain, with devastating consequences.

> I did not think it would ever be so long a time that I should not hear from you as it is I know you are very busy and I am very sorry that you are so deeply pressed with business that you cannot find time to write your mother a letter. I do not mean to complain but I would so much like to have one of your good long letters again. I try to pray for you and commend you to the Lord and his keeping.

A couple of years earlier Wellcome had complained that the letters from his brother George were mainly sermons, to which George had replied with some dignity on 12 October 1882:

> My heart was full of the love of God which I have since been destitute of & having dodged the will of God & tried so many times to run away from him by trying some other work yet he followed me all the way through & has driven me out until I have yielded to him to do his bidding.

There had in fact been a surprisingly long gap in their correspondence, George writing to their mother on 19 May 1882: 'Do you really think the Great amount of Biz Henry has is sufficient excuse for his not writing to me for more than a year? I don't know any reason, but that seems a little too thin.'

The rift was only temporary, but George and his family were desperately poor and depended on the millinery work of his wife, Cevilla. In asking his brother for a loan to set up her own business in January 1883, George revealed that 'we have to live mostly on her earnings as I do not bring in much. I have only rec'd about $18 this winter & that does not go far to keep a family & horse.' Wellcome responded at once and promised further assistance, which he was to give for many years. His reward was the intense gratitude of George and his family. For example, in a letter of 14 September 1887 George wrote to Henry:

> You say call on you for what I need. Henry I cannot; you have loaded me down now with kindness & how could I have the face to ask you for more? I tell you truly all I have rec'd from you has been greatly

needed & came just in the place & when you feel like doing anything for me it will never come amiss nor will it be wasted.

Wellcome's visit to his mother in September 1884 was quite short; a subsequent one to Garden City, which he had intended to make with Jacob Wellcome, but who was detained by an urgent brain operation in his new practice in Sleepy Eye, was a great disappointment. The thriving and expanding little community of the 1860s had fallen upon bad times, and Wellcome was shocked by 'a picture of ruin and decay, it was painful to see the wreck'. The family drugstore 'looks very dingy; it has never been repainted either inside or out'. Almost all his schoolfriends – at least those of enterprise and talent – had left to make their fortunes elsewhere, as he had, and were succeeding, especially George Palmer. It was a melancholy return to the scene of the happiest part of his childhood.

Wellcome's reluctance to return to America except on business did not mean that he had become so Anglicised that he wanted to forget his American nationality. He established himself as the founder and leading personality of the American Society in London, and made a point of entertaining American visitors to England. His sources of information about these visits were excellent, and most of his knowledge about the arrivals of politicians, diplomats and men of importance – who included his friends, Robert Lincoln and Russell Harrison, both sons of American Presidents – came from the American Legation, with whose officials he kept in close touch. The arrivals of members of the American drugs business were made known to him either directly or through his personal links. By 1885 Wellcome was being described in the social pages of the newspapers as 'a well-known American citizen resident in London'. He was a friend of the American Consul-General, Thomas M. Waller, a former Governor of Connecticut; and when George M. Horton, formerly of the *New York Herald Tribune*, came to London to represent a New York publishing company, Wellcome gave what was admiringly described as 'a complimentary and most sumptuous déjeuner at the First Avenue Hotel, attended by a number of gentlemen well known in the literary and artistic world'. Wellcome organised these occasions with great care and imagination, and ensured that they were well reported.

He was very willing, indeed anxious, to do them all favours, and when any of his English friends were to visit the United States, he provided them with letters of introduction and advice. He was invited to become an Honorary Commissioner of the proposed American Exhibition in London in 1885, and was dismayed to discover that it was to be located either in Battersea or at the Alexandra Palace. To put it in either place, he wrote, would guarantee failure 'and that a mortifying one'; his wise advice was followed, and the Exhibition took place at Earls Court in May 1887. It was a considerable success and was visited by Queen Victoria. Wellcome's prominent involvement in the 'American Exhibition of the Arts, Inventions, Manufactures, Products and Resources of the United States' gave him increased stature on both sides of the Atlantic.

Since Sudlow had introduced Wellcome to Masonry in 1885, he had become a very active Mason and had risen rapidly to elected senior positions. He was particularly attracted by its masculine character, the excellent company he found through his membership of several Lodges and The Savage Club, and the emphasis on philanthropy. Sudlow and Kirby, another enthusiastic Mason, had become close personal friends as well as employees, and through them Wellcome was introduced to a particularly influential element in British society.

One of Wellcome's new friends, and destined to be a lasting one, was an American-born woman of remarkable dynamism and attractiveness; indeed, she was one of the most extraordinary women of her time.

May French Sheldon, the daughter of Colonel Joseph French, was five years older than Wellcome. When she first met him in 1882, she had already made four world tours at the expense of her rich father and her husband, Eli Lemon Sheldon, who, although also American, had established himself as a successful businessman in London. Sheldon himself was an interesting young man, with a background that was also like Wellcome's. He had been born in Michigan in 1849, and although he had studied law and medicine, he did not practise in the latter; unlike Wellcome, he had inherited a significant sum of money from his father, and had practised law in Chicago between 1871 and 1876. When his partner died, he became the London manager of the Jarvis & Conklin financial house of Kansas City, his responsibility being to attract British capital to the United States, which he did with considerable success. He had married May French in 1876, and although, in total contrast to her, he was quiet, retiring and thoughtful, he was also a highly successful writer, under the name of Don Lemon, whose pocket encyclopaedia sold half-a-million copies. He was regarded in the City of London as a shrewd and talented businessman, but he was to leave his widow practically nothing, and his investments, as Wellcome discovered, were virtually worthless.

However, Sheldon's role in establishing the fame of his wife was very important. May Sheldon had decided to specialise in African travel, very largely because of her admiration for Stanley, but, one suspects, because the opening up of 'The Dark Continent' was the most exciting and glamorous of adventures. She created what was virtually a salon for African travellers in London, and Wellcome became a regular member of it. The Sheldons were quickly attracted to him. Here was a charming, intelligent and ambitious fellow-American, who also greatly respected Stanley – an opinion that was not at all universal – and who was fascinated by travel and African exploration; moreover, there was a mutual business aspect.

Wellcome had met Stanley briefly in New York, but it was not until the latter had returned to London in 1884 from his arduous, dangerous and highly controversial mission to the Congo that they came to know each other well, through Mrs Sheldon.

Stanley's was a deeply complex and not altogether attractive personality. His search for fame and acceptance in Britain never quite succeeded, and his celebrated greeting, 'Dr Livingstone, I presume?', became the subject of much mockery. But the fact was that he had conducted an epic expedition from Zanzibar through largely unknown land and hostile and treacherous tribes, had surmounted great dangers and disease, and, above all, had indeed found David Livingstone. He was the victim of vicious allegations about his brutality to the Africans, which were not wholly unjustified, but which were grossly exaggerated, and of good old-fashioned English snobbery and jealousy. Wellcome however considered him a genuine hero, even a genius of exploration, an opinion confirmed by Stanley's latest, highly critical, but scrupulously fair, biographer.*

As Stanley realised, the Burroughs Wellcome 'Tabloids', in their specially designed travelling cases, were the answer to the medical problems that had bedevilled his famous African expeditions to find Livingstone in 1871–2, his epic cross-African expedition of 1874–7 from Zanzibar to the Atlantic Ocean, and his highly controversial operations on behalf of King Leopold II of the Belgians in the Congo between 1879 and 1884. As he and his companions were to discover in their equally criticised expedition to 'rescue' Emin Pasha in 1887–9,** Burroughs Wellcome medicines could not combat most of the diseases and ailments that inflicted them, but at least they were portable, convenient to use and, in their cases, stood up well to the African climate. As we have seen, his was the first major African expedition that took Burroughs Wellcome products, provided free of charge in return for publicity; Mrs Sheldon's of 1890–1 in East Africa was to be the second.

It was also through this remarkable, if very difficult, woman that Wellcome made another of his great friendships. Arthur Jermy

* Frank McLynn, *Stanley: The Making of an African Explorer* (Constable, 1989) and *Stanley: Sorcerer's Apprentice* (Constable, 1991).

** 'Emin Pasha' was in fact Edouard Carl Oscar Theodor Schnitzler, born in Silesia in 1840, who, as a result of his service as a medical officer in the Ottoman Empire, called himself Emin Bey. In 1875 he had gone to Khartoum and, in 1876, was invited by Gordon to become chief medical officer in Equatoria. The Mahdist victories over the British–Egyptian forces in 1882–5, culminating in Gordon's death in Khartoum in January 1885, forced 'Emin' to the south, where he skilfully portrayed himself as a beleaguered 'second Gordon'.

Mounteney Jephson, also five years older than Wellcome, was totally unlike him and Stanley; he was a handsome Englishman, somewhat lackadaisical, a young man of little occupation but with some financial substance, keen on adventure and also absorbed by Africa. In a classic case of the attraction of opposites, Stanley liked and trusted him, and was to take him on the Emin Pasha expedition (particularly since Jephson could contribute £1,000 towards it) with many unfortunate consequences, not least on Jephson's previous admiration for him. Jephson was to find, as many others had, that Stanley's ferocious ambition and ruthless determination to succeed at almost any cost made him a brilliant but dangerous leader. In part, Jephson came to hate and despise him, but he also recognised that, for all his manifold faults, harshness and cruelties, Stanley was the greatest of all African explorers; he was certainly the bravest and, unlike so many other Europeans who were flocking to Africa, he had deep feelings for the African peoples and their cultures. Jephson's often bitter comments about Stanley in his journals must be read in the wider context of admiration for his leadership and astonishing achievements, grudging though they often were and severely qualified. Not many Englishmen, or others, who set out on Stanley's expeditions lived to tell the story, and their mortality rate – and those of the Africans who went with them – was very high. Jephson was destined to be one of the survivors, but at a heavy cost to his health. However, his insouciant and debonair courage and qualities of leadership made him immensely attractive to Stanley, Wellcome and May Sheldon.

May was certainly a woman of many talents. She was a gifted sculptor and artist, and fluent in French. Wellcome and Stanley were to be her chief advisers on her epic African adventure of 1890–1, which made her fame and completely turned her head. She was to become a grievous burden to Wellcome, who was often exasperated by her, although she was to have a remarkable revival of fortune. But she seems to have been the first woman who seriously attracted Wellcome, and he was with her so often that rumours began to circulate about their relationship, which continued until her death, shortly before Wellcome's, in 1936. By then she was the only survivor of his early years in London, and when she visited him a shrewd observer noted that they were 'on extremely friendly terms, not the usual respectful ones with Wellcome'.

When a handsome young man becomes the confidant of a highly attractive married woman, it is inevitable that tongues wag, and in the context of the mid-1880s they certainly did, particularly as Sheldon himself had a roving eye. The assumption that they had an arrangement may possibly have been true, but there is no evidence in Wellcome's correspondence with her that he was involved. It would certainly have been totally out of character for him to have a romantic friendship with the wife of a friend; it would have been wholly against his stern concepts of what being a gentleman and a man of honour involved, and, as his young wife was to discover on their marriage, he was sexually inexperienced, embarrassed and inadequate. His biographer has the strong impression that, at this stage of his life at least, he enjoyed feminine company and friendship, but was exceptionally cautious about any deeper relationship. It also struck his friends and contemporaries that in general he far preferred male company, and they believed that he would be a lifelong bachelor – a species that was then neither uncommon nor regarded with suspicion. In Wellcome's papers there is an unsigned anonymous handwritten note on May Sheldon:

> I knew Mrs French Sheldon very well indeed. She was a most remarkable woman, one possessed of unusual gifts of intellectual ability as well as a woman of great physical courage. . . . She was also possessed of a strong personality, and Wellcome once said of her (to me), 'God made one of his rare mistakes in making her a woman. As a man she would have achieved great fame and success.' A woman of this type was without doubt a rare character in the 'eighties, and being *persona grata* at the Court of the King of the Belgians, and a woman of literary ability, it was not surprising that Wellcome was friendly with her, a friendship that continued until she died in 1936. The mistake W. made was in defying the conventions of the Victorian Age, and thereby giving

rise to scandalous innuendo. . . . Today such an association would be regarded as quite a normal one.

Stanley, whom she was to nurse when he was stricken with malaria on his last expedition, wrote of her (29 July 1891) to Wellcome when she ended her African journey in triumph:

> Sheldon can be congratulated on having a wife who has distinguished herself in almost everything. Good woman, kind nurse, tender friend, cheery companion, translator, novel writer, sculptress, newspaper correspondent, female physician & African traveller. She is a paragon, and quite deserving of our love & respect. She has such a good friend in you that if kindness & attention will bring her round she will soon recover [from a bad fall].

The surviving correspondence between Wellcome and May Sheldon gives no indication of anything beyond warm affection and respect; tempered on Wellcome's side by rages about her financial follies, which, after her fame and the death of her husband, became monumental. None the less, it is clear that their friendship developed into a romantic attachment of some strength, although it is very doubtful indeed, as was often alleged, that they were ever lovers. Wellcome was always attracted to high-spirited and adventurous women with style – until he met his match.

The first of their joint ventures was disastrous, although not financially. In 1886 the Sheldons bought an interest in a small publishing company, Saxon & Co., to which Wellcome contributed part of the capital. The company's first publication was May Sheldon's translation of Flaubert's *Salammbô*, fulsomely dedicated by her to Stanley. Largely as a result of Wellcome's energetic publicising of the book in England and America, it was a substantial and highly controversial success. There is no record that Burroughs at this point objected at all. He wrote to Wellcome on 28 April 1886: 'Read *Salammbô* on the steamer coming over. Wonderful book. . . . It is such a remarkable book, so different from any other of modern times, that it will excite the curious interest of all literary people.' He also bought fifty copies as gifts for friends, as the book – as was the practice at that time – contained Burroughs Wellcome advertisements. However, the following year he professed himself outraged by what he described as 'this lamentable and near-pornographical work', and by the fact that his partner had been involved in its production.

Wellcome defended it strongly, writing about one critic that,

> I am not surprised that Mr Root does not fancy the book, as I have several friends who take the same objection, but we must remember that many people even disagree about the Bible. In fact I have some very good friends who will not allow a copy of the Bible inside their homes, regarding it as an indecent book for their families to read. I do not think that there are many who are inclined to treat this book as if it were a story of the present day. There is all the difference in the world. The Church people are finding great satisfaction in it, & believe that the book illustrates the great benefits of the Christian religion, which has raised the world from darkness & barbarism, & made Molochism an impossibility. I repeat to you what I said some months ago, that I believe so thoroughly in the morality of the book that I would not hesitate to have a sister of mine, sixteen years of age, read it. Still, I do not object to everyone holding their own views about such matters.

Even before publication Wellcome reported to a New York friend on 18 November 1885 that,

> I have positive information from N.Y. proving that some party or parties are underhandedly at work trying to poison the minds of journalists, & endeavouring to prevent publicity in the press. So far as the moral tone of the book is concerned I am willing to stake my reputation upon it. I shall rely upon you, as a friend, to confidentially give me all information you may gain on this score. The prospects are that I shall have a very lively fight.... I do not know but that it is just as well that ugly statements should be made about it in advance, for when it appears people will be pleasantly disappointed. I am glad to say I have not made a failure of anything yet & you can depend upon it that I shall not make a failure of this matter. My friends here seem to rival each other in their support & if America serves me well, we shall all be happy.

*Salammbô* was a considerable success, running to four editions and selling some twenty thousand copies; May Sheldon revelled in her celebrity, while Burroughs used the book as another weapon in his armoury against his partner.

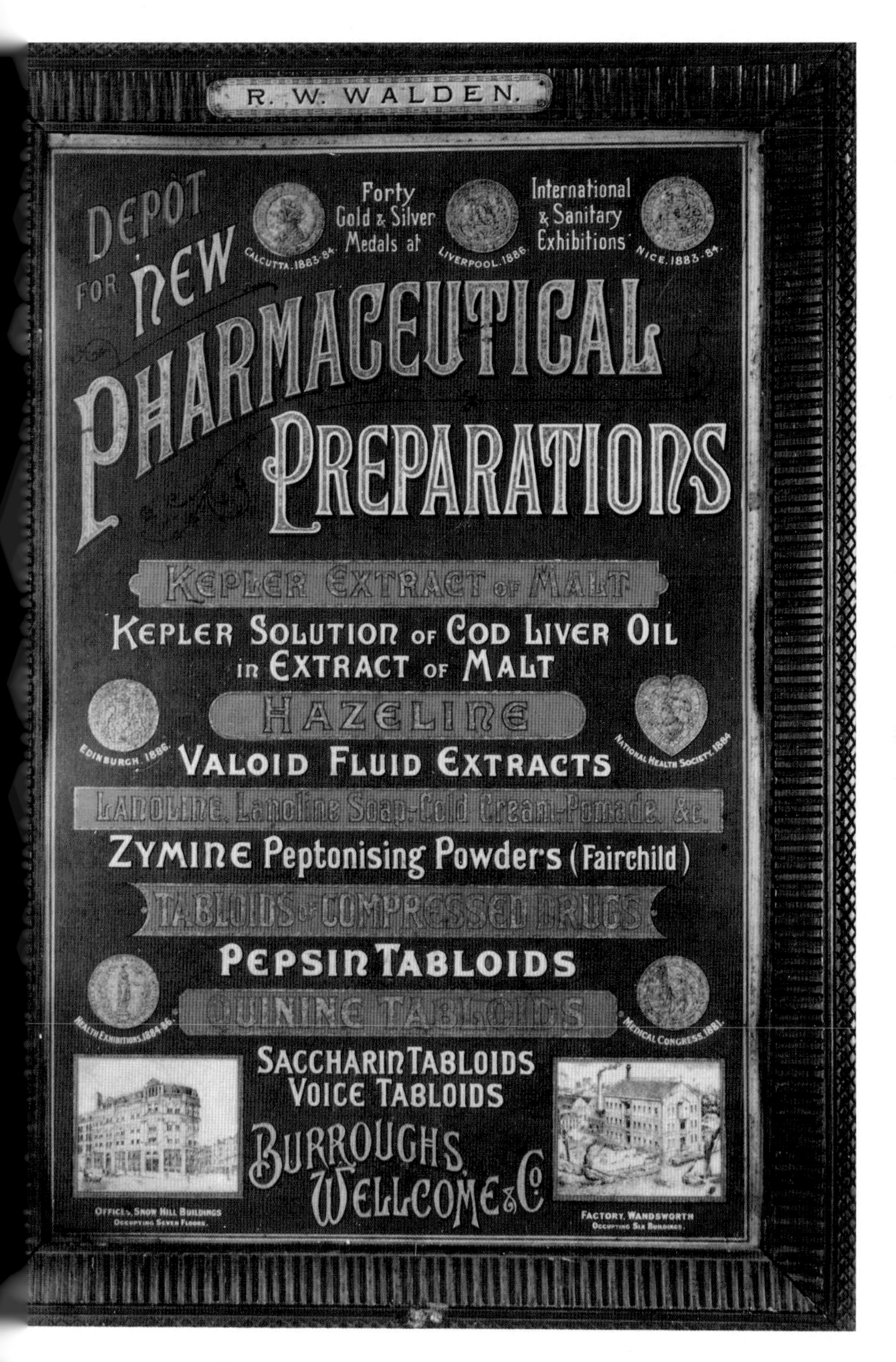


A pharmacy sign from *c.* 1885 advertising Burroughs Wellcome & Co.'s products.

"'HAZELINE' SNOW"
(TRADE MARK)
Gives
Radiant
Beauty
For the Skin
"'HAZELINE' SNOW"
Dainty
and
Distinct


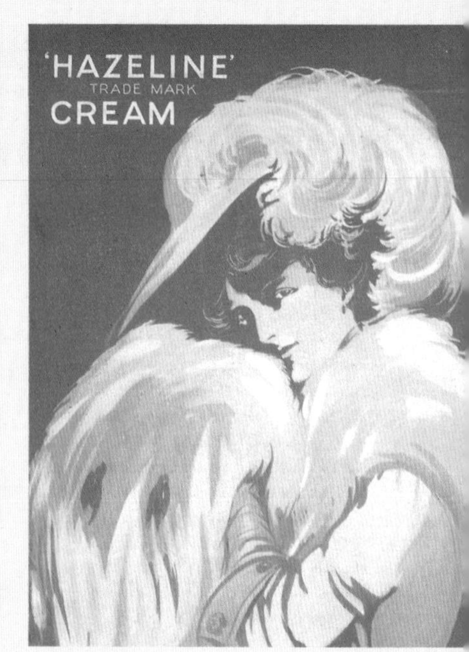

'HAZELINE'
TRADE MARK
CREAM

"'HAZELINE'
(TRADE MARK)
SNOW"
gives
fascination
to the
complexion
Printed in England

'HAZELINE'
BRAND
should be prescribed if the best product of Witch Hazel is desired.
It is unique in retaining the full astringent, styptic and anodyne principles of the fresh green bark.
WARNING!
This indicates the shape and appearance of an original bottle of the genuine 'Hazeline'.
TO PREVENT SUBSTITUTION—
Written prescriptions for original bottles (4 oz. or 16 oz.) are safer than verbal orders.
PREPARED BY
B W & Co
THE
"HAZELINE"
BRAND OF
THE ACTIVE PRINCIPLES
DISTILLED FROM THE BARK OF
WITCH HAZEL
HAMAMELIS VIRGINIANA
DOSE. One to three teaspoonfuls. (See full directions at back of this label)
A 65855 A
BURROUGHS WELLCOME & Co
MANUFACTURING CHEMISTS
LONDON, SYDNEY, & CAPE TOWN.

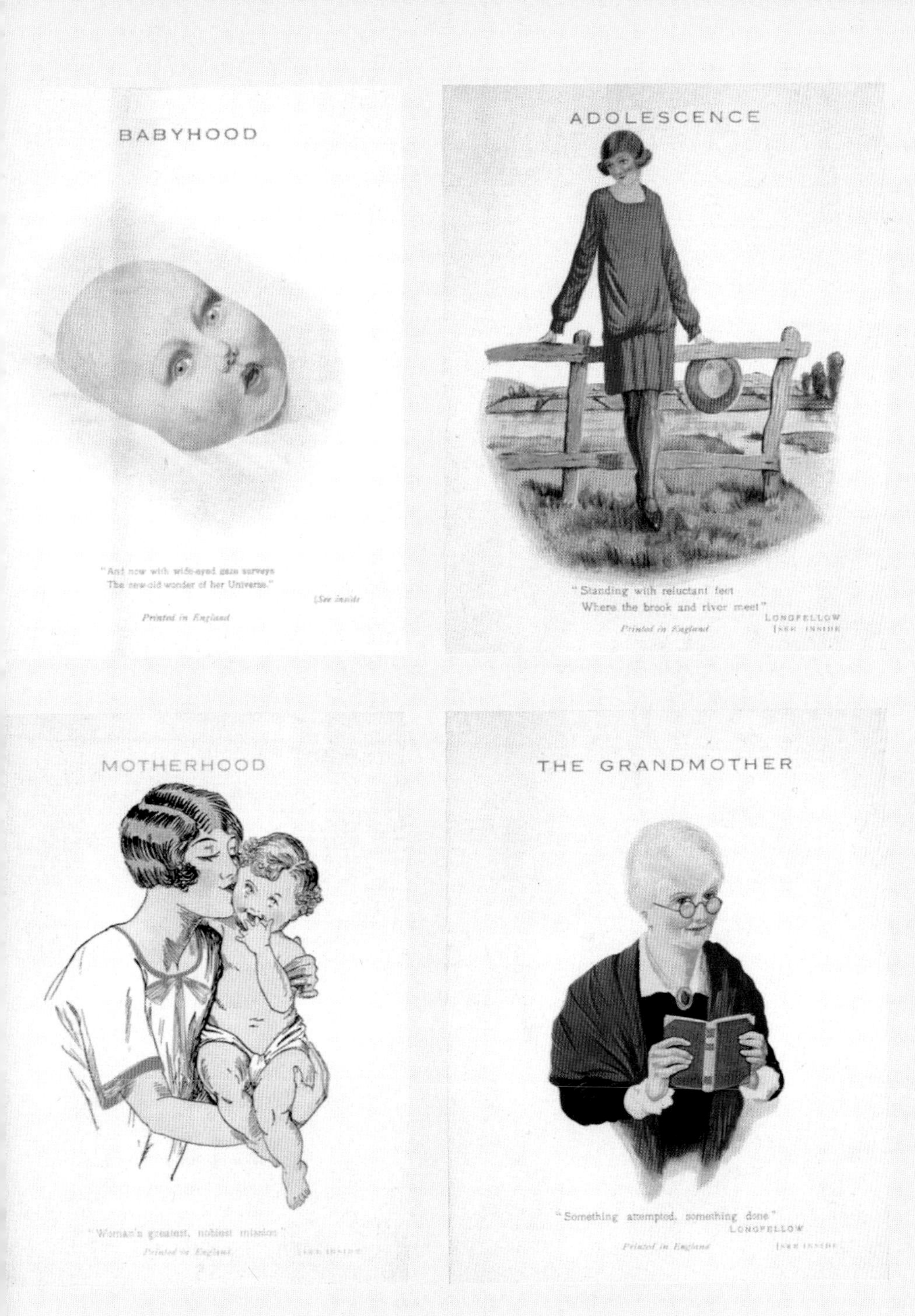


THIS PAGE *The Ages of Womanhood* (1927), promoting the use of cod-liver oil, is characteristic of the range of booklets produced by The Wellcome Foundation in the 1920s to promote 'Hazeline' and 'Kepler' products.

OPPOSITE PAGE One of The Wellcome Foundation's longest established ranges, 'Hazeline' products have been sold since 1880 and are available today in parts of the world. The advertisements illustrate the range of preparations offered over the period.

Henry Wellcome registered the company's famous trademark 'Tabloid' in 1884. It was applied to a variety of products including medicines, compressed tablets of tea, and medicine cases.

TRADE MARK 'TABLOID' Brand

MOTOR-CAR

MEDICINE ..

CASE .. .. ..

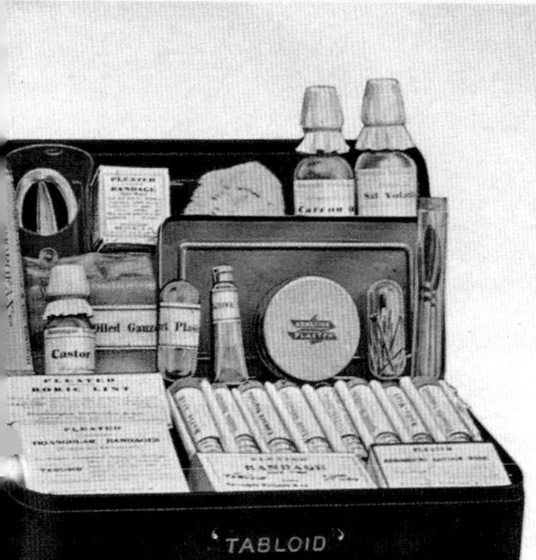


A COMPACT
FIRST-AID
EQUIPMENT
FOR MOTORISTS

'Tabloid' Motor-Car Medicine Case
Measurements $7\frac{1}{2} \times 4\frac{3}{4} \times 2$ in.

Advertising for Wellcome's non-prescription products has often been more creative and colourful than for the more closely regulated ethical range, as this panel of advertisements for cosmetic creams illustrates.

EPLER'
SOLUTION

'Kepler' products were based on cod-liver oil and malt, and their advertising was heavily dependent on nautical and fishing themes.

'KEPLER'
SOLUTION

COD LIVER OIL
AS A FOOD

FOR the greater part of a century cod liver oil has been recognised by the medical profession as the best food in wasting and conditions associated with poor nutrition. But its odour and taste render it repulsive to many, and weakened digestions frequently fail to assimilate it in its crude condition.

In wasting

In 'KEPLER' SOLUTION these difficulties have been overcome. Its flavour is acceptable to the most fastidious, and it is easily digested and assimilated, even by the weakest. In this lies the value of 'KEPLER' SOLUTION, for cod liver oil is a food and not a drug, and

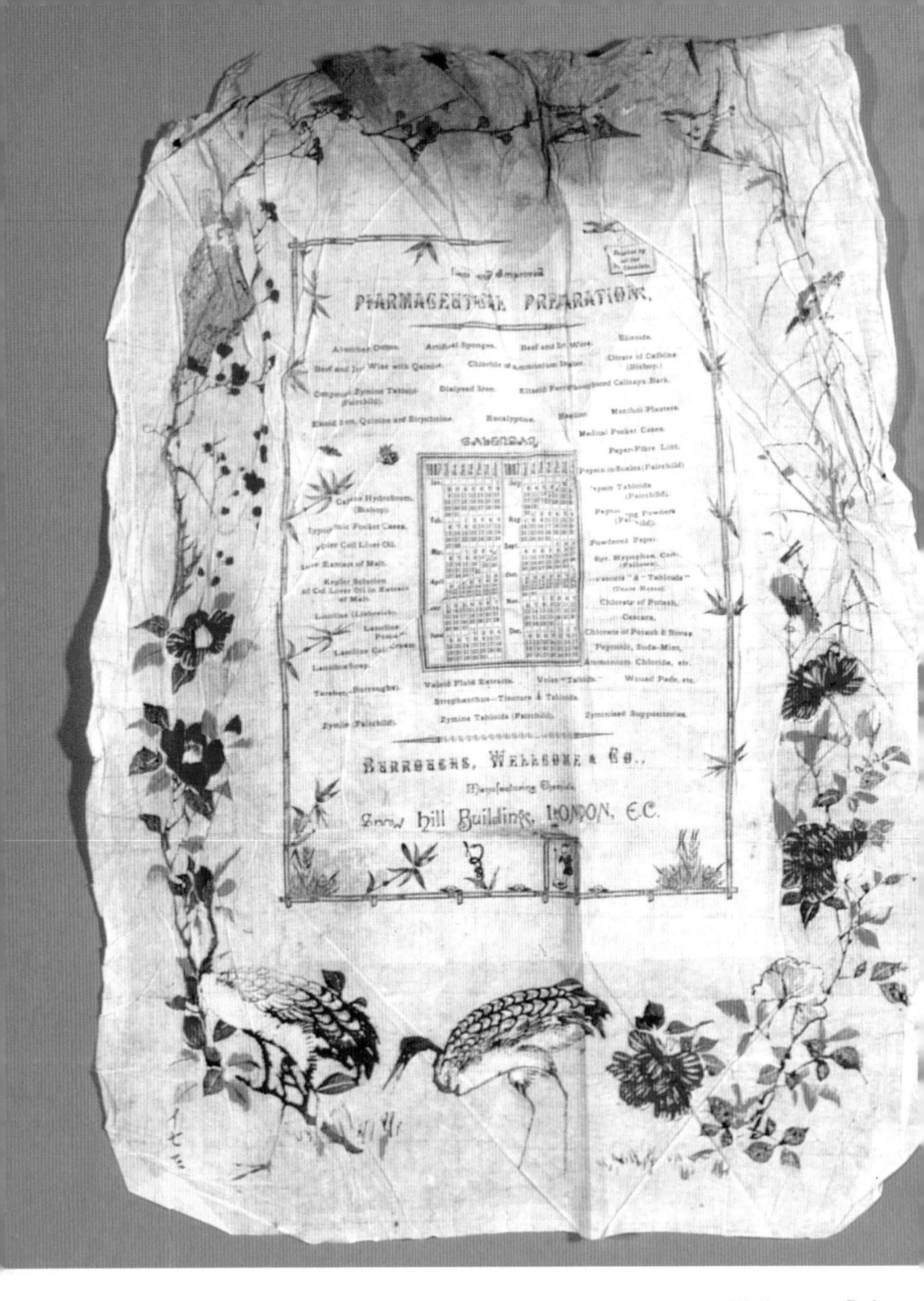


A 'Chinese-style' calendar for 1887 printed on one of Burroughs Wellcome & Co.'s own products, paper-fibre lint, used as a promotional gift.

# 5

# Burroughs v. Wellcome

At the beginning of 1885 the tension between Burroughs and Wellcome became more serious when Wellcome received a stiff letter from Burroughs's solicitors on 7 January charging that,

> During Mr Burroughs' absence from England from October 1881 till February 1884 the books of the partnership have been kept under your directions in a manner which Mr Burroughs regards as in some respects altogether erroneous. Since his return to England Mr Burroughs having been engaged in other matters has not made himself acquainted with the state of the accounts and it is only quite lately that he has ascertained that the accounts of the firm have been drawn up in a manner prejudicial to his interests. . . .
>
> . . . Thus far we have been speaking of your respective rights and liabilities under the Partnership Deed, but we are bound to add that Mr Burroughs considers the present state of affairs unsatisfactory and strongly suggests that you should without delay contribute to the business a capital proportionate to your two fifths share of the profits.*
>
> You will of course understand that this letter is written in a friendly way, and is intended to express Mr Burroughs claims fairly and firmly, and is in the legal sense 'without prejudice'.

* These are unclear, but the gross receipts from the business had increased from £17,811 in 1880–1 to £33,158 in 1881–2, and were £57,165 in 1882–3, testimony enough to Wellcome's conduct of the affairs of Burroughs Wellcome. Burroughs's contention was that Wellcome had only nominally equalled his capital investment, and that 'you altogether failed to qualify yourself as an equal partner'.

Wellcome's response to these 'friendly' charges has not survived, but it resulted in a new Deed of Partnership that was prepared and agreed shortly afterwards. Wellcome's capital in the firm until then was the same as Burroughs's – £3,277 15s 11d – but his Drawing Account was under £500, while Burroughs's was over £9,000. This was due to the fact that Burroughs had been abroad for almost three of the first four years of the firm's existence, but it emphasised that whereas Wellcome was living, and admittedly living well, on his income from his share of the firm's profits, Burroughs was living even better entirely at the firm's expense, in addition to his share of the profits. This in itself was a potential cause for friction and mistrust on Wellcome's behalf.

Burroughs was right that more capital was required, and under the new Deed it was increased to £15,000, of which Burroughs held seven-tenths (£10,500) and Wellcome three-tenths (£4,500), profits again being divided pro rata. This time, however, there was no provision for Wellcome to increase his holding to equal his partner's. There were other differences. Neither partner was to engage in any other business without the consent of the other, and the partnership was terminable at the end of five years if either partner gave the other six months' notice in writing, upon which the recipient partner could purchase the share of the one who had given the notice. Both these provisions were to have momentous consequences.

Wellcome's suspicions about his partner's intentions were clear in this provision, whose significance Burroughs had characteristically overlooked – and was to continue to overlook. Burroughs did have a valid point in that Wellcome's stake in the partnership was represented by guarantees rather than by readily available cash, but this was no longer relevant.

By now Wellcome was in a position, although principally by loans and guarantees, to buy an equal share in the business, and at first glance it seems curious that he did not press for it with the same vigour that he had in 1883. However, he put great importance upon the other provision, whereby the partner who *received* the notice of dissolution could become the sole owner. This is the first clear indication not only of Wellcome's ambitions, but also of his increasing mistrust of his partner's.

There were other signs of them going separate ways. Wellcome bought an interest in Saxon & Co., and Burroughs became a director of a tobacco company, Terry & Co. Under the new Deed each had to secure the written permission of the other, and did so.

*

Since a boy on the Watowan Wellcome had loved canoeing, and his new prosperity gave him the opportunity to design his own canoes, to be made, on his insistence, by American Indians, but to his own precise designs and specifications. This pastime nearly cost him his life and played a significant part in his deteriorating relations with Burroughs.

In the spring of 1885 Wellcome became unwell, the first signs of the illness that was to haunt him, undiagnosed, for thirteen years until it reached its crisis,* and he was advised to rest. He organised an expedition of eight of his canoes from Oxford to London with fellow enthusiasts, to whom Wellcome's authentic Indian canoes were an exciting novelty that aroused much interest on the Thames, as Wellcome had no doubt intended. In August he went up river from Oxford with a Doctor Burrows, who was a consultant to Burroughs Wellcome and a new devotee to canoeing, and, he thought, a friend. 'Our trip was a most delightful one, though we met strong headwinds and lots of rough water, I was however quite at home again,' Wellcome wrote to Burroughs, who was at home in Medina, New York. 'I used almost to live in canoes as a youngster, and was specially fond of shooting rapids in the Birchbark canoes.'

* I am most grateful to Lord Butterfield for his analysis of Wellcome's medical records and for his conclusion that he was suffering from ulcerative colitis – a diagnosis entirely confirmed by Chune Fletcher's own belated one in 1898. An alternative possibility was chronic amoebic dysentery, which could have been acquired in South America, but the time factor militates against this. Also, Fletcher's diagnosis of 'catarrh of the bowels' fits in exactly with the symptoms of ulcerative colitis.

But then disaster struck. In September Wellcome reported to Burroughs:

> This week I have had one of the adventures of my life. I was up for a day on the River with Miss Wakeman, the American authoress. We were going up through Boulter's Lock, with her in a canoe – about 2/3rd or 3/4ths of the way up to [the] front gates. The water was let in very suddenly from one of the flood gates and it burst like a grand fountain and in a flash swamped us. No possible effort could have prevented us from going over. Miss W was at once sucked down and the canoe over her. I at once made a dive after her and after a desperate struggle against the terrible currents brought her to the surface only to be sucked down again, but finally I saved her after the most desperate struggle I have ever experienced. Miss W showed the greatest pluck for she never struggled but allowed me to hold her without the slightest hindrance. . . . I did not feel the effects much at the time, but ever since I do feel very severely the dreadful reaction from the frightful exertion. I feel thankful to God for his delivering us out of the jaws of death.

Burroughs wrote at once 'to congratulate you upon your narrow escape from drowning and also upon your successful efforts to save another from a similar threatened fate. I hope that the shock and strain to the nervous system consequent upon the peril and exertion have now passed away.' They had not.

A large number of people had seen this near-tragedy, and Wellcome was highly praised for his courage and fortitude. The incident was widely reported in the national and American newspapers, and he was awarded the Bronze Medal of the Royal Humane Society, which was presented to him at a dinner held at the Savage Club. But the price he had to pay for his fame was to be a heavy one.

Wellcome had been seriously unwell for several months, his doctor declaring that he was unfit for work. The time he spent canoeing that summer was on medical advice, but the Boulter's Lock episode gave him a severe setback. It was difficult to determine from his medical records what was wrong with him, and the fact that the cure proposed by his own doctor and Sir William Jenner, the Queen's physician, was a complete change of scene and rest leads to the conclusion that they did not know, either. But Burroughs's later charges that he wilfully malingered and grossly exaggerated his condition are not sustainable.

Wellcome's condition worsened in the winter of 1885–6, and the Sheldons invited him to stay with them, so that they could nurse and look after him. He was visited by Dr Burrows, both as his doctor and as a specialist consultant to Burroughs Wellcome, and it transpired that it was Burrows who spread the word that Mrs Sheldon was Wellcome's mistress. Wellcome was enraged when he heard of this and threatened to horsewhip him if he ever repeated the story. It was quite true that she did visit him during the night when he was particularly ill, but this was with the full knowledge and agreement of her husband. Unfortunately, Burrows's allegations came to the ears of Burroughs. At the time Burroughs wrote from America: 'I hope your health and strength are reviving with the return of Spring, and that you will in due season be able to take a trip across the Atlantic.' 'The damp chill weather cuts into my bowels like a knife', Wellcome replied, 'and gives me the most terrible headaches.'

Wellcome's doctors prescribed that he should first go to the Isle of Wight to recuperate and then, when strong enough, to cross the Atlantic for a prolonged holiday in America. He stayed in the Isle of Wight for three months before sailing to New York, where he arrived early in August 1886 still feeling 'very ill'.

May Sheldon had sailed for New York on 23 April. When Wellcome arrived, he stayed at the same hotel as her for two nights; he was later the guest of her mother in her summer house by the sea, and subsequently of her sister in Philadelphia. Inevitably, with the publication of *Salammbô*, they met from time to time. These arrangements did nothing to reduce the rumours and allegations about their relationship, but it is worth noting that Sheldon himself was prepared to give evidence in court that they were false. However, there were many, then and later, who did not believe him.

Wellcome then went to Maine to hunt, fish and canoe, but the open-air cure was not wholly successful. 'I am feeling most wretched,' he wrote to Burroughs; 'the excessive heat so completely breaks me down. . . . Pray do not expect many letters or long ones from me, and ask all friends to be indulgent; it is an awful exertion for me to write in my present state of health.' But by November he reported to Sudlow that, 'After nearly two months' complete hermitage in the Northern forests, I am just out with improved health.' To Burroughs he wrote that he was going to extend his time 'out of reach of post and 'grams for two or three weeks longer. I am anxious to get back to the office again as of old, my season of ill health seems an age.'

It was certainly seeming so to Burroughs, as by the end of 1886 his partner had in effect been out of action for over a year. Burroughs was beginning to demonstrate signs of impatience, and letting them be known in the firm and to customers. He was also contemplating a major investment in the United States, as the demands for Burroughs Wellcome products now required expansion. Wellcome accepted the latter, but assumed that it would be in Britain. He had no knowledge of Burroughs's plans and had, in any event, plunged himself with unwise fervour into a completely different venture, which occupied him totally for several months in the winter and spring of 1886–7.

*

It was at this point that Wellcome met William Duncan again, whom he had first encountered in New York in 1878. Duncan was a lay missionary, who worked under the auspices of the Church Missionary Society of London. He was a Yorkshireman, who had gone to British Columbia in 1857 and had worked for five years among the notoriously savage Indian tribes, the Tsimsheans, at Fort Simpson. Duncan first learned the language (from an Indian called Clah)* and then worked along practical, educational and religious lines, 'preaching to the natives the simple truths of the gospel'. So that his work

* Arthur Wellington Clah (1831–1916), a Tsimshean Indian at Fort Simpson, who was one of Duncan's earliest converts.

would be able to prosper, in 1862 Duncan transferred his converts, who numbered about fifty, away from the corrupting influences of the trading post and established a native Christian community at Metlakahtla, which was the abandoned site of a former Indian village.

He built a model village and a Christian mission with certain strict rules. The settlement grew rapidly so that within a few years the population had increased to nearly a thousand 'industrious, law-abiding Christians'. The village included well-built houses, a town hall, a substantial church, a school, a profitable co-operative store, a guesthouse, drainage and other public works, all built by the natives under Duncan's instruction. Duncan taught 'right living, industry and thrift', and trained the natives to become competent craftsmen in various trades and occupations, for example, soap-making, carpentry, trading and fishing. All such activities were established and carried on as private enterprises.

But in Duncan's endeavours to remove the Indians from the temptation of alcohol, he had refused to serve them Communion wine. Having persuaded them of the evils of cannibalism and alcohol, he could not command them – as the Church Missionary Society ordered him to do – to accept the full ceremony of the Lord's Supper. The Society then instructed Bishop Ridley of Caledonia to take charge of Duncan's Mission and to withdraw all aid. The land attached to the Mission was declared to be not 'the property of the Indians, but that of the government of British Columbia'.

When the official surveyors arrived, they were met with such hostility – although not actual violence – that a warship was dispatched to maintain order. Duncan withdrew from the Society and disputed its claims to the Mission Reserve, but the British Columbia lawyers ruled against him. He then appealed to the United States Government and Congress to take responsibility for his converted Tsimsheans; he had found a site on Annette Island, Alaska, to which he wished to take his people.

Wellcome was enthralled by Duncan and his work for the Indians. He was also attracted, as he wrote, by 'his exalted Christian character, his unswerving devotion to God and to duty; his unique and very successful policies and methods in dealing with native peoples; his versatile and unusual ability as a man of affairs, and his administrative ability.' However, Duncan was a highly controversial man, and Bishop Ridley was not his only critic.

In Wellcome's voluminous papers on the Metlakahtla saga are seventy-two journals, account books and notes by Clah, which Wellcome bought from his family after Clah's death. These deal principally with the daily life of the settlement, weather notes and details of hunting, canoe expeditions, work, visitors, church services, sermons and, especially significantly, land claims. But Clah also gives details of the disputes with the Society and Bishop Ridley in his own style. Thus, for 12 December 1882 he wrote:

> News came up in our town to say Mr William Duncan and Bishop Realy [Ridley] both Quarling about Society. Society wants Mr Duncan out and Bishop wants take his place. All the people help Mr Duncan they not want let him go. 10 or 20 help Bishop.

Although Clah was ambivalent about Duncan, the ambition of Bishop Ridley and the Society to force him out and close the Mission, supported by the Canadian Government, prompted Clah to write (9 December 1881): 'I felt very sorry when I heard Duncan is out. I pray to Great God very much. . . . Queen sell out our land. That which is who is stronger, Queen and God (?) and who made this world. God or Queen (?) Queen sell our land.'

Wellcome vehemently supported Duncan in his plan to seek US protection, and established a committee that petitioned the United States Government for property on Annette Island for the Mission. He went to Washington with Duncan to present the petition and to sit with him in meetings with the Secretary of the Interior, other Government officials and members of the Supreme Court and of the Senate. Having mastered the substantial documentation on the history of the Mission and the disputes with Ridley, Wellcome was able to persuade influential Americans of the justice of Duncan's case, but, characteristically, he believed that it also needed publicity. Finance too was required.

Wellcome therefore wrote *The Story of Metlakahtla*, published by his company Saxon & Co., which described in violently partisan terms the growth of Duncan's Mission and the problems with the Church Missionary Society. It also included extracts from many who had praised Duncan's work. Wellcome's one enterprise into literature was a remarkable public success. One reviewer wrote:

> The bare recital of the facts of this story should make the ears of Christendom tingle with shame, and arouse popular indignation to make generous amends for the injustice which has been done. It is a book with a purpose which cannot fail to appeal to the justice-loving and liberty-loving American peoples. . . . [Wellcome] tells the tale in a remarkable, graphic, simple way, and subjugates literary effect to the recordance of fact.

Perhaps more accurate, however, was another reviewer who described it as

> A badly written book, but at the same time a striking one. The righteous indignation of the writer occasionally injures his style or weakens the force of the facts, better simply stated. The book is written with perhaps too many staccato marks, ill-represented by a too-strained punctuation, and a too-free use of capitals and italics, and the author's stirred feelings have a slightly hysterical expression here and there; for all that, and despite literary blemishes, it is a wonderful story of the vicious power of ecclesiastical red-tape, and the success of the simple gospel in the hands of an historic missionary. The book is well-printed, except that the use of the comma is absurd.

The stylistic criticisms were fully justified. Wellcome's book would be regarded as a powerful piece of writing had it not been so ill-written, but grammar was never one of his strong points and the book was written with intense passion in a matter of weeks. 'If ever the heart and soul of an author are shown in his writings,' one reviewer wrote, 'these pages exhibit them.'

If Wellcome romanticised the virtues of the American Indians, and over-praised Duncan for his endeavours to assist and understand them, it should not be forgotten that they were to be described in the standard school history of America by Allan Nevins and Henry Steele Commager as 'a war-like, cruel and treacherous people still in the Stone Age culture'. This was certainly the accepted opinion among Americans in 1886, although, as Wellcome's successful campaign revealed, many were beginning to have their doubts. Also, the fact that Wellcome himself had been involved in the Sioux uprising, and bore the Indian no animosity, had its impact.

One particularly hostile Canadian commentator did, however, have a point when he wrote:

> Mr Wellcome obtained all the material for his book from Mr Duncan alone, and thus has only one side of the story. The whole matter, which might have been made plain, and lost none of its effect, even from Mr Wellcome's uncompromisingly partisan standpoint, has been lengthened out to nearly 500 pages. The 'filling in' consists of diatribes against the government of the Dominion and the Province, the Church of England Missionary Society, the bishops and ministers of the church, residents of Victoria who were not disposed to reverence everything Mr Duncan said and did, and all, in short, who took a different view of the matter from that taken by Mr Duncan. These choice passages are relieved by panegyrics on Mr Duncan, and by dissertations on law, morals, missionary work and the Indian question.
>
> The panacea prescribed for all the ills of the Metlakahtlans is to settle them in Alaska under the mild and beneficent rule of the Washington Government. It is amusing when one reads this to think of the constant ill-treatment which the tribes in the United States have suffered at the hands of that government's officials, of the unconcealed villainy with which they have been robbed of their lands, of the outrages which for years they have had to submit to, of the massacres which have repeatedly taken place, and the Indian wars which have made the name of the United States a by-word for their usage of the native races.

The success of the book was immediate, in that it aroused such interest that the application to the United States Senate for the Alaskan transfer, commenced a few months later, was successful. The American authorities permitted Duncan and some eight hundred Indians to move to the 'New Metlakahtla' settlement in 1887, under 'the beautiful American flag' presented to them by Wellcome.

However, in the short run the book confirmed Burroughs's view that, although he had given his permission in writing for Wellcome to buy an interest in Saxon & Co., he had been in breach of his partnership agreement. From this claim much was to flow. Wellcome's error was that he had grossly exaggerated the situation, using language such as 'this is a story of outrage upon, and cruelty to, a civilised Indian community on the part of the Dominion of Canada', and called upon the people of the United States, with 'its Government of the people, by the people, and for the people, to save this stricken community from desperation, and perhaps from bloodshed'. Wellcome's claim that the land which Duncan had organised was Indian land was in fact untrue, and there was considerable justice in the Canadian objections that Wellcome had obtained all his material from Duncan alone, and had not taken advice or evidence from any other side.

The Canadian indignation was understandable. Wellcome, with his passionate concern for the American Indians, regarded Duncan as a saint, but there were others who regarded him as an undisciplined and domineering charlatan. This, also, was excessive, but it was a highly charged issue, and for once Wellcome had allowed his emotions to transcend his cool appraisal of the facts. One can applaud his deep feeling for the Metlakahtlans, which lasted throughout his life and many vicissitudes, and to whom he was immensely generous in time as well as in money, and his admiration for Duncan was justified. None the less, this emotional effusion, which may have helped Duncan and his Indians, was certainly a factor which increased Burroughs's distrust of the judgment of his partner.

Wellcome's passionate involvement in the welfare and concerns of the Metlakahtlan Indians proved to be a considerable disadvantage for him, in that it diverted his attention from his business concerns at a critical moment in the history of Burroughs Wellcome. In his genuine concerns for the plight of the American Indians, which redound so strongly to his credit, he had forgotten that he was primarily a businessman. He was now abruptly reminded that the Romantic view had to be temporarily abandoned for the Realist one.

*

The arrangement with McKesson & Robbins had ended somewhat sourly early in 1886. Wellcome and Burroughs had considered for some time that it had become too much to the advantage of McKesson & Robbins, and too little to Burroughs Wellcome. They therefore proposed that they should buy McKesson & Robbins's products at fixed prices and be permitted to undertake their sale, thereby 'so as not to render ourselves liable to petty aspertious criticism regarding our methods, &c.'. When McKesson & Robbins refused, Burroughs and Wellcome issued a notice of termination of the contract, to McKesson & Robbins's indignation. Wellcome brushed this off, noting that 'we have learned with very great pain that some of your members have behind our backs given utterance to some very unfriendly expressions & these entirely without warrant'.

But this was not the end of the matter. There was a heated dispute over the ownership of trademarks, which profited no one except lawyers, and which was to occupy much time in 1887. What upset and angered Wellcome was that McKesson & Robbins let it be known in the trade that it had abandoned its relationship with Burroughs Wellcome, when it had been the other way round, and continued to 'villify', in Wellcome's own word, the quality of Burroughs Wellcome products and the abilities of the partners. Inevitably, these campaigns, which are not at all uncommon in business and are always difficult to combat, were brought to Wellcome's attention, and he was particularly hurt that the firm 'in whose interest I have worked for with as much zeal as it is possible for any human being to work' was treating him in this manner. It was a sad note on which to end his relationship with McKesson & Robbins.

However, this was not the only relationship that had soured. Burroughs was claiming that during this period Wellcome had totally neglected the Burroughs Wellcome business. Although this was not the case, as his correspondence with Burroughs, and especially with Sudlow, demonstrates, the fact was that he had been away from London and the business for almost eighteen months, between the late autumn of 1885, when he first became seriously ill, and his return from the United States in May 1887. Although he had not left London for the Isle of Wight until May 1886, his business activities in the spring of 1886 had not been extensive because of his illness. Burroughs now asserted that his partner's time in the United States had been ill-spent on working on the publication of Mrs Sheldon's disagreeable translation and on his own book. Burroughs's own political views were becoming extreme, but sympathy for the American Indians was not among them. He let it be widely known that while he had been arduously engaged in the service of Burroughs Wellcome, his partner had been publishing obscene books and engrossing himself in the concerns of an obscure English missionary and an American Indian tribe. Wellcome was alerted by Sudlow, Kirby and others that Burroughs was sedulously and skilfully undermining his position and reputation, not only in the firm but also in the profession.

Moreover, Burroughs had planned an elaborate deception. Wellcome believed that the future of Burroughs Wellcome lay in Britain, with overseas subsidiaries and outlets. He had thought that Burroughs had accepted this strategy, but Burroughs, in conspiracy with Dr Otto Witte, was determined to establish manufacturing plants in the United States. Wellcome had for some time disliked and distrusted Witte, and with strong justification. He was to prove himself the greatest traitor in the history of Burroughs Wellcome.

Witte was one of Burroughs Wellcome's relatively few bad senior appointments. In particular, his failure to appreciate the crucial importance of quality control in production led to many complaints, especially about Malt Extract, which too often either fermented or solidified. The exasperated Wellcome wrote to him to say that

> This threatens us the most serious losses, & I must again urge upon you the vital importance of your taking such steps as will prevent any possibility of further fermentation or solidification. I can see no possible excuse for these continued mistakes. We may overlook isolated cases but this thing has been kept up for a twelvemonth almost continuously, disgracing us in every market while we are incurring enormously heavy expenses in the pushing of the goods; therefore we are obliged to hold you seriously responsible for it. . . . We now call upon you to prepare an Extract that will not ferment or congeal, that is palatable, & that has a fair amount of diastase. This is successfully accomplished by other houses & it is very rarely that they experience trouble from fermentation or solidification. As this is possible for others it is certainly possible for you. This is a matter of such serious moment that we cannot permit any further delays & excuses. It must be met fully and fairly at the present moment.

This episode confirmed Wellcome's low opinion of a man who was now in America with Burroughs, acting on a major development of the business, without his knowledge or consent.

The first Wellcome knew of Burroughs's American plans was when he was informed by cable from Snow Hill that Burroughs and Witte had sailed for America on the SS *Alaska*. He assumed that they were destined for New York, but then found that they had disembarked in Maine, and that Witte was there 'to prospect for good location for factory to make malt extract and malt milk', as Burroughs coolly informed Wellcome on 1 May 1887. Meanwhile, Wellcome had been fretting in New York, seeking news of the arrival of the *Alaska*. With considerable irritation he described his frustrations to Burroughs in some detail on 2 May: 'I am anxious to see you and learn of the condition and prosperity of the business. I have received hardly any information from you in regard to the general business since leaving England.'

Although Wellcome did not dismiss Burroughs's proposal for an American factory out of hand, he was not at all convinced, and wrote that 'nothing should be done until we have discussed the matter thoroughly and well scanned the pros and cons'. But Burroughs went ahead with buying new premises, ignoring Wellcome completely. Wellcome, realising, somewhat belatedly, that he was in danger of being excluded from the business by his prolonged absence, sailed to London on 25 June 1887, warned by Sudlow and others that Burroughs was determined to remove him from the partnership and take full control of the firm.

In London, Wellcome wrote to Burroughs on 28 July:

> Now that by the absence recommended by you and others, I have regained a full measure of health, I beg you will not spare me, but will throw upon my shoulders a large share of work, which I shall cheerfully bear. Our business is prospering, and its future looks very bright. I trust that with united feelings and united strength we may realise our best hopes.

Burroughs by then had returned to London; his reply that afternoon was a declaration of war:

> I am sorry to be unable to accept the explanations of the past, and the assurances for the future, contained in your letter. I have long feared that your failure to fulfil your partnership obligations would render a dissolution imperative, and I have now come to the conclusion that this can no longer be avoided or delayed. Under the circumstances, I have instructed my solicitors to write you a letter which you will no doubt receive today.

Burroughs's first salvo was rather too clever. It was not a formal notice of his wish to terminate the partnership, which would not have been possible before September 1890; also, if Burroughs was to be the instigator, Wellcome would have the automatic right to buy him out, which was exactly the opposite of what Burroughs intended. His solicitor's letter accused Wellcome of breaches of covenants, of 'general failure to discharge the duties of a partner', of neglect of the firm's business, of engaging in other business without Burroughs's consent, and of 'at length render[ing] the position intolerable to Mr

Burroughs, and he is determined to obtain the dissolution of the partnership and such other redress as the law allows him'. If Wellcome did not agree to a dissolution by mutual consent, Burroughs would apply to the courts for a decree of dissolution.

This was intimidatory bluff, as Wellcome knew. He made it plain that he intended to fight. Also, virtually all the charges were baseless, especially that of neglecting the business. Burroughs had, after all, in seven years spent two-thirds of his time travelling abroad, and not exclusively on the firm's business. He had also now made initiatives in the United States without any consultation whatever with his partner. There were other factors that made Burroughs's allegation preposterous. So were his proposed terms of dissolution, which would have ejected Wellcome at minimum cost to Burroughs. Wellcome stuck emphatically to the 1885 Deed and settled in for a long battle.

There is not much attraction, save perhaps to lawyers and those few who enjoy the perusal of fading legal documents, in the histories of litigation. Burroughs's affidavit was riddled with easily disprovable allegations, particularly concerning Wellcome's health, his recuperation in America and the alleged breach of agreement through his Saxon & Co. connection; Burroughs actually stated that 'I never gave my consent to the Defendant becoming interested in the business of Saxon & Co.', when Wellcome had his letter of full approval.* There were other glaring falsehoods.

In Wellcome's papers there is the following memorandum, in shorthand. It is unsigned, but is the detailed account of a conversation between an employee of the firm and Burroughs, in which the latter poured out his allegations against his partner, professional and personal, with a passion and untruthfulness that are acutely revealing, and demonstrate why Wellcome's antagonism towards Burroughs, although kept under strict control, had become so profound. They also raise questions about the balance of Burroughs's mind, as there

* On 20 March 1886 Burroughs had written: 'You have my full consent to interest yourself by taking a business interest in the firm of Saxon & Co., London and N.Y.'

seems little doubt that he had come to believe his extraordinary allegations:

Thursday 8th March 1888

I was invited by Mr Burroughs to enter the private office as he wished to have a little conversation with me. It was commenced by a remark that as he had heard Mr Wellcome was going round among the employees and saying it was his intention to take over the business and that he would promise to assure the position of those employees who would stand by him in the litigation which was now in hand. As Mr Wellcome was making these remarks, Mr Burroughs in self defence let certain of the employees know his feelings upon this matter.... [Wellcome] had joined this firm on the understanding that he was to take turn and turn about with Mr Burroughs alternatively in staying in London and travelling wherever it appeared necessary. Since then, he had only travelled once down to Brighton, and one or two other places on the South coast and took no orders but spent some money since then he had never travelled.

At the time when Mr Burroughs went away on his visit to India and Australia he was glad to have such a man as he then believed Mr Wellcome was to leave in charge of the business. But during that time he never wrote to him at all or when he did it was in a very ruthless and dictatorial tone. He soon learned how he had been deceived in his man. During his absence he took an absolute position in the business and had struggled hard to retain that position ever since. It was understood that the measures introduced by Mr Wellcome [were] likely to prove productive of profit and any compensation over his share of the good business had been made 35%. The business had proved a complete failure. Then Mr Wellcome gave instructions for the books to be kept in some way or another by which he tried to prove he had sufficient capital to entitle him to claim 50% of the whole profits. The capital he had brought in were mere pieces of paper and were altogether valueless. They could not have been negotiated. Anyone would have seen they were bogus drafts.

He had on every occasion treated Mr Wellcome with perfect politeness and in a kind conciliatory way. He had acted to him on all occasions like a brother and this was his reward....

[Wellcome] had for a long time past made all his acquaintances among a lot of literary professional and theatrical people. He preferred their company and their ways to those of straightforward business. In fact that was all a case of humbug at a time he said he was sick of living in . . . Square. He was incidentally introduced to a lady at the . . . Ball who said to him it is hardly necessary for us to be introduced Mr Burroughs I am Mr Wellcome's landlady and see you frequently at my house. Upon Mr Burroughs remarking that it was a sad thing about poor Wellcome's illness, she said she knew how to cure him in a couple of days. Mr Burroughs said 'You must be a great doctor.' She said there was nothing the matter with him, all he had to do was to pull himself together, get up at a respectable time in the morning and go to his business like a man instead of lying in bed all day, and getting up to dinner in the evening and then staying up three-quarters of the night with literary people and Mrs Sheldon.

His remarks were then to the fact that there was improper intimacy between Mr Wellcome and Mrs Sheldon. . . .

That contrary to the partnership agreement and in opposition to Mr Burroughs' views, he had associated himself with outside business affairs and without his permission had been spending the time he had to be in business in writing up these literary notes. That when he complained to him he treated him cold or the most undue insolence. And at last in self defence and over the good of the business he had instituted these proceedings by means of which he intended to get rid of him and his associations for ever as he wanted to have nothing whatever to do with him in the future. He had had just enough of him and could not endure the sight of him about the office any longer. . . .

. . . That Mr Wellcome was a first rate man as a servant but not one at all as a manager. That he was incompetent to manage a business of this distinction. That since Mr Burroughs had brought some pressure to bear upon him he had made some show of attending to business. That was just the sort of man Mr Wellcome was. He could never argue with anyone. He must always either be jumping on somebody, or to keep him in his place someone must jump on him. That he had made various offers with regard to closing the partnership, but he had delayed all his answers until Mr Burroughs was tired of making propositions to him. That by his obstinate insistency Mr Wellcome had lost him all his best friends. People who we need cannot be fooled about like this.

That Mr Burroughs had it in his power to pitch Mr Wellcome out in five minutes at the time that he held his bills, but instead of that he only required him to decrease his interest in the business. That all the capital he had in the business he had borrowed first of Mr Burroughs. Mr Burroughs had always left the arranging of the books in Mr Wellcome's hands and he had given instructions over them to be kept in such a way as would be most to his own advantage and secondary to that of Mr Burroughs. And now he was restored to health he only made pretence of tending to business – his whole time was taken up in arranging this litigation matter. All he did at the present time was to get down here between 11 and 12 and read his private correspondence then go and get his lunch and pick his teeth over the hour or two, then get a shave and come here early in time to entertain his theatrical and musical and literary friends. He said he was attending to the advertising but he did nothing of the kind. It was true he got a few orders over advertisements but anybody could do that as it was only a matter of spending money. He had never yet written up a page of ledger. It was either too much trouble or he could not do it.

. . . That [Burroughs] had offered Mr Wellcome an opportunity of settling the matter by arbitration, but he had played about over the whole fortnight and would give him no answer. And as he was disposed to play about with Mr Burroughs, who was essentially a man of peace, Mr Burroughs had but one alternative and that was to go into the courts when Mr Wellcome would have an opportunity of airing his various preferments before the public eye.

Mr Burroughs' mind was just made up and he was determined to bring this thing to a speedy showdown and in fact he was prepared to force matters in the law courts and he was about ready to begin at once, and no time should be lost.

Burroughs had always been impetuous and hot-headed, which was part of his very real attractiveness, but his cavalier approach to business and to politics was now transferred to what had become a vicious personal vendetta against Wellcome. He wrote to other companies and to the firm's representatives abroad to inform them that he was dissolving the partnership and that Wellcome was retiring from the business. But he had descended far lower than this, as this extraordinary tirade revealed. A significant feature of a legal process that took two years to come to the Chancery Division of the High Court was that the four principal employees of Burroughs Wellcome – Sudlow, Kirby, A. J. Spratlin, the assistant accountant, and Collett Smith, the correspondence clerk – gave depositions on Wellcome's side; Burroughs could only find one junior clerk, a J. W. H. Prevost, to appear for him, with unimpressive results.

One of the most puzzling aspects of the case was that Burroughs completely convinced himself that he could not possibly lose, and behaved as though he was already the sole owner of Burroughs Wellcome. Understandably, personal relations were, at best, formal. The firm's business still had to be transacted and, rather surprisingly, was.

It was in 1888, at the height of this personal dispute, that Burroughs Wellcome, having freed itself from McKesson & Robbins, did so from Wyeth. The relationship with Wyeth had never been satisfactory and, in February 1883, Wellcome had become so exasperated that he had travelled urgently to New York, where he found the Wyeth brothers

> very gushing and kindhearted as usual but they quietly manifested the same old greedy spirit . . . they hold out that they are our benefactors, while the simple facts are they show every disposition to bleed us. Our views regarding their real attitude have now been so plainly stated that they cannot possibly misunderstand them. I never spoke more plainly to any man in my life than I did to Jim Wyeth and I feel quite certain that he now recognises that we will not allow them to sit upon us or use us as tools.

The enormous success of compressed medicines by Burroughs Wellcome had inevitably provoked competition from other firms, and the Wyeth machines were now outclassed by others. To Wellcome's chagrin, although Wyeth still took its commission, it refused to permit Burroughs Wellcome to use its new, improved machines. As Wellcome wrote coldly, announcing the termination of their agreement on 5 September 1888:

> When we urged upon you the awkwardness of our position in competition with other makers, and our needs, you said that you did not care for the business and advised us to purchase any other compressing machines and in fact to go further into the business entirely on our own hook if we chose. You further stated that you only dealt with us in the matter from first to last from motives of friendship with Mr Burroughs and that you did not expect or wish to make money out of it.

In fact, Wyeth had unwittingly done Burroughs Wellcome a considerable favour. Burroughs was all in favour of ending the agreement with Wyeth, whereas Wellcome was initially more cautious, but it was plain that the old Wyeth machines were seriously out of date. Burroughs Wellcome bought other machines to test them, but, although they were better than Wyeth's, they still dissatisfied the partners, who decided to invent and make their own in their own workshops that would be fully automatic and be able to make those 'Tabloids' that previously could only be made by hand-operated machines. The result was a patented new machine capable of producing 600 'Tabloids' a minute, and of far greater accuracy. The cost was considerable, and would not have been possible if Wyeth had not behaved so arrogantly and churlishly over its improved machines. The Burroughs Wellcome one was much better, and, somewhat impishly, Wellcome told Wyeth – having secured the American patent – that

> we will be happy to give you the first refusal of this machine in the States. As it has been a matter of considerable expense to us we expect you will be willing to pay us a fair price for it. It is evident that in future the money to be made out of compressed goods is in small profits on very large quantities, and very rapid acting machines will be indispensable to manufacturers.

It was in fact Wyeth who terminated the contract with Burroughs Wellcome, and in accepting its decision Wellcome announced that Burroughs Wellcome would not only cease to pay commission, but also return its machines, having made a far better one itself. This was a vital episode in establishing the total independence of Burroughs Wellcome.

*

The partners' correspondence was now on formal terms, on a 'Dear Mr Burroughs' and 'Dear Mr Wellcome' basis, and often without the 'Dear' or the 'Mr'. But whereas Burroughs had worked himself up into a passion about Wellcome's alleged perfidy, incompetence and low morals, Wellcome took a cool, long-term view. We can now see that Burroughs had no case at all, however unwise Wellcome had been to prolong his stay in America to champion Duncan's cause, but at the time, to bewildered outsiders and even more bewildered employees of the firm, the situation did not appear to be so clear-cut. If the senior members of the firm emphatically took Wellcome's side, Burroughs's immense personal popularity in the company and in the pharmaceutical profession was such that there were many who actually believed his wild allegations against his partner. Wellcome, in contrast, appeared cold and rather calculating. He cut down severely on his social life and dedicated himself almost exclusively to business. His friends noticed a new tenseness and even acerbity, and that he made trouble over quite minor matters. Those closest to him appreciated the daily strain upon him and made allowances; others were puzzled by what seemed to be a change of character.

In such episodes a sensitive man, however confident he may be of the rightness of his position and the ultimate outcome, becomes prey to self-doubt and to gnawing re-examinations of past actions, pondering upon what might have been done differently, and asking himself whether the blame lay exclusively with his critics. Wellcome's loneliness was another factor. Burroughs had a happy, loyal family and his political friends, and, while Wellcome became more cautious and reserved, Burroughs became even more gregarious and outspoken. He radiated confidence and success. Wellcome however retreated into a suspicious silence, trusting only a few and appearing sad and morose to those who did not know him well. The whole business made him miserable, with an element of bitterness. To his good friends Sam and Ben Fairchild of New York he revealed his feelings in a letter of 11 April 1888:

> I have long delayed writing to you about my private affairs hoping to be able to give you some really definite and satisfactory information, but nothing has transpired that has in any way practically altered the situation.... The chapter of aggression has simply been continued and is most likely to continue for a considerable length of time. I have taken the very best legal advice obtainable and am assured that my rights are perfectly secure. Litigation will of course be expensive, but I have no fear of the ultimate result....
>
> I have taken matters as calmly and placidly as possible, assuming simply the defensive attitude, leaving the policy of aggression entirely to the adversary. I have not the slightest intention of selling, and I am quite prepared to purchase.... There was a very nice little plan arranged during my absence, and there has been a great deal of tall lying done in this case, but facts are facts and there will be very little difficulty in establishing the facts. I know the justice of my case and with quietness and firmness I shall stand by my rights. I know that an attempt has been made in every possible way to injure me but I am not aware that it has had any effect. Certainly the result here has been to bring on my side the pledged support of many leading business men on simply hearing the side of my adversaries. I may tell you that Mr B. has been a very subtle worker against us, and this as a result of my very generous treatment. It is very evident that he is working for a purpose, but it is not at all likely that he will attain his object.

From George Wellcome came a letter of support:

> September 4 1888
>
> You may well believe we were indeed much astonished to learn of the deep waters of trouble through which you have been called to pass & after all the battles which you have fought in defence & for the success

of the firm that it should result in this. We feel very sad at the thought on our part that you have kept this from us so long & even when you were here with us said nothing to us about it in the least & we have been allowed to enjoy your help when it should have been on the other hand & while we regret this we do honour you for the fortitude with which you have borne it. As soon as we read your letter we laid it before the God of us both & there we leave it trusting & hoping he will bring things about all right. . . . I trust Mr B. will come to justice in due time.

To his anxious mother Wellcome wrote at the end of 1888 that

I have not been able to bring things to issue, and probably cannot for some months yet, but every hope of ultimate success seems assured. Do not worry or feel anxious, for I have endured the worst and am now in good health and strength and ready for the fray. I believe that justice will prevail.

He wrote to Frank Lincoln in March 1889 even more revealingly:

Now my dear fellow I am going to tell you in a few words of my stern experiences of the past two years. On my return from America in '87 I soon found myself completely set about by enemies who had laid their heads together to wrest from me my business, which has now grown to greatness – fortunately I had returned with a new lease of life in the form of completely restored health and I met my adversaries without a halt. But manly battle was not the game they wished to play – 'twas subtle guerilla warfare they wanted to wear me out with and they've kept it up and are keeping it up.

Instead of being my best friend Mr B. is my worst enemy and he is endeavouring to secure to himself the fruits of my labors – this through jealousy and greed – noble motives these & this is a noble return for the success I have secured to the firm and which is known and understood by all who know the history of our success.

His pretext is that in going to America to restore my health I neglected the business & on this ground he claims the right to drive me out . . .

then he began litigation which [I have] promptly and frankly met while [he] has done nothing but delay & get extensions of time. Thus for nearly two years I have been under constant harassment – nothing has been too petty or contemptible to seize upon as pretexts to villify & deprecate me. But my dear old [man] I've stood by the rudder of the old ship – and have never once allowed the tempest tossing to break my serenity – I have met insolence and brutality with courtesy and firm composure. I sought from the first the best legal advice. I know that I have the right on my side and further that I have facts and documentary facts which will break his fiction. I will not bore you with details. It has been a hard struggle but I have never for a moment lost hope & hope! Oh what a blessing is hope. It has been necessary for me to watch every movement of the enemy [to] meet every card – and every card [so] far has told for me.

I have not written to you about this because I have preferred to bear it silently & tell it after. But then there is a limit & I fear you may hear my adversary's version and be disturbed thereby – Have not fear for me I have no idea of failure in this case and I have much at stake.

One of B's plans seemed to be to try to swamp me with legal expenses & then gobble me down – but in this he has failed – though the expense has been great. I am prepared to buy the entire business but I have no idea of selling – or submitting to any imposition he may attempt to force upon me.

It all began through intense jealousy of the social and business position I have won in London & his chagrin at his own failure to secure like recognition & this in spite of the fact that in vain I tried to introduce both him & his wife (who are jointly my sworn enemies) into society it is but one of the old stories – though it seems too silly to contemplate seriously.

You will now understand why I have neglected you. I have against my will become selfishly absorbed in defending myself in a continuous duel with an enemy who knows no rules of honour. Please do me the favour to read this carefully and then burn it immediately for it is not wise to tell these troubles to the world & I have told you the story in confidence. Here I have only told several very intimate friends who are my advisers.

The case of Burroughs v. Wellcome, when it eventually came before Mr Justice Kekewich in the Chancery Division on 24–25 June 1889, was a notable Burroughs fiasco, with some exchanges between judge and barristers that were worthy of W. S. Gilbert.

Burroughs's own testimony was somewhat bizarre, even suggesting that Wellcome had been responsible for Miss Wakeman's near-drowning in Boulter's Lock. He had to admit that he had given Wellcome written permission to interest himself in Saxon & Co., but most damning of all was his concession that the firm, far from being ill-managed by Wellcome in his absence, had prospered greatly while he had been abroad and Wellcome had been in charge. His only witness, Prevost, claimed that Wellcome usually came into the office at 'about eleven or twelve and left at various times in the afternoon', which Wellcome only mildly denied, but which clearly struck Judge Kekewich as eminently sensible. Indeed, before Wellcome was even cross-examined by Burroughs's Counsel, Judge Kekewich had heard enough. He had also been shown, in strict confidence, the company's accounts, and the firm's healthy profits had impressed him decisively. He had been considerably less impressed by Burroughs's claim that the profits had only risen during Wellcome's absence, and had become irritated by Burroughs's general demeanour and manner of answering – or not answering – questions put to him by Wellcome's barrister. There was one especially devastating exchange:

QUESTION: Have you taken the pains yourself to see the correspondence which took place between the firm and Mr Wellcome during Mr Wellcome's absence in America?
ANSWER: I have not looked at it minutely; I have glanced over it.
QUESTION: About when?
ANSWER: About two weeks ago.

From Burroughs's point of view there was even worse to come:

QUESTION: Are not the letters the partners write to the Manager put on the file?
ANSWER: I do not know. I never have looked into the file once yet.

To Wellcome's special pleasure the true story about Dr Witte came out in Burroughs's evidence. Witte had not only betrayed some of the firm's secrets to its competitors and had been dismissed, but was also being pursued personally by Burroughs for the theft of company furniture. Moreover, Burroughs was confronted by the glowing encomium he had written about *Salammbô*, and by the fact that he had bought fifty copies as gifts for his friends, even though he had subsequently described it as 'obscene'. He also said that it had been arranged that Wellcome should undertake some company business in Cuba while in America, which was proved not to be the case; in any event, in August 1886 there had been a major cholera epidemic there. Burroughs claimed, to general incredulity, that 'several of our customers think that Mr Wellcome is a myth in this business. They think there is no such man in the business as Mr Wellcome at all, never having seen him, or never having heard anything personally about him. He has lived in a literary atmosphere separate from the Drug business.' And the hapless Mr Prevost was then reduced to making a pathetic declaration about Wellcome's working hours: 'I am not prepared to swear to anything. I can only give my idea – that is all.'

Both Wellcome and Burroughs confirmed that they had regular business conferences and continued to lunch together from time to time, on which Mr Justice Kekewich commented with feeling that 'I hope they will do so again in a few minutes', and brought the proceedings to an abrupt ending. He did not see 'the slightest ground' for the dissolution of the partnership, but had some concern over Wellcome's involvement in Saxon & Co. Wellcome's barrister said that he was prepared to relinquish his interest in it immediately. That having been said, Mr Justice Kekewich, after some sharp comments as to why the case had come to the courts at all, refused the decree of dissolution, and suggested that the contestants should shake hands and that the costs should be borne by them in proportion to their shares in the firm – which, of course, put the main burden upon Burroughs.

On leaving the court Wellcome sent his mother a telegram containing the single word 'Victory'. In fact, it had been a rout. But whereas Wellcome accepted the Judge's advice, Burroughs proved a bad loser.

He felt his defeat and public humiliation keenly, and his wife even more so. They continued to intrigue against Wellcome, to belittle his achievements and character, and to attempt to retrieve Burroughs's own fallen reputation in the profession, which had been badly harmed by a case that had been followed closely by the medical and pharmaceutical professions and journals.

Within two weeks of the court judgment, Burroughs hit back, with a carefully planned and, in its way, brilliantly successful counter-attack.

Although Wellcome had strongly opposed Burroughs's attempts to establish new works in the United States, he accepted that Burroughs Wellcome had outgrown the Wandsworth plant, and the partners now sought a new site well out of London, with good communications, abundant water and substantial acreage, not only for the expansion of the works in future, but also for growing their own plants and establishing their own farms. The ideal site came on the market in the summer of 1888, when the Phoenix Paper Mills at Dartford, Kent, were advertised for sale; they fulfilled all the criteria that Burroughs and Wellcome had agreed upon. Also, the closing of the mills had caused dismay in Dartford, and the employment prospects of Burroughs Wellcome gave the company an immediate local popularity. Burroughs bought the mills for £5,000 and leased them to Burroughs Wellcome for forty-nine years at a rent of £250 a year. This was to cause prolonged trouble. But in spite of the deep tensions between the partners, the matter initially seems to have been arranged amicably, and they worked closely together on the conversion of the mills for the firm's purposes. Indeed, until it came to the official opening, this was perhaps the most effective and enduring collaboration in their partnership.

Their joint ambition was not only to establish their operations more effectively, but also to create a model community, on the pioneering lines of the great Quaker families. They went into considerable detail, down to the design of the gates; the small lake in front of the mills was drained and cleaned and an artificial island built. In less than a year the new works was in full production of Kepler Malt and 'Tabloids'.

This remarkable achievement was then spectacularly marred by Burroughs, who invited Henry George to be the guest of honour and speaker at the official opening on 6 July 1889, less than two weeks after the collapse of his case against Wellcome. Burroughs ardently supported George's radical gospel against the possession of land, and indeed most private property, but Wellcome felt strongly that the firm should not involve itself in partisan politics at all, especially those of George. Burroughs assured Wellcome that George's speech would be entirely non-political, and, as the invitation had already been sent and accepted, Wellcome reluctantly agreed to the situation, although with justified unease and suspicion. His fears were increased by the indignation of the local Conservatives, who angrily boycotted the ceremonies and denounced George's views as 'downright robbery', and worse. They were publicly and loudly contemptuous of Burroughs's assurances about the 'non-political' nature of George's appearance, and with good cause.

The great day began well, in perfect weather, and in spite of the Tory boycott over two thousand guests walked around the grounds and inspected the works. Two bands played, the sun shone and the refreshments were lavish. All seemed to be going well, although Wellcome was horrified to see huge banners hailing not only the guest of honour, but also Free Trade, which he supported, and Free Land, which he certainly did not. The official opening ceremony in the afternoon was uncontentious. Then came another event in the evening, organised by Burroughs and the Liberals and Radicals. Over two thousand attended this, with another crowd, estimated at over five thousand, demanding entry; they achieved a near riot and were undeterred by the police employing fire hoses to hold them back.

In these highly charged and emotional circumstances Burroughs opened the proceedings with the words 'Friends and fellow citizens of the world'. He then introduced George, who delivered his standard demagogic speech for over an hour, denouncing the rights of property, advocating the abolition of all taxes except those upon land, and his other controversial nostrums. This was rapturously received, as was Burroughs, but the room was so crowded and hot that Burroughs dramatically broke some windows to allow more air, receiving another ovation from the excited audience before haranguing the overflow meeting with the same message. There was then a splendid firework display, with 'a colossal fire portrait of Mr Henry George' and the blazing message 'The Land for the People'. It was all very dramatic, colourful and popular, and the dancing continued until three in the morning.

Wellcome was incensed by Burroughs's conduct. He had not attended the evening meeting, but, as he had expected, Burroughs had cheated him. His partner also printed and published George's speech, and circulated it to Burroughs Wellcome's customers, by whom it was ill-received. They and the Dartford Conservatives denounced the whole affair, but Burroughs was triumphant. In response to Wellcome's angry protests he said that there had been no political content in the *opening* ceremony; that was true, but the real attraction of the day was George, and neither the newspapers nor Burroughs Wellcome's customers differentiated between the two meetings.

Burroughs regarded it as a triumph for the firm, and especially for himself; Wellcome considered that, for once, such publicity was not helpful, and that Burroughs had betrayed and humiliated him quite deliberately, and had done the company harm, which he had to correct. Burroughs then impishly arranged for pamphlets advocating George's policies to be put in the cases of the firm's products, which caused more angry complaints from the recipients and from Wellcome. All this made relations between the partners even worse, but as Burroughs entertained his guests – who did not include Wellcome – at dinner at one o'clock in the morning, he could reflect on an especially satisfactory revenge. The fact that this extravaganza had been paid for by the company made it even sweeter for him, and considerably more bitter for Wellcome, who recognised that, for once, he had not only been deceived, but also totally outwitted. He resolved that there would be no repetition, but Burroughs was incorrigible. Exultant at this victory, he returned to the attack.

Then came another heavy – indeed much heavier – blow. On the afternoon of 12 September 1889 fire broke out in the Wandsworth chemical works; it quickly took hold, and the building was totally destroyed, with one fatality. Although a considerable quantity of machinery, equipment and stock had already been moved to Dartford, the bulk of production had been continuing at Wandsworth until Dartford became fully operational. If Dartford had not been producing at all, the loss of the Wandsworth works would have been a calamity.

Wellcome had been attending a BMA conference in Newcastle and hastened back to find what had been very much his own creation in ruins. There was talk of an explosion, and the coroner would not complete the inquest on the dead man until this had been investigated by a Home Office explosives' expert. The enquiry disclosed that although many of the chemicals would burn if ignited, there was nothing that could have caused an explosion. The verdict was accidental death, and the cause of the fire remained unknown. The buildings and their contents were covered by insurance, and there were reserves of goods in the Snow Hill warehouses and at Dartford, so what could have been a disaster and an excellent opportunity for Burroughs Wellcome's competitors was only a severe setback. Both Wellcome and Burroughs were distressed by the death of the fireman, Jacobs, and made good provision for his relatives, and Wellcome's constant concern over safety was increased at Dartford, which was now in effect Burroughs Wellcome's manufacturing centre.

The separation between the partners became virtually physical, Burroughs devoting most of his time to Dartford, where he became a local celebrity and much loved by the growing number of employees, who did not share the local Tories' fear of his Radicalism. After he took British nationality in 1890, he was pressed to consider standing for Parliament in the Liberal/Radical interest, to Wellcome's horror. Wellcome himself, when he was not travelling for the company, operated in London, and although 1889 had been unfortunate for the company, in other respects it achieved its first contracts with the Government for medicines and medical equipment for India and the Royal Navy; a year later it secured another with the Crown Agent for the Colonies, which had been the ambition of both for years. Wellcome's passion for photography resulted in 'Tabloid' photographic chemicals, which were an outstanding success; no less inspired was 'Tabloid' tea, which became part of the equipment of explorers and travellers, and revealed Burroughs Wellcome's almost uncanny eye for markets that others had not realised existed. Wellcome continued to plan for the company's own research laboratories to initiate new drugs; the increasing prosperity of the firm now made this possible.

Both Burroughs and Wellcome aspired to be model employers. Long before legislation, they instituted the eight-hour day. With their encouragement and the company's financial support, the firm had literary and musical societies, and even its own orchestra. Later, Wellcome instituted the custom of presenting every member of staff with a book for Christmas, and went to great trouble to find one that he thought would not only be suitable, but also entertaining. Programmes were arranged for staff outings and concerts, and a sports club was founded – one of the earliest of its kind. Wellcome's leasing of Acacia Hall in Dartford in 1898 for the Wellcome Club and Institute was presaged in the schemes he and Burroughs founded or encouraged long before then. The result was an exceptionally contented workforce, with a deep loyalty to the company and its principal partners. Nor was Dartford itself neglected, and Burroughs was the driving force and chief fundraiser for the Livingstone Cottage Hospital, whose foundation-stone was laid by Stanley in 1894.

But their relationship still deteriorated, in spite of their increasing success. At the end of 1889 Burroughs abruptly decided never to speak to Wellcome again and, from then on, they only communicated through Sudlow. Burroughs seemed to Wellcome to be engaged in a systematic attempt to discredit him, particularly with the employees; some of Burroughs's high-handed actions were trivial, at least to later eyes, but not to Wellcome's. A particularly sore point was Burroughs's arrangements for political meetings congenial to his own views held on the company's premises. Burroughs even tried to circumvent Wellcome by proposing an amalgamation with John Wyeth without telling Wellcome. Wyeth, with his experience of Burroughs, replied that 'your business could be managed with much stricter economy', and the matter was dropped. In 1893 Burroughs was plotting again to make Burroughs Wellcome a joint-stock company, with him as principal shareholder.

However, the real problems were over the ownership of the Phoenix Mills and Burroughs's cavalier prodigality with company money.

One of Burroughs's most perceptive, but unfortunately anonymous, obituarists emphasised that

> The influence of Henry S. Wellcome in cementing and organizing the business of the firm cannot be lost sight of in commenting on the brilliancies of the senior partner. While Burroughs was a man of intense mental, physical and commercial energy, of buoyant individuality and brilliant initiative, he lacked that steady persistence, that capacity for governing and directing others, that shrewder judgement and that love of executive work and care for detail that distinguished his partner. Burroughs threw off multitudes of crude, red-hot ideas; Wellcome, brimming over with energy and originality himself, had sometimes to work out Burroughs' as well as his own ideas before they could be given to the world as definite, artistic entities.

The same commentator also marvelled that Burroughs left a fortune of over £125,000, 'in spite of barbaric extravagances in all directions, and an almost spendthrift disregard of money', not appreciating that Burroughs had not been spending his own money, but the company's; it is not difficult to be lavishly generous with other people's money. Of all Burroughs's offences against Wellcome, many of which can be put down to ebullience and impulse, this one was the most grave, and the least forgivable. An American admirer later recalled Burroughs's generosity to his employees:

> Whenever he came to this city [New York] he would call on me and would be sure to say before he went out: 'What would you suggest as a good present for my men?' Then he would buy dozens of bottles of fine perfumery, or a lot of American-made articles to take to his employees, who always appreciated these little gifts, because they came from him.

They came, of course, out of the company's funds.

Wellcome maintained a studious coldness in public, but to his mother he could be frank, writing to her on 16 December 1890:

> Dear Mother
>
> It is too bad I have again delayed so long in writing you my heart has beaten in anxiety and my thoughts constantly fly to you but in this great cruel whirl of work with tired brain, I struggle in vain for moments when I can sit down & collect such happy thoughts as I would wish to convey to you. I fear in writing I may burden you with my overheavy burdens of care and worry – time speeds by and alas alas in spite of all good intent I find myself neglecting you. Oh how I wish it were possible for me to be near you or even so near I might more often visit you. Three years so full of life's most trying experiences have sped by since I last embraced you and enjoyed your loving counsel. I have thousands of kindly acquaintances, some true friends – but only one dear devoted mother the one to whose guidance I owe so much. I feel so anxious to visit you & at any cost I will do so ere many weeks or months at most.
>
> After my bitter experiences of the past few years I have found it necessary to stick to my post with the utmost vigilance to protect my interests. This has meant almost daily and hourly vigilance, my only holiday was one I took this summer when utterly worn out with work I went to Switzerland and visited Mr and Mrs H. M. Stanley who were then staying at Maloja & from there I went up into the highest mountains of the Alpine ranges and shot Chamois. I got two very fine ones. This over I took a short trip with the Stanleys to Lake Como & several other

places in Italy and then into France & up to Geneva where I left them and returned to my toil. This holiday did me a world of good. . . .

The destruction of our works by fire last year was a very severe blow and it is one of the reasons why it has not been possible for me to visit you but I feel quite certain I shall be able to make a hasty trip sometime this winter.

I am sending you and Geo. each two hundred dollars as a Christmas present to use for your comfort. I shall send it all to Geo. in one draft and he can get it cashed for you. Mrs Sheldon of whom you have heard me speak, as one of the dear kind friends who nursed me during my serious illness – is now in New York & has taken over some things for you & Cevilla & the girls. A rare Himalaya shawl for you a silk one I bought in Milan Italy for Cevilla & some thing for shawls or gowns for the girls, etc etc.

. . . If you get ill always get the best physicians obtainable and let me know the cost and I will send you the money.

I am taking great care of my health but am very very tired.

With my whole hearts love dear Mother & affectionate remembrance to you all believe me your very faithful Son.
Henry.

The increasingly bitter and constant disputes with Burroughs had a lasting effect upon Wellcome. Although he had won, it had severely shaken his faith in friendship, even though the bulk of his friends and employees had stood by him staunchly; but he seemed to be rather more aware of those who had not. He also realised that on one matter at least Burroughs had had a point. If the malicious portrait of him as someone much more interested in glamorous and interesting London Society than in business had been a travesty, Wellcome had made himself needlessly vulnerable to gossip and rumour. He decided to restrict his outside interests, and he attended to business more closely than ever to control Burroughs and to maintain his own rapidly increasing investment and wealth. 'Please remember that I don't want the facts of my troubles discussed among our friends,' he wrote to his mother. 'I want no sympathy from outsiders – I don't believe in the sympathy of the outside world.

They are not essential to my happiness, and [I] only care for general results.'

When matters between the two partners had become more embittered by June 1891, Wellcome wrote to Burroughs a letter headed 'Dear Sir'; in it he claimed that after the court case,

> I met you at your office and extended to you my hand and proposed that on both sides all differences of the past should be forgotten from that moment. You took my hand with apparently unfeigned pleasure and heartiness [and] expressed appreciation of my offer and called upon Mr Kirby to bear witness that the hatchet was at that moment buried and that all differences of the past should be mutually forgotten as from then. I meant this pledge with all my heart and have strictly observed it. You have now directly disregarded the sacred undertaking you then made.

Burroughs loftily replied that he would have answered earlier,

> but have been much engaged with attending to the firm's business matters. I will first refer to the fact that you are constantly in the habit of assuming an aggressive attitude towards me and you feel badly apparently because I will not put up with your false and slanderous statements or treat you as a gentleman when you cease to behave yourself as a gentleman. I have never entertained any malice toward you and never shall. I feel that you have treated me shamefully but it is not my business to punish you. For your own good I would like to see you reform your ways.

There was much more in the same vein. As everyone at Burroughs Wellcome knew, the partnership now existed in name only.

*

In 1891 Mary Wellcome discovered an ominous lump in one of her breasts, and the doctors' opinion was the obvious one. George wrote to his brother warning of the gravity of their mother's condition, but Wellcome could not, and would not, believe it, writing to her on 23 June:

Dear Mother

I am deeply grieved to learn from George that you are feeling depressed about the gathering. I must tell you that I am extremely doubtful about the serious report the lady and other doctors have given you. Not one case in five hundred that are pronounced cancers are really cancers, and it is a shame for doctors to worry and frighten patients by such imaginary reports. I have more confidence in Uncle Jacob's opinion than in any other surgeon in the West and I am anxious that he should as quickly as possible come & see you & make a careful examination and if he thinks necessary he should call in an eminent surgeon to consult on the case.

Do not I beg of you allow any more petty doctors to examine and worry you with their reports. I have requested to George to send for Uncle at any time necessary & to get whatever good surgeon from Chicago or elsewhere Uncle may think desirable and I will pay all expenses. I shall and I want you also to repose all confidence and reliance in Uncle. I have seen and known leading medical men in nearly all countries of the world and I would as quickly trust my life in the hands of Dr J. W. B. Wellcome as any man I know of in the world.

Don't fail to put your trust in his skill and his judgement and observe exactly his directions and wishes in all things. If it is the worst and an operation must be performed trust in God and Uncle's skill. More people are made wretched and unhappy by busy tongued people & these often are doctors who worry patients into illnesses instead of encouraging them to stand up against minor illnesses.

I am grieved beyond words that I cannot come to see you at once, but important issues hold me here. I shall watch with deepest anxiety letters from you & George and especially as to your cheerful or depressed state. With cheerful heart one may bear any ill but with heavy heart all maladies are deep afflictions.

Do not worry for me. I have had a hard struggle against circumstances but, fear not, God has been my guardian and your prayers at home have brought me this protection. I am in a stronger position and better able to maintain my rights than ever.

I am glad you have at last received the shawls etc only I am so sorry they are so very late. Mrs Sheldon left them with a servant in New York to forward and they were evidently forgotten.

Mrs Sheldon has since gone to Africa to lead an important expedition to Kilimanjaro and the Massai Land. She has successfully carried it out and has just returned to Zanzibar but severely ill. She will arrive in London about the end of July. Mr Sheldon and I are living together up at Hampton on the bank of the Thames where I keep my boats & canoes.

I find it difficult to write but I will try & send you a few lines as often as possible. And if any emergency should arise I shall go to you at once. But have courage put your faith in God and Uncle's skill and let the little doctors alone.

With much love your devoted Son, Henry.

May Sheldon had indeed triumphed, with Wellcome's strong personal involvement, but at substantial cost, to herself and others – notably Wellcome himself.

She had laid her plans for her African adventure with Stanley-like efficiency; indeed, Stanley was not only her inspiration, but also her guide and adviser. Her ambitious plan was to travel unaccompanied by any white companion from Mombasa to Mount Kilimanjaro, a route that was largely unexplored; there was also little information about the natives she would encounter. If the expedition had a madcap element about it, she was a serious explorer and a keen anthropologist and ethnologist. Wellcome advised her on her medical needs and supplied her with one of his specially planned and designed exploration medicine cases, already a Burroughs Wellcome speciality. But he also designed for her a 'Palanquin', principally made of cane and bamboo, to be in effect her travelling home. It was so light that it could be carried by four men with her inside (although she declared that she intended to walk most of the way) and would serve as her bedroom at night.

A contemporary describes its construction and amenities:

It is perfectly round, size 5 ft 6 ins in diameter by 2 ft wide. It is made of pulp cane on a bamboo structure, the joints of which are bound with Aluminium, this renders it perfectly strong and enables it to resist any weight that is brought to bear upon it. The chief object during building has been to keep the Palanquin as light as possible consistent with the strength required. The fittings are so arranged that every available space is utilised to the very best advantage; there are three lockers lined with waterproof, suitable for wearing apparel, etc., the seat and table are adjustable and can, quite easily, be converted into a couch; there are three down pillows covered with canary China silk, which will be used for the seat and back cushion during the day, and the whole forms a splendid bed for use on the couch at night. The awning is made of a green waterproof silk, edged with gold draped with China silk. The awning and curtains are made to run on cane rods, and can be raised or lowered at will by Mrs French Sheldon without removing from her seat. Among the numerous useful articles carried in the lockers are a set of four waterproof blinds, fitted with Mica windows for use during

**Mrs. FRENCH SHELDON'S PALANQUIN.**

is palanquin was made at Whiteley's for Mrs. French Sheldon, the "Lady Stanley" who is bound for Central Africa, from designs by Mr. enry S. Welcome (of Messrs. Burroughs & Wellcome, Snow Hill). It is a unique specimen of strong, light, and artistic cane and bamboo ork, and Mr. Wellcome must be congratulated on his excellent taste. The palanquin will be carried by four of Mrs. Sheldon's Zanzibari porters.

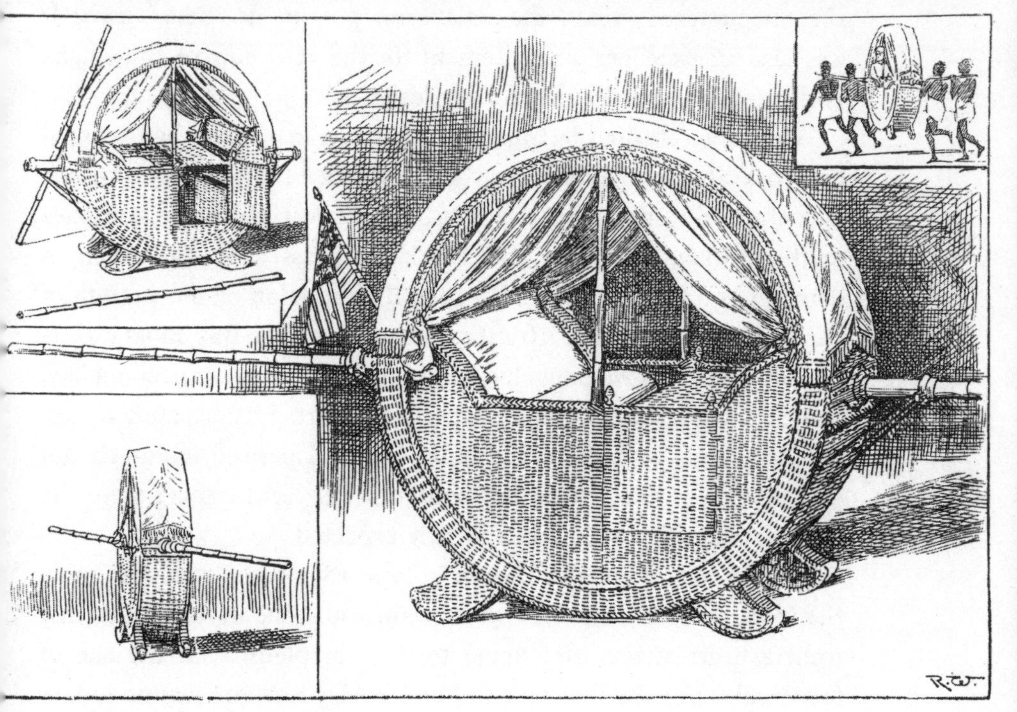

May Sheldon's palanquin, 1891

wet weather, and an extra waterproof awning trimmed with gold tinsel gimp and fringe, for use on State occasions only. The whole, besides having a very pretty effect, combines every luxury it is possible to fit in so small a space. The Palanquin is to be carried by four natives by means of long bamboo poles fitted at each end into fittings made of wrought iron and braced with steel.

The Sheldon Palanquin, constructed by the firm of William Whiteley in ten days, was the first sensation of her expedition when Wellcome showed it off to admiring newspapers and their artists. 'Mr Wellcome must be congratulated on his excellent taste,' the *Mirror* enthused. The praise was well deserved. The Palanquin was an admirable mixture of the attractive and the practical, and is one of Wellcome's most delightful creations; it not only proved itself throughout May Sheldon's travels, but was also – understandably – a source of wonder to her Zanzibari porters and to the African chiefs she encountered, when the Palanquin put on its 'State' garb. It was also an excellent advertisement for the versatility of Burroughs Wellcome, and particularly for its designer.

When she returned in triumph to London in 1892, it had seemed that May Sheldon had achieved all she desired from her epic African adventure. She was briefly famous, the subject of admiring articles in the British, American and European press. She was much in demand as a lecturer, making a special impression by the warmth of her references to all the Africans she had met. She was, most exceptionally then for a woman, elected to the Royal Geographical Society, and also addressed its American counterpart. Her account of her voyage, *Sultan to Sultan*, was published and praised, although not excessively so, but neither her book nor her lecture tours were the financial success she had confidently expected.

Then, while she was in Boston in June 1892 completing her book, Sheldon, who had just left her to return to London, died suddenly from a heart attack after being treated for pleurisy, at the age of forty-eight. For the first time in her life May Sheldon was no longer rich. Unable to believe this sad fact, she continued to live in her previous style. By May 1893 she was in acute financial difficulties and appealed to Wellcome for help. He did so, but emphasised that

> I must urge upon you the greatest possible prudence and economy in expenditure & cost of living and the avoidance of contracting liabilities, for your income is small and extremely uncertain and your own health is so uncertain that you can only place positive reliance on what you really possess. . . . I think under the circumstances you could in staying in a place for weeks or months secure apartments and board at about half your present expenditure and this quite as good, quite as comfortable and probably with better attention and more quiet and rest. I have no right to offer you this suggestion except that I am endeavouring to assist you out of your financial worries and I consider that economy in expenses is as essential as the production of funds.

But May Sheldon took no notice whatever of Wellcome's advice and lived in an expensive hotel without the means even to pay its bills. In September she appealed to him again for rescue, and he replied with considerable anger in a letter of six pages upbraiding her for her folly, which began:

> . . . I perfectly recognise the serious embarrassment of your present circumstances and am very anxious to aid you, but I consider it perfectly useless to render any further assistance if you continue to incur debts and expenses far beyond your means. . . .
>
> I have written this plainly and emphatically as a safeguard and warning to you – with but one motive, and that is to save you from the humiliation and disaster which is certain to befall you unless you entirely change your methods. . . .

Wellcome was not then the rich man that he was to become, and he had his family in America dependent upon him. Since Sheldon's death, he had given his widow nearly $4,000 (approximately £1,000), and she was now pleading for – or rather demanding – another $1,000. These were very large sums, and Wellcome's indignation at what he rightly described as 'pouring funds into a bottomless hole that simply enable you to get from one dilemma into another' was very understandable. However, he did add shrewd advice whereby she could 'with your exceptional talents, material, and experiences make a good fair income by a systematic series of lectures'. He also reluctantly agreed to come to her assistance again.

It would be pleasant to record that May Sheldon immediately came to her senses and followed Wellcome's advice. Perhaps she did for a while, but more correspondence in 1897 and 1898 reveals her 'in desperate straits' without even money for a cab fare, while she was still living in the Hotel Cecil in considerable style. She was utterly arrogant, grand and exasperating, but her friendship with Wellcome survived and, indeed, strengthened through the years. Somewhat surprisingly, she never remarried. Wellcome did not forget her kindnesses to him in his early years in London, nor her courage and achievements.

Happily, his faith in her, although often very sorely tried, was unexpectedly vindicated, as her fortunes were to change very substantially. Through Stanley she met King Leopold and expressed interest to him in exploring in the Congo. She must have bewitched the tyrant, because he issued an edict that

> Leopold commands that Mrs French Sheldon shall be the freest and most independent person throughout our Congo domain. She shall not be denied free access to any documents, and shall be given every opportunity of investigating every branch of all work done by natives at all times by officers in command.

This was to prove a fine investment, because her published accounts of the conditions in the Congo gave a roseate picture of benevolent colonial rule that was denied to other observers. If historians have been justifiably scornful, the fact was that May Sheldon became enamoured of everything Belgian, and especially of its royal family. Her financial situation improved dramatically as she could claim, with justice, that she was the personal friend of three Kings of the Belgians. She was to be a highly successful fundraiser in America at the beginning of the Great War for the Belgian Red Cross, for which she received the award of *Chevalier de l'Ordre de la Couronne*. She also gave all her manuscripts, ethnographical material and items she had gathered on her African travels to Wellcome to add to his by then formidable collections. As everyone in Burroughs Wellcome came to know, she was to be treated as a very special visitor and guest. When, much later in her long life, she had to appeal to Wellcome again for assistance, he did not fail her. Her extraordinary life ended in February 1936, at the age of eighty-eight, within four months of Wellcome's death. Each had fully repaid their debts to the other.

*

By the time May Sheldon returned, briefly famous, Burroughs and Wellcome corresponded principally through Sudlow, to whom Burroughs wrote on 2 January 1892 that

> a long and mournful experience has satisfied me that generous treatment is thrown away on Mr Wellcome, for the more money I have loaned him & the lower the interest when he appeared to think further favours were uncertain the more unkind has been his treatment toward me till I am utterly nauseated.

Wellcome's feelings towards Burroughs were not dissimilar.

A chronic source of difficulty was Burroughs's incessant search for new ways to spend the company's money, particularly on its employees. Thus, on 14 March 1893, he cabled from the liner *Teutonic*:

> Am indeed glad to learn that the bonus has been so good. No money is spent by me with greater pleasure than the payment of this percentage of the profits of the business as a gift to all who are engaged in it.
>
> I like the idea of every one in the business having the advantages of a partnership in the way of a share of the profits without having to incur any liability or take any risk of loss if the business should be a possible loss instead of a profit. I am indeed thankful for the great prosperity which has attended our mutual efforts the past year. I note with satisfaction the large sales of January last.
>
> When we can do a trade by the blessing of Providence of £200,000

> a year I shall be satisfied and not care to extend it beyond this because it seems as much business as our house can attend to and do it well.

None of this appealed to Wellcome: a generous bonus scheme was one thing; a mass partnership was very different. Nor would he be content with sales of £200,000.

Burroughs's genuine solicitude for the firm's staff was one of his most admirable qualities, and his papers, and the company's, give many examples. He gave tennis parties and other entertainments for the firm's employees at his large house and garden in Surbiton, and was in every respect the kindly and generous employer and friend. What irked Wellcome was that this splendid generosity was almost entirely at the company's expense – and, indirectly, his. A Mrs Mattox, who had been with the company a year, asked if she was entitled to a holiday; Burroughs cabled from Chicago: 'Send Mrs Mattox £5 as a present with compliments & best wishes to take the vacation and include her name in the list of employees to share in the profits.' When a Miss House fell ill, Burroughs cabled from Tangier: 'Let us do everything in our power to be of service during her illness and ask her doctor or her people to let us know if we can do anything.'

Burroughs considered that Wellcome's approach to the staff and the business was 'patronising' and mean. 'He ought to write a book as a guide to enterprising young men who wish to become possessed of partnership shares in businesses without putting up any capital by merely promising to do so sometime or who wish to become part owners of factories &c by means of something very like forced loans,' he had written to Sudlow from Nice on 30 December 1891, not at all untypically. It was, of course, another totally untrue charge, as Sudlow knew very well. Although Burroughs knew that Sudlow, who was the company's rock during these swirling tides, was totally loyal to Wellcome, he continued to write to him in contemptuous, vicious and libellous terms about his partner.

Then, there was the incessant problem of Burroughs's politics, which, in Wellcome's eyes, became odder and odder. His increasingly wilder statements, pamphlets, letters and speeches – he even tried to convert May Sheldon to the abolition of private property in letters of inordinate length – made Wellcome wonder whether his partner was deranged to some extent, a suspicion shared by his biographer.

A characteristic example of his growing obsession with politics occurred in 1890, when he proposed to challenge the rating assessment for the Dartford Works in the courts, not because it was excessive or unreasonable, but because it gave him another public platform from which to denounce the taxation system. Then, he seriously proposed to punish the 'absentee landlords' by actually selling the Phoenix Mills, 'with a deep regret that we ever went there at all'. Wellcome repudiated this insane proposal, and after Burroughs had reluctantly agreed to abandon it, Wellcome reminded him that while he had always supported the right of Charles Bradlaugh to hold his free-thinking opinions, Burroughs had taken a leading part in the campaign to exclude him from Parliament. Wellcome considered this 'neither just or manly', and evidence of 'cowardice and blindness', and added that, 'I don't think foreigners should interfere with the domestic politics of a country unless the people of that country are incapable of managing their own affairs.'

However, although Burroughs had dropped the idea of making a huge issue of the Mills, he took no notice whatever of his partner's other strictures. One who knew him well later wrote: 'It was impossible to talk with S. M. Burroughs for five consecutive minutes without impinging on that "Single Tax" of which Mr George is the modern godfather.' Then, although he had never been a teetotaller, he suddenly embraced the cause of Temperance with equal vehemence, flaunting for a time a hideous blue ribbon in his buttonhole to demonstrate to his amazed acquaintances and friends his wholly unexpected new allegiance.

One of the key differences between the two partners had become increasingly obvious. Wellcome buttressed his wide interests by reading a great deal outside medical and pharmaceutical matters, while Burroughs hardly read at all, especially as he got older. However, one friend may have exaggerated by writing that Burroughs's reading was limited to the Bible and a few books of travel, adding that, 'his political horizon was limited by the Herculean pillars of Free Trade and the Single Tax. Within these he had fathomed every depth, taken every bearing. Without surged a sea of problems where his searchlight had not penetrated.' Single-issue people are usually bores; interestingly, this was never alleged about Burroughs even by his most severe critics, and, understandably, his employees loved him, without apparently ever succumbing to his political beliefs.

Early in 1894 a journalist researching a long article interviewed Burroughs at Snow Hill and was impressed by 'a gentleman in the early prime of manhood – slight of figure, of medium height, with fair hair and a keen grey-blue eye which penetrates with unerring accuracy. But it is not the eye of a sharp and exacting person; it is full of kindliness and of sympathy.' She was awed by his accounts of his generosity to charities and impressed by his profit-sharing schemes. After he had spoken, inevitably, at length about George and the Land Tax, she said that he ought to be in Parliament, upon which Burroughs modestly replied that he had been asked often (which was true), but 'I could not give the time from my business.' He suggested that she should go to Dartford, which she did. She described it as 'a People's Palace':

> There was a beautiful lake, wherein swans and smaller waterfowl disported themselves; fruit and flower gardens, tennis courts and bowling greens stretched themselves around the works, and must, in the summer time, present a scene of picturesque loveliness. . . . Truly the employees at the Phoenix Works are a favoured people.

This was superb publicity – for Burroughs; Wellcome was only mentioned when the name of the company was referred to.

*

There is no evidence that Burroughs took any interest whatever in Wellcome's new project, which had been maturing for some time, indeed since 1890, when E. von Behring and S. Kitasato published their momentous research and findings that animals – particularly sheep and goats – could raise diphtheria anti-toxin by the serum produced by others. In 1894 P. P. E. Roux proved that the serum could be raised much more effectively in horses. The use of animals for research was not new, although strictly controlled by the Home Office under the 1876 Cruelty to Animals Act; what was new was the realisation that they could be the provider of drugs that had real possibilities for humans. The huge potential struck Wellcome immediately, and out of this stemmed his ambition to establish a physiological laboratory of his own in 1894, so that Burroughs Wellcome could be closely involved in this entirely new area, which opened the possibility of creating an immunising drug against a disease that was one of the major killers of the time, especially among children. He was also excited about the potential for sera from the same sources against erysipelas and puerperal fever.

In spite of the pioneering work of Lister, Pasteur and others, the profession of medicine remained crude. X-rays were only discovered in 1895, and it was many years before they were available and efficient and interpreted properly. There were virtually no vaccines or immunisations, except against smallpox; and, although operations could now be undertaken under anaesthetic and antiseptic conditions, the drugs available were pitifully few – the armoury available to a modern physician did not exist. But the research that was to produce such astounding results later was beginning to excite the profession with its potentialities, and Wellcome wanted his firm and name to be in the forefront. The anti-diphtheria serum could be the beginning.

The Dartford laboratory, like that at Wandsworth, was primarily concerned with testing and manufacturing rather than with research. In 1891 an 'experimental laboratory' had been established on the third floor at Snow Hill, but its purpose is not clear, and its results seem to have been nugatory.

It was Wellcome's concern at the inadequacy of the few effective drugs available to doctors and surgeons, and the importance of research being undertaken elsewhere – particularly in France and Germany – that was the strongest motivation of all. The medical profession had at its disposal a wretchedly small amount of proven drugs even at the beginning of the twentieth century – principally quinine against malaria, mercury for the treatment of syphilis, and digitalis for certain heart conditions, together with some anaesthetic and analgesic pain-relieving drugs, mainly morphine, cocaine and barbiturates. All of them were based on plants or on minerals, such as iodine, sulfur, iron and sodium bicarbonate. In spite of the work of Lister, the importance of aseptic measures in surgery was only gradually appreciated, and abdominal surgery was only introduced successfully in the 1890s, Wellcome being one of the beneficiaries of the new knowledge and techniques in 1898. Just as the founders of the Philadelphia College had realised the perils of quackery in the 1820s, medical scientists and the medical profession in the 1890s now appreciated how meagre were their resources. Also, it was in Germany that Paul Ehrlich was experimenting with dyes to combat bacteria, calling the process chemotherapy. In 1909 he found a compound, the famous 606, that was effective against syphilis, then a disease of major importance; he called it Salvarsan. The future sulfa drugs that were to revolutionise chemotherapy had their origins in Ehrlich's work, to be followed by that of another German scientist, Gerhard Domagk, in the 1930s, on the red dye Prontosil, a derivative of coal tar. All this, and antibiotics, was far in the distance in 1894, but Wellcome was sure that great advances could be made if dedication, resources and the best minds could be combined. Thus, although the Physiological Laboratories initially had a limited purpose, albeit a fine one, Wellcome's longer term ambitions were much larger, as he was to demonstrate in 1895 with the most important, single appointment so far in the history of Burroughs Wellcome – that of Frederick Power as the firm's chief scientific chemist and researcher into the unknown.*

* See page 206.

The dominant purpose of Wellcome's Physiological Laboratories was to produce diphtheria anti-toxin. 'We think it very important that we should be in the forefront with this,' he wrote eagerly.

One factor that made Wellcome so excited by these developments, and spurred him on, was his vivid memories of the terrible devastation of this disease in his childhood in Garden City, and the desperate attempts of his Uncle Jacob to save those afflicted by it. This possibility of immunising people, especially children, against this deadly bacterium was a marvellous one. One is never quite sure with him where the different strands of Wellcome the opportunistic businessman and Wellcome the philanthropist began and ended, particularly as they so often overlapped, and this was a classic case. One of the most intriguing aspects of Wellcome was that he so seldom put his ideas to paper. He was a prodigious producer of letters, memoranda and telegrams, but these dealt almost entirely with current problems and concerns. Some years later he said, very revealingly, to his second General Manager, George Pearson: 'My plans exist in my mind like a jigsaw puzzle, and gradually I shall be able to piece it together.'

Thus, although the Physiological Laboratories' first purpose was the production of the diphtheria anti-toxin, they were to develop in a manner that Wellcome certainly had not planned with any precision, but the *idea* became the eventual reality, as with so many of his ventures after 1894. He produced the ideas; others took them forward, but could not have done so had Wellcome not provided the conception and the means.

Wellcome claimed from the outset that his new laboratories were not to be considered a commercial operation, and that the sera were to be distributed at cost price; but the longer-term commercial rewards if Burroughs Wellcome could develop an effective diphtheria anti-toxin were clearly enormous. It is in no sense cynical to note these convergences; without the profits, the research and development of new drugs and medicines could not be undertaken, and services to suffering humanity were not to be any the less because they contributed to the financial strength of Burroughs Wellcome. Wellcome was understandably irritated by those academic researchers who affected to despise the commercial drug business, and not least because the latter tended to achieve more than they did.

This prejudice, once so strong in the United States but considerably less so than in Britain, had reversed in both countries, and promising young British medical researchers were too often advised by their superiors not to wreck their reputations by going into the pharmaceutical business. Wellcome was to lose a future Nobel prizewinner (Frederick Gowland Hopkins) as a result of these pressures – which were usually indirect and covert, but potent enough – and was nearly to lose another (Henry Dale). Fully aware of this, Wellcome heavily stressed the academic and altruistic aspects of his new laboratories, but the commercial possibilities were never far from his mind, either. In both he was entirely genuine. He was doing good, and also doing well out of it. The hundreds of millions who were to have the spectre of diphtheria removed from their lives would not cavil. Other very rich men, having made their fortunes by methods that do not bear close inspection, have assuaged their consciences with good works and benefactions later in their lives or after their deaths; Wellcome did so in the middle of his working lifetime. There is a difference.

Even before he could find and appoint a Director of his new laboratories, Wellcome had appointed Dr Thomas Jessopp Bokenham to produce an anti-diphtheria serum from horses stabled near Snow Hill in 1894. It was also being produced at the British Institute of Preventive Medicine (later the Lister Institute), but Burroughs Wellcome was the first pharmaceutical company to be involved in production of the serum, which was distributed to hospitals in Britain and the United States for testing and evaluation. To modern doctors this speed appears alarmingly irresponsible, but the response was so dramatic that initial supplies were quickly exhausted. The diphtheria anti-toxin had in fact been well researched at the Pasteur Institute by Roux; Wellcome's new, and at the time very modest,

Physiological Laboratories* and stables produced some anti-toxin, with considerable difficulties, in significant quantities for the first time, in itself an achievement. This gave the Laboratories an immediate prestige, which they were quickly to forfeit.

In April 1895 Wellcome formally appointed Bokenham to take charge of the Laboratories. However, his first choice had been Hopkins, who would have been infinitely better, and who was recommended to Wellcome by Dr (Edwin) Cooper Perry, the senior consulting physician at Guy's Hospital. But there was a delay in making the appointment, which was primarily the result of Wellcome's distractions with Burroughs at this crucial time, and there was also prejudice against young scientists going into 'trade'. As a result, Perry offered, and Hopkins accepted, a relatively junior post as an assistant in his physiology department at Guy's. This was one of the very few occasions when Wellcome lost a truly outstanding medical scientist.** Hopkins was a biochemist of genius – indeed, he, more than anyone, established it as a separate and important discipline. But in 1894 he was only thirty-three and had just qualified. None the less, Wellcome, on Perry's advice, had been fully prepared to appoint Hopkins. He can only have watched Hopkins's subsequent spectacular career with very mixed feelings, but it was a good example of Wellcome's excellent contacts in the medical profession, which were to bring others of Hopkins's calibre into his laboratories.

Meanwhile, the diphtheria anti-toxin had given the Wellcome Physiological Laboratories an immediate reputation that was to attract researchers and academics. Wellcome was particularly proud of the fact that his company produced the serum at so low a price that the firm actually lost money in its initial production and distribution; and,

* See E. M. Tansey and R. Milligan, 'The Early History of the Wellcome Research Laboratories, 1894–1914', in *Pill Peddlers*, ed. by G. Higby and E. Stroud (American Institute of the History of Pharmacy, Madison, Wisconsin, 1990), pp. 91–106.

** Hopkins later became Professor of Biochemistry at Cambridge and, as Sir Frederick, received the Order of Merit. He won the Nobel Prize and became President of the Royal Society; his work on vitamins was to revolutionise one aspect of modern medicine.

being Wellcome, he made this fact well known. It seemed that it was the true beginning of his reputation as a medical innovator and philanthropist as well as a sharp American businessman, host and self-publicist. But it was also to prove to be one of his closest brushes with disaster.

The Physiological Laboratories moved to 10 Devonshire Street and then, in 1896, to larger premises at 40 Charlotte Street. All seemed to be going well.

It has been argued that, as the senior partner, Burroughs must have known of Wellcome's decision in 1894, from which so much was to flow. But there were other distractions and differences at the time, and there is no reference to the matter in the disjointed and rasping correspondence between the two estranged partners in that vital year.

*

The relationship between Wellcome and Burroughs had gradually deteriorated further during 1894, as Wellcome reported to his mother on 16 March: 'Mr B has been away most of the time since my arrival but he has just returned and attempted some new tricks or old ones repeated, but without success – yet he will continue his course of procedure to the end.' On 17 November he wrote to her that,

> The year has been full of high pressure work – necessary business duties and much time wasted in the battle for my rights. . . .
>
> During the past few months negotiations for separation between B and myself have been going on but he has been tricky through it all and like a fela [*sic*] he will not stick to anything and has not yet shown any disposition to settle in a straightforward and equitable manner but rather seems to be trying to draw me into some trap so that he can secure the whole business without paying me value. Up to the present he has failed in all his attempts and I have had many signal victories but no one can predict the end with certainty. I have good legal and business advisers and am quietly standing by my guns. It is such a pity for our business is so prosperous and successful enough for us both. It is only the fiendish spirit that incites all this trouble.

However, at this point 'the fiendish spirit' was extinguished.

Some of the disputes between Burroughs and Wellcome were absurd, except in the context of their relationship, and the fact was that profits had been severely affected by the heavy cost of the alterations and new equipment at Dartford. Burroughs breezily considered this a temporary problem, but Wellcome became almost excessively cautious about expenditure, upbraiding his partner regularly for his prodigality with the firm's money without his authority, and often without consulting him at all. A serious dispute had arisen over the resale of the Mills from Burroughs to Burroughs Wellcome, coupled with his refusal to reduce the considerable amount he had in the firm on loan. Here, Burroughs was guilty of very sharp practice indeed, and it had taken until July 1892 for the property to be formally transferred to the firm. Then Burroughs refused to reduce his loan, which stood at over £13,000, and on which he was receiving five per cent interest, as he had been doing on his purchase of the Mills. He was, in short, getting a considerable additional income from the company, which then had to repay his loans in full. The fact that Burroughs was simultaneously writing articles, tracts and making speeches denouncing capitalism and the crime of private property made Wellcome's sense of injury and outrage even greater. But they remained locked in an indissoluble partnership, in which their fortunes were totally committed until 1895.

It was thus in the worst of atmospheres that negotiations for the future of the firm took place late in 1894. Burroughs began by claiming that as he held the larger interest the firm would be totally his on the expiration of the partnership. This was nonsense, but he then revived the idea of the joint stock company. His proposals were, however, studiously vague, but he and Wellcome at least agreed that each should nominate a friend to try to arrange a settlement. Burroughs chose a Liberal MP, C. S. Clark, who, significantly, shared his George-ite views on the Land Question, and who was also a qualified doctor; Wellcome chose his close friend Dr Chune Fletcher. There was only one meeting at which all four were present, on 13 December

1894, at the end of which Burroughs arbitrarily and unilaterally broke off the negotiations. Fletcher was trying to sort things out when Burroughs, suffering from a severe cold, abruptly departed for Monte Carlo for the benefit of sunshine, warmth and renewed vigour.

# 6

# Wellcome Alone

Both Wellcome and Burroughs were enthusiastic about physical fitness, but the latter was almost obsessive on the subject, and Wellcome's persistent ailments and illnesses had aroused his derision. An ardent bicyclist, Burroughs would arrive early at the Dartford Works, be active all day and then rapidly cycle home again to Surbiton; often, Burroughs would cycle from Dartford to Snow Hill, and thence back to Dartford. He seemed indefatigable.

But at the end of 1894 he found it difficult to shake off a persistent cold and bronchitis. His doctors advised a warmer climate, and Burroughs travelled to Monte Carlo, by himself, to stay with his sister, leaving his wife and daughters in London. He continued to ride his bicycle daily and caught a chill, which developed into pleurisy and then to pneumonia. On 6 February 1895, before his wife, urgently summoned, had arrived, Silas Mainville Burroughs was dead.

Wellcome faithfully observed the proper formalities on learning of Burroughs's death, but his public tributes were understandably muted. His attitude to his partner had become one of tense and suspicious exasperation and impatience rather than of hatred, but the private note of relief at his unexpected deliverance from a man whom he no longer either trusted or liked is very apparent, especially in his letters to his family, although he always recognised the more positive aspects of Burroughs's personality and his unique role in the establishment of the original firm. Wellcome now took steps to gain total control of it. This was to prove another embittering experience.

Wellcome received a considerable number of letters of sympathy, but several were realistic. George Wellcome's condolences were very similar to his brother's thoughts:

> That was a sad end for Mr B., but the Lord who has had the oversight of all the past only knows how those matters would have ended & now do not allow yourself to be overburdened & that you will keep yourself as fresh for your work as possible.

'I have just heard of Burroughs' death,' one friend wrote. 'I never spoke of him to you but I knew well how things stood & know how much freer this change has made you.' Another wrote in similar vein from New York that 'it will make matters more comfortable for you, at least I hope so'; this was also the theme of Wellcome's friend, Fred Hoffman, who wrote from New York that Burroughs's death 'has largely altered your position and, as your many friends here hope and trust, may tend to better and to strengthen your position and to secure and enhance your prosperity in London'.

Burroughs's widow, Olive, detested Wellcome deeply and was resolved to retain her husband's interest in the firm he had founded, which she now regarded as hers. Therefore, she and her advisers proposed – again – that it should become a limited liability company with Burroughs's dominant interest remaining. But Wellcome was now in a position to exercise his right to buy his partner's share of the business, and was determined to do so. He was absolutely within his rights, but Burroughs's executors and lawyers, urged on by his widow, challenged him vehemently and often insultingly, putting upon him pressure reminiscent of that of Burroughs himself. Wellcome once again resisted them strongly. 'The business will continue on the same lines as in the past,' he wrote to an enquirer in the trade, 'and the executive direction, which has always been in my hands, will continue the same and there will be no relaxation of zeal and energy. I regard our business as in its infancy.'

However, buying out Olive Burroughs's interests was prolonged, unpleasant and very expensive. The sum involved was calculated at precisely £113,099 15s 11d, the whole to be paid off in three years by six half-yearly payments. But Mrs Burroughs's executors fiercely contested this sum, demanded earlier payment, denied Wellcome access to the safe where the Phoenix Mills deeds were deposited, and refused to transfer to him Burroughs's interest in the firm's trademarks or his shares in Kepler. In response, Wellcome was obdurate. In September Olive Burroughs unwisely took legal action against him, and Wellcome responded successfully with a counter-claim for an Order to give him the sole ownership of the Mills and all the assets of the partnership.

It was a grim and unhappy affair, which Wellcome deeply resented. To add to his indignation he had to postpone planned visits to his very ill mother, to whom he wrote on 12 June 1896:

> My darling mother
>
> From what I have already written you you will understand something of the situation that compels my constant presence here. Not only the important changes made in my staff of employees by death and ill health – but what is more the fact that during the past year I have been constantly defending myself in contests with the executors of Mr B and in protecting my interests in law cases which I believe were incited from the same source – the success or failure of each of these meant very large sums of money and apparently the motive was to crush me out of existence. Perpetual vigilance, the utmost caution and every nerve of power has been required on my part to thwart the tricks which have been attempted. Two of the cases consisted in attempts to break large agency contracts which had great value to me and if broken might considerably reduce my income and render it more difficult for me to pay my liabilities to the executors – and naturally it would be profitable to the parties concerned to reap all the benefits of my firm's expenditures on these agencies. Step by step I won every point in each of these cases but almost daily new points come up that required to be met and disposed of. You will be rejoiced to learn that I have been completely victorious in both these cases; the second one was completed only a few days since not only by the parties concerned completely surrendering

to me but further still – in both cases new contracts have been made which are much more favourable to me than the old ones and the parties are now both on friendly terms with me – so instead of being crushed in these cases I have won everything I could have expected but also have gained great additional advantages.

He wrote again in July to report developments:

My contest with the executors is however still in progress and it has been a most wearisome affair – trick after trick has been resorted to but tho. I have won at every step they bob up again like a cork. The lawyers on the other side know they have no case but have counted on worrying me into some large sacrifice for the sake of peace. At the first I made the most liberal proposals possible and much beyond what was due them but they preferred to show fight and they have had a fruitless year of battle (except as regards the lawyers) and my position has gained in strength every moment for I have paid off the instalments even before they fell due and their chances of crushing me have lessened every day.

. . . it is gratifying to find that under my single-handed administration the business and profits have enormously increased and this too greatly aids me in my payments and in my contests.

. . . I have vast responsibilities – not only the responsibility on behalf of my own kin but also for the welfare of the hundreds of employees who range under my banner. Though I am very tired my health is and has been excellent.

In another letter dated 14 September he wrote:

My darling mother

Every plan I have made to get away to you has been thwarted by the emergencies that have come up week after week. Especially as regards the litigation with Mr B's executors – the final matters have come for hearing repeatedly and then they manage to get it put off and so adjournment after adjournment has taken place causing me the greatest possible inconvenience and naturally considerable anxiety also for fear they may succeed in some sharp trick, though as a matter of fact I have won every point up to now and believe that I shall continue to do so. My absence would give them many chances and be a great danger to all issues. I'm certain they cannot delay much longer and I don't believe the court will allow them. It is now quite positive that I cannot get away for some weeks but when I do go I shall be able to stay longer than if I had gone earlier – so this will be a sweet consolation to us.

George writes me of your great suffering and of your great bravery and trust in God. I do pray that the Heavenly Father may give you strength & ease your pains so you can sustain all this terrible ordeal and that you may be spared to greet me – so that as a happy little family circle we may live over again in our memories and interchange of thoughts the many joyous years gone by.

For many years I have been pulled down by worries and cares, now I am relieved of all real worries – I am fatigued but that is nothing & my health is better than it has been for years – and soon when I get clear of debt I can take life easier and devote myself more to the welfare of my fellow men.

All my business plans which I have carried out since I have been alone in business have proved successful in the highest degree and this enables me the sooner to free myself from debt and will the sooner enable me to put things so I can spend more time with you which is my most anxious thought. You know my darling mother I will hasten to you at the earliest possible moment. My thoughts are constantly centred in you and I pray that God may grant that we soon shall embrace.

With my whole heart's love, ever affectionately your son, Henry.

Wellcome's motives are clear enough; Mrs Burroughs's are less so, although vengeance was obviously not absent. If her object was additional money, she certainly succeeded, Wellcome eventually being compelled to pay her an additional £40,000* for the Phoenix Mills title deeds, as Burroughs's executors had found, no doubt to their delight, that Burroughs had had the only key to the deposit safe and, although the deeds had been signed by both partners and the Mills

* As Burroughs's Will was proved at over £125,000, Olive Burroughs was an immensely rich widow after the final settlement with Wellcome. This in no way reduced the intensity of her feelings against him.

were unquestionably a major asset of the partnership, they refused to release the key until Wellcome had agreed to their extortionate demands. But, in spite of paying Mrs Burroughs the enormous sum of nearly £140,000 in total, it was not until July 1898, after more unpleasant litigation and immense harsh correspondence, that Mrs Burroughs was forced to surrender all her husband's interests in the former partnership, and the shadow of Silas Burroughs was at long last removed from Wellcome's life. Neither his widow nor her daughters ever forgave him, and one took particular pleasure in writing to the company complaining of the poor quality of Wellcome products, as opposed to those in her father's lifetime.

*

If 1895 had brought relief in one respect, although with future problems, it also brought tragedy, and one that greatly affected Wellcome. On 4 October he wrote to his mother that,

> I am grieved to say I have just lost my Assistant General Manager – he met with a most serious accident by explosion of gas in his kitchen – was so terribly burned that he died in three days; he is not only a great business loss but I was deeply attached to him from his most beautiful and noble nature he had been with us for the fifteen years since the firm was founded and worked his way up from office boy to chief accountant – cashier and Asst Genl Manager. He was most loyal and true throughout all litigation and I held him in the highest estimation in every respect: his name was W. H. Kirby. I am sorry to say that my General Manager Mr R. F. Sudlow is in poor health so that the load is very heavy on me – but my health is better than it has been for ten years.

Wellcome felt Kirby's wholly unexpected and tragic death deeply. He had been with the firm from its early days, had been staunchly loyal to Wellcome, had become a close friend as well as an employee, and was a fellow-Mason. Wellcome took immense trouble over the funeral arrangements and ensured that Kirby's family was well provided for, as well as lavishly consoled and comforted. Their gratitude was substantial and moving. Wellcome, with much experience of the opposite, had come to value loyalty and friendship more than any other qualities, and the loss of Kirby at this time made him particularly melancholy.

His responsibilities weighed heavily upon him, as he wrote to his mother on 25 November:

> . . . More and more I realize the responsibilities upon me – those I care for and whose future welfare I have at heart and to whom I hope to be an aid, and most seriously too the welfare of the more than 400 people I employ and to whom my success or failure means their prosperity or otherwise. I feel that I have a life work of usefulness that with God's help I shall devote myself to and the fruits of my labour under his guidance will not be selfishly employed.

With Burroughs gone, Wellcome could take his ambitions further, and one was the establishment of his own chemical research laboratory to conduct pure research. And he knew exactly the person he wanted to take charge of it.

*

Wellcome had often lamented that he had not followed his early ambition to work with Frederick Power, and now, with almost indecent haste, within a week of Burroughs's death, he approached him again.

He had maintained close contact with Power, whom he admired and liked more than anyone else, and was devoted to his children, who called him 'Uncle Henry'. Power's career had reached a crisis in 1895. His period as the first Director of the Department of Pharmacy at the University of Wisconsin had been a triumph, but in 1892 he had accepted the offer of Scientific Director of Fritzsche Brothers, at Passiac, New Jersey. The move was a disaster. The Powers hated New Jersey and, after the warm friendliness of the Midwest, found the people of the East cold, selfish and bleak. Also, the transition from a benign academic world to the competitive commercial one did not suit Power's temperament. Within six months of leaving Wisconsin Power realised that he had made a terrible mistake. 'We do not yet feel at home here, and do not now anticipate that we ever shall,' he wrote to his friend and successor Edward Kremers. 'The atmosphere of scientific and literary culture is utterly wanting in a manufacturing town, and even those who are amply endowed with the material things of life seem to care for little else than the passing amusements of the hour.' He found that the facilities he was given made him 'disappointed and disheartened', and the local schools were 'antiquated in their methods and miserable'. In December 1892 he lamented that 'The condition of things does not improve with time, and is frequently almost intolerable.'

Kremers was anxious for him to return to Wisconsin, but Power, although grateful, considered that that chapter of his life had been closed.

> What my future here might be, and how circumstances might change in the course of years, it is of course impossible to prognosticate, but under present conditions, with no time for scientific reading or for independent scientific or literary work, and to be constantly, week after week, so completely isolated from all congenial companionship, tends to make me feel quite out of my proper sphere, and therefore decidedly miserable.

Then, in December 1894, after the birth of a son who lived for only a few days, his wife, Mary, also died, and Power was plunged into even deeper distress, with a young daughter and son to raise. His daughter, Louise, later wrote:

> He was the idol of my childhood, no dolls, no toys, no diversion of any kind could take the place of his Sunday afternoon stories to us children, and no event of the week so swelled me with pride (and I doubt not he shared in it) as when I walked by his side on my way to Sunday School, knowing that when I was brought home he would be watching to open the door in response to my privileged ring.

But this had been in Wisconsin. New Jersey provided, as Louise wrote, 'the most unhappy period of my father's entire life'.

The Powers' anguish was deepened by the complete indifference of their neighbours and Power's colleagues to their loss. 'I believe it was 10 days after our return from Hudson [for the funeral] before a soul came to us to speak a word of sympathy, except the pastor of our Church,' he informed Kremers, adding that his employer, Fritzsche,

> has written to me but once since we have been here, and that over 2 years ago, and also did not call at our home when he was here about a year and a half ago. . . . I am now more desirous than ever that we should get away from Passiac, where the cup of sorrow has been drained to the bitter dregs, and should be glad enough to get into an atmosphere where dollars and cents are not the ideal and inspiration of life. It is unfortunate that without money one can do so little, and there has perhaps never been so much destitution in the land even among the worthy.

Wellcome knew of Power's unhappiness with the Fritzsches and of his devastation at his wife's death. On 14 February 1895 he wrote to Power:

> Dear Fred
>
> On Wednesday last my partner Mr Burroughs died from pneumonia at Monte Carlo after only two or three days illness. I cannot express to you how deeply this sad event has pained me – a pain so greatly intensified by my thought of the unhappy relations that have existed between us during the past few years. I can only now, and want only now, to think of the time when we were close friends. But there is one great consolation to me, and that is, that during these years of strife I have never retaliated upon him nor said or done a thing to injure his name. To have done so while associated with him as partner would be but to foul the firm's good name, and more he had been my friend, and a 'friend' means a great deal to me.
>
> Now Fred by the rule of fates I have become the sole proprietor of this great business into which I have put my heart and the best years of my life. I feel even with the added responsibility in one sense, a wonderful relief from the strain of worry that has weighed me down so long.
>
> My first thought is to desire you to come to London. I feel that I

could aid you in your progress, and I know you can greatly aid me. What I suggest is that you come and let me fit up for you a most thorough and complete Experimental Laboratory near my Offices, and for the first year or two, or longer if you like, devote your time exclusively to my work – both scientific research and literary work – and if at any time any professional opening might offer [itself] you could accept if you like.

I want you for constant consultation as I propose to enter much more into scientific medical chemical products. Whatever you are receiving from your present firm I would pay you more, and Fred how dearly I would like to renew the companionship of twenty-one years ago. I would like it if we could live together and be chums again. You are the one I look to and I feel now that I could serve you. We have drifted apart [but] not in heart.

. . . Do write me as soon as possible and tell me all about yourself and if and when you could come: I would not desire you to, and I know you would not leave your present firm without fair notice. Even if engaged for a term perhaps they would release you. I should not ask you to take up any business cares of actual manufacturing drudgery but only experimental, and strictly scientific work etc. such as I know is most congenial to you.

Power has been described as 'the most distinguished investigator in the field of phytochemistry that this country [the United States] has produced'. For his examination of the resin of Podophyllum, his Philadelphia thesis, he had been awarded the Ebert Prize of the American Pharmaceutical Association in 1877, at the age of twenty-four. At Wisconsin he had concentrated upon investigations into essential oils and alkaloids, and other constituents of drug plants, which he continued at Passiac. His work on the oil of bay, which seemed at the time to be merely of scientific interest, later assumed great importance in the production of synthetic rubber – a classic example of how pure research can have quite unexpected consequences.

Power was a true scholar, manifestly ill at ease in a commercial context. What Wellcome offered him were the conditions, facilities and staff he required. The proposed Wellcome Chemical Research Laboratories would be entirely separate from the Dartford Works and its own research staff, and from the Physiological Laboratories. It was Wellcome's intention from the outset that they 'are not ordered in any narrow commercial spirit, and are engaged in many purely scientific enquiries that have no direct commercial significance'.

Nothing can demonstrate better the gulf of attitude that had existed between Burroughs and Wellcome. The latter believed in research for its own sake, recognised its complexities and disappointments, and had no illusions about its cost. But he also believed that if he could recruit the best people, the firm would not only acquire an increased status, but might also be able to make significant medical advances that could have a commercial application. However, the latter was not the priority.

The combination of Power's wife's death, his unhappiness with his work and Passiac itself, and Wellcome's urgings and promises gradually outweighed in Power's mind the domestic difficulties of moving to London. None the less, Power did not accept Wellcome's first offer, writing on 1 May 1895:

> Now, my dear Henry, I do not want you to feel that I am at all lacking in appreciation of your most kind and generous interest in my welfare, but I cannot begin to express to you my thanks for all your good and sympathetic heart prompts you to do. Were it not for the domestic affairs, and if I were alone, I should be glad enough to avail myself at once of the opportunity of travel or any diversion to relieve my burden of grief. Perhaps in the mutations of time there may be again some brighter days.

Wellcome hastened to emphasise that it was not only kindness in his friend's bereavement that had prompted the invitation, but also that he was serious about establishing a real scientific laboratory independent of the firm, and of which Power would be the head. Power began to weaken and agreed at least to discuss the prospects; by February 1896 he was writing to Wellcome to say that, 'guided by your wise judgement and kindly interest, everything may develop propitiously for a future career of success and usefulness. It is needless for me to say that in any course upon which we may decide my own best efforts will be joined with yours.' To his mother Wellcome wrote that 'I shall not only have the benefit of his valuable service but also of his pleasant companionship.'

It was one of Wellcome's greatest and most important personal and professional achievements, and was characteristic of his vision for his company – now that it was indeed his. He was a moderately wealthy man, and the company was prosperous and expanding, but he was singularly uninterested in material matters for himself. As he later remarked, when appointing another brilliant man, Henry Dale, he could have spent his money on fine houses or racehorses, but chose instead to spend it on scientific research. His rule was to be to find and appoint the best person; give him the equipment, budget and staff that he needed; and to leave him to get on with whatever line of research attracted him. He was always interested in the work of his laboratories, but he rarely interfered except when he had good reason, and was modest about his own qualifications. It was to prove a brilliant strategy, and one which also gave him the time to build up his own collections and medical library, and to travel. He was not only free from Burroughs, but from the daily grind of business. His horizons were opening.

Power's children went to stay with their aunt in Hudson and, in the early summer of 1896, Power sailed for London. On 21 July Wellcome gave a lavish dinner in his honour and, in introducing Power to a distinguished audience, publicly announced the establishment of the Wellcome Research Laboratories.*

They began, modestly, at 42 Snow Hill, and the first of a multitude of published papers – by Power's assistant, Dr Hooper Albert Dickinson Jowett – appeared in the *Journal of the Chemical Society* in 1897. Jowett had been chief assistant to Professor Wyndham Dunston at

* They were not titled the Wellcome Chemical Research Laboratories until May 1898.

the Pharmaceutical Society and had been engaged in alkaloid research at the Imperial Institute. In January 1898 another protégé of Dunston, Francis Howard Carr, took over the newly established Chemical Department at the Dartford Works. In April 1898 Dr S. B. Schryver joined Power's team, but was to return to academic life three years later, and eventually to become Professor of Biochemistry at Imperial College and a Fellow of the Royal Society. Power himself was to prove a prolific author of learned papers of exceptional quality and importance over the next eighteen years, and to establish the fame of the Wellcome Chemical Laboratories.

Power may well have been initially disconcerted when he discovered that, instead of conducting original research, he and Jowett were at first almost wholly preoccupied with production difficulties and quality control at the Dartford Works, and in 1897 Power wrote 292 letters and reports on these matters. Jowett was also closely involved in plans for a new plant to produce Malt Extract at Dartford. Then serious difficulties arose over the Chemical Department, its high cost and non-commercial attitude, ironically, particularly arousing Power's criticisms and inducing an incorrect analysis by the chief analyst that caused the company considerable embarrassment. But the Chemical Laboratories eventually assumed the role that Wellcome and Power had envisaged with a team of young scientists of high quality.

The personal bond between Wellcome and Power had always been strong, and Power had described him to his future wife in 1882 as 'one of my truest and most faithful friends'. Unlike Wellcome he disliked club life and was totally dedicated to his work. He lived a rather solitary existence in his apartment in Torrington Square, but, assisted by Wellcome, he made many friends and developed a very Wellcome-like love of travel, preferably with his children; he saw them in America every two years, and they came to Europe regularly for family holidays. Like Wellcome, and quite contrary to Wisconsin legend that he was teetotal, he enjoyed good wine and cigars, and aroused a devotion among his friends and colleagues that was quite exceptional. From every possible point of view it was a perfect association, Power once writing to his daughter that 'I desire above all to be loyal and true to Uncle Henry, who has done so much for me'.

*

Freed from the incubus of Burroughs, Wellcome now entered into the most active, remarkable, inspired and constructive period of his life. The Physiological and Chemical Laboratories were established in 1894 and 1896, and, as will be seen, the Wellcome Tropical Research Laboratories in Khartoum in 1902. In 1898 the Physiological Laboratories moved to Herne Hill. In 1899 he leased Acacia Hall at Dartford to establish the Wellcome Club and Institute, formally opened that year with characteristic publicity and style. The Hall had substantial grounds, which were laid out for sport, including cricket, football, tennis, boating and swimming. There was a club house, a library and a gymnasium, among other amenities. It was one of the few Wellcome projects of which Burroughs would have totally approved.

Then, in 1897 there appeared the first *Wellcome's Medical Diary and Visiting List Combined with Excerpta Therapeutica*, which replaced *The A.B.C. Medical Diary and Visiting List* published by Charles Letts & Co. and distributed by Burroughs Wellcome, but with no reference to the firm or its products. Wellcome bought a half interest, so that after 1892 it was a joint publication, but he remained dissatisfied at regularly missing such a valuable promotion aid. He rightly put great importance on the *Diary* becoming a widely respected publication in the profession, and took great trouble over the design, layout and style, as well as the contents. It is clear that this idea had germinated before the *A.B.C.* became a joint publication with Letts in 1892, but, as with so many of Wellcome's ideas, it is impossible to determine when it began. But, as in the case of the Laboratories, one can trace the thinking over a number of years, until he suddenly took action. He was often impulsive in moments of crisis – as in his offers of medical equipment in both the Spanish–American and South African Wars, and to virtually all serious expeditions – but the key decisions evolved over a significantly long time, unlike Burroughs's ideas, which hurtled out of his fertile mind and imagination virtually on the spur of the moment. The Wellcome *Diary* has been described as 'the firm's most famous publication'; it would be more correct to say that it was the most celebrated and admired one up to that point.

But Wellcome was also to have to endure one of the darkest and most worrying periods of his career.

The production of the diphtheria anti-toxin continued to cause considerable problems, and by the time the Physiological Laboratories had moved to Charlotte Street in the middle of 1896, Wellcome had become convinced that animal experimentation was essential, not only for this work, but also for expanding research on and testing of animal-derived and chemically manufactured drugs and preparations. This took Burroughs Wellcome into a new, and crucial, league. Also it possibly required the premises to be registered with the Home Office to comply with the 1876 Cruelty to Animals Act, but this was unclear.

This Act, like so many well-meaning pieces of legislation introduced by the intense political pressures of what was already a highly vocal and well-organised anti-vivisectionist campaign, was capable of a number of interpretations and posed questions not dreamed of in 1876. For example, did the raising of diphtheria anti-toxin from horses, which inflicted no pain or cruelty whatever, require registration? And did testing the serum come under the Act? To these queries there were precedents on both sides of the argument, as usually occurs with legislation that has become seriously out of date. In mid-1896 the Home Office ruled that the former did not require a licence, while the latter did. Thus, officialdom had come up with the remarkable solution that the raising of the serum could be done on unregistered premises, but that its subsequent testing on rodents – primarily guinea pigs – had to be done on registered premises by scientists and researchers each holding his own individual Home Office licence. In spite of the palpable contradictions of this, Wellcome made his application in June.

There was no precedent for a licence to be issued to a private laboratory and therefore, if it were granted to Burroughs Wellcome, other pharmaceutical companies would surely treat it, with good cause, as a precedent of major importance, a decision which would require the involvement of the then Home Secretary, Sir Matthew White Ridley, himself. Also, the discovery of anti-toxins and the necessity of testing them on rodents had presented the Home Office with a peculiarly sensitive problem with public and press opinion on the subject, with which any politician in Britain in the 1980s (when the 1876 Act was amended) will strongly sympathise.*

The Home Office Inspector, Dr Poore, visited the new Wellcome premises and was greatly impressed by them, 'being fitted, as perfectly as possible, for Bacteriological work'. He recommended that they should be registered, but also observed that, 'if the use of anti-toxins of various kinds should increase, it seems not improbable that every manufacturing chemist in the Country will want facilities equal to those accorded to Messrs B & W'. This, of course, was the snag, and the application was refused.

Foolishly, Bokenham considered that this was an insulting reflection upon his reputation and decided to fight the decision in a way that the officials justifiably considered 'ill-mannered'. 'In my earliest days of contact with the Home Office', he wrote loftily to Wellcome, 'it was carefully impressed upon me that a policy of civility did not altogether pay with them & that the best chance of obtaining any concession from the Department was afforded by claiming as a right what one wanted & NOT asking for it as a privilege!' Wellcome was not at all sure that this belligerent approach was the right one,

* By a most curious coincidence the author, when Member of Parliament for Cambridge, became closely involved in this complex matter, and had the strange experience of attending a meeting of his constituents at which he was the only person present who was not a Nobel prizewinner or a senior Fellow of the Royal Society! He invited them to submit a paper to the Secretary of State, William Whitelaw, and to be careful to have it signed personally by each of them. They did so, and the document caused a considerable stir when it was delivered to the Home Office. The subsequent amending legislation closely reflected the – of course confidential – advice of this awesomely august body.

and ordered that Chune Fletcher should be consulted at all stages.

At this point *The Lancet* published a specially commissioned report on the relative strengths of diphtheria anti-toxins produced by nine institutions, of which three were British, including Burroughs Wellcome. The findings were a deeply unpleasant shock to Wellcome. Burroughs Wellcome was claiming 600 anti-toxin units for each vial; the tested strength was from 45 to 300 units in the liquid serum and from 40 to 300 units in the dried serum. To make matters even worse, the quality of the anti-toxin produced by the European institutions, particularly the German ones, was of far higher quality. Curiously, in the resultant storm, which included questions in the House of Commons about the poor quality of the British pharmaceutical industry as opposed to the European, the severely inhibiting effects on research and testing of the 1876 Act were totally ignored, even by *The Lancet.*

Although Wellcome saw the point of this difference between the work easily possible on the Continent but severely constricted in Britain as a result of the Act, and the real fear imposed by the rabid anti-vivisectionists upon the medical profession and politicians, his alarm was the possible deep harm to the reputation of Burroughs Wellcome, who had in effect been accused and convicted of deceiving its customers. Bokenham then made matters considerably worse by writing imperiously to *The Lancet* to state that 'I *know* that the results obtained by your Commissioners are incorrect', and claiming that his experience and expertise were considerably greater. In publishing his letter, *The Lancet* justifiably called Bokenham's allegations 'preposterous' and called upon Burroughs Wellcome to place the matter 'on some more satisfactory footing'.

Wellcome entirely agreed. He had already sought the legal and scientific advice of a man whom he had come to regard very highly, Fletcher Moulton, who was not only a QC but had also been an MP until he had lost his South Hackney constituency in the general election the previous year (he was to be returned as Liberal MP for Launceston in 1898). Moulton was a youthful prodigy, whose law papers at Cambridge had achieved the highest marks ever awarded, and had become a QC at the age of forty-one.

Moulton was not only an outstanding lawyer, but also a mathematician and scientist of exceptional ability, having astonished the scientific world as a young man, in conjunction with the President of the Royal Society, Dr Spottiswoode, with a famous paper entitled 'The Sensitive State of Electrical Discharges through Rarefied Gases', which identified electrons in the mass as something distinct from rarefied gas, and described, under the title 'free electricity', some of the leading phenomena by which they may be recognised. They also gave a precise account of some X-ray tubes they had constructed, and with which they had experimented; the crucial importance of their work was later confirmed by the work on X-rays in Röntgen's laboratory. This extraordinary achievement was done while Moulton was a busy junior barrister, but his scientific work was so esteemed by the French that he was awarded the *Légion d'Honneur* before he was forty. Although his legal and political careers prevented him from continuing a career in science and medicine, he kept closely in touch with developments and in 1910 was to become the first Chairman of what was to develop into the Medical Research Council. Both Wellcome and Power admired him intensely – Wellcome primarily for his legal wisdom and advice, and Power for his exceptional scientific knowledge, Power writing of him after his death in 1921 that, 'had he devoted himself to the pursuit of science, he would assuredly have been one of its most brilliant exponents'. In November 1914 Kitchener was to ask him to take charge of the production of explosives; it was Moulton who persuaded the reluctant military to abandon TNT as its standard explosive and to replace it with Amatol. The production of explosives under Moulton's leadership rose from one ton a day to 1,000 tons a day. Also, his knowledge of the dye industry was unparalleled.

Although he received many honours, including a Fellowship of the Royal Society, Moulton was a noticeably modest and quiet man, and it was not surprising that Power especially found him a congenial and fascinating companion and friend. They had first met at the great banquet Wellcome had given to mark the beginning of his Chemical Laboratories in 1896, by which time Moulton had become a vital participant in the rise of Burroughs Wellcome. It was Chune Fletcher who had first drawn Wellcome's attention to this unquestionably rising legal and scientific star. Wellcome therefore retained Moulton to prepare a detailed and serious reply to the Commission's findings.

To achieve this he needed information about serum samples from Bokenham rather than intemperate public letters and private ones berating important Home Office officials, whose goodwill Burroughs Wellcome very much needed if it was to obtain its licence. But Bokenham had departed for a European tour, ostensibly to study foreign anti-toxin production. Wellcome was now so exasperated by him, and suspicious, that he demanded reports on his investigations. None seems to have materialised, and on Bokenham's return in August he was very reluctant to test any of the samples supplied by *The Lancet.* Indeed, as E. M. Tansey has noted, 'Bokenham performed, or admitted to performing, no testing experiments at all during 1896.'*

The situation was hopeless, and Wellcome cast around for someone else to unravel the matter. Fletcher came up with the name of Dr Alfred Kanthack, the thirty-three-year-old Director of the Pathological Department at St Bartholomew's Hospital. On 16 October he was approached directly by Fletcher, at Wellcome's request, to undertake the investigation. After some hesitation and consultation with his superiors, he agreed. On 3 December Wellcome wrote to Bokenham that '*I am determined* that the sources of error shall be discovered whether it be on the side of the *Lancet* or ourselves', and ordered him to give Kanthack the facilities 'for carrying the matter through on the lines indicated'. Wellcome had a high regard for *The Lancet*'s integrity and impartiality, and the evidence of the Commission's findings was compelling. The products of the European

* 'The Wellcome Physiological Research Laboratories 1894–1904: The Home Office, Pharmaceutical Firms and Animal Experiments', *Medical History*, vol. 33, 1989, p. 13.

companies had been subjected to exactly the same testing methods as those of Burroughs Wellcome, and were of a consistently higher strength and reliability. He did not want a controversy; he wanted to know what had gone wrong, and how the crisis could be resolved.

It was by now a genuine crisis, threatening not only Wellcome's much-vaunted new Physiological Laboratories, but also the entire reputation of Burroughs Wellcome. Months had elapsed since *The Lancet*'s devastating findings, and all that Bokenham had done had been to write his disdainful letters.

But worse was to come. On 21 December a letter was received from Dr J. W. Washbourn, a respected bacteriologist,* which came as a thunderbolt to Wellcome. It read:

> Dr Lucas of Burwell, Cambridge, sent me an unopened bottle of your Anti-diphtherial Serum today for examination. I am sorry to inform you that it is full of bacteria, and consequently unfit for use. I thought it wise to let you know at once because Dr Lucas has had two deaths from vomiting and diarrhoea occurring shortly after injection with Serum obtained from your firm.

The firm of Burroughs Wellcome had had difficulties and disappointments before, but this had particularly terrible potentialities. When Sudlow discovered that Washbourn was advising Lucas to publish these fatal cases, their alarm reached new levels. Bokenham was ordered to see Washbourn immediately, but, significantly, the offending sample was sent not to him but to Kanthack for analysis. Sudlow insisted that Bokenham send him a copy of his letter to Lucas before it was posted, suspecting that it would be contemptuous and personally offensive. It was. Sudlow wrote a more emollient one. Somehow, and somewhat mysteriously, Dr Lucas decided 'for many reasons' not to publish; Tansey has suggested that 'The reasons can only be conjectured, although the affair may have reflected badly on Lucas himself.' It would have reflected appallingly on Burroughs Wellcome.

* He was later Physician to Guy's Hospital, but was to die at the early age of thirty-nine in 1902.

By now Wellcome had had enough of the arrogant and incompetent Bokenham. Dr Walter Dowson was another of Wellcome's discoveries, working at the Department of Pathology at Cambridge as a bacteriologist, as was Louis Cobbett, who was recruited on a temporary basis to test the sera in the Cambridge laboratories; already, on Cobbett's advice, Wellcome saw Dowson as Bokenham's successor. Bokenham greeted the new recruits sourly, would not take the Cambridge tests seriously and refused to co-operate with Kanthack. He also refused to disclose any information about his own work to anyone. The only puzzle is why Wellcome waited until September 1897 to dismiss him, by which time Kanthack, Cobbett and Dowson had discovered how to produce anti-toxins free from contamination and of the necessary strength. In the meantime, some two years had been lost, and, thanks to Bokenham, the carefully built-up reputation of Burroughs Wellcome had nearly been imperilled as well.

Wellcome handled the matter courteously, regretting to Bokenham that 'the almost constant friction which has for a long time existed is incompatible with that cordial relationship essential to successful working, and I have no doubt I am acting in our mutual interest in asking you to place your resignation in my hands'. This letter was written on 29 September; Bokenham's successor, Dowson, would be announced on 2 October. But Wellcome also offered Bokenham six months' salary and assurances that his professional reputation would not be affected. In view of Bokenham's lamentable performance, this might be regarded as exceptionally generous treatment; but Wellcome was reluctant to admit to one of his few major mistakes.

However, Dowson's was a strange appointment in many respects. He had no qualifications whatever for the direction of research, being a doctor who had retired from the medical profession in middle age to take a course in pathology at Cambridge, when he was introduced to Wellcome. He was not remotely comparable to Hopkins in either intellect or experience or vision. As events were to demonstrate, he was technically incompetent and slapdash. But as one who knew him has written, 'he had an energetic and generous temperament, and was eager to create a true atmosphere of research for younger colleagues'. This he certainly did, and it was clearly this aspect of his rather turbulent character that appealed to Wellcome. Viewed in the short term, it was to be an unfortunate appointment; in the longer perspective, it was to prove inspired, because Dowson was to find, appoint and encourage some of the most talented young men in British medical science and research, who were to make the Wellcome Physiological Research Laboratories famous. Not especially talented himself, he proved to have a remarkable eye for talent in others.

When the problems of producing the diphtheria anti-toxin had, it was thought, at long last been resolved, the Physiological Laboratories quickly outgrew Charlotte Street, and even before Dowson took over as Director from Bokenham in October 1897 Wellcome had been looking for new premises. He found them at Brockwell Hall, in Herne Hill, in south London. He took a long lease on the property and oversaw its conversion, 'at very great expense, and no pains, labour, or money spared in rendering the equipment and appointments most complete'. When Dowson and his then small staff moved there by May 1899, they were described publicly as the Wellcome Physiological Research Laboratories and were opened to the inspection of professional journals and the profession itself, *The Chemist and Druggist* being particularly admiring of the experimental laboratories, incubation chambers and associated facilities, and not least the stables that accommodated fourteen horses.

Far more important was the fact that the Laboratories could employ more staff. Most remarkable were two boys recruited from Alleyn's School, A. T. Glenny and A. J. Ewins. Dowson had contacted the senior master, Harold Baker,* about employing school-leavers with a science background. Glenny was to remain with Wellcome for the whole of his working life and was one of the key personalities in modern immunology. Within a remarkably short time of joining the

* Baker was the chemistry teacher at Dulwich College, the 'parent' school of Alleyn's, whose headmaster he was to become in 1902.

Laboratories, he realised that the method of inoculating the horses with diphtheria toxin and bleeding them at irregular intervals was not only haphazard and unscientific, but also often meant that the horses were bled a long time after the highest anti-toxin titres had been reached. He accordingly introduced a simple system of records for each horse, with the result that the production of anti-toxin was greatly increased. His 'horse-cards' have survived. If this was all quite elementary, no one had thought of doing it before.

Ewins, like Glenny, was only seventeen when he joined Burroughs Wellcome, for whom he was to work with much distinction until 1914, when he joined the new Medical Research Committee (later Council) under Henry Dale.* In 1917 he joined May & Baker as its Director of Research, where his continued studies on the chemotherapy of infections resulted in Sulphapyridine, the astonishing M&B 693, the most potent anti-streptococcal agent yet discovered and produced. In 1943 it was to save Winston Churchill's life when he fell seriously ill with pneumonia; it was also to save countless others. At Burroughs Wellcome Ewins was to concentrate upon the distribution and action of acetylcholine, becoming head of the chemical division in 1909 at the age of twenty-seven. He was the joint discovery of Baker and Dowson, rather than of Wellcome personally, but Wellcome had instilled into Dowson his policy of looking for young talent and seeking the best advice possible. Glenny and Ewins were among the most talented that Burroughs Wellcome ever recruited.

*

Then, Wellcome was able to begin to fulfil another long-felt ambition: the assembly of a collection of books and artefacts relating to the history of medicine and pharmacy. He had always been a collector, although with no particular emphasis or theme until the early 1890s. Again, there is no precise moment when he decided to create a formal institution; he himself later said that although he had been fascinated

* See page 325.

by history, medical science, anthropology and archaeology since a boy, the idea of a specific museum only came gradually.

At first he collected artefacts important in the development of medical knowledge; then he added pictures, prints, manuscripts and books, including a number printed in the fifteenth century. Now that he had the means, it became a devouring passion. At the early stages it seems to have been almost entirely a personal search, principally in Britain, the United States and Europe, but even then he was buying instruments and documents on ancient medical practices through agents in Greece and Egypt. As he was virtually the only person in this particular field, it is doubtful whether his rapidly growing collection cost very much, although the sharper dealers began to hail his arrival with much pleasure. Although he did not publicly advertise until 1903, the nucleus – and it was already a very substantial one – was there long before then, stored either in his London home, at the Burroughs Wellcome offices at Snow Hill, or at Dartford.

But although he could now well afford to leave the daily workings of Burroughs Wellcome to the able men he had appointed, which gave him far more time for travelling and collecting, he was closely involved in the expansion of the company. In 1897 an Analytical Department was established at Dartford to test raw materials and to improve the quality of ingredients; to meet ever-increasing demand a new Tabloid Building was built and opened in 1900; a year later full electric power was introduced for the Works, and the Materia Medica Farm was planned and planted. Wellcome was one of the earliest enthusiasts of the fledgling motor-car, and in 1902 Burroughs Wellcome began to replace its horse-drawn vans with motor transport.

War was to become a convenient, and important, source for the development of Burroughs Wellcome. It gave medical supplies to the Americans in the Spanish-American war, but wisely did not advertise the fact. But the South African War, when it broke out in 1899, was an easier proposition. Lady Randolph Churchill, another fellow-American and the mother of Winston, set up a charity to equip a hospital ship, renamed the *Maine*, to be staffed entirely by Americans, and financed by Americans living in Britain. When Wellcome read of this, he at once offered to supply all the medical equipment, medicines and drugs required. He also designed an especially elaborate medical chest, admiringly described by *The Chemist and Druggist* as

> covered with Carthaginian cowhide tooled with allegorical designs representing Britain and America united in aid of the wounded. Portraits of Washington, Queen Victoria, President McKinley, as well as of Lady Randolph Churchill and other members of the Committee were also included. The Union Jack, the Stars and Stripes, a representation of the hospital ship itself, Britannia and Columbia supporting a banner of the Red Cross, as well as representative units of the British Army were also depicted in the design.

When the City of London Imperial Volunteers sailed for South Africa, they took with them medical supplies also presented by Wellcome. These fine and patriotic gestures were, unsurprisingly, very well publicised.

Less well so was the scandalous way in which they were used by the British medical corps, which contributed to the appalling fact that out of the 22,000 British troops who perished in the war, 16,000 died from disease. The Royal Army Medical Corps was not only incompetent, but also venal. Bertrand Stewart, the son of Wellcome's solicitor and friend Charles Stewart, went to the war with the Royal West Kent Yeomanry, taking with him on Wellcome's advice two telescopic sights, which Wellcome had found of remarkable value for long-range shooting. But Stewart soon became disillusioned and reported back to Wellcome that,

> with regard to medical matters, I'm delighted to hear a Committee has been appointed to come out here & enquire about it. From what I hear the supply of drugs etc. in the country has been quite sufficient but that often they have not been transported to the places where they were required. The complaints of the men are more directed against the treatment which they receive from many RAMC & the hospital orderlies – many of the former they say give them very insufficient attention

> when they are sick & many of the latter the most scanty attention when they are in hospital besides using comforts for the sick for themselves. I myself was asked the other evening to a hospital orderlies supper at which there would be brandy & fiz etc. – it was not procurable in any other way. I refused but someone else no doubt went – & so the game goes on.

On his return to England in January 1901 Stewart wrote Wellcome a very long letter about his experiences, in which praise for his commanding officers, the RAMC and the conduct of the war was notably absent. He added that the

> complaints about food amounts – as I think I've told you before – 'we don't complain about what we can't get – but about what we ought to get & don't get'. A general can't always give his men full or nearly full rations – but when we are very short we do complain that the Quartermaster Sergeants & men on the waggons & the Army Service are on full – a portion of which is what they keep back of our rations – & many officers are far too much occupied in looking after their own food to bother about such matters. With all due deference to them I doubt if an officer in the VIIIth division main body was really hungry – whereas the men & particularly the infantry were for days together. We don't grudge the officers theirs – they are quite right to do themselves well if they can – but the men expect them to look after their rights more than many of them do.
>
> My saddle medicine case was most useful more for doctoring than surgery – but one day one of the men was badly wounded in the thigh & no surgeon was out, so a qualified man in the ranks dressed him & bandaged him with my case – the poor devil would have had a baddish time without your case. Your big flat tin case was also most useful as a store case which I carried on the waggon & doctored numerous cases in camp every week & replenished the saddle case. If there was one bright star in the muggy atmosphere of indifferent medical arrangements in several moving & stationery hospitals & indifferent medicals & robbing hospital orderlies – it was THE TABLOID. The hospital question has no doubt been well thrashed out – & there have been many excellent arrangements – but tho' most of the good will have been brought

> forward, much of the bad is of necessity kept back – many men never had the chance of speaking or others who had didn't do so for fear of the consequences. I am not sufficiently informed to propose remedies – but many of the RAMC & orderlies at all events require a far closer supervision by the PMO of the hospital or brigade as the case may be.

Wellcome drew these shocking facts to the attention of his medical and other friends in London, and Stewart, on his return, was to add further information about the way the RAMC sold drugs intended for the soldiers. The only positive aspect was that the quality of the Burroughs Wellcome 'Tabloids' had become recognised, and inspired Wellcome in 1902 to establish a permanent depot and agency in Cape Town.

Also looking abroad, Wellcome opened a depot in Milan in 1905 and a Canadian branch in Montreal in 1906. He then decided on the move, in 1906, of the firm's Australian branch, from Melbourne to Sydney, including the building of a complete new Works.

This was the fulfilment of Burroughs's original dream of making the firm one of the world's greatest drug companies, but his ambitions of 1881–4 had been premature, as the firm was in no position then, either financially or in its products, to enter world markets except through the British Imperial and military routes, which it had done successfully. Now was the time for further advance.

Wellcome planned this development personally, even involving himself in the details of the location of the new Sydney office and the building of the Australian Works, sending out Pearson to supervise the construction and to ensure that the hard-won experience at Wandsworth and Dartford was put into good effect. In spite of their small populations, Australia and New Zealand had proved to be good markets; with his eye on the future, Wellcome was convinced that they would become even better, which they proved to be.

*

If the establishment of the new Laboratories, and especially the arrival of Power, heralded a more sophisticated scholarly aspect to Burroughs

Wellcome, former methods were still employed. Some of what would now be described as 'gimmicks', in which Wellcome the showman specialised, were distinctly odd. In 1896 the annual conference of the BMA was to be held in Carlisle, and, as usual, Wellcome was determined that the Burroughs Wellcome exhibit would be the main attraction. He devised the idea of illustrating the principal sources of 'Lanolin' and 'Kepler' products by having on the Burroughs Wellcome stand a live sheep and a live cod. A. W. Haggis's deadpan account merits inclusion:

> There was no difficulty concerning the former [the sheep] but transporting cod alive in a tank was no easy problem. Mr George E. Pearson, then the firm's West End representative, was sent to Grimsby to obtain live cod and if possible transport them to Carlisle in time for the exhibition. Attempts had already been made by Grimsby merchants to send live cod to the Fisheries Exhibition in London, but although only about half the distance from Grimsby to Carlisle their effort had proved a failure. Getting the live cod was not a difficulty, but to possess any chance of keeping them alive Pearson had to charter a special tug to take him twenty miles out to sea to get water of the proper density. Six live cod were placed in a tank 6 feet by 4 feet and a special wagon hired from the Railway Company to take them by train to Carlisle via Manchester. Notwithstanding continuous pumping of air into the tank throughout the long and tiresome journey, one fish expired at Manchester and another between Manchester and Carlisle. However four fish arrived safely at Carlisle and were exhibited at the British Medical Association where they created considerable interest. Wellcome was particularly pleased with that achievement.

The establishment of the Physiological and Chemical Laboratories were formidable achievements, and particularly securing Power, but in his struggles against Burroughs and then his widow, Wellcome had not only suffered, but had also lost something.

A fact that is often neglected, not only by biographers, is that people *do* change, and that one cause can be success. This sometimes leads to arrogance and over-confidence. Success can make people happier and nicer than they were on the way up, or more selfish and grasping. It can also kill the creative energy that made the success, and can ultimately be as corrosive as failure.

Before he was forty-five years old Henry Wellcome had achieved all his early goals. He was now the sole owner of an expanding and esteemed company, and was a well-known personality socially as well as professionally. With Burroughs gone he could mould his company as he wished, and particularly fulfil his ambition for it to become a major research exploratory force. He was now personally rich and could indulge himself in whatever pleasures he desired. But one certainly does not gain the impression that he was a happy man.

He had become colder, lonelier and more acutely sensitive, and one can suddenly detect even at this stage the beginnings of that reclusive, almost secretive, last phase of his life.

His religious affiliations had also become vague. Power's daughter Louise thought that he was a Methodist, but there is little evidence for this. There are suspiciously few references in his personal letters, even to his mother, to church attendance or his earlier enjoyment of sermons. He was considered by his friends to take an increasingly relaxed view of the virtues of religion, and his early scepticism about Adventism, and his belief that 'God only helps those who help themselves', look increasingly significant.

One apparently puzzling, but important, sign was his neglect of his mother. He was her favourite son and she had supported him devotedly through all vicissitudes, and yet he only visited her once after 1886, even when it was obvious after 1891 that she was seriously ill. He financed her generously, as he did his brother and his family, and wrote fairly regularly, although in their view not regularly enough. He thought that he did all that a grateful and loving son and brother could do – except to put business and pleasure aside and visit them, which he could have done. He had time for the English social season, with Henley and Cowes prominent; he went cruising with friends in hired yachts; he always had time for travel and for increasing his already serious collection of medical books and artefacts; but he never seemed to have the time to go to South Bend, Indiana, where she was now living with George and his family, a journey of some ten days from London. When his mother died in 1897, he did not even attend her funeral. His subsequent ambition to build a mausoleum for his parents in Garden City may be seen as evidence of a certain, and justified, guilt; and he was later to fall out badly with George.

It was not until June 1893 that Wellcome went to the United States to visit his mother again. Apart from visits to the Chicago Exhibition and some business trips, he remained with her until 10 November. He wrote to Uncle Jacob that 'Mother I find more comfortable than I expected, but I fear that the case is grave and developing rapidly.' To one of his staff, Mr Searl, at Dartford he wrote that 'unfortunately nothing can avert the fatal end, which must come soon'. When he had to leave her, he was convinced that she was 'very rapidly drifting to the sad end, but with peaceful trust in Our Master the Most High'.

But her ordeal was to be prolonged for another four years, in the course of which Wellcome never visited her; nor was he to see her again, although he wrote to George that 'I shall come to you at once in case of any serious emergency', and provided the funds for her to receive the best medical treatment and nursing.

It would indeed have been difficult in the fraught period of 1894–5 for Wellcome to have left England, but after Burroughs's death, for all the problems with his widow, the pressures upon Wellcome were far less. But he did not make the journey to Indiana. Nor was he seriously deceived by the reports from her and George of her miraculous cure; as George eventually wrote sombrely, 'She has cancer most decidedly, and it is now growing and deepening.'

Wellcome's conduct is difficult to understand, unless one accepts that certain less attractive aspects of his personality, especially his self-absorption, which had always been present, now began to dominate. It is a melancholy story, of deep sadness, that does Wellcome little credit, but has its importance.

As has been recorded, it was in December 1890 that Mary Wellcome had told her younger son that she had noticed a lump in her right breast. Wellcome did not, perhaps would not, accept that her lump was cancerous. Indeed, writing a year later, all seemed to be well, as she reported joyously on 2 July:

> Henry My Dear Son it is with a light heart and with praise to the Lord that I take my pen to tell you what the Lord has done for me. I know George has written to you the particulars of the rapid growth of my cancer and that we had gone to Chicago for treatment and stopped that night with brother Nelson's folks old friends of ours. The next day instead of going to the Dr I went to a meeting that was conducted by Rev. J. A. Dowie called Divine Healing through faith in Jesus, and I presented myself as a subject for prayer. I then had a talk with him, and he laid his hands on the cancer & prayed. Immediately the pain left it, the inflammation ceased and one forth [sic] diminished in size & received strength that I had not had for weeks and have kept improving and I feel as well as I have for months. We came home yesterday.

George wrote that 'we went prepared for an operation one done cutting altogether and the other used plasters which would be longer and surer work but when we got there we found a better and safer way as I have written to you'.

On 11 December Mary Wellcome wrote:

> Dear Henry
>
> It has been some time since we have heard from you and have been looking for you this fall you spoke in your last letter as if you should visit us this fall. I have been very careless myself in not writing before this my health has been very good since I wrote to you with the exception of an attack of the flu in the summer there still remains a lump in my breast but it does not trouble me it is not more than one third of the size that it was last spring. We are all well with the exception of colds we are very comfortably situated and George will stay another year the children both go to school they are both very anxious to see you as well as the rest of us we had a letter from the Dr yesterday saying that he had not heard from you for two months and wants to come and see us all when you visit us we are expecting every day to hear from you hope we shall and hear that you are coming. If you have not started write us

soon as you get this and not fail for we are very anxious to hear from you if we cant see you it is too bad that you should be so afflicted & tried by one that you had esteemed as a friend but trust in the Lord my Dear boy you know his watchful eye is over all and while you can trust your Heavenly Father, he has nothing but this world to trust and he will have to leave it all and what will his reward be in the future keep up good courage and come and see as soon as you can, and remember you have our prayers from Mother down to Ethel that the Lord will bless you bring you home once more now good bye for the present much love from us all your own dear Mother Mary C Wellcome.

George wrote to his brother that 'Instead [of] employing any Doctor at all we went to the Great Physician & I believe he had done a safer & quicker job than any skilled man in the world. All Glory & Praise to Jesus of Nazareth.' But the reports from George grew steadily more ominous, and he wrote on 9 October 1896:

My dear brother Henry

. . . we daily think of your perpetual trial with those opponents but we trust as God has so far sustained you he will see you safely through as long as you *honor Him*. Never lose sight of that.

Mother has enjoyed a large degree of comfort the last two weeks but this afternoon she is taken suddenly worse with stomach & bowels. It may not prove so bad as before I have felt quite encouraged that she would rally up & be much better now that the weather is cooler, but there is no certainty in the case she may drop away very suddenly & she may linger for months yet. God grant she may get better & live long, the dear old mother.

We have had much expense this summer & fall although we have tried to economise all we could but we are again short & if you are fixed so you can I would like some more help. I do dislike to call on you like this especially when you are having such a struggle, but I can do nothing to bring income.

. . . Your letters are a good tonic for Mother. I wish you could write her oftener. Good night. Your aff brother George.

Henry immediately sent $250 to George and wrote rather 'oftener' to his mother, but not conspicuously so.

There had been some last flickers of hope, but the indications from George's letters were clear enough. For example, George wrote on 19 December 1896:

> My dear Brother Henry
>
> I write now to tell you of a lady who professes to be able to remove cancers. She does it by plaster & poltice. This lady does all the nursing of the case until it comes out & if successful asks $50 when well, nothing before . . . it will take from 14 to 18 days for the cancer to come out or about a month to do it up clean but we shall wait to hear from you first. Mother thinks she cannot suffer much more in the treatment than she has [had] to at times without it. Your aff brother Geo.

But, still, Wellcome had not gone to see her. Instead, in the late summer of 1896 he had been sailing for a month, with unfortunate results, in the English Channel.*

Wellcome was in New York for business discussions early in 1897, but there is no record that he visited his mother. Indeed, from the absence of any reference in his letters and in those of Mary Wellcome and George to the fact, one can only conclude that he did not. The only surviving documentary evidence of this visit is his insurance claim, when, on the return voyage in the White Star liner *Majestic* from New York to Liverpool, 'I was walking the deck at noon when a heavy sea struck the ship – the lurch of the ship threw me down, & bruised & strained my right leg and cut my right arm.' He was, he attested strongly, 'perfectly sober when the Accident occurred', and that as a result he had been confined to his room for weeks after his return to London at the First Avenue Hotel in High Holborn, able to conduct business 'only partially & when brought to my room'.

* See page 229.

His compensation fee on his policy was for £27, to cover his medical costs.

On 19 September 1897, in South Bend, Indiana, where she had lived for five years, Mary Wellcome died. In the words of a friend, 'with humble and trusting submission she rested, like a sick child, in the confidence and trust of her dear children, always grateful and appreciative for what was done for her, patiently suffering'. George wrote to Henry:

> Our darling mother fell asleep this morning at 1.05 after 18 hours of terrible suffering. Her circulation was so bad that Morphine could not be used – she breathed out her life into a sweet peaceful sleep and while we have lost that loving sympathising mother whose care was unceasing, for a little season I was glad for her after witnessing her agonies these years, to see her at rest, but O how I shall miss her.

His brother cabled: 'Blessed rest. God will comfort.'

Not long before she died Mary Wellcome wrote Henry her last letter to him:

> My dear Henry
>
> As George has been writing I thought I would try and see what I could do at it and I will try and wish you a happy greeting. Your mother likes you better than she can write, and would be glad to see you and hope I may some time but some time think my time has come and I must go. Your Mother.

*

As his personal prosperity increased, Wellcome was able to pursue his love of sailing, which had come to him rather later in life than is usual. He developed the habit of a regular early autumn cruise with Charles Stewart, and his son Bertrand, to the islands off Western Scotland; and he delighted in the empty and romantic Norfolk Broads, then almost unknown as a sailing and wildlife paradise. But he rose to more expensive ostentation. He became a member of the Royal London Yacht Club at Cowes, and would charter large yachts, with crew, and invite friends to cruise with him.

In the summer of 1896 he chartered the yacht *Madge* from the esteemed Herbert Blake of Southampton. The weather was bad and *Madge* turned out to be seriously unsatisfactory; at the first serious puff of wind the main shrouds gave way and *Madge* had to retreat to port for repairs. Then the gaff broke and Wellcome had to abandon his plans for crossing to France. Wellcome was incensed, writing angrily to Blake:

> You have certainly assumed a very grave responsibility in sending out a yacht in such a dangerously unseaworthy condition – jeopardizing the lives of all on board. As to the *builder* and *Lloyds Agent* who surveyed her – Keel hauling would be much too light a punishment for them, even though luckily no lives were lost.

Blake was equally angry at these 'libellous' charges against 'this new first-class yacht'. Wellcome refused to pay for the work he had ordered, claiming that 'the yacht was returned to you in better condition than when it went out', and reserved the right to sue for damages and report Blake to the Board of Trade, 'with a view to rendering it impossible for ship-builders and ship-agents to hazard the lives of yachtsmen and sailors', as was the case with the *Madge*. Blake denied all Wellcome's claims, but agreed to a private settlement. The sums involved were small, but Wellcome said that it was not a matter of money but 'one of principle, and one involving a duty to the public'.

This was a good example of Wellcome's increasing tendency, when causing trouble, to raise himself to lofty issues of principle and pursue quite trivial matters with an almost obsessive passion. It is clear that he and his guests had had an unpleasant experience in an ill-found boat, but the intensity of the aftermath was now characteristic. Blake indignantly brought the matter to an end, writing that he was 'much surprised at receiving such a letter from *you*', thereby finding himself in the same company as others who had crossed this charming American in his mid-forties.

Another instance of how prickly and difficult Wellcome had become also occurred in 1896, when he was Chairman of the American Society. It was decided, on his initiative, that the Society should especially honour Thomas F. Bayard on his retirement as the first United States Ambassador to Britain. There would be a lavish dinner in his honour with British and American celebrities, and Wellcome also proposed the gift of a loving cup wrought in gold, on a silver base, surmounted by a bust of Bayard. The design was by Wellcome himself, over which he took his customary care and imagination. The grand dinner was held at the Hotel Cecil on 26 November, with Wellcome in the chair, but, embarrassingly, with the guest of honour notably absent, as he had been commanded to dine with the Queen at Windsor. Wellcome had also commissioned a large, leather-bound volume of nearly 150 pages for each of the 300 guests containing the menu and programme, and histories of Anglo-American relations and Thanksgiving Day. It was generally agreed to have been a splendid banquet, in spite of the fact that Bayard was not there; the food and wines were excellent, the speeches were admirably appropriate, and the Chairman, Wellcome, was in particularly fine form.

In fact, Wellcome was locked in an unseemly quarrel with other members of the committee of the Society over payment for the loving cup. He had guaranteed the cost of the cup, £2,000, but donations considerably exceeded this and his guarantee was not required. At first it appeared that everything had gone well, but Wellcome then took umbrage at what he thought was an allegation that he had kept the surplus for himself, when he certainly had not. Again, it became 'a matter of principle and honour', and he fiercely demanded apologies. The other members of the committee wrote to deny totally that any of them had even thought of such a charge, let alone made it, but Wellcome pursued the matter relentlessly to the understandable amazement of his friends. The correspondence on the almost laughable Bayard Cup Affair reached absurd dimensions, until Wellcome imperiously resigned as Chairman, and thereafter took little part in the affairs of the American Society. It was as ridiculous as the mini-tempest over the *Madge*.* and dismayed his friends, who, like Mr Blake, had had no previous experience of Wellcome's excessive zeal to protect his reputation, which, in so doing, actually damaged it.

However, one fact that had been underrated, indeed hardly appreciated except by those who knew him best, was Wellcome's consistent ill-health since the crisis of 1885–6. His energy was so remarkable, his intellectual and physical powers so formidable, and his achievements after Burroughs's death so dramatic, that only very few realised that he was a sick man. His own concerns about his health had made others than Burroughs consider him a hypochondriac, unnecessarily troubled about his ailments, and put down his variable moods to non-medical causes.

There is a particularly sad irony in the fact that Wellcome was the victim of a series of disastrously wrong diagnoses by the most eminent physicians. It was not until the spring of 1898 that the real cause of his chronic, if intermittent, illnesses was at last discovered.

Deeply unwell and miserable again, on the advice of Chune Fletcher he sailed to Madeira for rest and sunshine, the virtually invariable Fletcher recipe, but his old internal problems continued. Fletcher once again diagnosed 'catarrh of the bowels' and stress from overwork, too much strain and travelling. When the agonising discomfort continued, Wellcome went to a local doctor in Madeira, M. C. Grabham, who treated him for 'catarrh of the bowels' as Fletcher had advised. But he felt no better, and the voyage home was acutely painful and unpleasant. Immediately on his return to London he went straight to Fletcher, who was puzzled why his patient had not responded to his treatment. He belatedly decided on further examination, which revealed two menacingly large bowel ulcers. The resultant emergency

* Wellcome's ill-fortune with his boats seems to have been chronic. On 10 June 1903 he wrote to John Harvey of Littlehampton, Sussex: 'Referring to the injury to my sailing craft caused by the bull, perhaps the best way for the butcher to adjust this matter will be for him to take the boat off my hands for a fair price. I would be quite willing to leave it to you to say what that should be, or perhaps he will make me an offer.' Research has failed to reveal the circumstances under which Wellcome's boat was attacked and damaged by a bull.

operation was entirely successful, but it was remarkably unfortunate that Wellcome's mysterious illnesses had not been diagnosed much earlier. In his relief, Wellcome blamed neither his friend nor Grabham, and was thankful at the prospect of returning to full health. His biographer can only remark on this professional ineptitude.

*

The increase in Burroughs Wellcome's business was reflected in its workforce: in June 1897 the total number of employees at Dartford was 349, with a relatively small Snow Hill staff; by April 1899 the total number of employees was 769, and this did not include travellers, agents or the Australian staff. An interesting aspect was the preponderance of women at Dartford, and an internal memorandum of January 1905 states that,

> We have clearly demonstrated that male labour saves us from 40% to 50% in packing, although the workers cost 25% more in wages. At the same time female labour is much quicker and cheaper for folding, insetting, collating, etc., and a case has been made out for joint male and female labour for the future.

The average wages seem startlingly low to modern eyes, but were considered above average in the context of the time, when an annual salary of £23 per annum for a lady's maid was regarded as generous. Also, the Dartford employees in particular worked under almost ideal conditions, and visitors were impressed by the skill with which the derelict land and stagnant water had been transformed by clearing out the pond and turning it into a freshwater lake, complete with artificial islands; trees had been planted, ornamental shrubs abounded and tennis courts laid. Sam Fairchild, admittedly biased because of his close friendship with Wellcome, called it 'a triumph of American ways of doing business' and particularly admired what had been done at Dartford: the creation of a factory 'in the form of a garden'.

Until his marriage Wellcome never had anything resembling a home; he lived in either rented houses, apartments or hotels. By 1896 he was installed in a somewhat grand apartment in Suffolk Place,

Thanksgiving Day banquet in London, 1896

Pall Mall, with balconies that were put to good use by him on Queen Victoria's Diamond Jubilee on 22 June 1897, when he invited friends and, principally, Burroughs Wellcome staff and their families. He also bought a considerable number of copies of *Sixty Years of the Queen's Reign*, a notably lavishly produced, glowing tribute, and sent most of them to friends and associates in the United States, Australia, Canada and South Africa as well as in Britain. So strong was his commitment to Britain and almost everything English that it puzzled his British friends that he had not followed Burroughs's example of taking British nationality; the reason was probably that he had no wish to follow his former partner's example in anything. His American accent had almost disappeared, and there were many, including his own employees, who thought that he was British. However, there is evidence that, for all his appreciation and enjoyment of British institutions, entertainment and the country, there remained an ambivalence.

In November 1899 a young American admirer, whose parents knew Wellcome, wrote to ask him for advice. Wellcome answered:

> In reply to your request for advice, I shall be very pleased if I can say anything that will be useful to you.
>
> What I shall say will consist merely of hints and suggestions, for I make it a rule of life never to take the responsibility of advising anyone to do anything, for the reason that people are often inclined to be blindly governed by the judgment of others, who may know little of the premises.
>
> Success in life may often be assisted by the counsel of friends, but every individual who has a well-balanced mind should use that mind to decide for himself, after gleaning information and opinions from others. . . .
>
> But locality is only incidental. The success or failure of any man lies more in his own personal qualities than in the accident of location. Integrity and the strictest sense of honour and good conduct form an essential corner stone to a career; then, qualifications suited to the business or profession chosen as a life occupation; then energy, singleness of purpose and devotion to the chosen calling are requisite. Few men can hope to succeed in these days of active competition unless they be willing to sacrifice convenience and pursue their calling with real earnestness. A thorough education is most important, but if one has not had full advantages, or if they have been neglected, it is important that he should educate himself by reading and studying such works as will best strengthen him in his occupation.
>
> America today, of any country in the world, undoubtedly opens the finest field for young men. . . .

His feelings towards America led him to make another contribution to Anglo-American relations, which ended more happily than the Bayard Cup Affair.

One is never quite sure, particularly at this turbulent stage of Wellcome's life, what his motives were. He was so much a self-publicist that some of his most generous gestures could be, and often were, misinterpreted by his critics. A good example is the Pocohantas portrait.

The story of Pocahontas certainly appealed to Wellcome's romantic nature, and to his strong feelings for the American Indians, a subject on which his sincerity was intense and totally genuine. He had learned the Pocahontas story as a child in Garden City,* and its Anglo-American aspects also attracted him. It was, accordingly, understandable that in 1891 he bought an excellent copy of the portrait of her by Simon de Passe that was painted in 1616 and hung at Booton Hall in Norfolk, the former house of the Rolfe family. It was characteristic, also, that Wellcome exhibited it prominently at the 1893 Chicago World Fair, where Burroughs Wellcome as usual had one of its striking exhibits. What is not clear is why he then decided to present it to the United States Senate. There was a subtle mixture of motives – a romantic feeling for the first American Indian to come to England and to die there, his desire to strengthen Anglo-American ties and his pleasure in making flamboyant gestures; but the realisation that this would also bring considerable publicity could not have been altogether absent.

However, it turned out not to be simple to present a portrait to the Senate. Wellcome thought that all he had to do was to bring it over with him to Washington, where it would be gratefully and prominently received, and his generosity applauded. He was quickly disabused. Senator Daniel from Virginia, Pocahontas's home State, had to be persuaded. The Vice-President, as President of the Senate, had to give his consent. And then the Committee on the Library had to be convinced that it was a genuine work of art that was appropriate for the Senate. These processes were tortuous and prolonged, involved

* When Captain John Smith, leader of the early colonists of Virginia, was captured by the Indians, he was condemned to death. He was about to be executed when the beautiful young Pocahontas threw herself upon him and begged for his life. Her wish was granted; she herself was subsequently taken prisoner and married Captain John Rolfe, who took her to England, where she was a sensation. She was presented at Court and was the object not only of intense curiosity, but also of admiration. Sadly, she found the English climate unbearable, and was returning to Virginia when she fell ill and died at Gravesend on 29 March 1617.

a startlingly voluminous correspondence and visits to Washington, and tried Wellcome sorely until all the authorities had given their approval; that inevitable hazard of democracy, elections, had not helped, as in the six years it took for the Senate to accept the gift, key figures had retired from the scene, whether voluntarily or otherwise. But all was eventually resolved, and Wellcome's great day came on 28 February 1899, when he formally presented the portrait to the Senate.

Senator Daniel, in the best traditions of Senators from Virginia, made a flowery speech, declaring that

> The charm of romance will ever hang over the story of Pocahontas; and that flower of the wilderness will ever shed its brightness and its fragrance over the rude, sombre and cruel scenes of our people's earliest struggle to get a foothold in the land whose inhabitants are as the stars of heaven, the leaves of the trees, and the sands of the sea.

Senator Cullom, who had become a personal friend of Wellcome's during the protracted negotiations, more prosaically extolled Wellcome as 'a gentleman of the very highest character, of a very generous and kindly nature, and one who has taken a very large interest in the welfare of the Indian race in the United States'. Senator Hansbrough, the Chairman of the Committee on the Library, formally accepted what had now been, at long last, agreed to be 'a genuine work of art'. The Senate then unanimously approved the Resolution authorising the Committee to accept the portrait.

It was one of the happiest days in Wellcome's life up to that time. The charm of the episode lies in the fact that, whatever Wellcome's motives may have been – part sentimental, part calculating – he achieved all his purposes. The United States Senate and the Washington press rang with his praises; expressions of gratitude were universal; he was a Washington celebrity; and his portrait had found the best of homes. It was a triumph, and one which, in his quiet way, he understandably relished.

Wellcome also had difficulties with another of his ambitious Anglo-

American ventures. In 1898 he proposed presenting to the Grand Lodge of England a life-size portrait of George Washington in Masonic clothing, to mark the centenary of his death in 1899, 'to serve as a constant reminder of the tie of blood, as well as of the tie of Masonic brotherhood which binds together the peoples of America and the Motherland'. The offer was accepted, but then the difficulties began.

Wellcome commissioned his friend Robert Gordon Hardie, a distinguished American portrait painter of the day, but the only original of Washington in Masonic dress was considered not only a poor likeness, but also of dubious authenticity. Wellcome then asked Hardie to paint an original portrait based on the best in existence. Hardie was told that there was another portrait of Washington hanging in Alexandria, Virginia, in Masonic dress, but this turned out not to be of him at all. Hardie was then refused permission even to draw the apron. When he became ill, months passed with no progress made at all, to Wellcome's increasing alarm. The year 1899 came and went, and by April 1901 Hardie had only made a few sketches. Eventually, he found a Masonic apron of the correct period in Philadelphia, which had been embroidered and presented by the widow of the famous Marquis de Lafayette. It was not until June 1902 that the portrait commissioned four years before actually reached London, which might be regarded as something of a dilatory record for the profession. On 8 August 1902 it was finally formally presented to Freemasons' Hall in the presence of the American Ambassador, Joseph H. Choate, and the Earl of Warwick, the Deputy Grand Master of England. As in the case of the Bayard Cup and the Pocahontas portrait, the matter generated a disproportionate amount of time and correspondence, and cannot be considered one of Wellcome's most fortunate ventures.

*

After Bokenham's departure from the Physiological Laboratories, Dowson's team was completed by Dr Stanislaus Pinkus, who was not a success and left in 1901, and H. J. Sudmersen, who certainly was.

After the near disaster at its outset, the Wellcome Physiological Research Laboratories now had the opportunity to recover, but it was essential for them to be registered, under the 1876 Act, particularly because the anti-vivisectionists were active in monitoring the Laboratories and complaining to the Home Office about their testing work; Dowson's view was that as this caused no pain, it was not covered by the Act. Wellcome willingly permitted the Home Office Inspector, Professor Thane, to examine the Laboratories and 'every room and cupboard in the house from roof to cellar', which he duly did and was, like his predecessor, greatly impressed.

In February 1900 Wellcome again put his case for registration to the Home Secretary, setting out his arguments at considerable length and remarking that, 'It is not going too far to assert that the administration of all powerful remedies to human beings should first of all have a sound basis in laboratory experiment.' Where he was on less certain ground was when he claimed, again, that

> These laboratories are entirely separate and distinct from the works and business departments of Burroughs Wellcome and Company. They are under independent direction and are conducted as strictly professional institutions. They are not carried on as a source of profit but are maintained at a heavy cost by funds derived from other sources.

In reality, all the Laboratories' staff were employed by the company and were already engaged on work for it, in addition to raising diphtheria anti-toxin. The fact that the latter was sold below cost price was not the real point.

Wellcome now sought the support of prominent men for his petition to the Home Secretary; these were primarily medical, but he tried also to enlist the backing of a future Conservative Prime Minister, Arthur Balfour, and the former Liberal Prime Minister, Lord Rosebery. Balfour replied sympathetically, but said that he could not sign a petition directed to a government colleague, while Rosebery characteristically responded by writing that he no longer had any influence. There were others who declined, principally from the more academic medical world, on the now familiar excuse of being unwilling to become involved in commerce, however indirectly. But eighteen leading doctors did sign the petition, which Professor Thane referred to the Royal Colleges of Surgeons and of Physicians, and also to the Pharmaceutical Society. Their conclusions were not favourable.

Wellcome then sought supportive newspaper attention for his new Chemical Laboratories. This was duly achieved, and his concentration on good public relations and the cultivation of individual journalists and editors again resulted in excellent publicity. However, the fundamental problems continued to exercise the Home Office. Indeed, Dowson discovered from Thane that a letter of refusal was about to be sent to Wellcome. This discussion took place at University College and Dowson, realising 'that a crisis was on us', went immediately to the Home Office and was able to persuade the senior civil servants not to post it, thus giving Wellcome more time to represent additional material in support of his position.

This initiative by Dowson, and his personal meetings with Thane and Sir Kenelm Digby at the Home Office, were crucial to the history of Burroughs Wellcome. The additional time given to Wellcome was used well. His enquiries demonstrated that no other major country producing drugs and medicines had restrictions on research comparable to Britain, and Rosebery at last came out in Wellcome's defence, declaring in *The Times* that 'In these days we need to be inoculated with some of the nervous energy of the Americans.' The anti-vivisectionists, particularly in their principal journal, *The Abolitionist*, reviled the Wellcome claim and sneered offensively at the Burroughs Wellcome policy of producing cheap serum. There was still strong opposition in the medical profession, which Dowson was able to reduce only slightly after long and patient personal canvassing, while Fletcher Moulton – now in Parliament again – worked on the legal and political aspects.

This occupied much of 1900. The second submission, presented in February 1901, was more careful and less flamboyant than the first. This time the initial response was more encouraging, and it was decided to recruit another physiologist to concentrate upon the precise details now required by the Home Office. This was John Mellanby of Emmanuel College, Cambridge, regarded as 'a young man of great attainment' with 'a brilliant future'. Mellanby was not in fact Dowson's first choice for such an important task, the principal reason being apparently his age, twenty-two. He was to prove another major Wellcome discovery, although his later eminence occurred after he had left the Laboratories in 1904; he eventually became Waynflete Professor of Physiology at Oxford. The Wellcome recruitment system, based almost entirely on word of mouth and individual recommendations, and Wellcome's personal 'hunch' about people, had produced another winner. In this case Hopkins had been the prime advocate of this young man, and both Wellcome and Dowson came to value his judgment highly.

Mellanby's responses to the Home Office enquiries persuaded Thane, and then Digby, to recommend to the Home Secretary that the application should be granted. Digby did so with reluctance, 'because I think besides the outcry which will no doubt be raised by the anti-vivisectionists, the Home Office will be taking a new departure, which will lead to some difficulties, but which in my view is inevitable'. On 6 September 1901 a letter was received stating that the Wellcome Physiological Research Laboratories had been registered under the 1876 Act. It was the end of a protracted campaign, and the beginning of a new era not only for Burroughs Wellcome, but also for the British pharmaceutical industry. It was a famous victory.

Wellcome received the news in Switzerland, where he was staying with his wife.

# 7
# New Adventures

Although Wellcome's name had been linked with several women, in addition to May Sheldon and Genevieve Ward, and Burroughs had not been the only person to make allegations, they appear to have been without foundation. To his friends and family Wellcome seemed to be a confirmed bachelor, who enjoyed the company of women but had no inclination to marry. In fact, for all the absorbing interests of his business and career, he was anxious to find a wife and to have a family and an heir, but had not found someone whom he was prepared to consider suitable. And then he fell in love, but not immediately.

Syrie Barnardo, the daughter of the celebrated Doctor Thomas Barnardo, was eighteen when Wellcome first met her in 1897. By then, if Wellcome had become very well known and respected, Barnardo was a humanitarian legend, whose work for impoverished children was justly internationally recognised and admired.

But Barnardo was a complex and controversial man. He was born in 1845 in Dublin, where he was brought up and educated, unhappily, in St Patrick's Cathedral Grammar School, where the headmaster, the Rev. William Dundas, exerted a harsh tyranny. Barnardo later recalled him as 'the most cruel man as well as the most mendacious that I have ever in my life seen. He seemed to take a savage delight in beating his boys.' On leaving school, Barnardo was apprenticed to a wine merchant for a while, but then had a religious conversion; he first had a believer's baptism into the Baptist Church. He then joined the Church of Ireland, but left to become a member of the Plymouth

Brethren, firm believers (like the American Adventists) of the imminent Second Coming, in which his brothers were active. Through them he came to know George Muller, the founder of the orphan homes in Bristol. He then joined the China Inland Mission, inspired by Hudson Taylor's oratory about 'a million a month dying in China without knowing Christ'. He left Dublin for London in April 1866; shortly after his arrival cholera ravaged the poverty-stricken East End, killing over three thousand people, including many children.

He registered as a medical student at the London Hospital, but only passed the preliminary examination. Then he abandoned the China Mission project, his medical aspirations and the Brethren. He preached in Stepney and taught at a 'ragged' school in the Mile End Road, of which he became superintendent. He soon quarrelled with his committee over finances when he raised funds for a juvenile mission of his own, and resigned to start his own home for destitute children. His later version that his work for children began in a 'transmogrified donkey shed' was suitably picturesque, but untrue. But although his accounts of the origins of Doctor Barnardo's Homes tended to the dramatic rather than to the totally veracious, and serious questions were raised about his methods and the disposal of funds, the fact was that he was a genuine saviour of the emaciated orphans of the British cities, about whom few others cared.

It is probable that Barnardo's father, a German immigrant from Russia, was Jewish. His wife was the sister of his first wife, a union that would have been illegal under the Deceased Wife's Sister Act – immortalised by W. S. Gilbert in *Iolanthe* – but for the fact that he was then a Russian subject, married in London in a German church. However, the Barnardos not only concealed their alleged Jewishness, but also consistently denied it. In spite of Barnardo's remarkable achievements, it is rather difficult to warm to him and his wife.

Syrie (pronounced 'Sirry') was born on 10 July 1879. Although she was christened Gwendoline Maud Syrie (the last her mother's Christian name), she was known in the family as 'Queenie'. Her three surviving brothers went to expensive private schools, and one, Cyril, to Oxford University. Her sister, Marjorie, was mentally retarded from birth. Syrie was privately educated at home, and there is no evidence whatever that either she or her imperious and improvident mother, with very expensive tastes, had any serious personal involvement in the work of the Barnardo Homes.

Cyril Barnardo evidently found the family home too limited, and disliked the spiritual atmosphere and emphasis on religion. He had a kindred spirit in Syrie. There is much truth in the comment of one of her biographers that

> Beneath Syrie's gay exterior existed a sober, hard-working person who proved herself to be no less determined, ruthless, and opinionated than her father. Like him, she turned these unexpected traits to her own benefit. Religious she was not, nor particularly charitable.*

There is a temptation, however, to which some writers have succumbed, to depict Syrie as a trapped gilded bird in a gloomy cage, desperate to escape from a dreary life of Good Works and God. In fact, the Barnardos were worldly and lived very comfortably in houses that got progressively larger and more comfortable; they had servants and coaches, and although Syrie's mother, known as The Begum, was widely regarded as a trial, and an extravagant one as well, there was much more to her father than was generally realised, as became evident when Lady Wagner meticulously exposed the real man behind the myth.**

His enemies had pounced on the fact that he had not been a doctor at all; there were also serious questions asked about his affluence and high standard of living, the clear implication being that not all the money he had raised had gone to destitute children. His own accounts of how he began his work in the East End proved to be not wholly accurate; indeed, many were alarmingly fictional. He had a domineering personality and, as Lady Wagner comments:

* Richard B. Fisher, *Syrie Maugham* (Duckworth, 1978), p. 7. This is a work, like many others on her, to be regarded with caution.

** Gillian Wagner, *Barnardo* (Weidenfeld & Nicolson, 1979).

> Temperamentally Barnardo was always intolerant of authority, and it was his domineering personality as much as anything that seemed to be the obstacle. . . . His dislike of examinations was another manifestation of this trait and his aversion to submitting himself to any form of outside judgement was to remain a dominant characteristic.*

Barnardo was a brilliant self-publicist, and a fine and moving writer, but he had many enemies and sceptics who doubted his claims to sainthood as much as they questioned (rightly) his claims to an aristocratic Italian family background. They would have been even more questioning had they known that, for all his religiosity, he was not at all averse to the pleasures of the table. His was not a puritanical home.

When Barnardo died in 1905, Wellcome, who had not only arranged his funeral but had also paid for it, ensured that there were no bottles in evidence at his house in Surbiton when the mourners arrived. They had been removed from both his study and his own carriage. Wellcome was not at all shocked by this; he was only anxious to preserve Barnardo's reputation for moral blamelessness, which, as he well knew, was open to challenge. One can appreciate why they understood each other.

But Barnardo, although complex, was not a hypocrite. He had a perverse pleasure in quarrelling with almost everyone, and he enjoyed the fame he had justifiably achieved, but the truth was that he did a great deal for the wretched children whose cause he espoused. The fact that he had very human weaknesses, and was to many a highly unattractive and arrogant little man, was of far less importance than what he achieved. Although he was much subjected to criticism, his work with young people merited his contemporary eminence.

Syrie adored her father; about her mother she was more ambivalent, in which she was not alone. She inherited his small size, vivacity, resourcefulness and fierce individuality – and, in later years, his imperiousness, ruthless determination and lack of scruple. She was

* *Ibid.*, p. 23.

not called 'Queenie' inadvertently. However, she certainly did not inherit his strong religious views. She put up with them as a child and young woman, but although her father was more tolerant than most, his own family was not. They remained emphatically Plymouth Brethren after he had moved on to a more relaxed, although totally sincere, Anglicanism, as the style of his life and habits demonstrated. Syrie was to carry this relaxed attitude considerably further in her own life.

Barnardo was very much the kind of man that Wellcome admired. Like Stanley, he was not only famous, but was also human and warm, and his positive contribution to relieving misery demonstrated a remarkable character, energy and compassion – all virtues that Wellcome especially respected.

By 1899 the Barnardos were living in St Leonard's Lodge, Surbiton, an imposing house close to the Thames, and in which Wellcome had occasionally stayed as a paying guest. Wellcome rented a house nearby, ostensibly for his canoeing, and it was during that summer that he first got to know the Barnardos, and Syrie, well.

She was beautiful, high-spirited, amusing and intelligent. Contrary to some later accounts, she was not at all wounded by a broken engagement – if it had ever got that far, which is unlikely. When she was seventeen, she had been much taken by a young man of good family, but her parents had forbidden any match; as she was so young, and revered her father, she accepted their decision. The young man then had a serious riding accident on Ham Common and died some weeks later from his injuries. When, many years later, she related the episode to one of her greatest friends, Rebecca West, it was without any criticism of her parents.

In spite of the large disparity between their ages – twenty-six years – there was obviously a strong mutual attraction between her and Wellcome, greatly assisted by the fact that her father and Wellcome had so much in common. By May 1900 they were corresponding regularly on matters of mutual interest, and Barnardo was on several occasions Wellcome's guest at functions in London, including at the

Savage Club. And, when Barnardo sailed for New York on his way to Canada in July 1900, Wellcome arranged with Sam Fairfield for 'My friend Dr Thomas J. Barnardo' to have the courtesies of the Union League Club extended to him, and made the same arrangement directly with the Lotus Club. Wellcome also introduced him to the novelist, Marie Corelli, who, Barnardo wrote to him, 'was perhaps a little too effusive for my modesty. I felt dreadfully shy and abashed on hearing all the flattering things she said to me when I was first introduced to her. I am not accustomed to such resonant adulation.'

Wellcome invited the Barnardos to join him at Henley; and showed Barnardo the Dartford Works, Acacia Hall and the Wellcome Club. Barnardo was genuinely impressed by 'all that you have done for your employees to make life sweet and enjoyable for them'. The Barnardos invited Wellcome to the annual Barnardo's Founder's Day – 'it will give me great pleasure if I could see your face among my guests,' Barnardo wrote – and Wellcome responded by inviting him to speak at a large official luncheon, with Stanley present. Barnardo responded by telegram: 'You confer too high an honour upon me of which surely some other is more worthy but I cannot refuse the King to hear is to obey. I am your obedient Barnardo [10 July 1900].' In a letter on the same day he asked to be spared the ordeal of making a speech: '*You* must be responsible if it is a failure, and upon your head I am afraid the failure must lie.' Barnardo's wife also wrote often. Wellcome was a generous contributor to the Barnardo causes and was regarded as a personal friend; he was always very welcome at St Leonard's Lodge.

It is entirely due to Wellcome's unpublished biography by Haggis, made available by his Trustees to other historians and biographers, that the legend was created, and often repeated, that Syrie and Wellcome did not meet until 1901 in Egypt. As will be seen, it was there that they decided to marry, but they had known each other for nearly three years before then. They had corresponded often, but in his agony in later years Wellcome destroyed all her letters to him, except those relating to the future of their son.

Syrie had had a happy and pampered childhood, and her broken teenage engagement had certainly not made her broken-hearted. Nor does it appear that she was particularly looking for a husband. But Wellcome was not only attractive to her parents, but also to her. He was handsome, charming and interesting, seeming, with his energy and enthusiasm, much younger than he was; he was also kind and generous. Additionally, he was now successful and rich. She was by no means the first woman to regard him as an exciting and romantic personality. At what point friendship developed into something deeper it is impossible to say, but the vital initiative was to come from her and her parents, especially her mother. The myth that Barnardo so disapproved that he did not even attend their wedding is negated by the fact that he signed as one of the witnesses, and strongly defended his daughter's decision when it was criticised by other members of the family.

However, when Wellcome sailed for the Sudan at the end of 1900, nothing had been decided – at least, not by him.

*

At this point Wellcome was becoming involved in what was to prove one of his most important ventures.

His interest in African matters went far beyond commercial ones, and he was enthralled by the accounts of his friends, Stanley, Jephson and Sheldon. He bought, and read eagerly, the considerable amount of new literature on the subject, as the 'scramble for Africa' developed in the 1890s, when the British, Germans, French, Belgians and Italians seized, by various means, vast tracts of the continent.

In the early 1880s the British had suffered serious military reverses in South Africa, and even more notably in the Sudan, where the death of General Gordon at Khartoum at the hands of the Mahdi's forces in 1885 had been considered a national disaster and humiliation. It was certainly catastrophic for the people of the Sudan, whose sufferings under the Mahdi's successor, the Khalifa Abdallahi, became gradually known in Britain, and well advertised by the British authorities in Egypt, who were resolved, under the populist cry of 'Avenge

Gordon', to recapture and pacify the Sudan. There had been small chance of such a venture being approved in London so long as Gladstone was in power, but in 1894 he ceased to be Prime Minister; a year later the Conservatives took office and, most significantly of all, Joseph Chamberlain became Colonial Secretary.

The key figures in Cairo were Evelyn Baring, created Lord Cromer in 1892; the Sirdar of the Egyptian army, General Herbert Kitchener; and Colonel Reginald Wingate. Cromer had first gone to Cairo in 1876 at the age of thirty-five to represent British interests concerned with the massive debt problems of the then Khedive. After three years in India he had returned to Egypt as 'British agent and consul-general'; he was in reality the true ruler of Egypt. As Winston Churchill later wrote of him:

> He was never in a hurry, never anxious to make an effect or sensation. He sat still and men came to him. He watched events until their combination enabled him to intervene smoothly and decisively. He could wait a year as easily as a week, and he had often waited four or five years before getting his way. . . . He rejected all high-sounding titles; he remained simply the British Agent. His status was indefinite; he might be nothing; he was in fact everything. His word was law.

Wingate, the head of Military Intelligence, published in 1891 *Mahdiism and the Egyptian Sudan*, a powerful and accurate account of the wretched condition of the people of the Sudan under the Mahdi's evil rule. It also ensured the widest publicity for Slatin Pasha's *Fire and Sword in the Sudan*, which, in addition to being a remarkable adventure story of Slatin's capture in 1884 by the Mahdi when he was Gordon's governor of the province of Darfur, imprisonment and escape in 1895, also gave a suitably horrific portrait of the tyranny and cruelty of the regime. It was political propaganda, but based on fact. Its impact upon British opinion was considerable.

Cromer had not approved of either the disastrous attempt in 1883–4 to recapture the Sudan, or Gordon's fatal mission to Khartoum. In 1885 he used his developing powers to achieve the complete withdrawal of British and Egyptian forces from the Sudan, with the exception of the Red Sea port of Suakin, while he concentrated upon the affairs of Egypt, which he did with brilliant success. This achieved, he and Kitchener then turned to the unfinished business to the south. The Egyptian Government was opposed to occupying the Sudan and the British Cabinet was unenthusiastic, but Cromer's authority was now such that he carried the day. The result was the immensely long campaign that culminated on 2 September 1898 at Omdurman close to Khartoum, when the Dervish armies were totally destroyed, with insignificant British and Egyptian casualties. The Sudan was conquered, and Kitchener became a national hero. But, as in most conquests, the problem now arose of what to do with it.

Wellcome had followed these events with keen excitement. For his Christmas book gifts to his employees and friends in 1898 he bought 800 copies of G. W. Steevens's *With Kitchener to Khartoum* and 870 copies of Slatin's book. But it was Kitchener's ambitious plan to introduce 'civilisation after conquest', and to begin with education, that especially enthralled him. The fact was that the problems of this vast territory, depopulated by war, famine and disease, were so enormous that this attracted a particular type of person, of whom Wellcome was one.

When Kitchener issued a public appeal for £100,000 to build a college at Khartoum in the name and memory of Gordon in November 1898, Wellcome immediately wrote to him enclosing a personal contribution of 100 guineas. He also offered to donate 'a complete medical equipment and stock for the Dispensary in connection with the College'. Kitchener's appeal was immediately successful. There was also another, somewhat unexpected, personal factor. Kitchener must have been one of the very few persons in British public service who had heard, and read, about the Metlakahtlan Indians, who had actually met Duncan, and who had become a friend as well as an admirer. He had also read Wellcome's book, another oddity. When he told Wellcome of this remarkable fact, the latter's enthusiasm became even greater, and in the autumn of 1900 he sailed to Cairo with letters of introduction to Cromer and to Wingate, who had now replaced Kitchener – dispatched hurriedly to South Africa to assist General Sir Frederick Roberts after the early British disasters in the Boer War – as Sirdar of the Anglo-Egyptian Sudan. His journey there was not fortunate, as Wellcome somehow managed to fall into an open hatchway, badly injuring – although not breaking – his right leg and arm, and being described by the doctor as 'totally disabled'. This appears to have been a considerable exaggeration, but his insurance company paid up after a sharp correspondence conducted by Snow Hill on Wellcome's cabled instructions.

Kitchener, Cromer and Wingate welcomed him warmly, as he was among the first civilians from England who wanted to visit the Sudan, and who, moreover, had something to contribute to helping the terribly impoverished people of the country they had annexed. They offered him all possible assistance. Wellcome later recorded his first impressions:

> It was my purpose to study the existing conditions of the native peoples, as well as to observe their ethnological characteristics. To aid me the Sudan Government converted a native sailing craft into a *Dahabeeyah** to enable me to cruise on the Upper Nile and visit the native settlements. During my visit to one of the small islands of the Nile, just above the Shabluka Cataract, there were perhaps thirty or forty inhabitants, everyone lying helplessly prostrated, weak and emaciated, suffering from malaria in an extremely virulent form. I am sure that no-one could have seen those mere skeletons of men, women and children without being moved by deep emotion to do something to mitigate the pitiful condition of these poor and sorely distressed peoples. . . . At that time no provision had yet been made for medical and sanitary research work in the Sudan.

The conditions in Khartoum itself were appalling, and the damage inflicted by the victorious British troops had been far greater than Wellcome (or anyone else in England) had realised before the first

* A houseboat with sails.

edition of Winston Churchill's classic *The River War* was published in 1899, which also contained strong criticisms of the treatment of the Dervish wounded, notably toned down in later editions.

The combination of a total lack of sanitation, water-borne disease, malaria, cholera and malnutrition was lethal, and inflicted far more fatalities on the Anglo-Egyptian army than the Mahdi's armies had. The predicament of the poor Sudanese was infinitely worse. What were needed, as Wellcome pointed out, were the provision of basic necessities, such as clean water and food, and an all-out attack on the sanitation problem. There was no immunisation against, or cure for, malaria except by giving daily doses of quinine and by doing everything possible to dramatically improve sanitation. Wellcome promised drugs and medicines, on which Power and Dowson were already working in London and at Dartford, for dispatch early in 1901, but common sense showed that immediate action was needed. Both Cromer and Wingate accepted all his recommendations. The Dispensary was in itself invaluable to the hard-pressed medical officers, and, as Wingate wrote enthusiastically at the beginning of a correspondence and friendship that lasted until Wellcome's death, both he and Cromer were 'fully alive to all the possibilities you have opened out for us, possibilities, which, without your assistance, would have been postponed well nigh indefinitely'.

Wellcome wrote that the climate was such that he was 'completely regenerated and made well again', and the challenges of the Sudan inspired him. He had already conceived a far more ambitious plan, which he unfolded to Cromer when he returned to Cairo. He proposed to establish in Khartoum a tropical research laboratory, which would have as its first task the reduction of disease by the application of known preventive methods and treatment; secondly, it would conduct serious scientific research into the particular diseases of the area. He would provide the complete equipment, but the laboratory should be self-sufficient by 'the charging of such reasonable fees as will aid in covering the cost of maintaining them', while the Government of the Sudan should maintain it and meet the salaries of its Director and staff. The offer was speedily accepted, and Power and Dowson were instructed to expand their work on the Gordon College Dispensary to equip a complete laboratory of the highest quality, to be 'equal to those of any institution in Europe'. Wellcome also promised, on his return to London, to take advice to find a Director who 'shall be skilled and resourceful and be prepared to direct and carry out with zeal and energy all branches of work for which the Laboratories are equipped, and a man who is willing to devote his life to the work of the Institution'.

He was to prove in every respect as good as his word. One example of his almost excessive attention to detail was to insist that all the laboratory's woodwork and fittings were to be of the highest quality teak, to be baked at a high temperature for several months to season it for the Sudan climate.

His search for the first Director found Dr Andrew Balfour of Edinburgh University, who had served in the South African War, spoke Arabic, and had specialised in tropical diseases under Sir Patrick Manson, the founder of the London School of Tropical Medicine in 1899 and, most famous of all, the parasitologist whose brilliant work in China and Hong Kong had established the school of medicine that developed into the University and Medical School of Hong Kong. The possible connection between mosquitoes and malaria had been suspected for some time, but never conclusively proved; Manson's work in China and then in London strengthened the case. It interested and impressed a member of the Indian Medical Service, Ronald Ross, who, under Manson's patronage, returned to India on special leave and, in one of the most remarkable of modern medical researches, identified the secretive, night-flying Anopheles mosquito as the transmitter of malaria. It earned Ross the Nobel Prize for Science in 1902, at the age of forty-five, and has been described as 'a revolution in medical science comparable to the discovery of the Double Helix in 1953. It created a new speciality of Tropical Health and Hygiene.' There was no cure for malaria (nor is there nearly a century later), but the villain had at last been clearly identified. Titled 'the father of tropical medicine', Manson had become a friend of Wellcome when the latter had suddenly become fascinated by this new area. Manson had suggested Balfour; it was to prove another of Wellcome's great appointments.

Balfour was only twenty-nine when he went to Khartoum to establish The Wellcome Tropical Research Laboratories in 1902; he was also appointed Chief Health Officer, with formidable powers to enforce his instructions. Characteristically, he learnt conversational Arabic. He was to reduce the death rate in Khartoum alone from sixty per thousand to seven, and to make it one of the healthiest cities in Africa and Asia. This all lay in the future when Wellcome sent him off with a lavish and well-publicised banquet in London in his honour attended by all the most notable medical men in the country, including Manson and the President of the Royal Society, as well as Stanley, which must have been a somewhat intimidating audience for someone so young.

Public health was one of Balfour's principal interests; his 1898 MD thesis had been on the pollution of rivers by the dyestuffs industry, and his BSc in Edinburgh in 1900 had been in public health. He had also played rugby for Cambridge and was a noted athlete. He was an enthusiast, immensely energetic and in a hurry. When he went to the Sudan, his staff consisted of one British laboratory assistant and two Sudanese – one of them a small boy. By 1911 he had nine European scientists, two Sudanese clerks and other laboratory assistants. But he was not content with this. His ambitions matched – indeed, exceeded – those of Wellcome himself. He was an obsessive worker, fascinated by his subject, immensely intellectually energetic, but whose romantic novels, which endeavoured (unsuccessfully) to emulate Stevenson, were not comparable to his medical and scientific achievements. But one can clearly see why Wellcome thought so well of him and his variety of interests.

There was another result of Wellcome's expedition to Egypt and the Sudan: it was then that Wellcome first met Alfred Tucker, the Bishop of Uganda, and was deeply impressed by him and the work of the Church of England Missionary Society in East Africa. From Tucker he learnt of the work of the Cook brothers – Albert and Howard – who had opened a modest hospital on the northern shores of Lake Victoria Nyanza in 1897. It was Howard Cook who had discovered, and reported, the scourge of sleeping sickness in Uganda.* The hospital was so successful that it was replaced by a larger building in 1900, but the dispensary was destroyed by fire two years later after it had been struck by lightning. When Tucker wrote to Wellcome to report this disaster, Wellcome at once offered to build a new one, provide all its fittings and equip the dispensary for six months; in 1910 he paid for a large medicine and drug store, and contributed to the Society for the rest of his life.

But Wellcome's visit to Khartoum was distracted by a wholly unexpected event during his return to Cairo. A large Nile steamer arrived, with a party of English ladies on board. One of them, to Wellcome's astonishment, was Syrie Barnardo.

*

Syrie's dramatic arrival in Egypt has never been adequately explained, and certainly took Wellcome by surprise, but it must have been quite deliberate. The speed of their engagement, and subsequent marriage, baffled Haggis and others, who had not realised that they had known each other for so long. Syrie had clearly missed Wellcome, and certainly made most, if not all, of the running. Wellcome professed himself deeply in love; almost certainly, they both were.

So little has survived from the Wellcome marriage, in correspondence or subsequent recollection, that it is not even known where they actually met again in the Sudan; however, circumstantial evidence implies that it was at Assuit, when Wellcome was returning to Cairo. Nor is it clear when Wellcome proposed and was accepted, but by

* Two seconded RAMC officers, Howard Ensor and R. G. Gayer-Anderson, while working for Balfour respectively mapped the distribution of tsetse flies in the area, and created the natural barriers to the spread of the disease by turning back people travelling into the Sudan from areas infested by sleeping sickness, establishing isolation camps and clearing river-bank vegetation.

the time they sailed from Alexandria to Italy they regarded themselves as definitely engaged. It was from Florence that Wellcome wrote to her parents to seek their permission to be married; in view of the Doctor's poor health – he was recovering from a severe attack of angina at the resort of Bad Neuheim – Wellcome suggested that the wedding should be in Frankfurt. The speed of this justifiably took the Barnardos aback, and it was decided to have the wedding at St Mark's, Surbiton, on 25 June, ten days after Wellcome was due to return to London. By this time he had rented The Oast House, at Hayes, in Kent, then in the countryside, well south of London, as his first real home.*

There is no doubt that Syrie's mother ardently wanted her to marry Wellcome, and was probably responsible for her mysterious trip to Egypt; Barnardo's position is less easy to assess. His biographer has written that 'Barnardo is said to have been saddened at the idea of his daughter's marriage to Wellcome, a man so much her senior, and he was ill and away from home at the critical time.'** But Barnardo had always got on well with Wellcome, and when there was family disapproval of her engagement to an American so much older, he wrote in vigorous defence of her decision.† Wellcome maintained good relations with him, although not with his mother-in-law.‡ Each admired the other's achievements and character, and it must have appeared to Barnardo that, in spite of the age difference, Wellcome was the ideal son-in-law and husband for his lively daughter, who had certainly inherited her parents' expensive tastes. Lady Wagner states that 'Syrie herself would seem to have had some doubts about the marriage . . . but was overborne by her mother.' But there is no

* Hayes was then little more than a village, in quiet and attractive countryside. The Oast House was built in 1873 for Lord Sackville Cecil, the half-brother of the third Marquis of Salisbury. It was a substantial property, with extensive grounds.

** Wagner, *op. cit.*, p. 283.

† *Ibid.*, pp. 283–4.

‡ When a friend wrote in complimentary terms of her, Wellcome wrote in the margin: 'You don't know her.'

evidence that Wellcome was aware of any such doubts, and was eager – as was Syrie – to have the wedding as soon as possible.

The journey home was unpropitious, as their cases were robbed. Syrie's large trunk was 'hacked open and completely cleared out'. Wellcome was swiftly on to his insurance company. He had no better luck with two monkeys he brought home with him as a present to Stanley. One came from the shores of the Blue Nile and another from the White; they were sent to the Zoological Society's Gardens in Regent's Park, but quickly died.

Wellcome's friends were overjoyed by the news of his engagement. Mounteney Jephson was still ill after his grim African experiences, from which, physically, he never fully recovered. He wrote to 'My very dear Hal' on 4 June:

> The news in your letter of your engagement to Miss Barnardo touches me very closely, for you know, dear old man, that I have the same affection for you that I wd have for my own brother. I recognise that you are a person who would be made or marred by marriage – one might say that of many people, but it is more true of you than anyone I know.
>
> You say in your letter 'I want you to like her, & I want you to say God Bless the Union.' The first I already have done, & the second I do, old man, from the bottom of my heart.
>
> I know Miss Barnardo so little, but what I do know I like extremely. I know that she is bright & full of life & you could never get along with a dull wife. . . . But of course I only know her as a bright, pretty taking little Lady, who dresses very well! I don't know anyone who needs a wife more than you do, for your work has made you into a sort of Moloch & you have sacrificed too little to the graces of life. Miss Barnardo will I am sure change all that, or at any rate modify it a good deal!
>
> A woman with tact & who really cares for you will improve you most enormously. And for her, for the little Lady herself, I know what a really good sort she is getting for a husband, for I've tried you, dear old man, many a time & never found you wanting all these years of our close friendship. . . . This is a very stupid letter, Hal, but somehow

> when one feels a thing very deeply it is difficult to express oneself, a grip of your hand would express it so much better. . . .

The Stanleys, who had met Syrie on Wellcome's introduction in the previous year 'in all her sweet young beauty', in Dorothy Stanley's words, were among the many who wrote to Wellcome letters of delight, congratulations and hope that now read poignantly. One recalled at Henley the previous June 'the splendid agility with which [Syrie] sprang from a sinking canoe through the window of a barge'.

Differences of age do not necessarily lead to unhappy marriages, and there are many examples to prove how successful they can be. The real problem in the Wellcome marriage was a severe clash of temperaments and attitudes to marriage. Wellcome clearly thought that by marrying into a public-spirited, religious family he had obtained a suitably devout wife. That, it became swiftly evident, was a serious miscalculation. Syrie was escaping from a religious family, as had her brothers. Nor was she much interested in Good Works, as Wellcome was, nor in his work. She dutifully attended the many Wellcome functions, dinners and sports days, without enthusiasm or enjoyment, and had no interest whatever in his business, his enthusiasms, his collections (which she derided as his 'curios'), their motor-car expeditions over appalling roads in England and Europe, and particularly his enjoyment of travelling abroad to inhospitable and uncomfortable places. This she especially hated, going, as she wrote to a friend, to 'places I detested'. Wellcome, with his background, enjoyed the privations of exploration and discomfort; she, with hers, did not. What he regarded as adventures, she considered torments.

Much more serious was that she was young for her age, not at all intellectual and in many respects immature. She was clever, amusing, charming, and had style, wit and spirit, qualities that entranced Wellcome – and, later, many others – but she was a woman of emotion whose horizons were limited to the immediate. It is not surprising that she aroused intense reactions from those who knew her – some adulatory, others very much the reverse. In later years Rebecca West, among many other friends, spoke and wrote of her with affection and admiration; but others spoke of her differently: 'pure poison' was one of the phrases this biographer has heard used of her from some who had professional and personal dealings with her. It is fairest to say that she was a controversial personality, which Wellcome had not at all expected when he married her.

Syrie at the time of her marriage had few real friends – those that she had were of her age – and no experience of London Society. The trouble was that Wellcome's friends and their wives were much older than she, and their idea of enjoyment was different from hers. They were agreeable, kind and intelligent, but uninspiring and certainly not Fun.

Wellcome only slowly realised that Syrie was a restless young woman, aware of her attraction to young men, and unwilling to conform to his notions of an obedient and patient wife. She was also strong spirited, with a hot temper and a sharp tongue. She was one of the forerunners of The Emancipated Woman, a species Wellcome could not comprehend, especially in a wife. Their respective ideas of adventure were totally different. The age difference did not help, but it was not decisive.

The wedding was a private one, with Jephson as best man. There was no reception, nor a honeymoon. Syrie, whose near-genius as an interior decorator had not yet developed, did her best with The Oast House while her husband was preoccupied with his business, especially the establishment of the Khartoum venture. In September they travelled to Paris at the beginning of a long European tour, which included on Wellcome's part much collecting and visits to museums; they did not return to England until May 1902. An unfortunate pattern had already been established, but although it was a life that did not appeal to Syrie, there do not appear to have been any difficulties at this early stage. Only Barnardo seems to have deduced that his beloved daughter was unhappy. Wellcome's friends, and not least the Stanleys, considered the marriage a happy one, particularly when Syrie had a son on 26 June 1903, named Henry Mounteney

Dr. & Mrs. T. J. Barnardo
have the pleasure to announce
the approaching marriage of their daughter
Gwendoline Maude Syrie
with
Mr. Henry S. Wellcome.
to take place. D.V.
at St. Marks Church Surbiton.
on Tuesday the 25th. June. 1901.
at half past two.

Owing to the condition of Dr. Barnardo's health,
the wedding will be of a quite private character.
There will be no reception after the Ceremony.

St. Leonard's Lodge.
Surbiton.

Announcement of Syrie Barnardo's marriage to Wellcome, 1901

after his two godfathers, Henry Stanley and Mounteney Jephson; his parents always used the second name. The christening was at St Michael's, Chester Square, with a reception afterwards at Claridge's.

On the surface, they appeared a happy couple, excited by the birth of their son. Wellcome was certainly proud of his attractive and stylish young wife; only shrewd observers like Chune Fletcher appreciated that in reality they had nothing in common beyond their genuine devotion to their son, for whom Wellcome had high, and understandable, ambitions to inherit and lead Burroughs Wellcome. As Syrie cared neither for business, nor for Burroughs Wellcome, this did not appeal to her.

In one of the most shrewd comments in Haggis's otherwise somewhat lacklustre unpublished biography of Wellcome, he observed rightly that,

> All his life Wellcome loved events such as Banquets, Receptions, Presentations. He seldom missed an opportunity for associating his name with some function. Any important occasion, an appointment, a resignation, an anniversary, an official opening, he seized upon as a reason for lavish entertainments, yet all the numerous functions he held were planned with careful discrimination. Whoever was the guest of honour, whatever the purpose of the celebration, when the demands of courteous hospitality were satisfied, Wellcome would bask in the limelight of the occasion.

Except when entertaining at their home, Syrie appears to have been given no role in the planning of these festivities. This fact caused considerable surprise to those who knew her later, when her talents as a hostess flowered to the point when she was the obvious victim of the malicious short story by Mary Borden, 'To Meet Jesus Christ', about a London hostess of great ambition arranging The Ultimate Party, at which the guest of honour was Jesus Christ, who, inexplicably, failed to turn up. Wellcome seems to have had no idea whatever of his wife's various talents, while at the same time having such a good judgment of the potential abilities of other people, especially young people. There is little doubt that he was the central figure at Mounteney's christening party, which he had himself planned and organised. Modest about his own achievements, and usually very careful about the concerns and sensitivities of his employees, and regarded as a true, thoughtful and generous friend, the element of The Showman, apparent from an early age, was always there. Only Burroughs, on the famous occasion of the opening of the Dartford Works, had ever upstaged him, and his young wife was never given the chance to do so.

There is also the fact that Wellcome understood men far better than women. To the latter he could be charming, considerate and flattering, but, with very few exceptions – May Sheldon and, later, Ada Misner being two of the most conspicuous – he had very few women friends remotely as close to him as Sudlow, Stewart or Fletcher. And his biographer can only reflect again on his neglect of his ageing and dying mother, always finding the excuse of business or illness not to visit her, while any man with the remotest idea of the centre of a woman's life would have realised that she desperately wanted to see her son's face and hear his voice.

This basic lack of understanding of women, or even of sympathy, does not condemn Wellcome as heartless or totally selfish. It can best be described as thoughtlessness where women were concerned. When May Sheldon was being feckless and extravagant, he did not go to see her to upbraid her, but wrote stern letters of rebuke. When his mother was dying, he wrote to her consolingly, but nothing more. He entirely failed to understand his wife. She certainly had faults, which were to demonstrate themselves more clearly later, but Wellcome never seems to have appreciated that she was, in her way, an exceptionally gifted person. Although the age difference was a problem, it need not have been insuperable; nor would it have been, if he had been more sensitive to her. She was not, by birth, upbringing or temperament, cast to play a minor role in life, but this was the role in which Wellcome unthinkingly placed her. It was a terrible mistake, for which he was to pay a grim price.

Another unhelpful fact was that Wellcome had become something of a celebrity, the result of years of self-promotion, but also of real achievement. In January 1903 he received his first academic honour, appropriately from the Philadelphia College of Pharmacy. In the autumn of 1904 he took Syrie and Mounteney to Canada and the United States. They went to Minnesota, so that Wellcome could introduce his wife to his relations and friends of his childhood. Then, rather surprisingly, Wellcome presented the Chicago College of Pharmacy with a large, silver loving cup; Thomas Whitfield, in whose pharmacy he and Power had worked, was present. When they reached St Louis for the Exposition, the Burroughs Wellcome stand received one Grand Prize and one Gold Medal. In addition, Power and one of his colleagues received Gold Medals, as did Dowson and George Barger, another Wellcome appointee. In Washington they were the guests of General John W. Foster, a former Secretary of State, and not only attended the inauguration of the re-elected President Roosevelt, but were also personally invited to the White House. They then processed to Philadelphia, where Wellcome presented another inscribed loving cup to his old College, this time gold-plated and also designed by him. He was then the guest of honour at a dinner attended by the Mayor and the President of the American Medical Association.

This succession of triumphant occasions did not give Syrie the pleasure that they did her husband. She disliked this seemingly endless travelling, particularly with a small baby, and Wellcome's friends were unknown to her and, significantly, much older than she. The real root of future difficulties was boredom, and one can hardly criticise her for this. If she had shared Wellcome's years of struggle and disappointment, she could have appreciated better the satisfaction he felt at the recognition he was now receiving from academic bodies in the United States. But she had not, and did not, which Wellcome found incomprehensible and wounding. But no serious problems between them had yet arisen.

Barnardo's health had continued to decline. He never received any official recognition for his work during his lifetime, his enemies and detractors being as active as Stanley's had been. He died, after a series of heart attacks, in September 1905 at the age of sixty. Wellcome took charge of the funeral arrangements, which were magnificently done, almost on the scale of a state funeral. Barnardo had always liked Wellcome and admired him as a kindred spirit; the affection and regard had been fully returned. His death was another blow to an already fragile marriage.

*

There was another loss that affected Wellcome considerably more than his wife. One of Wellcome's principal concerns was Stanley's health, which deteriorated badly after 1900. In April 1903 he had two strokes, and Dorothy Stanley wrote to Wellcome that 'I have no hopes of his precious life'. In fact, he achieved a partial recovery during the summer and autumn, and Wellcome was a regular and devoted visitor to him in the last year of his life. On 1 May 1904 Dorothy Stanley wrote to Wellcome that 'My beloved husband, the doctors tell me, may no longer be spared to me. His heart is rapidly failing. He is just conscious.' By this stage Wellcome saw Stanley daily, and on one occasion Stanley talked very coherently about Jephson, himself seriously ill. Stanley died on 10 May.

He had asked Wellcome to be one of his pallbearers at his funeral and burial in Westminster Abbey next to Livingstone, and, knowing Wellcome's abilities, to make all the arrangements for the service. This Wellcome willingly agreed to do. To his astonishment, the Dean of Westminster, Joseph Armitage Robinson, refused burial in the Abbey, and also refused to give his reasons. Wellcome was incensed by his attitude and argued that it was not only Stanley's dearest wish, but also his right. Robinson was obdurate. Then Wellcome sought the assistance of the American Ambassador, Choate, and the Livingstone family. Robinson did not even reply to Choate's letter and was deaf to the appeals of the Livingstones. He was prepared to permit the funeral service in the Abbey, but not the interment. The real cause was that Robinson had heard of the stories of the violence and cruelty that surrounded Stanley's reputation, and considered these more important than his achievements and courage. As McLynn records, as 'Mark Twain's friend William D. Howells put it . . . Stanley was "refused a grave in Westminster Abbey by a wretched, tyrannical parson"'.* This was exactly Wellcome's opinion. Robinson could only have been overruled by the King, but Wellcome's advisers appear to have decided to accept the compromise of what Robinson called 'second honours'.

The service went ahead, everything planned and organised by Wellcome. The other pallbearers included Livingstone's grandson and Jephson. Wellcome used all his gifts of drama and occasion, spurred on even more forcibly by his fury against Robinson.

Dorothy Stanley married again, three years later, but always called herself Lady Stanley and dedicated herself to his memory, not always with success. But in Wellcome she had a staunch supporter and friend. Neither ever forgave Dean Robinson for denying Stanley's greatest wish.

*

It was also unfortunate for the Wellcome marriage that it coincided with the flowering of Wellcome's new passions, collecting, motoring and travelling. It does not seem that at that early stage Wellcome was contemplating a medical museum, but rather an exhibition. He was writing to a Mr Holmes in December 1903 that

> I am gratified that I can count on your valuable assistance in connection with the Exhibition which I am anxious to make a great success. I want it to be free from any shoppy elements, and to be a thoroughly scientific and instructive display. I am sure you can contribute greatly to the attainment of this object.

He was also learning guile, writing to an American friend about their proposed 'round amongst the book stalls':

* McLynn, *op. cit.*

If you are not too proud, may I suggest that it will be better not to wear fine raiment. I usually put on very plain clothes for such expeditions. A top hat usually excites the cupidity of the dealer, and the higher the hat the higher the price.

Until 1896 Wellcome's collection had been entirely personal, but in that year he employed Dr C. J. S. Thompson to undertake research into the history of medicine and to acquire objects for the proposed exhibition. In 1898 Thompson became a member of the staff of Burroughs Wellcome, with which he was to remain until his enforced retirement in 1925, by which time he had been the Curator of the Wellcome Historical Medical Museum since 1913. One of his first known purchases was in 1897, when he bought a 1692 manuscript, *Receits of Phisick and Chirurgery*, for £2 10s. He was also responsible for a series of booklets on aspects of medical history published as advertising material by the company; but Thompson was an author in his own right, of several books on pharmacy and toxicology.

By 1902 the search was on in earnest, Wellcome writing to leading authorities that,

I am very deeply interested in the origin and development of the sciences in ancient Egypt, especially in connection with Astrology, Alchemy, Medicine and Surgery, and should esteem it a great favour if you would kindly inform me of any sculptures, carvings, paintings, or papyri having reference to these subjects which there may be in the Museums or in other collections within your knowledge. I shall also be grateful to you if you can let me have any information about the early physicians of Egypt, and if you can tell me of any portraits of them. I will, of course, bear any expenses incurred in procuring the above mentioned information. Perhaps you can delegate some member of your staff to procure it for me.

I beg acceptance of the enclosed booklet, the text of which will indicate to you the direction of my interest in the matter.

PS In addition to the above, can you refer me to any matter illustrating or bearing upon ancient Egyptian Hospitals, Laboratories, or representations of chemical operations and apparatus, surgical instruments etc.

In 1903 he appointed Dr Louis Sambon to 'give me your entire time for six months, and . . . devote yourself to such matters in connection with the forthcoming historical, medical etc. exhibition as I may indicate. The honorarium in return for the six months' service to be Two Hundred Guineas.' Sambon was a lecturer at the London School of Tropical Medicine. Wellcome agreed that he could continue his lectures while in his employment, and sent him to 'the principal centres in Holland, Belgium, France, Switzerland and Italy', with all fares paid and travelling expenses. It would appear that Sambon was the first person outside Burroughs Wellcome who was specially employed for the purpose of purchasing books and artefacts for the exhibition, but in January 1903, a year before Sambon set out on his travels, Wellcome was writing to his agent in Genoa, stating clearly his methods, which, even at this comparatively early stage, did not lack cunning:

Dear Mr Curry

When I was in Vienna last winter, Dr Friedlowski of Kreisbach, near Wilhelmsburg, via St Polten (Kreisbach, I understand, is a small town or village near Vienna), told me that he had a collection of 10,000 – ten thousand – portraits of medical men, ancient and modern, the collection embracing many very rare and valuable ones. Immediately you arrive in Vienna I would like you to send the enclosed letter to Dr Friedlowski. For your information only, I am sending you an English copy of the letter. The letter in German only should be sent to Dr Friedlowski after you have added your signature and Vienna address.

It is desirable that you should handle this matter with the utmost discretion and secrecy. This man, in common with most people in Austria-Hungary, possesses the characteristic subtlety and craftiness, and is inclined to open his mouth very widely, so that you will need to be very carefully on your guard as he is likely to ask you many subtle questions as to whom you are and how you got the information about him, etc.

Do not under any circumstances mention Mr Wellcome's name, but say that you learnt through another party that he had this collection which he was anxious to sell, and it occurred to you that you could purchase it if he were prepared to sell at a reasonable price which would afford a fair chance of disposing of it to advantage. Do not let him think you are purchasing it for yourself, but leave the impression in his mind that you are a dealer or that you are buying it as a business speculation.

As a result of the letter to Dr Friedlowski, I anticipate he will ask you to visit his home to see the pictures. In that case, it will be necessary for you to take an interpreter, who should not however be connected with the trade or profession in any way. He should merely be a medium of speech, and one who is not likely to divulge any part of your mission. I tried to get Dr Friedlowski to bring the collection to Vienna, but he said it was too much trouble and that they were too bulky, etc. etc., and tried to induce me to go to his home. His asking price for the portraits last winter was something like 2000 kronen.

When you see the pictures, I want you to inspect them very carefully and take special notes as to the approximate ages and dates, the quantities of the pictures covering the different centuries – note if they are arranged in chronological order to enable you to do this – how they range in sizes and whether they are fine prints or ordering cuts, etc. etc. I know you have not had much experience in these things, but try and form the best judgement you can as to their value. Dr Friedlowski alleged that the portraits were collected by an eminent Austrian medical author, who had made the collection a life study.

Of course the collection may consist largely of good old engravings or woodcuts, or it may be mostly made up of clippings from illustrated journals, etc., but on the other hand the collection may be perfectly unique and extremely useful to me. I rely upon your great care and discretion in dealing with the matter, and when you have arrived at an opinion, please cable the firm indicating as below your opinion of the pictures and what you think they are worth, the price he asks and the price he is likely to accept.

| | | | |
|---|---|---|---|
| Excellent | Worth £ | Asks £ | Possible £ |
| Good | | | |
| Fair | | | |

Please give English money to prevent mistake.

You will be able to form a pretty conclusive idea of the minimum amount he will accept by bantering with him.

It is possible Dr Friedlowski may depart from the old asking price of 2000 (two thousand) kronen, and he might even ask more than that to begin with, but I think you should see the portraits just the same and make the careful inspection and report.

In order to visit this town, I recognise it will take you a day or a day and a half.

Yours truly

Henry S. Wellcome

Wellcome's stratagems – and those of Thompson – were elaborate, as the eminent book dealer, M. L. Ettinghausen, later discovered:

[Before 1914], while I was still in Munich, a letter arrived from a London firm by the name of Epworth and Company, with offices in Newman Street, inquiring for medical, pharmaceutical and other scientific manuscripts. At the time, in the stock of Ludwig Rosenthal there were masses of such manuscripts, of varying degrees of interest and all manner of dates. Very soon case after case left Munich for London. We were puzzled that a firm not in the *Booksellers' Directory* should need such quantities of manuscripts, for which they paid considerable sums in the course of some years. On my next visit to London I called at Newman Street; the offices of Epworth and Company seemed to be one room on the second floor, and I was informed by the caretaker that the owner of the firm visited his office only to fetch letters and parcels. I looked through the letter box and saw nothing but bare walls. The firm remained most mysterious, till one day some book was returned by them and I found that the paper used for packing came from Burroughs Wellcome and Company, the famous manufacturers of Tabloids and other medicines.

Later, on my return to London, after the First World War, while passing the chemist shop of Bell & Croyden, I found that there was an entrance, in the basement, to a Medical Historical Museum open only to medical men. I visited the basement and was amazed at the marvellous

Syrie Wellcome *née* Barnardo (1879–1955). Drypoint by Paul-César Helleu

LEFT Henry and Syrie Wellcome

BELOW Syrie Wellcome with Henry Mounteney Wellcome

Wellcome on a collecting tour in Spain and Portugal in 1908. The photograph of the car was probably taken by Wellcome; inside is his courier and interpreter John Ferreira

Syrie Wellcome (second from right) entertaining guests at The Nest

Walter Dowson, Director of the Wellcome Physiological Research Laboratories from 1899 to 1906

Scientific staff of the Wellcome Physiological Research Laboratories, 1906: from left to right, C. T. Symons, Henry Hallett Dale, Walter Dowson, H. J. Sudmersen, George Barger

ABOVE General William Crawford Gorgas (1854–1920)
RIGHT Sir Reginald Wingate, Governor-General of the Sudan 1899–1916

BELOW Henry Wellcome (seated centre) with the staff of the Wellcome Tropical Research Laboratories, Khartoum. To the left of Wellcome is Andrew Balfour, Director of the Laboratories

ABOVE Alfred Chune Fletcher (1856–1913)
BELOW Sir Henry Hallett Dale (1875–1968), Director of the Wellcome Physiological Research Laboratories 1906–14, Chairman of the Wellcome Trustees 1938–60

ABOVE Sir Andrew Balfour (1873–1931), Director of the Wellcome Tropical Research Laboratories in Khartoum 1902–13, and Director in Chief of the Wellcome Bureau of Scientific Research in London 1913–23

RIGHT Charles Morley Wenyon (1878–1948), Director in Chief of the Wellcome Bureau of Scientific Research 1924–44

Frederick Belding Power, Director of the Wellcome Chemical Research Laboratories 1896–1914

RIGHT C. J. S. Thompson (1862–1943), Curator of the Wellcome Historical Medical Museum 1913–25

BELOW The Wellcome Historical Medical Museum at 54a Wigmore Street, London, soon after its opening in 1913: the Hall of Statuary

The Jenner section of the Wellcome Historical Medical Museum at Wigmore Street

Major J. S. Uribe in Wellcome's House of Boulders at Jebel Moya, 1938

RIGHT Henry Wellcome on the north-west terrace at Jebel Moya

BELOW Wellcome's camp at Jebel Moya

The Wellcome Bureau of Scientific Research in Gordon Street, on the site of the later Wellcome Research Institution (Wellcome Building), with gardens to right along Euston Road

BELOW Stonework for the Wellcome Research Institution (Wellcome Building) at Trollope and Colls's yard, with Wellcome (second from right) and the architect Septimus Warwick (second from left), 1931

The Wellcome Research Institution's building, Euston Road, London (the present Wellcome Building), constructed 1931–2

BELOW Entrance Hall of the Wellcome Research Institution (Wellcome Building), 1932

ABOVE The Pocahontas portrait presented by Henry Wellcome to the Senate of the United States in 1899

LEFT Father William Duncan (1832–1918), founder of the Metlakahtla Mission

LEFT Sir Henry Wellcome with Captain Peter Johnston-Saint (1886–1974), Conservator of the Wellcome Historical Medical Museum, at St Augustine, Florida, 1935

BELOW LEFT Dr Paira Mall (1874–1957), collector of Indian manuscripts and paintings for Sir Henry Wellcome 1910–25

BELOW Ada Misner (later Reed), Sir Henry Wellcome's secretary

Wellcome, 1932

exhibits there of medical antiquity and interest. I soon met Dr C. J. S. Thompson, the author of a number of popular works, such as *The Mystery and Romance of Alchemy and Pharmacy* (1897), and found that he was the director and librarian of Sir Henry Solomon Wellcome, the owner of Burroughs Wellcome and Company, multi-millionaire and collector of everything that pertained to the human body. After a time Dr Thompson confessed that he had figured as 'Epworth and Company', one of the pseudonyms behind which Sir Henry liked to hide for the purpose of buying.*

Wellcome told a Royal Commission on Museums and Galleries in 1928 that 'I have been gathering material all my life', but although this was true, it was only after Burroughs's death that it gradually became a dominating factor in his life. Syrie, who had no interest whatever in his collecting mania, nor in his business, found to her dismay that their extended visits in Europe and elsewhere were almost exclusively for these purposes. As she wrote in 1910: 'Ever since our marriage, the greater part of our time has been spent, as he well knows, in places I detested, collecting curios . . . sacrificing myself in a way I hated, both to please him and gather curios.' Her husband did not consider them 'curios' at all, but the creation of something unique and permanent, of real value to anthropology as well as to the history of medicine – the History of Man, in fact. Syrie considered this a tiresome hobby that wives had to put up with, like golf. She never appreciated that her husband regarded this task as something even more important to him than the creation of a famous and successful company. This would be his permanent monument, by which he would be remembered, whatever happened to Burroughs Wellcome and Co. There were to be other causes of friction and difficulty between them, but this was a very important one – indeed, it was fundamental.

The collection, and eventual exhibition, came to absorb Wellcome totally. Before long a formidable amount of time, effort and money

* M. L. Ettinghausen, *Rare Books and Royal Collectors* (Simon & Schuster, 1966).

were being devoted to the proposed exhibition. To Thompson he wrote:

> I would like you to keep a careful list of all the Curio & antiquity shops, books, &c also junk shops, Pawn shops &c [in Portugal, Asturia Galicia] everything useful to us with addresses and a brief note on each as to character and nature of business and kind of objects etc. so that by reference you can recall any point or special articles. Get the clear address of each – get a card or invoice or letter heading etc. if possible – such a register with notes will be most useful for us.
>
> Pawn shops Blacksmith shops and rag & bone dealers are amongst the most likely to yield results. The roughest places are often the best – but they require patience. Priests can do much for you.
>
> I find it best to always make a rapid survey of a town & incite the people to hunt out things and always give an earlier date for departure than I intend or they will put off until the last minute and be too late.
>
> There should be some good books in the libraries [in Saragossa] and there are some good antique book shops but as 'keen as razors' quite a number of curio shops in private houses a good guide is necessary to root them out. The leading antique book shop is nearly opposite one of the principal hotels – this man issues catalogues. He had a lot of books on calligraphy at big prices I bought half a dozen at a moderate price, not his best you may make a better deal. He is a clever & cranky but drowsy looking old man in bad health – he may be dead, his son did not seem so keen.

Helen Turner, in her account of Wellcome's collection, has described it as possible

> to trace in the Wellcome records the day-to-day, ant-like activity which built up this vast collection. The central, directing figure is Wellcome himself, with Thompson as his chief assistant. At the turn of the century, when he began buying in earnest, the first targets were the leading British auction rooms, and these continued to be regularly visited throughout the next thirty years. . . . Wellcome himself seldom attended sales and he tried to keep his extensive buying secret by every possible means. He never used dealers to bid for him, but employed junior

members of his staff. . . . They were given sums in cash to cover what they spent. Pseudonyms were used on all records and goods were collected in a discreetly unidentifiable van. But it was all to no purpose, for the London dealers inevitably found out what was happening, and certainly some mixed lots were made up round items which would catch Wellcome's eye.*

In fact, although Wellcome seldom went to sales personally, he was himself an avid purchaser when travelling – not only from shops, but also from markets and private individuals – and his agents were instructed to follow his methods. He also had the virtue of persistence. In 1896 he visited an exhibition in Cardiff to mark the centenary of Jenner's epic discovery of the anti-smallpox vaccine, and discovered that this important collection was the property of Frederick Mockler. Wellcome at once tried to buy it, but Mockler refused. In 1903 Wellcome again approached him, only to find that Mockler, under severe financial difficulties, had sold it to a Mikael Pedersen, who was equally reluctant to part with the collection. But Wellcome and Thompson persisted and finally acquired the major part of the Jenner collection in 1911 for £500, and the remainder at auction in 1918. He bought anything connected with another hero of his, Lister, but few items were available in Lister's lifetime; it was not until 1926 that he was able to create his Lister collection for public display.

One of Wellcome's greatest interests was in old pharmacies, to be reconstructed with as much fidelity as possible, for which he collected furniture and fittings; the eventual results were to be of real historical value, as well as being visually dramatic. A particular triumph was John Bell's Pharmacy in Oxford Street. In 1908 Thompson was walking down Oxford Street when he saw that it was being demolished, and bought it on the spot; the others were clever reconstructions, but this was the real thing. The episode also demonstrated that Thompson had the Wellcome touch.

* Helen Turner, *Henry Wellcome, The Man, His Collection and His Legacy* (The Wellcome Trust and Heinemann, 1980).

It is not clear when Wellcome began to think in terms of creating a museum rather than only an exhibition, and even the most detailed examinations* of his papers and records have failed to give the answer. When he came to give evidence to the Royal Commission on Museums and Libraries, he could, characteristically, make it all seem logical, in retrospect, as though it was part of a master-plan. This was certainly not the impression he gave at the time; nor was it. As Henry Dale remarked, 'It may be doubted whether anyone knew him with sufficient intimacy to do more than speculate as to his real feelings and motives.' This was as true about his collecting as about anything else after Burroughs's death.

Wellcome later claimed that he had spent 'years' studying the collections in the British Museum and was very much aware of the extraordinary collection of the soldier-turned-archaeologist, General A. H. L. F. Pitt-Rivers, accepted by Oxford University in 1884. There was also the factor that archaeology at the end of the nineteenth century attracted huge public interest; the excavations of Schliemann at Troy and Arthur Evans at Knossos were dramatic and made the men – temporarily, at least – major international figures. Wellcome also took to heart Pitt-Rivers's injunction 'to collect the everyday'. The result was that there was no discernible theme in his collecting, as his buyers – and the dealers – soon realised. The collection, eventually five times the size (in terms of number of items) of that of the Louvre, with an expenditure on acquisitions far higher than that of the British Museum, was an astonishing hotch-potch, including medical instruments, weaponry, statues, human and animal remains, instruments of torture and criminal weapons. One consignment contained 'lamps, leather items, military equipment, costumes, fabrics, camping equipment, horn and ivory placques, musical instruments, silver and plated ware'. This was not at all untypical.

But there was one essential point about Wellcome's collection, and

* Ghislaine M. Skinner, 'Sir Henry Wellcome's Museum for the Science of History', *Medical History*, vol. 30, no. 4, October 1986.

the eventual Wellcome Historical Medical Museum: it was not to be for the benefit of the general public – rather patronisingly referred to by him as 'the stragglers'. It was to be 'the laboratory where cultural and technological problems would be solved'. If this was the case from the outset, Thompson was an odd choice as the first Curator, but his work in creating the collection had unquestionably earned him the appointment. As a buyer and traveller Thompson may have had many qualities, but his other abilities were journalistic rather than academic, and his freelance writing – which was eventually to sunder his employment with Wellcome in 1925 – should have made this as obvious to Wellcome as it was to others. His biographer has the clear impression that Wellcome was a compulsive collector of virtually anything, and then subsequently rationalised it. But his purpose was a serious one and the results were considerable. The fact that his collection went far beyond the history of medicine reflected the width of his interests; and, if he acquired much dross, there was also gold, to which any student of the development of medical science can testify. But the process of acquisition further imperilled an already strained marriage.

# 8

# 'A Morbid Misery'

In 1905 Robert Clay Sudlow, whose health had not been good, decided to retire. He had seen the tiny firm of S. M. Burroughs & Co. emerge through many vicissitudes into a major manufacturing company with a substantial international reputation. But he was far more than a highly efficient General Manager, crucial though that was, particularly when the mercurial Burroughs was the senior partner; his knowledge of the other employees, the nature of the business and Wellcome's ambitions was unique. He had become Wellcome's personal friend and was trusted totally by him; they both enjoyed Masonry, male clubs and organising major occasions. Wellcome was the showman and the man of ideas; Sudlow, more than any other individual, turned them into practical facts. Calm, industrious, but with imagination as well as an accountant's eye, his part in the survival of Burroughs Wellcome and its subsequent triumphs was, as Wellcome knew better than anyone, vital. While the two egos of Burroughs and Wellcome clashed so fiercely, and near-disastrously, the company itself had to be carried on; without Sudlow, it is difficult to see how it could have done so.

Wellcome not only gave his friend a sumptuous farewell banquet and a magnificently bound souvenir volume for all who attended and for Wellcome's friends and business associates in Britain and abroad, but also appointed him to a new position as Treasurer of the company, which Wellcome described as a 'new and highly honourable and responsible position', but which in fact involved very little work and a good salary. In 1900 Sudlow's fellow-employees had subscribed to present him with a silver loving cup and Wellcome had given him an inscribed gold watch. At Sudlow's retirement dinner, he presented him with a gold medal, and in 1909 – on the anniversary of his thirty years with the company – a set of cufflinks of gold encrusted with diamonds. This was not simply the ostentatious gift of a now rich man to a devoted friend and employee. It had deep meaning. If one of Wellcome's less attractive features was his capacity for not forgiving enemies, that of never forgetting real friends – and especially those who had been there at the beginning – was the most engaging. This in particular struck Frederick Goodman, Wellcome's old American friend and former colleague at Thomas Whitfield in Chicago when they were working together in his pharmacy, who was now Professor and Dean of Pharmacy at the University of Illinois:

> Mr Sudlow has reason to be grateful. Had he lived here [in the United States] and been overtaken by sickness the chances are he could not have had the opportunity of resigning but would have been told to step aside and make room for a young and more active man. This being what we expect, we are all the more surprised to witness the royal treatment he receives and the magnanimity with which he is provided for in the future.

Wellcome's personally designed gold medal for Sudlow had the tribute '*Honoratus Fidusque*'.

But Sudlow was irreplaceable. Wellcome's choice for his successor was George Pearson, who had joined the firm at the age of twenty-seven as a traveller, having, by a curious coincidence, previously worked at the same Oxford Street pharmacy of John Bell & Co. which was rescued by Thompson for the Wellcome Historical Medical Museum. Wellcome had sent Pearson to South Africa on the outbreak of war in 1899 to superintend the distribution of Burroughs Wellcome products to the army and, after the war, to establish the firm's Cape Town branch. In 1901 he had gone to Australia to organise, under Wellcome's strict instructions, the transfer from Melbourne to Sydney.

Prior to his appointment as General Manager he had been the head of the Foreign Department, rapidly becoming one of the most important members of staff.

Although Pearson had received the qualification of the Pharmaceutical Society, his academic and scientific ranges were somewhat limited; he was a good salesman and an efficient organiser, but Burroughs Wellcome was now a very different company to the one it had been even ten years earlier. Wellcome was recruiting scientists and technicians of the highest quality he could find, and they were moving into entirely new and exciting fields of research and discovery. Pearson was not intellectually in their league; furthermore, he was not remotely on the same confident terms with Wellcome as Sudlow had been. Sudlow had been in effect, if not in title, virtually a partner rather than the senior employee, and had a close and almost intuitive understanding of Wellcome's thinking. He also had no fear of disagreeing with him, nor of raising practical objections to his schemes. They had, after all, been through so much together for twenty-five years.

What neither Wellcome nor Pearson anticipated in 1905 was that, although Wellcome had made it plain that he wanted to remove himself from the routine management, he would move into fields far removed from pharmacy and business and absent himself from Britain for ever-increasing periods. Pearson was not to have the almost daily contact with the firm's owner that Sudlow had enjoyed. Sudlow had, moreover, grown with the firm; Pearson took over when it was a very large international business that was constantly expanding and changing. It would be unfair and unreasonable to describe Pearson as a nonentity; it would be fair to say that Wellcome would have done better to follow his practice on the scientific and medical sides of looking outside Burroughs Wellcome for talent. He seems to have thought that now the firm was so well established and operating so smoothly, it required prosaic and efficient management rather than leadership – which he himself was not to supply for much longer. The gradual decline in the pre-eminence of Burroughs Wellcome can be traced to Wellcome's decisions in 1905 to move on to other interests and his appointment of Pearson.

*

Meanwhile, further dramatic advances had been taking place at Burroughs Wellcome. The firm's products may have become celebrated, but in 1905 Wellcome sought a distinctive design that would make them instantly recognisable. None of the suggestions attracted him until someone – and his papers do not indicate who it was – suggested a unicorn, the fabulous animal with the body and head of a horse, the hind legs of a stag, a lion's tail and a single horn in the middle of the forehead, with alleged healing properties. It is probable that it was Wellcome's own idea, but it was certainly he who embraced it and registered it as the company's emblem. It remains so to this day.

Wellcome was also anxious to find 'a really able man' to extend the Physiological Laboratories' diagnostic work. As his relations with Dowson were personally uncomfortable, and were to deteriorate further, it is probable that he was also looking for a successor to a man as irascible, moody and over-confident of his abilities as Bokenham had been. But when he raised the subject with Chune Fletcher, his close friend formally again raised a matter with him that was causing him considerable concern.

For all Wellcome's claims about the independence of his Laboratories from the company, he was offering contracts that imposed a total commitment to confidentiality 'and respect as my property all my manufacturing processes, formulae, apparatus, etc., and all improvements therein, and also any inventions or new discoveries which may be made by you or anyone else in my employment'. These conditions also covered work done outside the Laboratories, and publications in professional journals and elsewhere had to be submitted to the Laboratories' Directors for their approval.

Fletcher rightly considered that such conditions would deter exactly the kind of person that Wellcome wanted; he also pointed out to Wellcome that three weeks' holiday a year was quite inadequate for high-calibre professional men. 'The trouble and anxiety which we

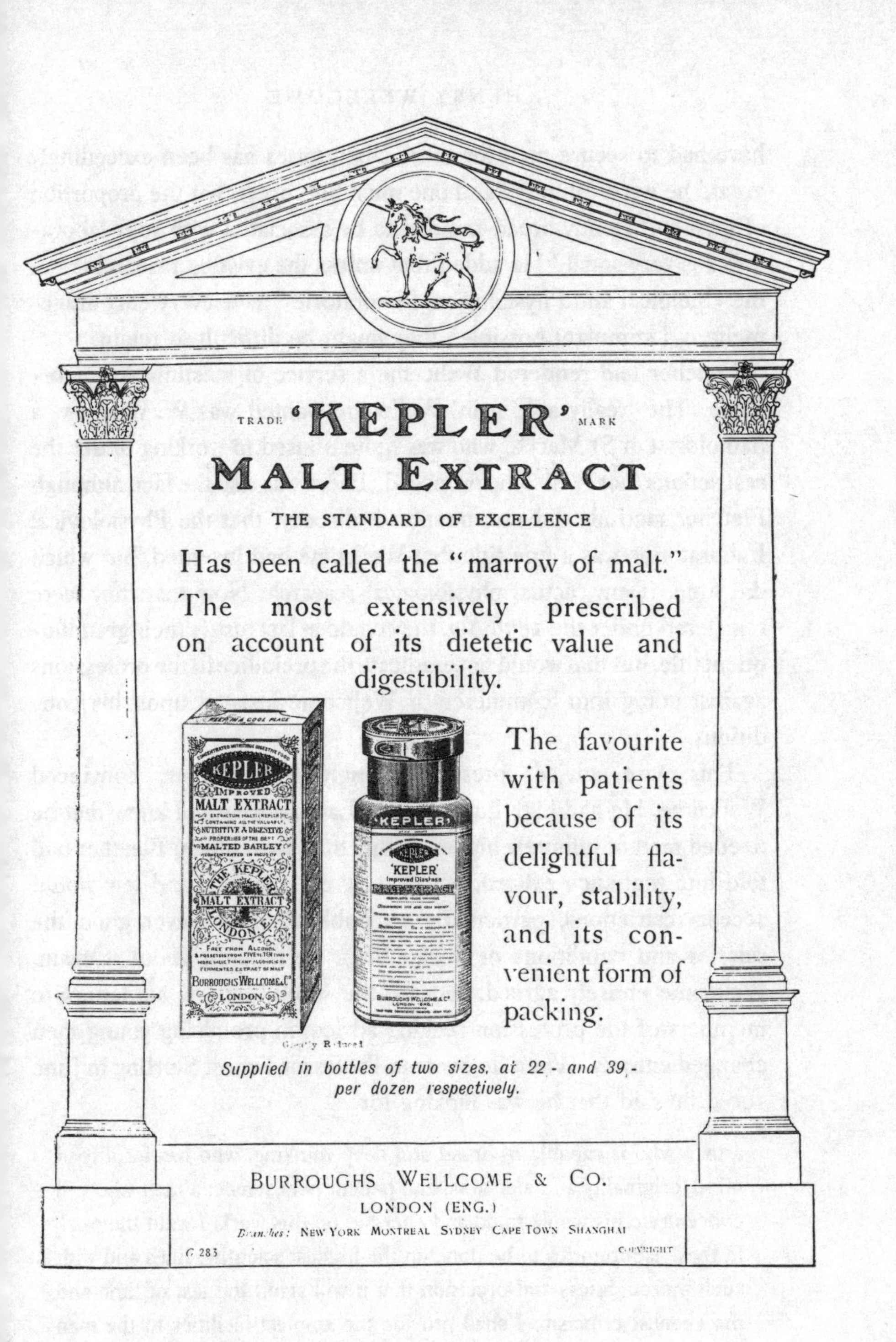


One of the first Wellcome advertisements featuring the unicorn, 1909

have had to secure men for these laboratories has been exceedingly great,' he wrote bluntly, 'and one must not forget that the proportion of men sufficiently broad-minded to be associated with your laboratories is very small.' He added that unless the existing researchers in the Chemical and Physiological Laboratories 'have every encouragement and stimulant possible', they might be difficult to retain.

Fletcher had rendered Wellcome a service of inestimable importance. The 'really able man' Wellcome wanted was W. V. Shaw, a pathologist at St Mary's, who was quite unused to working under the restrictions that Wellcome proposed. There was also the fact, although Fletcher tactfully did not mention it directly, that the Physiological Laboratories was a fine title that Wellcome had invented, but which did little, if any, actual physiological research. Now that they were registered under the 1876 Act, they could at last justify their grandiloquent title, but that would not eradicate the prejudice in the professions against going into 'commerce' if Wellcome insisted upon his conditions.

This wise advice, pressed strongly by Fletcher, convinced Wellcome. He had high hopes for his Laboratories and knew that he needed men of infinitely higher quality than Bokenham. Fletcher had told him that such existed, but in no great quantity, and few would accept restrictions, particularly on publication, however good the salaries and conditions of work. When he thought about it again, Wellcome entirely agreed. Indeed, the whole tone of his letters to members of the profession seeking advice on promising young men changed entirely. When he wrote to Professor Ernest Starling in June 1904, he said that he was looking for

> a man who is capable of broad and deep thinking, who has fertility of mind, originality and alertness, and patient persistence; a man who will concentrate his whole mind and energies on this work. I want the work in these laboratories to be done on the highest scientific lines and with such thoroughness and precision that it will stand the test of time and the keenest criticism. I shall provide the amplest facilities to the man who will rise to the occasion and make himself a master in this work.

Starling strongly recommended Henry Dale, a Cambridge graduate of twenty-nine, a natural scientist, then holding a studentship under him at University College, London. Dale had not given much evidence of his subsequent eminence and fame apart from an excellent degree at Cambridge, but on Starling's recommendation – backed by others, including the ever-present Fletcher – Wellcome appointed him, on the clear understanding, as Wellcome wrote to Dowson, that 'our attitude must be that we do not want Mr Dale unless he wants to come. I do not want any man who has to be persuaded, and I expressed this very plainly to Mr Dale.' Dale himself was warned by his colleagues and some former tutors that 'I should be selling my scientific birthright for a mess of commercial pottage', but accepted the offer on the new terms that Fletcher had created. It is obvious that if Fletcher had not changed the whole approach, Wellcome would have lost Dale and the subsequent history of Burroughs Wellcome would have been entirely different; it would also have been very improbable that so many of the early recruits to the Laboratories would have become Fellows of the Royal Society. Of all the services Fletcher gave to his friend, this was perhaps the greatest of them all.

Later recalling his first, and frankest, discussion with Wellcome, Dale wrote:

> He made it clear that research, giving results which could be applied in increasing the prosperity of his business, would have an added claim on his appreciation, but only as giving him eventually a yet wider opportunity to support research. I believe that to have been a perfectly sincere statement of his attitude, and his whole subsequent career has justified it.

But there had also been an important practical aspect to Fletcher's advice, as there were those in the Home Office who remained very doubtful whether the Wellcome Laboratories should have been registered at all. This surfaced again when Shaw applied for a licence to conduct cancer research in January 1902. Thane was again consulted. To Wellcome's relief he came down firmly on his side in a detailed and thorough report, which stated that, 'In the eyes of many persons it will be a merit that scientific work is done in the laboratory in addition to trade work.'

This was the last occasion on which the doubts were expressed. Nor did the successful Wellcome registration lead to the feared burst of applications from other companies. In 1905 the Newcastle firm of Brady & Martin successfully applied; the real increase did not occur until the First World War and its aftermath, May & Baker being only the third company to be registered in 1916.

The importance of Wellcome's contribution to the British pharmaceutical industry by removing the taint of 'commercialism' from it by establishing standards as high, if not higher, than the best academic medical institutions is impossible to exaggerate. The sheer quality of the work of Power and his colleagues in the Chemical, and Dale (who became Director in 1906) and others in the Physiological, Laboratories established the reputations of both remarkably quickly. Although Wellcome and Dale had a considerable disagreement over the latter's use of the word 'Adrenalin' in a paper published in 1905–6 – Wellcome being fearful of infringing a competitor's (Parke Davis's) trade name – Wellcome followed Fletcher's wise advice about not curbing publications of serious and often important papers. Indeed, while being naturally cautious about the possible dangers of unwittingly assisting his competitors by revealing processes and discoveries that they could exploit without his expenditure upon research, he quickly came to take pride in them and to encourage his young men to produce more, with the result that there was an astonishing output of papers and contributions to learned and professional journals that was, in quality and originality as well as in numbers, far superior to that of most universities.

Nor was Wellcome's role purely that of the creator of, and the appointer to, these remarkable institutions that bore his name. When he personally invited Dale to join the Physiological Laboratories he suggested, almost casually, that perhaps Dale might investigate the properties of ergot, which demonstrated that he was familiar with the work of the Cambridge physiologist, Thomas Renton Elliott, who had just amazed the physiological world with a communication on the results of his researches at Cambridge on adrenaline. Dale and Elliott became close colleagues and friends, conducting their research on the effects of ergot and adrenaline in Elliott's Cambridge laboratories and in the Wellcome ones, thereby beginning one of the most famous collaborations in modern medical science, Dale taking the first steps towards his Nobel Prize; both were to become Wellcome's first Trustees.

Precisely why Wellcome was so interested in ergot of rye is difficult to determine. Neither he, Dale, nor anyone else knew in 1904 that it could unlock the door to the isolation and identification of acetylcholine, tyramine and histamine. It could have been an inspired guess, but this is highly improbable, as there had been considerable scientific interest in its properties, but their importance was not disclosed until Dale turned his intense concentration on them.

Dale has related* how 'many friends had advised me against' accepting Wellcome's offer, but

> I was attracted to the offer, not only by a conscious desire to earn a marrying income, but also by an instinctive feeling that it would be a good thing for me, at that stage, to be obliged to stand scientifically on my own feet, to find my own problems, to plan my own experimental attacks upon them, to learn and devise methods for myself, and to make my own mistakes. When I accepted the appointment, Mr Wellcome said to me that, when I could find an opportunity for it without interfering with plans of my own, it would give him a special satisfaction if I would make an attempt to clear up the problem of ergot, the pharmacy, pharmacology and therapeutics of that drug being then in a state of obvious confusion. Pharmacological research was for me a complete novelty, and I was, frankly, not at all attracted by the prospect of making my first excursion into it on the ergot morass.

* Sir Henry Dale, *Adventures in Physiology* (Pergamon Press, 1953).

In fact, Dowson had already done some tests on extracts of ergot, but his reports had not impressed Power, Jowett or Wellcome. As a result, George Barger, a chemist and former Cambridge acquaintance, had been appointed also to work on ergot, 'in response, no doubt, to a similar prompting', and had prepared a number of extracts. 'I thought that I might make a beginning by testing some of these,' Dale later wrote, 'for the kind of pharmacological activity which was within reach of my limited technical competence. So I began with their effects on the arterial blood-pressure of the anaesthetized, or, more commonly, the spinal cat. All of them . . . showed an initial, noteworthy pressor action on the spinal preparation.' This provided unremarkable results. But, 'by one of my greatest strokes of good fortune, however, it was to give me an immediate opportunity of making a mistake of my own – a really shocking "howler"'.

A sample of dried suprarenal gland substance was sent from the Wellcome factory for testing the proportion of adrenaline. Dale tested it on the same cat; successive injections unexpectedly reduced arterial pressure, and he condemned the sample. 'By another and incredibly fortunate coincidence of events this was repeated in detail a week later. . . . My first tottering attempt at practical pharmacology had thus ended in what might have been merely a humiliating crash.'* It was, entirely by chance, a demonstration of the interaction of ergot and adrenaline, and riveted Dale's attentions – and Elliott's. Dale joined in research with Barger and Francis H. Carr, of the Chemical Works. Dale's first paper, 'On Some Physiological Actions of Ergot', was published in the *Journal of Physiology* in 1906 and began his rise to fame.

Dale's work caused immense excitement in the Laboratories, Dowson writing to Wellcome on 25 February 1905 that,

> You were quite right about our new physiologist [Dale] . . . but so was I. His energies are all in the right direction and you will be glad to hear that he is doing epoch making work at ergot – or rather I should

* *Ibid.*, p. XI.

> say with Chrysotoxin, one of its active principles. There is no doubt he is going to make a fine pharmacologist and this ergot work will give the new departure a splendid kick off. Dr Barger is also doing fine work in separating the active principles for Dr Dale to test. Curiously, the latter has quite turned the tables on him. Previously Dr Barger could not get his things tested. Now, with such a brilliant operator as Dr Dale to help him, he cannot get things out fast enough for the physiological labty [laboratory].

One episode in Dale's career had particularly intrigued Wellcome. While working at the Institute of Physiology of University College, London, he was under the charge of Ernest Starling, who, with his brother-in-law William Bayliss, had discovered secretin, the first identified and known hormone. Two Swedish anti-vivisectionists attended a live animal demonstration and then publicly stated that the dog was not anaesthetised and accused them of cruel and illegal practices. Bayliss issued a writ for libel, and Dale, who had been an assistant at the demonstration, was a key witness and completely convinced the court that the charges were baseless. Bayliss used the damages he received to endow a scholarship in Physiology at University College.

It was also significant that in the dispute between Wellcome and Dale over his paper on adrenaline, it was Dale who won. One of his letters to Wellcome made a particular impact:

> The question is at bottom a practical one. The connection between chemistry and commerce is an old and honourable one: that of physiology is a new thing to England and regarded with jealousy and suspicion by the 'professionally correct' medical and physiological people. You may not know [that] my predecessor, Dr Shaw, was blackballed by the Physiological Society merely on the grounds of his supposed connection with commercial interests. The situation needs delicate handling, and I am sure I may rely on you for any possible concession to old-fashioned prejudice, provided that it is compatible with dignified independence and due regard to your firm's interest. You will see how difficult it is for me to press a matter of this kind when there are people always ready to detect commercial manoeuvre in the policy of these laboratories.

Curiously, Dale later came to wonder whether he had been right. 'I am not nearly so sure now, as I was then, that I was completely justified as to the merits of the case. I am very sure, however, that I won an important victory for the staff of the laboratories.'

By standing up to Wellcome so firmly and bravely – and it must be remembered that he was only thirty and had just married – he won Wellcome's respect and admiration. 'I consider him [Dale] the best man in his work I have ever met for a young man,' Wellcome wrote, 'and he is developing well & I want him to develop my ideals in this physiological work – in which we are far ahead of others.' Although Dale did not know it, Wellcome's opinion of Dowson had declined further as a result of Dowson's indignation at having his position questioned, and not being adequately consulted. 'I am afraid that Dr D is and has been throughout this discussion in one of his "moods",' he wrote to Fletcher. 'Dr Dowson lacks tactfulness and as we know from past experience when in one of his moods stirs up & fosters discord and suggests bad motives and uses regrettable expressions.'

At this point, unfortunately for Dowson, but very fortunately for Dale, another serious problem arose over the quality of the Burroughs Wellcome anti-toxin serum. A consignment imported into the United States was claimed to be contaminated when examined by the US authorities. Like Bokenham before him, Dowson strongly contested their findings and thereby put his reputation at stake. Wellcome was especially sensitive about the quality of what was the first major new product of his firm, and employed independent experts to examine the consignment. They confirmed the contamination; Dowson, like his predecessor, was given the option of resigning, and wisely did so. Wellcome promptly appointed Dale acting Director and then full Director shortly afterwards. At a very young age, and after a career of no great distinction, Dale had been given his chance and was to use it brilliantly.* Although Wellcome took a keen interest, and pride,

* E. M. Tansey, *The Early Scientific Career of Sir Henry Dale* (unpublished University of London PhD thesis, October 1990).

in the work of the Physiological Laboratories, he never tried to interfere again.

Indeed, as a result of Wellcome's increasingly long absences abroad after 1905, he and Dale do not seem to have seen much of each other, and Dale never believed that he had known Wellcome at all. 'The real trouble is, of course,' he wrote many years later to his close friend Elliott, 'that Wellcome took elaborate pains to "present" to his staff and to others the conception of himself which he wished them to receive: there is hardly anybody, and certainly nobody in recent years, who has any notion of what he was really like.' This was not in fact true in 1906, but Dale's comments emphasise the remoteness of his relationship with Wellcome.

Dale's first task was to resolve the contamination problem, which required drastic measures, including the construction of a specially designed new building fitted with a one-way ventilation system using only sterile air for processing and packaging the serum. This was designed by Dale and Glenny, and worked so effectively that within months Burroughs Wellcome serum was allowed into the United States. Wellcome was quite untroubled about the expense and delighted with the results.

But Dowson had also tried to produce an anthrax anti-toxin by the same method used for producing the diphtheria anti-toxin. The inoculated horse died, but then the carcass was not disposed of properly, with the result that other horses exercised in the field began to die. When Dale realised what was happening, the area had to be totally isolated and was not used again so long as Dale was Director.

Then there was another disastrous result of Dowson's reckless enthusiasm. Another of his ambitions had been to produce an anti-toxin against Malta Fever. This was a very difficult and potentially dangerous procedure, as was proved when all four members of the team working on the project contracted the fever, and the leader, Dr Allen MacFadyean, a former Director of the Lister Institute, whom Dowson had specially employed, died. Dale had to close down the entire operation. 'I wonder if you ever realised what a hopeless mess we were in at that juncture on the bacteriological side of the activities of the WPRL,' he later remarked to one of his junior colleagues, who had joined after Dale had sorted out his grim inheritance from Dowson. Dale also made some important changes in personnel, recruiting, among others, his former pupil P. P. Laidlaw, with whom he was to make his major achievement to date in discovering the physiological roles of histamine. Before Dale joined the Physiological Laboratories nothing had been achieved in any area of research, and the Laboratories had proved to be incapable even of producing totally uncontaminated serum, which had been the whole purpose of their establishment ten years before. After Dale's arrival, and the creation of an outstanding team, the fame of the Laboratories really began.

The success of the Physiological Laboratories was not confined to research. Their production rose from 84,000 packages in 1905 to 239,000 in 1910, and to 627,000 by 1915. The most dramatic single increase was in diphtheria anti-toxin serum after Dale had overcome the problems that Dowson had bequeathed him. By 1910 the Laboratories were producing 268 million units a year. By 1912 the sera produced included diphtheria anti-toxin, anti-colon, anti-staphylococcus, anti-typhoid, anti-puerperal fever, anti-rheumatic fever, anti-venom, scarlatina, ulcerative-endocarditis, anti-meningococcus, anti-streptococcus (erysipelas), anti-dysentery and tetanus, and vaccines against a number of diseases and ailments, including typhoid, cholera and Mediterranean fever. The Laboratories also produced eleven varieties of tuberculin and greatly expanded the Burroughs Wellcome list of veterinary products. The scepticism with which many, especially his competitors, viewed Wellcome's protestations that the Laboratories were primarily for pure scientific research became increasingly justified, but he fulfilled his promise to put the firm's very substantial profits, and his own resulting personal wealth, back into more research, more highly qualified staff and better facilities. With Power's pioneering work at the Chemical Laboratories, and Balfour's work in the Sudan, Wellcome had created one of the most talented and powerful research bases in the history of modern medicine and pharmacy.

Of particular importance was the concentration on diseases becoming rare, if not unknown, in Britain, the United States and Europe, but prevalent throughout most of the British Empire; the firm's products therefore were much in demand from expeditions and from the British military and civil authorities. Few precise figures of the firm's sales and profits have survived the total destruction of the Snow Hill headquarters building in 1941, but it is almost certain that Wellcome was a millionaire before 1910, and that the firm's profits were very large indeed, and growing significantly each year, thus giving Wellcome personally more time and opportunity for pursuing other interests. It was his concentration on these that caused Dale to call him a 'poseur'; but he had not known the younger Wellcome, and did not know the older one very well, either.

Dale and Wellcome never really got on with each other and were to part in 1914 with some coldness on both sides. Dale was himself a difficult man in many respects and was to make some sharp private comments on Wellcome in later years, resenting his obsession with his exhibition, archaeology and constant travelling. But he was always grateful to Wellcome for giving him his great opportunity and wrote to him, very prophetically, in 1906, when he became Director of the Physiological Laboratories, that, 'I hope some day to see the aid of commerce by physiology recognised as an important & desirable brand of medical science in England, & to see your laboratories recognised as the pioneer institution.'

*

There were other 'pioneer institutions' in the name of Henry Wellcome.

Since the beginnings of Burroughs Wellcome, the American market for its products had been distributed by Wellcome's friend, Sam Fairchild of Fairchild Brothers & Foster, and since Wellcome's dispute with Burroughs in 1887 there had been no manufacturing or production of any of the company's products in the United States. But by 1906 improving American sales justified the establishment of an associated house in New York, managed by Thomas Moore, who had had a successful experience in establishing the firm in South Africa. Two years later the company rented several floors in a large building on Hudson Street and began manufacturing; in 1910 the expanding business moved closer to Fifth Avenue while manufacturing continued at Hudson Street. The number of staff was modest and the equipment notably inferior to that in England. Unsurprisingly, the company never made a profit until 1919, and Wellcome was constantly being urged by its accountants to close it down, but refused, claiming that what was needed was better staff and equipment and the adoption of methods that had been so successful in Britain. Furthermore, he had, rightly, great faith in Thomas Nevin, who had been the Manager of the Canadian Wellcome house before being moved to New York in 1911. Wellcome's very modest investment in his country of origin initially paid very poor dividends; it was only many years later that his obstinate refusal to accept his accountants' advice was justified.*

Balfour and his staff were achieving remarkable results in the Sudan, most notably in his insistence upon strict sanitary rules and a relentless assault upon the mosquitoes' breeding grounds. Balfour organised camel caravans with laboratory equipment to travel across the country, collect specimens for research and combat avoidable disease, particularly among cattle. The conditions were harsh and two of his British staff died. Although Balfour and the Army Medical Service were able to prevent sleeping sickness and the dreadful tsetse fly penetrating the Sudan, there was no shortage of other diseases.

In 1905 an eminent Egyptologist, Sir Wallis Budge, visited the Sudan and was amazed by Balfour's achievements, particularly in Khartoum itself. But he pointed out in a letter to Wellcome that, although

> they are doing wonderful work up the White Nile in respect of the cattle diseases, the distance of the field of work from Khartoum kills some of the results. What is really wanted is a laboratory in a boat,

* See pages 377–8.

> which could move from place to place, so that it might be possible to draw off blood from a suspected beast and deal with it at once without waiting for it to get to Khartoum and be there tested. . . . It is hopeless to look to the Government for such a thing, but it seems a dreadful pity that so good a work should be hampered and probably stopped for the want of a little floating laboratory and plenty of materials at Khartoum.

Wellcome considered this a brilliant idea – which it was – and, in close co-operation with Balfour, agreed to finance a fully equipped floating laboratory, together with a steam tug* to take it to the upper reaches of the Nile. In 1907 Charles Wenyon was seconded to Wellcome for a year from the London School of Tropical Medicine to join the floating laboratory. He made extensive collections of parasites from humans and animals, and this provided him with the experience and much of the material for his future work, books and papers on protozoology, and the beginning of a remarkable career with Wellcome, culminating with his eminent directorship of the Wellcome Bureau of Scientific Research from 1923 to 1944. Here was another example of how the pioneering works of Burroughs Wellcome drew outstanding young scientists into its operations by reputation rather than deliberate recruitment. While Wellcome was always asking his friends and contacts in the profession to recommend young men of exceptional promise and talent, the name and fame of Burroughs Wellcome was now such that they were applying to become part of the most exciting – and best-funded – area of British medical research. Wenyon's secondment was in one sense accidental; in another, it was not. Burroughs Wellcome's laboratories had become a magnet for men of ability and ambition, as Wellcome had always intended.

Wellcome was now moving in very exalted company, having been appointed a member of the General Council of the Gordon College, whose other members included Kitchener, Cromer, Wingate, Lord

* This was originally drawn by a large rowing boat, which was not satisfactory.

Rothschild and Sir Ernest Cassel. He undertook to publish the reports of the Tropical Research Laboratories' work, and did so with his customary lavishness. In his honour a new species of mosquito discovered by Balfour, captured after it had 'boarded the steamer in the evening at Baro, and bit freely', was named *Anopheles Wellcomei.* When the Khartoum Laboratories were totally destroyed by fire in May 1908, Wellcome at once financed their complete rebuilding and restoration, to even higher standards than before.

*

However, a problem closer to home had to be resolved. The substitution and infringement of trademarks became steadily more serious as Burroughs Wellcome's fortunes continued to improve. Wellcome now had Moulton on a retainer fee, and also made use of the advice of Sir Edward Clarke, one of the most formidable courtroom lawyers of his generation, who had been a Conservative Solicitor-General, but who subsequently fell out with his Party. There was no shortage of work for Wellcome's lawyers, in Europe as well as in Britain, in the campaign to protect the firm's rights and reputation.

The result was a series of successes. Some challenges never came to court; when they did, the legal artillery that Wellcome deployed was devastatingly triumphant. In September 1900 Wellcome sued three pharmacists in Milan who were selling imitations of 'Tabloid' brand products, and successfully obtained an injunction against them. There were two major court actions in Britain in 1902, but by far the most important occupied a great deal of Wellcome's attention in 1903.

The Liverpool firm of Thompson & Capper was manufacturing and selling pills it described as tabloids. When Wellcome protested that it was infringing his trademark, it responded that the word was descriptive and, accordingly, not a trademark. When the case eventually came to court in December 1903, Wellcome's team, headed by Moulton, contained three King's Counsel; they had marshalled seventy-two witnesses and intimated that they could produce as many again. Mr Justice Byrne sensibly declined the suggestion.

Wellcome was the first, and obviously principal, witness, and his evidence occupied nearly fifty pages of the printed evidence. The names of his supporters who gave evidence was virtually a list of the most prominent members of the medical profession. The defence mustered fourteen witnesses, of whom ten were professional men, principally from Liverpool, but six of them were described as homeopathic doctors and chemists. Mr Justice Byrne ruled totally in favour of Burroughs Wellcome; surprisingly, Thompson & Capper appealed, but were again defeated.

This victory was not only important for Burroughs Wellcome, but also for their legitimate competitors, with their own trademarks to protect. 'The Tabloid Case' was therefore followed with considerable attention and concern in the profession. Wellcome's invented word entered the dictionaries as specifically describing the products of Burroughs Wellcome. The court's decision also by clear implication protected other pharmaceutical trademarks as well.

*

By 1904 Wellcome's other interests, and his passion for travelling, had become so dominant that he engaged a business efficiency consultant to reorganise the management of the firm, and specifically the Snow Hill head office, one of the principal purposes being to free him from business detail and the regular running of the firm. As everyone in Burroughs Wellcome knew, Wellcome always kept a very close eye on the company's business and research activities, and did so until his death, but after 1905 it was usually done from a distance, and often a substantial one. If his fascination for medical science and history, and his regard for the best minds in the field, never abated, the pursuit of money for its own sake did not interest him any more. He was now rich, but he did not own a great house or acquire any of the other usual appurtenances of wealthy self-made men. When the Wellcomes left The Oast House in 1904 to move to another on Hayes Common, inappropriately called The Nest, leased for £152 per annum, it was not as large; although a substantial modern house, it was of little distinction and certainly no grandeur.

But the Wellcomes were not in either of their houses very much. They were in the United States from the beginning of September 1904 until the following April; in the autumn of 1905 they went to Madeira after travelling through France, Spain and Portugal, not returning to England until May 1906. Then, Wellcome became enraptured by the motoring craze. In the autumn of 1906 he was exploring Kent; emboldened, he planned a long European motoring expedition for the following year. These were allegedly vacations, but, as with his frequent business trips to Europe, with a serious purpose, the purchase of any objects of medical interest for his great exhibition. While he – and Syrie – concentrated upon France, Spain, Portugal and Madeira, Thompson went further afield, including Germany and Scandinavia.

Syrie found these prolonged expeditions a purgatory. The worst of all was an interminable wander by motor-car through France, Spain and Portugal in the winter of 1907–8. There were frequent punctures, the cars kept breaking down, the roads were terrible and the weather was bad. There was an endless stream of cables from Wellcome to Snow Hill demanding new tyres and spare parts to be sent to him immediately by train. There was also an acrimonious altercation with an offensive Portuguese customs guard, which resulted in a letter of protest to the authorities of several pages; as Wellcome had actually been arrested and marched off surrounded by an armed guard of several soldiers, he had reasonable cause for complaint. When they got to Lisbon, they found that King Carlos and his elder son had just been assassinated, and riots were in progress, in which a number of civilians and soldiers were killed. The Wellcomes eventually returned to England after having been away for over six months – and six very unpleasant ones. Wellcome seems to have enjoyed the adventure, and not least the Lisbon riots; his wife considered it a nightmare, and, surveying the mass of telegrams and messages that poured into Snow Hill as their cars proceeded from one misfortune to another, it is easy to see why. These trips, with Wellcome's constant searching for items for his exhibition, put strains on their relationship that were becoming unbearable for her, and the tensions between them were dangerous. It was during another long absence from Britain that the virtually inevitable rupture occurred.

They sailed for New York in September 1909, then travelled by train to California. The principal purpose of this extended visit was for Wellcome's health, which had again deteriorated with the recurrence of his ulcerative problems, and which lowered his morale and made him exceptionally irritable. This was now, disastrously, accompanied by severe quarrels with his wife.

On their return journey to the East, the Wellcomes stayed in Washington at the request of the Secretary of War, J. M. Dickinson. The reputation of the Khartoum Laboratories had by now become international, and their publications, expensively printed and distributed, were read with mounting excitement and interest by all engaged in the new field of tropical medicine. Dickinson asked Wellcome personally to undertake a detailed inspection of the health and sanitary conditions in the insalubrious and disease-infested Panama Canal zone. The work on improving these conditions was being undertaken by General William C. Gorgas, himself a distinguished expert on tropical diseases, but the entire Canal project was now under threat from a Congress and a press that was seriously challenging its vast cost and the severe death toll from illness and disease incurred in the construction of the Canal. There was also criticism of Gorgas personally, and Dickinson was anxious to obtain a dispassionate outside opinion.

It was exactly the kind of enterprise that appealed greatly to Wellcome, whose health seems to have recovered slightly from the Californian holiday, but not at all to Syrie. The new plan was for them to travel to Quito to stay with some American and English friends, from where Wellcome would go to the Panama Canal zone for his inspection. It was in Quito that the explosion occurred.

The invitation to them came from Jordan Stabler, then at the American Legation to Ecuador, in Quito. He had befriended an

Ecuadorian political prisoner, Major J. S. Uribe, who was hostile to the regime and who, after his release from prison in November 1909, was given asylum in the American Legation. Stabler was anxious that Uribe should be removed from Ecuador under American protection, and asked Wellcome to take him back with him to England, as Uribe's life was clearly in danger. Wellcome agreed, and a myth was subsequently created that he had saved Uribe from a firing-squad by bribing an officer. What is probable is that Uribe might well have met such a fate if Stabler and Wellcome had not intervened.

Also staying in Quito with Stabler was Archer Harman, then aged fifty, an American railroad builder and financier in Ecuador, 'who came to exercise a powerful influence in the internal progress of the country'.* He, Stabler and Uribe were all enthusiastic polo players.

This long and wearying journey might in itself have been the last straw for Syrie, but it was in Quito that Wellcome suddenly and angrily accused her of having been unfaithful to him with Harman. The vehemence of Syrie's indignation and denial seem genuine,** but as she was later to regale her second husband, Somerset Maugham, with tales of her alleged amorous adventures, it might appear that Wellcome's suspicions were justified, although Maugham came to believe that they were fictitious. The scenes between them were obviously violent and bitter, and Syrie angrily left him for New York. Although it is not literally true that they never saw each other again, they never again spoke to each other. Wellcome refused to reply to her letters, handing over the painful role of intermediary to the hapless Chune Fletcher.

* *Encyclopaedia Britannica*, 11th edition (Cambridge University Press, 1910).

** Mrs Uribe has written (7 February 1994) that, 'It would seem hardly likely to me that the latter [Harman] may have been involved in the quarrel of Sir Henry Wellcome and his wife, since I can clearly remember conversations when Archer Harman's name was frequently mentioned in a natural and amiable manner between Sir Henry and my husband, which surely would not have been the case otherwise.' It is a fact, however, that Wellcome demanded a written assurance from his wife that she would not see, or communicate with, Harman, to which she agreed, under strong protest.

The normally admiring and supportive Haggis rather surprisingly turned against Wellcome over this disastrous episode, accusing him of intolerance, injured vanity and 'a self-righteous hypocrisy incapable of distinguishing between the quality of Mercy and weakness'. This severe judgment ignores the fact that Wellcome was genuinely convinced that his wife had betrayed him. Haggis considered that he then fell into

> a morbid misery only to be soothed by a vicious preoccupation in his own interests . . . [that] soured his character for the rest of his life. His outward charm remained, but he inclined to a mistrust in human nature, his friendships became fewer and shallower as the years rolled by, until he was left almost to himself and his work, an egocentric human force believing that the world had little to offer him save the material success of his projects and the plaudits of the onlooker.

This was not true; nor was Haggis's charge that Wellcome's generous settlement on his estranged wife 'was more than likely inspired by an anxiety to secure the approval of the outside world', not least because 'the outside world' knew nothing about either the separation or the settlement. Wellcome took considerable care to ensure that as few people as possible knew about either.

There was another factor that may have played some part in Wellcome's reaction: at the time of his fatal quarrel with Syrie, he was undoubtedly seriously unwell and was to remain so for several months, at a critical time in his personal life.

One of his best and most valued friends was John Ferreira, whom he had met on his first visit to Madeira in 1897, when he was trying to recuperate from his 'catarrh of the bowels'. He employed Ferreira immediately as his courier, interpreter and friend in Spain and Portugal, as well as looking after his interests and collections in Madeira itself. Most unusually for Wellcome, his letters to Ferreira are addressed to 'My faithful John', and even 'My dear and trusty friend', and it was to him and no one else that he confided that he had become ill again, and that his fateful visit to California in the autumn of 1909 had been for health purposes. In the summer of 1910 he wrote to Ferreira that 'I have been obliged to undergo a series of severe operations. I am now progressing towards recovery. This illness is all the result of the severe cold and influenza I caught at Seville when I did not follow your good advice.' It was in fact a severe recurrence of the old ulcer problem, complicated by influenza, and it was not until June 1911 that he could report to Ferreira that 'my life in the Desert has substantially restored me to health'.*

While Syrie was returning home with her son, in burning indignation, Wellcome undertook his Panama inspection. The enraged and embittered husband was now replaced by the cool analytical Wellcome. He made three visits to the zone between the beginning of March and 30 May, when he submitted his report to Dickinson.

In its way it was one of Wellcome's masterpieces. Together with Gorgas and his chief assistant, he undertook long cruises through the swamps, visited hospitals, laboratories, drainage and sanitary systems, and examined the scientific records. In the main he was impressed by what Gorgas and his team had achieved, especially in curbing the mosquitoes, which, as Wellcome wrote, formerly made 'life in Panama a terror, as I well know from personal experience'. Gorgas was well aware of Balfour's achievement in Khartoum and had applied the same methods of treating all stagnant water meticulously with larvicide, using Derris, an immense and complicated task in the swampland. But, while Wellcome was impressed by Gorgas's work, and had begun a particularly warm friendship with him, he drew on his Sudan and Balfour's experience to recommend special Inspection Laboratory Cars for field experimentation work, on the lines of his Nile floating laboratory, and the establishment of a training school of tropical medicine and hygiene, with publication of

* Wellcome never saw Ferreira again after 1914, but regularly sent him and his family money and other gifts, regarding him as still being in his employ, although, as his eyesight and health declined, he could do no work for Wellcome. Nor did Wellcome forget him in his will, giving him an annuity for life, writing that 'I often think of our many happy experiences and adventures together'.

its findings. He also emphasised the problems that could arise from external diseases when the Canal was opened. With his usual wide ambitions, he saw the Panama development as an object lesson and example to all Latin American countries, where, as he well knew, ignorance of tropical medicine was virtually total.

Not all his recommendations were accepted, but the bulk were, and his report was widely circulated in the American Government, particularly to the Surgeon Generals of the army and navy, and summaries of it were published. The unjustified criticism of Gorgas and his colleagues virtually ceased, and despite continued mutterings about the cost of the project, the Canal's construction continued with a significant further reduction of deaths and illnesses from preventable diseases. It would have been better if such an enquiry had been undertaken at a much earlier stage. The scientific knowledge, equipment and drugs did not exist then to make the pestilential area free of disease, but the combination of the Nile experience and practical common sense on sanitation and hygiene had almost as dramatic results as Balfour had achieved in Khartoum.

Having received Dickinson's warm thanks and praises, Wellcome sailed back to England summarily to resolve his marital crisis.

There is no question that Wellcome was embittered by Syrie's conduct, but so would most men who believe that they have been cuckolded, and especially one of Wellcome's standards and background. It does not seem to have occurred to him that his wife's unhappiness, which was obvious to her own family, was in any way his own fault. There is also evidence that the sexual aspects of the marriage had not been satisfactory, but Syrie never claimed, as others have done on her behalf, that he physically ill-treated her, or had done anything that could have given her grounds for a divorce. She had discovered that she and her husband had virtually nothing in common, and his insensitiveness to her palpable dislike of a life of boredom in a suburban villa punctuated with long and tedious travelling mystified his friends, who knew of the warm and generous side of his personality. But it is not unknown for men to be sympathetic, tolerant and understanding to their friends and employees, and less so to their own families.

For all his success and achievements, Wellcome was already a wounded man before his marriage. To be an expatriate working in another country is seldom a wholly satisfactory or happy experience, and although Wellcome had tried hard to assimilate himself into English society and to be accepted by the English, perhaps he had tried too hard. It is significant that, outside business, he gravitated naturally towards fellow-Americans who had settled in Britain – the Sheldons, Stanley, Genevieve Ward, Hiram Maxim* and Power most particularly – and had relatively few close British friends. Sudlow and Kirby could certainly be so described, but they were company colleagues. Chune Fletcher and Charles Stewart were perhaps his closest English friends and confidants, but here, also, there were professional as well as personal connections. After Mounteney Jephson was married, their close relations seem to have become more distant as Jephson's employment as a courier took him abroad even more than Wellcome's incessant travelling. Thus, they also drifted apart.

But the deepest wounds had been inflicted by Burroughs, and then his widow and her financial and legal advisers. They had tried to destroy him on several occasions and had demonstrated a degree of malignity against him personally that had at first astounded him, and then embittered him. He had started out with an enthusiastic faith in most people; he now began to suspect and mistrust them. His friends noted a new wariness, accompanied with an authoritarian approach in personal as well as in business matters.

He had also become intolerant. One employee at Dartford was summarily dismissed when found smoking a cigarette by the lake; a

* Hiram Maxim was a resident of Dartford. Born in Maine in 1840, he was the inventor of the revolutionary Maxim gun, capable of firing 666 rounds a minute, which was adopted by the British army in 1891. Maxim was also one of the aircraft pioneers, although an unsuccessful one. Like Burroughs, and later Wellcome, he became a naturalised British subject and was knighted in 1901.

personal servant, after his marriage, had to sign a solemn declaration in the presence of witnesses that he would never drink alcohol again. The cheerful 'Hal' had been replaced by a more driven, difficult, enigmatic Henry. His friends were mystified; his young wife was made unhappy.

The terms of the separation were generous. Syrie received £2,400 a year and would have custody of Mounteney until he was eleven. Wellcome would pay all his educational and medical costs, and Mounteney would spend three months a year with his father; after going to boarding-school, he would be with his father for half of his school holidays. What was far less generous was Wellcome's insistence that he should have the power to decide whether certain people were, or were not, desirable company for his son, Chune Fletcher arbitrating in such cases. Wellcome had come to the inflexible opinion that his wife was a deeply immoral woman, who might well expose his son to people like her and, thereby, in some respects corrupt him; he therefore insisted upon this condition. It was another indication of the depth of his feelings against her and the company she best liked to keep.

However, one of the most puzzling aspects of the matter is which of them insisted on the separation in the first place. The dispute in Quito had clearly been terrible, and violent words had been spoken on both sides. But their friends both there and in England assumed that there would be a reconciliation of some kind, if only for appearances and Mounteney's sake.

It was Wellcome's clear understanding after Quito that his wife was determined to leave him. In a letter to her of 29 April, he wrote:

> I do not know how much money you have by you, BUT in case of emergency and under any circumstances I do not want you to be dependent upon nor to receive money from others, though you are preparing to desert me. Here are six hundred dollars for you to have in hand and this should more than cover any necessary expenditures for some time. I must forbid you to incur any debts on my account hereafter.

She wrote to him on 24 May from a hotel in London: 'What do you propose for the future? You can hardly suggest after your recent treatment of me that life together is possible.' She did not expect this separation to be permanent. She was enraged by Wellcome's allegations, but clearly assumed that the storm would pass, and could have salutary results on the behaviour of her husband. When she realised how embittered he was, she sought his forgiveness and understanding; but it was too late, and the wound was too deep. To her dismay, Wellcome began proceedings for a legal separation as soon as he returned to London. When she asked to see him, he refused.

His friends, especially Dorothy Stanley, implored him to be reasonable – Syrie was contrite and did not want a separation – but Wellcome now revealed a cold bitterness that astonished those who knew him best, which they had never suspected and which he had never revealed in his disputes with Burroughs.

On 8 June Wellcome wrote to Mounteney Jephson's wife, Anna: 'I feel I ought at once to tell you that grave trouble has arisen between my wife and myself. I know I have only to ask that when you and I meet no reference be made to the subject.' She replied:

> Your letter is a great shock, and I can only say that it is also a real sorrow to me. I know how little any words can mean in times of trouble, but if I can ever be of any help to you or Queenie I am sure you know how gladly I would do anything possible. I quite understand that you are numbed by this great anxiety, but whenever you feel able to come to us, there will be a warm welcome waiting for you now and always.

To another friend in America Wellcome repeated his request for silence (24 August):

> ... I cannot tell you how I appreciate the sympathetic heart beats indicated by your letter – which is truly characteristic of you and yours in loyalty and faithful friendship. I warmly thank you and Mrs Curtis for your kind offer but there is absolutely nothing that you or any one else, however wise and willing, can do that will be helpful except to

observe absolute silence. I cannot forget that my wife and I lived together on affectionate terms for nine years – that I adored her as the idol of my heart, and that she is the mother of my child. I want nothing unkind said about her.

From the first I have not allowed myself to discuss the trouble with even my closest friends. I feel that this course is best for all concerned. I am sure you will realise my distress of mind about it all. It seems as if the light of my life was put out. Our happy home is broken up. . . .

All offers of assistance were rejected. Dorothy Stanley tried very hard, as did Anna Jephson, with no success. Dorothy Stanley wrote on 13 June that 'You may count on my absolute silence – indeed, spoken sympathy would be intrusive and a liberty. I just strongly feel how good and splendid you are.'

On 20 July she appealed to him:

I see your little Queenie as often as I can, as much for your sake as for hers. Oh, dear Mr Wellcome do forgive her any folly or imprudence. She is so all alone and needs your love & protection. Then, for your boy's sake do not separate from his Mother, it will be bad for him. They are both children and need infinite indulgence: we all need indulgence & forgiveness let us then give it freely to one another. The more you feel wronged, the grander to forgive, and Queenie will forgive you for thinking she had done you a wrong she has not done. You only have to ask her to. The public know you have been ill, that is all, there need be no scandal, no talk: if only you would forgive and let her come back to her rightful place – & trust her. Show trust in her (she has had her lesson). She looks ill and very worn, do, do forgive her.

When little Mounteney grows up, do not let him feel there has been a slur on the character of his Mother. Stop those horrid lawyers from drawing up their cold-blooded agreements: let Heart and Soul speak I know that I have only heard one side, but anyhow, whatever you think or even feel – just forgive. Don't abandon poor little Queenie. What will become of her!! I will do every mortal thing I can to take care of her. No one knows I am writing – not H.J. [her husband], not Queenie; but write to you I must, as I would to a dear Brother.

Wellcome replied from Hampstead, where he had rented a house in Holford Road, on 28 July:

With all my heart I appreciate your high motives in writing me as you have. I know that you speak from your heart, but I must tell you quite frankly and definitely that what you suggest with such whole souled good intentions would – under the actual circumstances – only bring unhappiness.

Every point you have presented has been well before me from the first and the course I have pursued has been well and anxiously considered with an aching heart and guided by my most earnest desire to safeguard so far as possible under the circumstances both Mother and Child.

If I am misunderstood and misjudged because I think it best to avoid discussing the case even with my trusted friends I must stand it. I know how easy it is to form strong conclusions when only one side is heard.

I fear that any encouragement of the ideas you have suggested with the best of motives can only do harm, and will not facilitate settlement.

I am trying to arrange matters in a considerate manner for a friendly settlement without publicity. If this fails I shall be profoundly sorry.

Again please let me assure you that I do not fail to realise and appreciate your friendship and lofty motives in writing to me as you have. Believe me I am not insensible to any of your many touching passages many of which go to the very heart core.

She replied, sadly, on 1 August:

I realise by your letter the finality of it all. Death brings no such bitterness in its sad separating. It is true, I have only heard one side, and even the side I have heard revealed nothing that seemed irremediable, so I worried you and perhaps even hurt you with a letter. No one can realise what you have gone through, how awfully you have suffered. . . . I always knew you had the nerves of a fine racehorse, those nerves alone enabled you to win your many races, but on the other hand those very nerves make you suffer far more exquisitely than many another type of thick skinned man. How I wish there were any possible words or deed in my power to testify to you my sympathy and affection. But there is, I realise now, nothing one can say or do.

I ought to have realised that no decision of yours was arrived at lightly, or to be altered by friendly appeals. I wrote mainly because of my immense regard for you. I so longed to find it was only an unhappy dream, a misunderstanding, which could be swept aside. I felt, if I could conceive a misunderstanding between me and Stanley, that I would just lie down at his feet and die there rather than not be forgiven, and that even if I believed I was in the right I would accept being in the wrong – anything but separation from Him. Nothing – no power – Not Himself could have kept me from Him. So I felt I would try to get you to forgive as I should crave to be forgiven – but everything is different, I suppose. How I wish H.J. & I had you here to take care of you & nurse you, and prove our love, but you want to be away and alone and wish you had done with life and living and all the bitterness of things. I will not speak again of all this. How I recall the two short phrases of Bula Matari's* 'It's no use' and 'Let it be'. Do get well, and let me see you again. . . .

Your affectionate friend Dorothy Stanley.

On 6 August Syrie wrote to Wellcome from Henley:

Dear Hal

As regards Mounteney & quite apart from any agreement you & I may come to – you know as I do that he has a great chest delicacy, that our most earnest wish is & always has been that he should outgrow this delicacy, that in spite of any terrible misunderstanding between ourselves we are absolutely at one in wishing to do the very best for our boy and we both know it is absolutely necessary that he should spend a large part of every winter abroad. To do this is very expensive as you well know & I do not think you can or will refuse to make me a seperate [*sic*] allowance for this specific object – £500 is I believe a very moderate and fair one to make under the circumstances. You know how the travelling & keep of him & his governess adds to expenses, and as you also must know I personally would not dream of leaving England, or going so far afield, if it were not for the boy. I thought I would write

* Her nickname for Stanley.

you myself on this subject as I feel sure that with regard to the boy our wishes will always be in accord.

I always speak to him of you & he has your photo in his room & prays every night for you. I also constantly tell him how you are etc. so that he shall not at any time cease to care for you & I think you will believe me when I tell you that I always want him to love you as he always has. I dont want him ever, at any rate for years, to know there is any trouble between you & me. Children dont notice the living apart & I think if I talk lovingly of you to him it wont suggest itself to his mind to wonder.

Hal all the years we were married I honestly tried to make you happy & to please you & now you are turning your back on me. Won't you try & make things as easy as you can for me? You know best whether you wont feel happier in knowing you have tried to make life easier for me – and you must know how hard its going to be – how hard it must be for a woman without the husband she has been accustomed to look up to & lean on & depend on, & you know how I did depend on you, how it seemed as if I never could do without you, now we are out of each other's lives & I am sure it must make you as unhappy as it does me.

I am told you want me to write a letter about not seeing Mr Harman. Whilst I refuse to admit there is any ground whatever for me doing this still if it will make you any happier I shall be perfectly willing to write you to this effect – when we have come to a definite understanding & agreement.

I do hope you are better* & that the change to Harrogate will do you good (I thought it was by the sea but of course it isn't). I am not very well but I hope when all this worry & anxiety is over to be better, Your wife Queenie.

However, she wrote to Chune Fletcher on 14 August rather more bitterly:

* On his return from South America in May, Wellcome had caught a severe chill 'which brought back my old troubles of last year'. As a result, he had to undergo an operation in August.

Surely he owes me a little consideration & generosity now. I am the mother of his Child & as he well knows I've given him the best years of my life, my youth & health & the future is blank for me. All that should surely weigh with him in his treatment of me now. He knows as no one else can how I have given in to him & cared for him & it seems to me intolerable to have to plead & beg for fair treatment now when I should have thought he would have wanted to make things easy for me.

Why he asks me for instance to write a letter about Harman, a thing he has no justification for doing but which as I say I will gladly do if only as a courtesy & as he wished it, but surely he in his turn should be prepared to do things that he wont feel. I mean give up things that he wont miss, for me. I put this all to you as of course the actual clauses of the agreement are best left to the lawyers but these matters it seemed to me we could best settle ourselves.

These things may seem trivial to you but they comprise so much of a woman's life & I cannot be turned out with nothing to make life beautiful & livable even though happiness has gone. You know a woman of my age etc. must have those surroundings if life is going to be livable if she has not domestic happiness to make up for the lack of everything else. Surely it would be wiser & kinder to make my life possible and peaceful. I would suggest making a list of such things as I would like for our home from the Nest.

*

In defiance of the rules of chronology, the ending of Wellcome's marriage to Syrie Barnardo may be included at this point.

Her period of separation from Wellcome between 1910 and 1915 seems to have been an active and merry one, but as one of the principal narrators of her alleged affairs and adventures was to be herself,* they may be approached with considerable caution. It is not even clear that, as Somerset Maugham alleged, Gordon Selfridge

* These were related to Somerset Maugham, who fictionally portrayed her as 'Lady Grayston' in *Our Betters*, written in 1915 when they were living together in Rome, and first performed in London and New York in 1923, and who wrote about her, in his sour dotage, in *Looking Back*.

bought Syrie a house in London and that she was his mistress. Selfridge was depicted as Arthur Fenwick in *Our Betters* as a 'red-faced, grey-haired, cigar-smoking, poker-playing American who runs a London department store'. There have been allegations of other loves, and a lifestyle that was considerably more extravagant than even Wellcome's generous allowance could have afforded. One story had it that she had a special doormat made for her Regent's Park house with the word 'Wellcome' on it. (This, it must be said, has the ring of truth.) It is not even known when she met Maugham, already famous; some accounts date it in 1911, others in 1913. What was true was that they became lovers and lived together, and that in 1915 Syrie gave birth in Rome to a daughter, whom they called Liza.

Wellcome and his legal advisers must have been aware of the rumours attached to his wife's name, and on 23 July 1915 his solicitor, Henry Brenton, reported to him that, 'About two weeks ago some information which seemed to me most important came by chance to my knowledge. I thought it necessary to have some enquiries made in Paris and Rome.' These confirmed that 'Mrs Maugham' had indeed had a baby, and the doctor in attendance had identified Syrie as 'Mrs Maugham'. Maugham later claimed that she had told him that she had an arrangement with her husband, who knew of her affairs and condoned them; there is certainly no evidence for this in Wellcome's correspondence with his lawyers, and it is highly improbable. Maugham later thought so, also. It is probably true that, within limits, Wellcome had no interest in what his wife did, provided that she did not morally contaminate their son. But these limits did not include the scandal of her living almost openly with a young writer and playwright, who had achieved fame at a remarkably early age, and producing a child by him. There is no evidence that he was actively seeking a divorce; Wellcome was very well aware of the stigma that this cast, even on the innocent party, in English Society, in which he still had ambitions to rise. The suggestion, by some of Syrie's friends and others, that he was anxious to end the £2,400 a year allowance to Syrie can be dismissed; although it was a large sum, it was of little consequence to Wellcome. It is certainly the case that Syrie's finances were in a dangerously chaotic condition, and that she could ill afford to surrender her allowance from her husband. But these matters are more appropriate for the biographers of Syrie and Somerset Maugham than for one of Wellcome.

Faced with incontrovertible proof that his wife had been living with another man and had had a child by him, Wellcome instructed his solicitors. No defence was offered. Wellcome was awarded a decree nisi, with costs, and custody of Mounteney, on 14 February 1916. Syrie married Maugham at a civil ceremony in Jersey City in May 1917, by which time Maugham's homosexuality had become dominant. The marriage was a disaster and ended in 1929, when Syrie had already established herself as the most fashionable (and one of the most expensive) interior decorators on both sides of the Atlantic. She had many detractors, but also many admirers and close friends, who always rallied to her defence. When she died in 1955, Maugham wrote of her:

> It would be hypocrisy on my part to pretend that I am deeply grieved at Syrie's death. She had me every which way from the beginning and never ceased to give me hell. My hope, for some years I have been told, was that she would survive me. I wonder, when she looked back, if she ever did, whether it occurred to her what a mess she had made of her life.

In his old age, and virtual senility, he wrote a savage attack on her in *Looking Back*, which was so appalling that it was never published in Britain apart from some extracts in a Sunday newspaper; the fierce American reaction, and that of Syrie's friends, may have persuaded even Maugham that he had gone too far. Noël Coward, amongst others, hit back on Syrie's behalf with *A Song at Twilight*, about an eminent homosexual author in his old age confronted by a former mistress with some compromising letters he had written to a male secretary. Coward played 'Sir Hugo Latymer' and, just to make the point absolutely clear, had himself made up as Maugham.

The real Maugham was to attempt to deny his paternity of Liza, by then Lady John Hope, and to try to disinherit her; a miserable, but necessary, court action was needed to prevent this.

After her death, Rebecca West, Cecil Beaton, Oliver Messel and Sacheverell Sitwell made a public appeal for contributions to a memorial to Syrie. The response was substantial and enabled them to purchase a bust of Catherine the Great by Shubine, presented in her name to the Victoria and Albert Museum.

It is very probable that Wellcome's feelings against his former wife were as bitter as those of Maugham. But he did not reveal them. His only subsequent dealings with her, usually sharp, were over arrangements for her seeing their son. After their separation they only met once, when Wellcome was in a London cab with Mounteney. The cab had stopped and suddenly the door flew open, Syrie rushed in, kissed her son almost frantically and then, with only a quick look at her former husband, was gone.

Apart from these remote contacts, first through Chune Fletcher and then through lawyers, Wellcome never spoke of her, and it was understood by his friends, acquaintances and colleagues that it was a subject never to be raised in his presence. Syrie seldom spoke of her first husband to her daughter and then, Liza recalled, 'without affection'.

It is impossible, and perhaps unwise, to make judgments from afar on such matters. Wellcome was probably an unsuitable husband in many respects, Maugham certainly in every one. Syrie's friends put all the blame on them and none on Syrie, which seems equally exaggerated. But if Syrie did indeed make 'a mess of her life', she had inflicted deep wounds upon Wellcome. The physical and mental energy remained, but the spark had gone.

In Wellcome's absences Chune Fletcher had to cope with Syrie's frequent complaints, usually about money, but then, ominously, about Mounteney's health. He was a charming and kind little boy, but he was often sick and making disturbingly slow mental progress. Syrie even wrote directly to 'Dear Hal', ending her letter: 'That you should have a pleasant winter & derive great benefit to your health is the sincere wish of your Wife'. There was no acknowledgment. Fletcher was an admirable and understanding go-between, on occasion stepping in personally to pay pressing bills on Wellcome's behalf, once after a furious letter from 'Queenie Wellcome' that 'I will neither have to barter like a Jew nor beg like a pauper'. After Fletcher's death in 1913, she again tried to contact Wellcome directly by writing a long letter to him. She wanted to visit his Historical Medical Exhibition, 'as for so many years I was with you while you were collecting and was extremely interested in the project'; she also wrote about some items she wished to have and about the time that Mounteney should spend with her. This was a recurrent problem and was to remain so. Again, Wellcome did not reply to her letter, but passed it on to his lawyers with the curt instruction that the terms of the separation were to be adhered to rigidly. Whenever Syrie attempted to put her relationship with her estranged husband on a more civilised basis, she was bleakly rebuffed. She had been dismissed from his life.

*

In the autumn of 1910 Wellcome returned to Africa. But there was another event in 1910, on 28 October, when the Home Secretary, Winston Churchill, signed the document that made Henry Solomon Wellcome a British citizen. He had renounced his American citizenship in July 1905. On 1 November 1910 he took the Oath of Allegiance to King George V.

# 9

# Collector and Archaeologist

When Wellcome had first visited the Sudan in 1901, he had been intrigued by the evident opportunities for archaeological research, and had visited some promising sites, and in July 1909, on the invitation of Professor John Garstang of Liverpool University, he became a member of the Sudan Excavations Committee of the University's Institute of Archaeology. Garstang had established a considerable reputation for his excavations in Egypt and was, like Wellcome, fascinated by the possibilities in the Sudan. Wellcome had contributed to the costs of Garstang's work, and that of others in the same field, for a number of years, and had been in correspondence with Wingate about his financing and actually leading an expedition of his own. Wingate warmly encouraged him, but the opportunity had not arisen until the disasters of 1910.

By the late summer of that year Wellcome was a lonely, unhappy and frustrated man. He was rich and successful, but with the collapse of his marriage and the passing of many of his friends,* combined with continuing poor health, he was in low spirits. Also in 1910, his brother George remarried after the death of his first wife, Cevilla, and his second wife, Fannie Garwood, and Wellcome seem to have disliked each other from an early stage in George's marriage. To judge from the comments of the children of the first marriage,

* Many of his friends died relatively young. Between 1909 and 1914 he lost Jephson, Fletcher and Sudlow.

Wellcome's opinion was probably right, but the previous warmth of the relationship between brothers had faded sadly into acrimony. Contrary to Haggis's version, Wellcome did eventually make new friends after his separation from Syrie – his close friendship with Wingate developed later – and his creative zeal was wholly unaffected, but if he took some time to recover from the shock of the collapse of his marriage, this is not to be wondered at, nor censured.

Therefore, he was looking for new interests and adventures, at least now knowing that he did not have to bear the incubus of a sour and rebellious Syrie on his travels. His doctors considered that a warm and dry climate would be good for his health. So, he returned to Egypt and the Sudan in the autumn of 1910 to open another chapter in his life.

Wellcome's own writings are unhappily few, but in September 1912 he described to the archaeological section of the British Association for the Advancement of Science in Dundee his return to the Sudan:

> Chartering a *dahabeah* at Khartoum, I cruised up the Blue Nile so far as navigable water permitted, and explored both the eastern and western banks for some distance inland, finding several sites of ancient settlements. On my return journey, I halted at Sennar, and then trekked westward to a range of granite hills, known as Jebel Moya, lying about twenty-five kilometres distant from the Blue Nile. These rugged hills are of considerable height, and rise abruptly from the plain. They consist mainly of gigantic boulders and ledges, to which cling a few scattered trees of acacia, baobab and ebony. Several wells within the recesses of the hills, yielded a meagre supply of brackish water. On the failure of this supply most of the natives were obliged to migrate with their flocks to the Blue Nile, until the next rainy season. Years of severe drought and famine have caused much suffering.
>
> A native village of thatched bee-hive huts stood in the plain, at the northern extremity of the range, and contained on my arrival about eight hundred inhabitants, while in the vicinity, several nomad tribes were encamped with their herds.

Having found what he believed to be an important site, Wellcome was confronted with a major problem. The local chieftains were hostile and the potential workforce was indolent, totally unskilled and much addicted to robbery and conflict, especially under the influence of *merissa*, a potent liquor. Wellcome initially made the American mistake of offering high wages, which encouraged their greed, but not their confidence in him. They claimed to be devout Moslems, but in every respect were not. Characteristically, Wellcome had studied the Koran, which he now invoked in the face of hostility and violence. Murder was not at all uncommon, and Wingate was among many who warned Wellcome that his life was in real danger – which, unquestionably, it was.

When Wellcome first viewed the principal site, a valley at the south of the Gezira plain between the White and Blue Niles, it was littered with potsherds, a multitude of stone implements and other signs of human occupation. Wellcome became convinced that he had found a prehistoric site of great antiquity. 'It has been suggested', he said in 1912, 'that here also we should seek the veritable birthplace of human civilisation itself. Do the sands of this land of enigmas still hide within their depths an answer to the eternal enigma of man's beginnings and a record of his first steps upon the pathway of knowledge?' The Omdeh, the local native chief, was suspicious and, while promising assistance, consistently put obstacles in Wellcome's path. As a result, Wellcome began his great work with only a dozen men and some boys. But, 'having satisfied myself as to the real importance of this site, I applied to the Sudan Government for official authority to carry out excavations. This was granted.'

Wellcome's claim to have found the site himself has been questioned by Frank Addison, who wrote in 1949 that,

> In later years he liked it to be thought that he himself had discovered the site, but having regard to its situation, it seems hardly likely that he actually did so. It is more probable that, when he broached his scheme to the authorities in Khartoum, he was supplied with all available information relating to known, but unexcavated, ancient sites.*

* Frank Addison FSA, *The Wellcome Excavations in the Sudan, vol. 1, Jebel Moya* (Oxford University Press, Oxford, 1949), p. 2.

This does not mean, however, that Wellcome did not actually choose Jebel Moya himself.

Wellcome may indeed have been keenly interested in the subject, and the area, for many years, but he was not in any respect anything more than a rich amateur – although, it might be added, rich amateurs have contributed a great deal to modern archaeology. He had come to his conclusions very quickly, without any professional advice or examination of the items he had found lying on the ground. Even when it was later conclusively proved that the site was very late neolithic, and, although of interest and some importance, was nothing as exciting or novel as he had deduced from his somewhat cursory examination, Wellcome was never fully convinced by the expert evidence arrayed against him. He was sure that if his men dug really deep, and dug at other nearby promising sites, he would eventually find evidence of far greater antiquity and achieve fame comparable to Schliemann and Evans. For once, despite considerable expense and intense personal commitment and organisation of what became a very major undertaking, he failed.

But if Jebel Moya turned out to be archaeologically a disappointment, its story is an important one in the life of Henry Wellcome. Although in the end something of a failure, the manner in which Wellcome met and solved the formidable problems he faced was in its way one of his more notable triumphs.

Confronted with problems of man-management unique in his experience, Wellcome hit upon the idea of offering prizes for finding objects. This appealed to the gambling instincts of the natives, and also got round the difficulties caused by the Omdeh. He also gave much prominence to the high wages he was offering. Gradually the number of volunteers grew to 500; by 1914 there were over three thousand men working for him at the sites. One of their tasks was to build his house out of huge boulders of rock, which was known, unsurprisingly, as The House of Boulders.

Curing them of drink was considerably more difficult, but gradually the regularity of payment, and Wellcome's patient exhortations and practical incentives to them to save rather than spend, were effective. He also invited orthodox Moslems to come to Jebel Moya to tell his men, and their wives, that by drinking alcohol they were offending deeply against their religion. In addition, he pointed to the practical fact that the non-drinkers were making more money than the slaves to *merissa*, and winning more prizes. Another typical Wellcome innovation was his creation of the Wellcome Order of the Peacock. This took the form of a peacock feather which was bestowed, with much solemnity and public ceremony, on workers who had not drunk the evil *merissa* for two months. So successful was it that peacocks had to be specially imported from Britain to show the Sudanese the source of the feathers; again, it is impossible to assess the cost of this particular imaginative venture, which must have mystified Snow Hill, but which dutifully complied with Wellcome's bizarre order. The fact was that this strange combination actually worked; eventually, over ninety per cent of his workforce had sworn on the Koran never to drink alcohol again. Apart from the other results, this dramatically cut down the violence, murder and injury that had been common, and which had made Kitchener and Wingate fearful for Wellcome's safety and life. All weapons were banned, and Wellcome set up a savings bank; he also ensured that his workers had good food, principally the native corn, *dhura*, at low prices. When in 1913 the price rose sharply, Wellcome subsidised the cost of *dhura*, even importing consignments from India.

As conditions improved, Wellcome brought in European engineers and carpenters to man his workshops and to train the Sudanese, who were quick to learn and eager, as they were when Wellcome introduced them to football, hockey and athletics. In a relatively short time Wellcome had created a contented, reasonably hard-working and sober workforce out of a drunken and dissolute rabble, and he was acclaimed not only in Cairo and Khartoum, but also by Moslem leaders, who came to Jebel Moya to see for themselves what this strange Christian white foreigner had achieved.

One most unusual innovation by Wellcome was aerial photography of the site. Obviously, Wellcome had no aircraft, but as an enthusiastic photographer, he and the photographer, A. G. Barrett, conceived the idea of sending up a large box kite as a platform for a camera that Wellcome had had specially designed in London, with automatic devices. The technique was extraordinary. Perhaps even more extraordinarily, it actually worked. Addison has described it:

> It was about this time, too, that Mr Wellcome instituted, and Barrett carried out, some of the earliest experiments in archaeological air photography. The development of the aeroplane was then still in its infancy and large kites were used. No written account of these experiments is preserved in the records, but from the photographs it seems that two methods were tried. In the first the camera was lifted directly by the kite, the shutter release being operated by a string from the ground. The photographs taken in this way were those looking directly downwards. The second method was more complicated but enabled angled photographs to be taken and from greater heights. Here the main kite carried into the air a light wire cable, and along this a 'kite trolley' carrying the camera was sent, in much the same way as a schoolboy sends a 'messenger' along his kite string. . . . The sail was held open – presumably against a spring – on the upward journey and was folded up so that the trolley would slide down again by its own weight. To judge from the photograph, the trolley carried a mechanism which would, after it had travelled a predetermined distance upwards along the cable, operate the camera shutter release and immediately afterwards trip the spring which held the sail open, so that the trolley and camera would come down again. According to Major Uribe the chief difficulty encountered in these experiments was that of controlling the kites in the eddies and wind pockets induced by the surrounding hills, and more than once the apparatus was dashed to the ground.
>
> Yet the experiments on the whole were successful and excellent results were at times obtained. . . . Today, when photography from the air is a commonplace, and hardly a day passes without some example or other appearing in every newspaper, these photographs in themselves will excite no comment; but they were of unusual interest at the time they were taken and they represent a triumph over many difficulties.

> From a purely archaeological point of view the kite photographs are of limited value because, from the nature of the site, they reveal little that was not already discernible from the ground; but that the experiments were undertaken at all is evidence of Mr Wellcome's determination to avail himself of every aid contemporary science could furnish.*

But not all Wellcome's European assistants were successes, and he dismissed two – one of whom had hit a Sudanese worker without cause – who then spread malicious stories about him in London, which were published in Horatio Bottomley's notorious *John Bull*, to the consternation of Wellcome's friends and colleagues. Wellcome was accused of 'gross ill-treatment and cruelty' and of methods that 'practically amount to Slavery'. There was dismay and astonishment in Cairo. Wellcome totally denied the accusations, denouncing the accusers as disgruntled sacked ex-employees with a personal grudge, and expected Wingate to consider this sufficient. With London demanding information, questions being asked in the House of Commons, and Bottomley – himself an MP – sticking to, and blazoning, his story, Wingate had little choice but to instigate an immediate enquiry. Although the enquiry totally exonerated Wellcome of the charges of ill-treating his workmen, questions were raised about the legality of the Indenture which Wellcome insisted all his men had to accept when they joined his service. This particularly incensed Wellcome, who wrote angrily to Wingate that it had been drawn up first by a London solicitor, then checked in Cairo, where it was revised by a prominent Egyptian lawyer and translated into Arabic under his supervision:

> The Indenture is a part of the paternal system of welfare work which I have explained. . . . No wrong, difficulty, or grievance has ever arisen out of it. No complaint has ever been made against it to my knowledge,

* *Ibid.*, p. 6. Contrary to some accounts, this was not the invention of the subsequent eminent aerial photographer, Osbert Guy Stanhope Crawford, who was recruited for the fourth season (1913–14) as an archaeologist. Wellcome's remarkable technical innovation was patented in 1913.

> except the absolutely fictitious one which has been withdrawn as unfounded. . . . I do not know why I should be singled out as the one employer of labour in the Sudan for such delicate treatment. My thousand and more happy and well-fed workmen of today with plenty of best Indian *dhura* at four piastres per twenty pound measure can, I fear, hardly realise the deep solicitude now being felt for them in Khartoum. Had equal anxiety for their welfare been manifested three months ago when in vain they petitioned the Government for protection against fraudulent practices which prevented them from obtaining food to alleviate the pangs of hunger, they might have easily understood the generous spirit of it.

This bitterly sarcastic protest prompted Wingate, who liked and admired Wellcome, to issue a total and unequivocal endorsement of his methods and treatment of his workforce. As the government inspector had found not a scrap of evidence to support the allegations, and had himself apologised, Wellcome for a time felt sore that Wingate should not have taken his word as sufficient; but on their next meeting Wingate apologised with such charm and sincerity that good relations were immediately restored. Indeed, after his return to London, Wingate and his wife were to be among the closest of his friends, in what became a very limited company. Kitchener, who had visited Jebel Moya in 1912, also wrote an emollient and flattering letter. In *The Sudan in Evolution*, by Percy Martin, published in 1921, Wellcome's contributions to 'the moral, intellectual, and general improvement of the Sudanese, and the influence of his work', were warmly praised. But Wellcome's satisfaction at what he had achieved remained shadowed by charges which, in his view, should not have been entertained for an instant.

This unpleasantness arose in the spring of 1913, by which time the excavations were proceeding efficiently and well, and Wellcome was regarded as a saviour by his men. He enjoyed the desert climate and life, and not the least of his achievements was to instil into the Sudanese his love of animals, which were essential to the work. His policy was to buy only the best horses, donkeys, mules and oxen, and treat them well as valuable assets, to be kept healthy and contented; this had not previously been the Sudanese practice, but it became one at Jebel Moya. Wellcome himself developed a taste for racing camels and claimed that he had bought the finest in the Sudan. Affection for camels is not universal, but Wellcome found riding a fast camel across the desert one of the most exhilarating experiences of his life. He also enjoyed naming them: there was Great Belly (Abu Querah), Skittish (El Zozajh), Frightful (Hayav), Piercing Wind (Muserak-El-Hawa), Snow White (Dabalan) and Never Late (Zalqook).

One of Wellcome's principal assistants was his follower, later appointed Camp Commandant, Major J. S. Uribe. As has been described, Wellcome had met him while he was in Quito at the time of his violent quarrel with Syrie, when Uribe was a major in the Ecuadorian army. He became one of Wellcome's most devoted personal servants. After Wellcome left Jebel Moya in 1914 – as it happened, for ever – Uribe stayed on to continue his work, including the building of a school for the children of the site employees, again financed by Wellcome. Uribe and his family were to be among the beneficiaries of Wellcome's Will, to this day. This is another example of how Wellcome prized devoted loyalty above all other human qualities.

Wellcome took a close personal involvement in every aspect of his sites and insisted upon detailed excavation reports and records, often questioning the evidence and the conclusions reached from them. When a cemetery was considered to be mediaeval, he was incredulous; he ordered deeper digging, as 'the graves beneath the coins may be older'. 'He evidently wanted the cemetery to be much older than it is,' a reviewer of his notes later commented. When one of his more expert assistants, Oric Bates, wrote that 'There is a striking absence here of series of implements which, beginning with prototypes, produce primary, secondary, and further derivatives. This means that the people came here from outside with a culture already well-developed, and that they did not stay here long enough to evolve a complete set of new types', Wellcome retorted: 'This is based on a very meagre study of only a small portion of one section of the whole site.' Bates's journals, covering his work on the site between December 1911 and the late spring of 1912, reveal considerable confusion:

> The inventories are disgraceful. . . . Cameras came up yesterday, but no developing material. Only Derry & myself seem to appreciate the gravity of this: the rest of the staff, because there are some Tabloid chemicals and some small cameras for which there is ammunition, seem to think that we 'ought to be able to get along somehow'. . . . Men layed off as tomorrow the Bishops of London and Khartoum are to visit the site, and the men are to be seen working. . . . It being Friday there should have been no work, but Mr Wellcome had some work which could not wait. A fairly large number of locals struck and remained below in the village.

Another assistant, James Dixon, recorded in exasperation: 'Mr Wellcome wants another photograph taken of the deep pit 100/1027, which I have just had carefully covered up at his request.'

Crawford's later account pays considerable tribute to Wellcome's energy and resourcefulness, but comments that, 'I, too, like nearly everyone else, had differences of opinion with Wellcome.'

Such difficulties and strains were inevitable in an operation of this magnitude, but no amount of digging could confirm Wellcome's insistence that the sites were much older than in fact they were. The findings were by no means of negligible importance – indeed, some were of real interest and attraction – but however deep the men dug, or how wide the search areas, Wellcome could not find the evidence to confirm his rash early estimate of its age. Meanwhile, crates containing a startling variety of items were shipped in great quantities to London for further inspection and storing; as with Wellcome's other collections, the latter was now becoming a major problem.

*

By 1912 Wellcome considered that, as a result of his own collecting and the international response for gifts and loans of items (most of which he subsequently bought), he now had enough material to launch his great historical medical exhibition in London, to coincide with the meeting of the International Medical Congress, at 54a Wigmore Street. It was Thompson who had suggested to Wellcome that the planned Congress provided a unique opportunity, and the Wigmore Street site was occupied in 1911; in 1912 the Historical Medical Exhibition became the Historical Medical Museum and was accepted as the official Museum of the Congress.

While Wellcome was in the Sudan for the winters of 1911–12 and 1912–13, Thompson and his staff faced the daunting task of selecting items and organising displays from the vast amount of miscellaneous material at their disposal. Sambon had to examine and choose items from the mass of surgical instruments that Wellcome had acquired. When Wellcome returned to London, after intense activity and work, much of the exhibition was in place, but Wellcome at once made criticisms and ordered changes. A considerable number of the firm's employees and additional staff had to be pressed into service before he returned, but more had to be employed before Wellcome was satisfied. It was formally opened on 24 June 1913 by Sir Norman Moore, President of the Section of History of Medicine at the International Congress. Wellcome announced that the Museum would become permanent, and in the autumn of 1913 it became the Wellcome Historical Medical Museum, with Wellcome as Director and Thompson as Curator.

It was the sheer variety, as well as the scale, of Wellcome's collection that was so remarkable. Helen Turner gives some examples:

> From Bethlehem Hospital: a pair of ancient shackles, and a pair of handcuffs used in the 18th century for chaining up a violent lunatic: 9s 6d.
>
> From Mrs Helesdon, Andover, wife of the medical practitioner: bell mortars, weighing nearly 30lbs and bearing the remains of an inscription and dated 1659. Four pairs of primitive midwifery forceps entirely covered with leather. Four old dental keys. One lithotomy forceps, 17th

century. One extractor, 17th century. One lithotomy knife, 17th century. A curious dental instrument for extracting teeth. An ancient curved amputating knife with a carved wooden handle. Inclusive price for the above items: £2.10s.

Purchased in the East End of London – an amulet necklace that had belonged to an old Jewess. Composed chiefly of old jet beads, and strung with them numerous amulets, one of metal bearing on it in Hebrew characters a prayer to Jehovah against sterility, and others in the form of hands. Stated that the necklace was worn for a time by each child, and after the child had recovered from a complaint, a lamb bone was placed on the necklace to prevent the illness returning: £1.

Knocker from front door of house in Herne Hill where Ruskin was born, purchased from 'the people demolishing the house': £1.

Despite the disparate quality, which can be too easily mocked, the general reaction to the Museum, inside and outside the profession, was of awe and admiration. In 1912 Wellcome had announced the annual award of a gold and a silver medal for the best two student essays on any aspect of the history of medicine, the competitors to be judged by assessors from the University of Edinburgh. He also insisted that the Museum was a place for research and study, and not a collection of interesting historical curiosities. Accordingly, the library was its strongest feature, but Wellcome insisted that it was not to be opened to readers until sorting and cataloguing had been completed. It was not to open until 1946.

Even in 1913 only a small part of Wellcome's collection could be displayed. Meanwhile, to the dismay of Snow Hill, more shiploads of crates were arriving from the Sudan.

*

At this point, in 1913, Wellcome casually made a disastrous decision.

The achievements of the Chemical and Physiological Laboratories under Power and Dale had been phenomenal; inevitably, there had been considerable overlapping of research, but this in fact had been wholly beneficial. Balfour's work at Khartoum, however, had a special place in Wellcome's affections, and from it derived his decision to establish in London an institute for the study of tropical medicine and hygiene, not only for research but also for the training of students, to be headed by Balfour. This was a fine and ambitious concept, which was to have admirable long-term results, but Wellcome, without consulting either Power or Dale, or indeed anyone else, announced also the creation of the Wellcome Bureau of Scientific Research, whose 'Director-in-Chief' would control the Chemical and Physiological Laboratories. This would be Balfour.

Balfour had wanted to expand further the Khartoum Laboratories, but his health had deteriorated – including, ironically perhaps, from malaria – and, as Wingate noted, he was over-worked and fraught. Wellcome knew this, and there were strong compassionate grounds for bringing him back to Britain. The mistake was in the new position he was given.

Both Power and Dale, in their different ways, were indignant. Neither knew Balfour, except by reputation, nor were they consulted; they therefore felt slighted. Power was hurt rather than angered; Dale was evidently very angry. Power decided that he had had enough of his solitary life in London and told his old friend, to the latter's dismay, that he intended to retire and return to America. Moulton upbraided Wellcome strongly for his folly in unnecessarily losing Power, writing to him that 'there is no-one in Europe who could fill his place', but it was too late. Dale resigned. His reputation was high, and in 1914 he was elected a Fellow of the Royal Society. He had considered that he was being asked to undertake too much routine work and testing rather than research, but it was Balfour's appointment over his head that was the decisive event. Dale was approached by members of the new Medical Research Committee – at the suggestion of Gowland Hopkins – to join the new National Institute for Medical Research. After receiving assurances about his role, he accepted and was appointed as from 1 July 1914. Barger and Ewins were also appointed to the fledgling Committee. Barger was appointed to a Professorship at Goldsmiths' College in London, subsequently becoming Professor of Chemistry in relation to Medicine at Edinburgh and Regius Professor of Chemistry at Glasgow University. Laidlaw left, also in 1913, to become Professor of Pathology at Guy's Hospital, and later Deputy Director of the National Institute for Medical Research, recruited by Dale in 1922.

Wellcome had lost five of his key people, wholly unnecessarily, and as a direct consequence of his absorption with his collecting and archaeological passions. Also, his proximity to Balfour in the Sudan had led to his over-valuing him. Having Balfour leading a tropical research institute in London was one thing; to make Power and Dale report to him as their leader, after years of running their own laboratories, was entirely different.*

Wellcome may have half-expected Power's decision – Power was sixty and had told both his successor at Wisconsin, Kremers, and Wellcome of his desire to spend 'my advancing years' with his children and their families in America. Moreover, his personal output, although not that of his laboratories, had fallen dramatically – in 1912 he wrote only thirteen letters and reports.**

Dale's decision, however, was a real blow; furthermore, as Wellcome belatedly realised, it was final. But their exchange of letters, although somewhat formal, and revealing on Wellcome's part genuine unhappiness, was not insincere. When Dale's election to the Royal Society was announced in the summer of 1914, Wellcome wrote him a particularly warm letter of congratulation, to which Dale responded: 'When I entered your laboratories I had no thought of the opportunities there afforded me would lead to such an advance in my scientific

* Balfour was succeeded at Khartoum by Albert Chalmers, the author of a classic textbook on tropical medicine, written in collaboration with Aldo Castellani, and commemorated by the Chalmers Medal of the Royal Society of Tropical Medicine and Hygiene. He went to India in 1920, where he died; he was succeeded by Robert Archibald, Balfour's former pathologist, who was Director in Khartoum until the virtual sequestration of the Wellcome Laboratories by the Sudan Government in 1935.

** Power was replaced by Frank Lee Pyman, who had joined the Experimental Department at Dartford, under Jowett, in 1906.

position that a position elsewhere will be offered to me which I shall feel obliged to accept.' Wellcome wrote to 'reciprocate your kind expressions regarding our long and pleasant association which has proved so mutually satisfactory. While deeply regretting the termination of this association, I desire to wish you every success in your new position.'

In fact, the association was far from 'terminated'. They were in touch throughout the 1914–18 war, when Wellcome put the resources of the Bureau at the disposal of the War Office, a fact handsomely recognised by the Medical Research Committee. When, in 1922, Dale went to Canada to assess the importance of the discovery of insulin on behalf of the Committee, he recommended its production in Britain, in which Burroughs Wellcome was to play a prominent role. In 1932 Dale was to propose Wellcome for exceptional election to the Royal Society. He shared with him his knighthood in the same Honours List in 1932, and was to be his most conspicuous and dedicated Trustee. Dale owed Wellcome a great deal and, although he often complained strongly about him, knew it, and repaid the debt handsomely.

Dale's successor, Dr R. A. O'Brien, proved to be another outstanding appointment and, like Glenny, a product of the Physiological Laboratories' high recruitment standards. If he was not of Dale's calibre as an innovator, he was to prove an exceptionally gifted and practical researcher. Fortunately for Wellcome, he and Glenny stayed with Burroughs Wellcome. If they had followed Power, Dale, Barger, Ewins and Laidlaw out of the research laboratories, Wellcome's entire research structure would have been in danger, and thirty years of patient, and sometimes inspired, creation would have been severely imperilled.

Wellcome had drifted dangerously away from his real purpose. He had total control of the company, which he increasingly regarded as his private property, but long before the disaster of his marriage he had become grievously diverted from pharmacy into the role of amateur archaeologist, museum-creator, well-publicised benefactor and compulsive traveller. The process of disengagement from the firm that had begun in 1905 now reaped its unhappy harvest.

But it is not an unusual story. People who have created great institutions become bored by them. Other interests and diversions beckon, and the mainspring of their genius and ambition weakens, and eventually breaks. In 1914 Wellcome was having to face these unhappy realities, but did not do so.

*

Dale and Barger's first action after their appointment to the Medical Research Committee was to visit Germany to make contact with their German counterparts and to seek their advice for the establishment of their new department. With the single-minded concentration of scholars, they were wholly unaware of the looming conflict until, in Strasbourg, they were warned by the Professor of Biochemistry that mobilisation was imminent and were advised to return home. They did so barely before the declaration of war.

The Great War opened equally bizarrely and unexpectedly for Burroughs Wellcome & Co. Snow Hill received a letter marked 'undelivered' by the Post Office, on Burroughs Wellcome paper, enclosing £100 in notes addressed to a Mr A. Stafford in Glasgow. There was no record of a Mr Stafford, and it was certainly not Burroughs Wellcome policy to send cash in envelopes. Someone also realised that the notepaper of the company had been forged. The police were informed, and their investigations uncovered a German agent, a Doctor A. Karl Graves, who had been sent to Edinburgh in 1911 as a spy, specialising in naval affairs, posing as an Australian doctor undertaking a postgraduate course. Part of the subterfuge was that his German masters corresponded with him on forged Burroughs Wellcome notepaper, the letters posted to Snow Hill from Berlin and automatically forwarded to him in Edinburgh by the company. For reasons that remain obscure, Graves's masters considered that his usefulness, if any, was at an end and quite deliberately sent his instructions and money to someone they knew did not exist in a Burroughs Wellcome envelope, knowing that it would be returned to

Snow Hill. When Graves was found and arrested, the police discovered that in his *Wellcome Medical Diary* was the code he was using to communicate with the German intelligence authorities.

In the long list of utterly incompetent spies, Graves rates rather highly, which was almost certainly why his masters decided to expose him. Graves was tried and convicted for espionage, but expiated his offence – and saved his life – by agreeing to write (or at least to publish) a book titled *The Secrets of the German War Office*, declaring of his betrayers that 'the B & W mark was upon me'. Wellcome was always enthusiastic for publicity, but not of this sort.

One of Wellcome's principal objectives was to make use of his personal and professional friendships and contacts in the United States to urge American involvement in the war. A particularly important one was Robert Lansing, who became Secretary of State in 1915, and to whom Wellcome sent British newspapers and any publications relating to the war. But, even after the sinking of the *Lusitania* in May 1915, Lansing and Wellcome's other friends in the administration and Congress sent somewhat evasive replies to his urgings for greater American assistance. He took the robust, if inaccurate, view that the American pacifists were 'mainly the tools of German agents and perhaps a few cranks', and he decried the weakness of President Wilson – although, wisely, in private. As an American-born British citizen he felt the American neutrality intensely and was ashamed of it. However, until the end of 1916 his American friends listened to him politely and, as politely, disagreed with him. Wellcome was convinced from an early stage of the war that the Allies desperately needed the American involvement, although he was fully aware of American military limitations; he urged a substantial increase in the United States army and navy, so that when and if America intervened, her role could be decisive. On this, at least, he had a sympathetic response.

In one sense the war could have been a disaster for Burroughs Wellcome because much of its export market was closed by order of the Army Medical Department. But when it became grimly evident that the army was going to require drugs and medical supplies on a vast scale, the situation changed dramatically. In 1917 the Dartford Works had to be considerably expanded, Wellcome buying an additional 250 acres.

The reputation of the Wellcome Laboratories was such that at the outbreak of war they were asked to meet a particular emergency. One of the first results of war is an increase in venereal disease and syphilis, and the only known drug to alleviate it was Salvarsan, which was a German product. Within a remarkably short time the Laboratories had produced an alternative, called 'Kharsivan', which, after testing, was declared to be as effective as the German product. This was a joint venture involving other companies, the work co-ordinated by Dale for the Medical Research Committee, but the Wellcome role was of particular importance. By January 1915 'Kharsivan' was being produced in large quantities and the demand for it seemed almost unlimited throughout the war.

This was only the beginning, as it was realised how heavily dependent the British drug market had been on imports from Germany. The Wellcome Laboratories and Works now had to prepare and produce a wide range of drugs and medical goods of which previously the Germans had had a virtual monopoly, a revealing commentary upon the overall condition of the British pharmaceutical industry. Burroughs Wellcome chemists even had to produce a British version of aspirin. Nothing demonstrates Wellcome's contribution better than the fact that the medical and military authorities turned immediately to Burroughs Wellcome for help, and invariably received it. Much of the work of the Laboratories was now concentrated upon devising processes for the production of substitutes.

O'Brien had been working on the development and production of a tetanus anti-toxin on a moderate scale since 1912; it was now required in huge quantities, and the fact that it was reflected O'Brien's own abilities and the skills not only of the Laboratories, but also of the Dartford Works. But harsh experience revealed the urgent need for a gas-gangrene anti-toxin. Glenny, in a work of true brilliance and improvisation, came up with an anti-toxin that gave full protection against tetanus and all three known gas-gangrene bacilli; the trouble was that it had to be injected quickly into a wounded man, and this was not usually possible in the ghastly conditions of the Western Front. Indeed, so many men perished from gangrene that doubts were expressed about the Burroughs Wellcome anti-toxin, which were subsequently disproved; it, and its successors, have proved to be among the most remarkable life-saving drugs ever created. Like O'Brien's tetanus anti-toxin, the demand was awesome; over two-and-a-half million doses of gas-gangrene anti-toxin were manufactured by Burroughs Wellcome for the British army in the course of the war. Another product of the firm was typhoid vaccine, again urgently required in quantities undreamed of in peacetime.

Wellcome's insistence on quality now also paid immense dividends; his young researchers and everyone at the Dartford Works had had this fact instilled in them deeply. Years of trial and error, mistakes made and rectified, the pursuit of excellence and reliability daily preached by Wellcome and everyone in senior posts in the company, were now manifested in drugs and equipment that were totally trusted. The sudden move to mass production could have been disastrous; it was not.

The figures themselves were remarkable. In 1910 the Physiological Laboratories alone prepared and dispatched 239,000 packages; this rose to 627,000 in 1915 and to 1,554,000 in 1918. The production of the American company also expanded dramatically, particularly after the entry of the United States into the war, and in 1919 recorded its first-ever profit, while Australian production also flourished.

But Wellcome did not see the war, which increasingly appalled and distressed him, as an opportunity for making money. At the outbreak he told the War Office that all the resources of his firm and Laboratories were wholly at the disposal of the Government, and the Physiological Laboratories in particular concentrated almost entirely upon sera and vaccines required by the military. The new Bureau of Scientific Research trained and instructed medical officers in tropical diseases and medicine, and undertook research into specific illnesses encountered by British troops in the Dardanelles and Mesopotamia campaigns. Balfour, who had been honoured with the CMG in 1912 for his work in the Sudan, was now regarded as an international expert on tropical diseases, and much consulted. Before the outbreak of war in 1914 he had visited Venezuela and Colombia (having taught himself Spanish) and sent back a paper to *The Lancet* identifying the howler monkey as a reservoir host of yellow fever. In 1915 he and Wenyon, whom Balfour had appointed 'Director of Research in the Tropics', were given the ranks of lieutenant-colonel and were key members of the medical advisory committee of the Mediterranean Expeditionary Force. Balfour was its president and it became known as 'Balfour's travelling circus'. Amongst other aspects, the experience gave Wenyon the opportunity to make some of his most important findings on intestinal infections, while Balfour advised General Allenby on anti-malarial measures in Palestine.

The miserable ineptitude of the Royal Army Medical Corps, which seemed to have learnt little from the South African War, was not Wellcome's responsibility. He provided the facilities of the Bureau entirely free of charge and initiated research into the production of a mechanised field ambulance; the British went to war with horse-drawn ambulances, as did most armies. Wellcome offered a prize of £2,000 for the best design, but the winner was produced by an army engineer, who was refused permission to accept the award. Wellcome was indignant at this characteristic example of military bureaucracy, and diverted the money to designing and building a mobile medical field laboratory for use in the Middle East. However, by the time it reached the area early in 1918, most of the medical havoc had already occurred. But the achievement prompted Wellcome to offer $10,000 to his old friend General Gorgas, now Surgeon General of the US army, for a similar one to be used in France by the American forces; the offer was immediately accepted.

Wellcome's personal and his company's commitment to the war effort was total – perhaps too total for the company's long-term

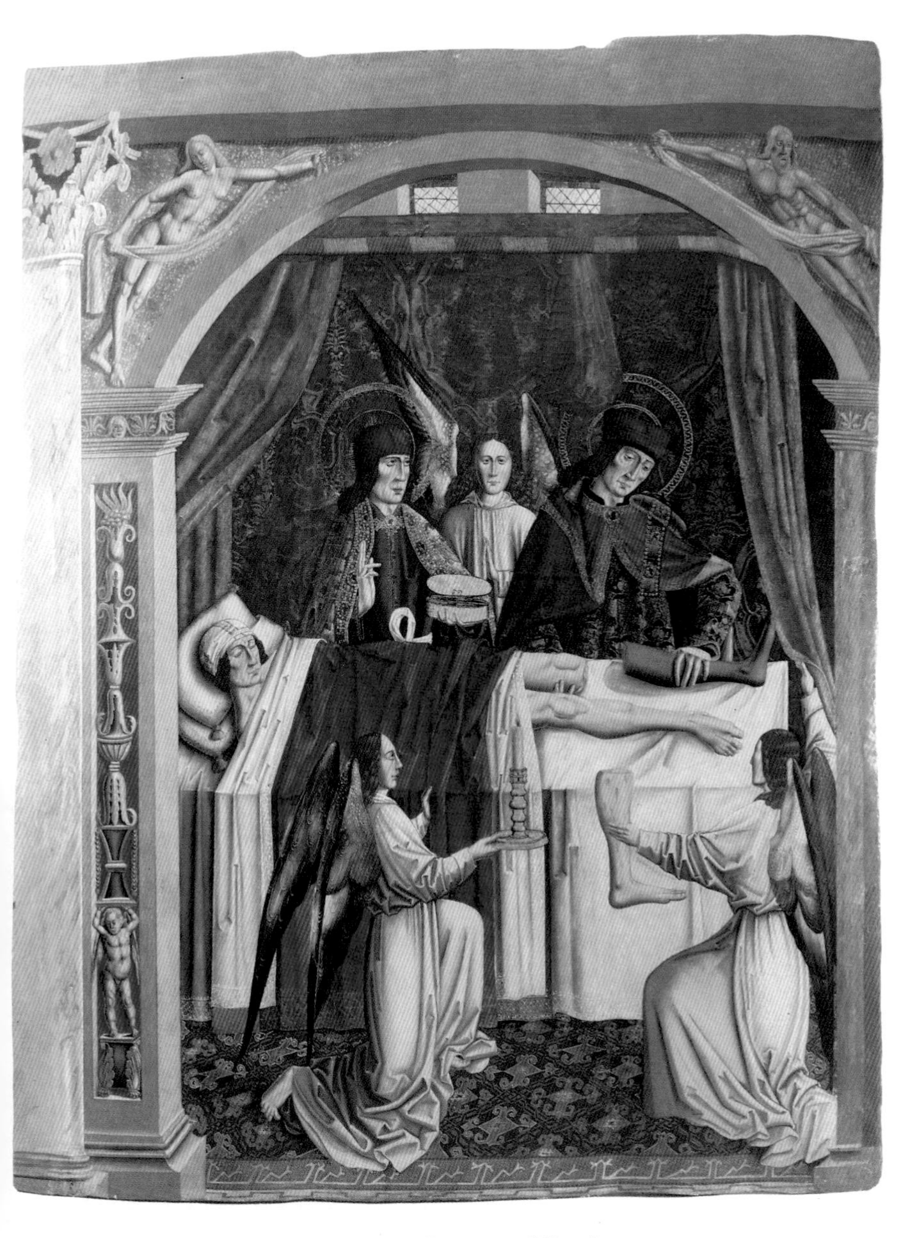

A miraculous surgical operation by Saints Cosmas and Damian.
Oil painting on panel by Alonso de Sedano, Burgos, *c.* 1495.
Bought for Wellcome by Peter Johnston-Saint in Spain in 1930.

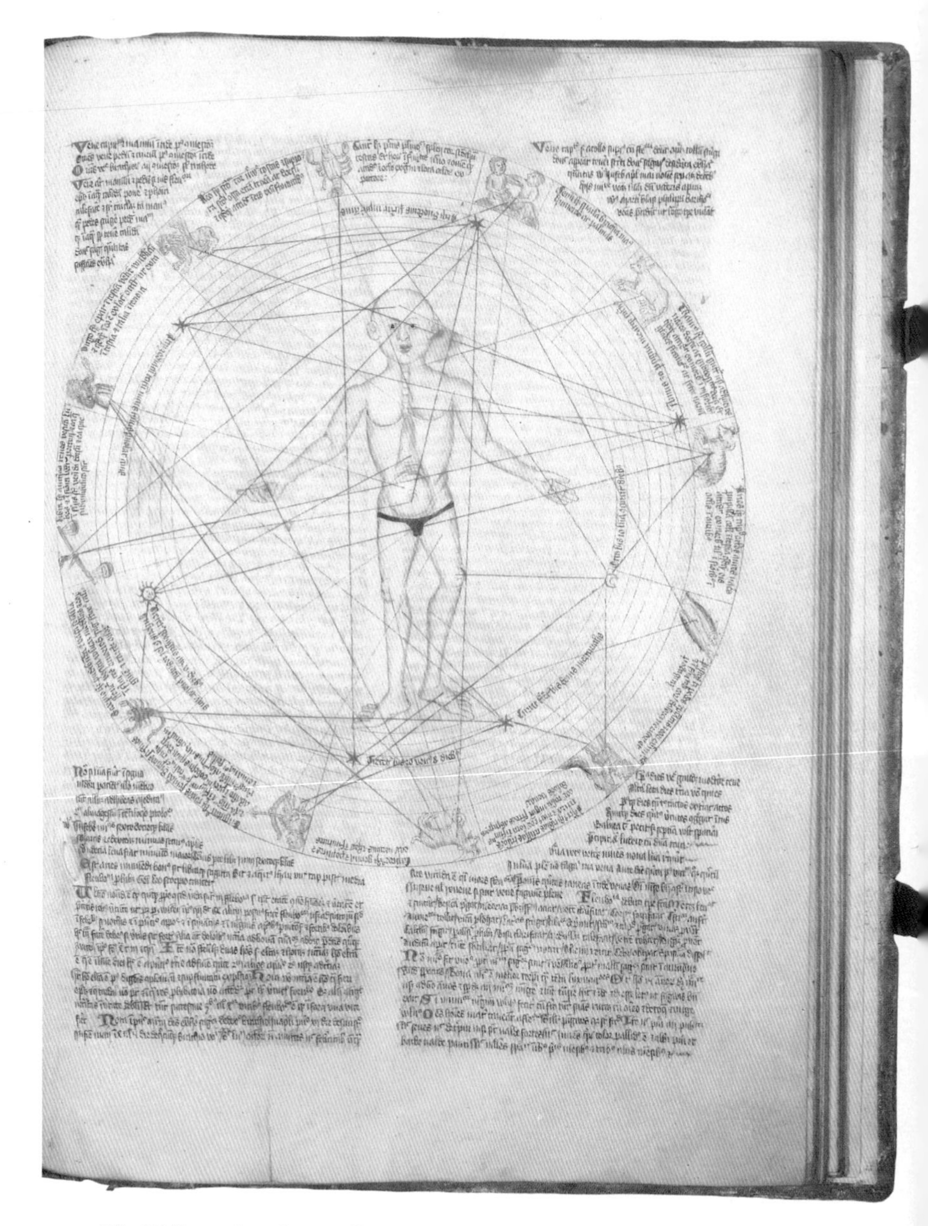

*The Wellcome Apocalypse*, a German manuscript of the early fifteenth century containing sacred, medical and allegorical texts, richly illustrated. Bought by Wellcome at Sotheby's in December 1931 for £2,300.

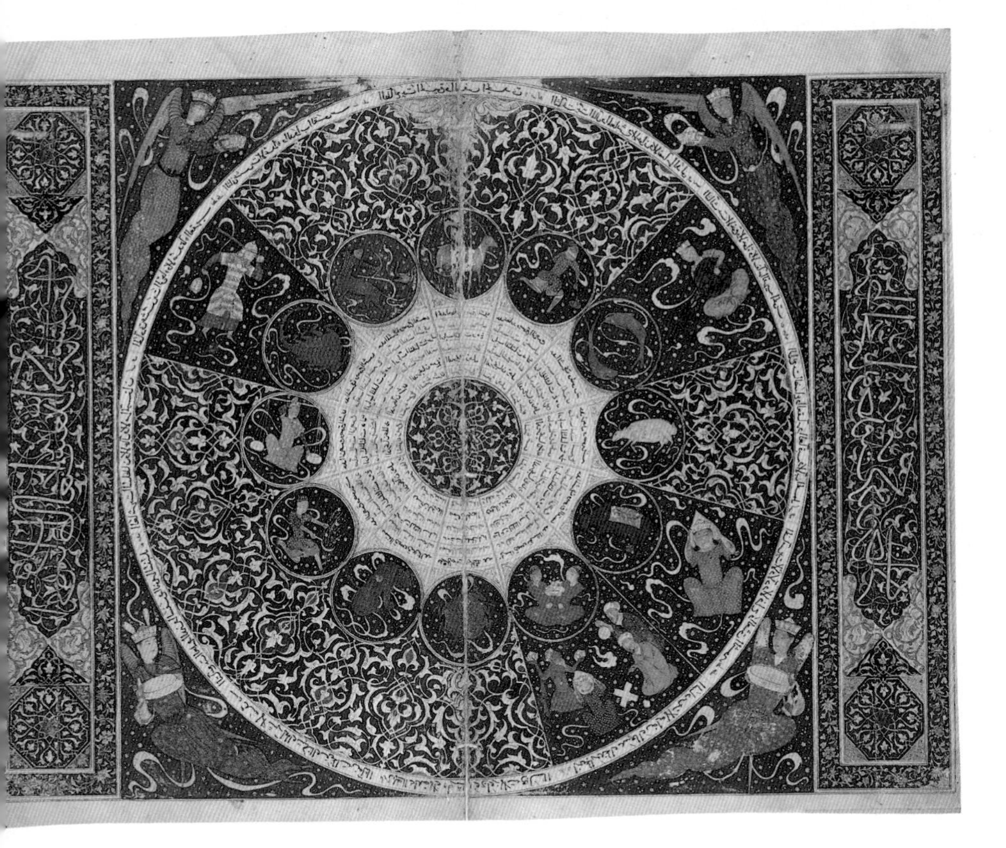

ABOVE The *Horoscope of Iskandar Sultan*, Shiraz, AD 1411. Formerly in the collection of the orientalist John Herbert Harington (d. 1828). Bought by Wellcome at Sotheby's in 1923 for £6 15s.

LEFT Saint Catherine of Siena, *The orcharde of Syon . . . with ghostly fruytes & precyous plantes for the helthe of mannes soule*, London, printed by Wynkyn de Worde, 1519. Bought at Sotheby's in December 1898 for £151, this is one of many books which Wellcome acquired from the library of William Morris.

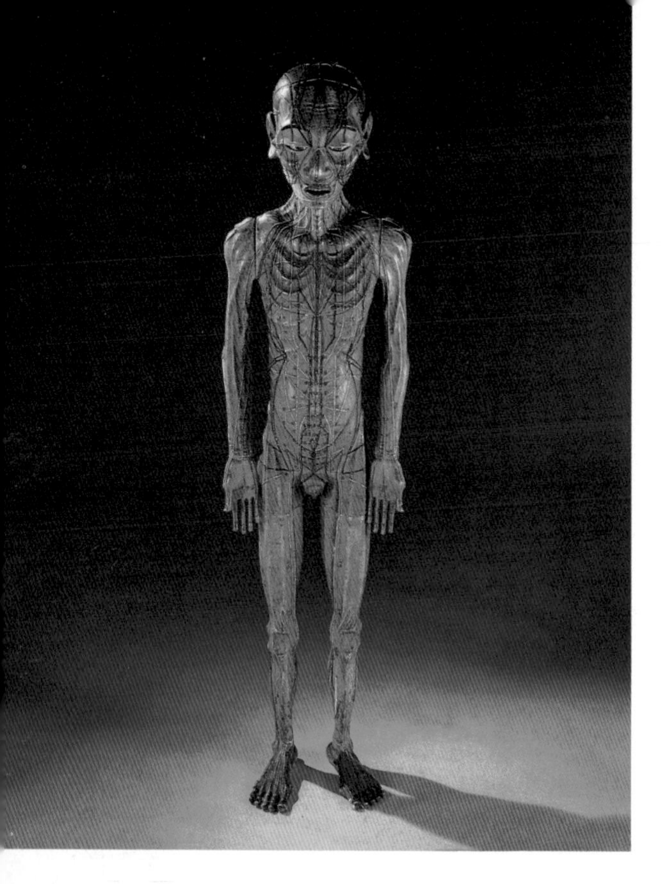

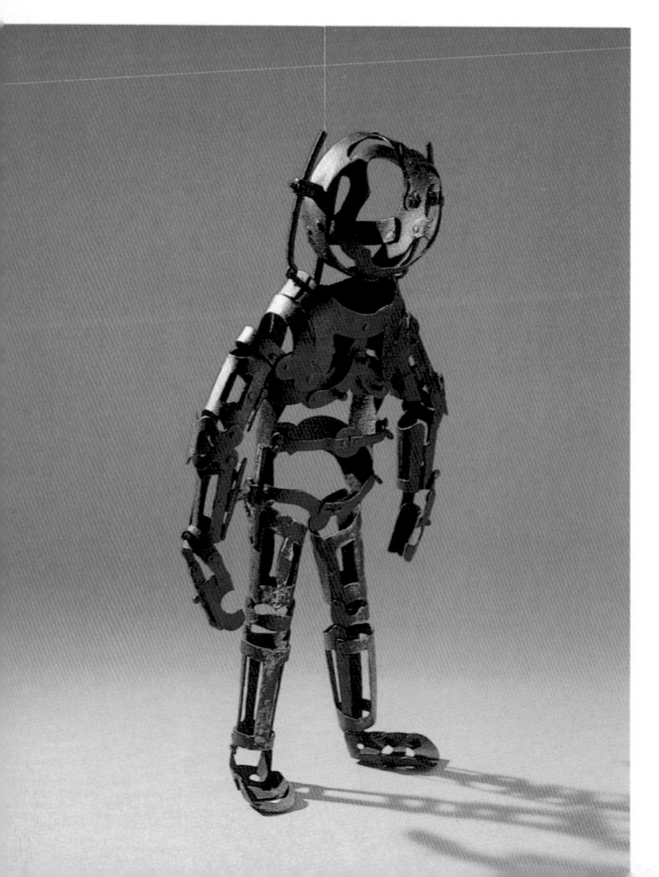

LEFT A Chinese acupuncture figure, seventeenth century (?), bought by Wellcome in 1917.

BELOW LEFT An articulated iron manikin following the forms of the human body as published by Fabricius ab Aquapendente in 1614. Bought by Wellcome at Stevens's auction house in London in 1928.

OPPOSITE ABOVE The Giustiniani medicine chest. Named after Vincenzo Giustiniani, *podestà* of Chios 1562–6, who is believed to have been its first owner. Acquired by Wellcome in Rome in 1924.

OPPOSITE BELOW Three Italian pharmacy jars from the many (some original, some replicas) in the Wellcome Museum of the History of Medicine. Bought in Italy in 1910.

SEM: D'APP
A|G

ABOVE John Bell and Co. pharmacy, 225 (formerly 338) Oxford Street. John Bell's historic pharmacy opened on this site in 1798. The shop front and fittings were rescued from demolition by Wellcome's museum curator, C. J. S. Thompson, in 1908.

LEFT An English wing-fronted medicine cabinet from Richard Reece's Medical Hall, 171 Piccadilly, 1813.

A French etching with gouache satirising vaccination, 1800. Bought for Wellcome by Peter Johnston-Saint on one of his collecting trips in Paris.

BELOW Physiognomical heads of terracotta for diagnosis of human character traits, nineteenth century.

A gallery in the Wellcome Museum of the History of Medicine at the Science Museum, 1994, showing some of the museum objects collected by Wellcome. In the foreground, a statue of St Sebastian, patron saint of plague-sufferers.

BELOW The Reading Room of the Wellcome Institute Library in the Wellcome Building, 1994. The Library holds the printed books, manuscripts, paintings, prints and documents collected by Wellcome.

interests, as all the resources of Burroughs Wellcome were devoted to it, and to testing and production rather than to research. Also, too many of the products had a totally wartime demand – 'Kharsivan' being a case in point – while others would have a considerably smaller peacetime sale. This did not trouble him at all. As he wrote to Charles Stewart, 'In every way practicable I am trying to assist as best I can the cause which stands for civilization and humanity.' In addition to the cost, the company lost some of its best young men in action, including two out of five of the Museum's professional staff.

Wellcome's health had again begun to deteriorate; again, the cause was not detected. It was thought that it was a recurrence of his ulcerative colitis, and it was not until 1916 that it was discovered that he required a partial prostatectomy. He went to the United States in 1915 by way of Cadiz and Havana, visited his brother, now living in Los Angeles, and George Palmer in Mankato. He was operated on in April 1916 and in August returned to America, still feeling desperately unwell, but responding to another appeal for help from William Duncan. A new chapter in the Metlakahtlan saga had opened and was not to end happily.

Duncan, having fought the Canadians, had now come into conflict with the American authorities, who had not accepted his 'squatters' rights' position and had gradually absorbed the New Metlakahtla into the American educational and social system. Duncan appealed again to Wellcome, and Wellcome responded by using all his influence in Washington, and through publicity, to maintain Duncan's purposes on Annette Island. He did not wholly succeed, but again he invested much time, energy and money into this cause in a period when he was unwell and much preoccupied with other matters. But he was not to give up lightly the cause he had taken up with such fervour as a young man, and whose roots were so profound. Once more, he came under much criticism, even more now that he was no longer an American citizen, but his faith in Duncan's Mission – which lasted after Duncan's death in 1918 – endured until his own. If this dedication may have seemed to others to have been excessive, and the expense even more so, his biographer can only admire a remarkable consistency to an ill-treated race he had respected since childhood, and which he never abandoned. The American Indian never had in modern times a greater individual supporter than Henry Wellcome.

The war had eventually severely limited Wellcome's collecting, and the Museum was used for illustrating military surgery. Afterwards new staff had to be recruited, but before long Wellcome was again in full cry, this time with a dashing young man, Captain Peter Johnston-Saint, 'used to the best society, much travelled and a good linguist, the driver of a series of sporting cars'. He had served in the Indian army and the Royal Flying Corps, and had joined the Museum in 1920, becoming Secretary; when the Australian anthropologist, L. W. G. Malcolm, succeeded Thompson as Curator in 1925, he took on Thompson's collecting role. He became Foreign Secretary in 1928 and succeeded Malcolm in 1934. He was to prove a considerably more discriminating collector than Thompson, and his vivid letters on his travels were particularly appreciated by Wellcome. Very well-connected – the Queen of Spain was a childhood friend – his greatest coups were the Library's collection of French medical caricatures, some notable Spanish sixteenth-century paintings and, most outstanding of all, a collection of memorabilia of French scientists and medical men, which earned him and Wellcome the *Légion d'Honneur*.

Some of the Wellcome agents were scholars – notably Miss Winifred Blackman of Oxford, an expert on Egyptian antiquities – but others were conspicuously not. Wellcome demanded detailed reports from Johnston-Saint and his agents, and some notable collections were purchased in addition to the Lister one. The agents bought for cash, and there is no record of how much Wellcome spent on his collection, but as it amounted to nearly one million items by 1936 it cannot have been less than £1 million, and was probably twice that.

It was the random nature of the collecting process, with no particular theme and with the agents given virtually unlimited resources, that caused the trouble and which was chaotic. The Museum store in

Willesden was filled with crates; while trying to sort out the vast amount of arms and weapons, Johnston-Saint came across a dozen stuffed crocodiles and snakes. After the Second World War David Attenborough was shown thousands of African knobkerries from the Wellcome collection being sold off by his Trustees for £1 each; to his lasting regret he did not buy one, estimating in 1992 that each one would be worth several thousand pounds.

But although this was very much Wellcome's personal collection, and reflected the width of his interests, as Helen Turner has rightly written, 'What Wellcome attempted was nothing less than the recreation of man's medical past, rather as the archaeologist seeks to recreate from objects the periods of prehistory, before there were written records.' His collection of microscopes, for example, numbered some fifteen hundred, and includes the prototype achromatic one made for Lister. His purpose, in his own words, was 'to conserve antique objects and as far as possible to trace each step from the period of their origin throughout the whole course of development'. Only a fraction of his enormous collection has ever been on view; much still remains in the London Science Museum's store, but the final result – only achieved many years later after his death – was an educational and research museum of medical history in London of unique value. It is easy to criticise the methods by which he collected, and to deride much of what he did collect, but the eventual benefit was incalculable. And it reflected his approach to medical research and the essential, questing nature of his character. 'If you do not seek, you do not find' was the dominant philosophy of his life, which became stronger as it progressed.

*

Syrie's marriage to Maugham had not eased Wellcome's personal difficulties and concerns. There were recurrent disputes, sometimes acute, about her access to their son and her alleged abuses of the terms of their divorce settlement, but far more worrying to Wellcome was Mounteney's slow mental development. He believed for some time that Mounteney's lack of progress was due to idleness and 'slacking', on which topic he wrote his son many stern Victorian-father letters. He also urged Mounteney's tutors to be stricter with him, to 'keep him up to the mark' and to punish him severely if necessary. 'No boy that is pampered and taught to avoid the difficult pursuits of life is likely to develop self-reliance or sense of honour or duty,' he wrote to Pearson from the United States in 1917. 'One of the greatest gifts a father can give to his son is preparation to take responsibilities and qualifications that will insure his self-support. Strict discipline of Spartan parents is far kinder than any softening indulgence.' He wrote on these lines to Mounteney's tutors, and to Mounteney himself.

It was only gradually that he and Syrie realised that the boy whom they both loved, and often fought over, was not going to develop as they had both hoped and expected. Wellcome, disconcerted and troubled, began to enlist medical advice. The results were confusing rather than illuminating, but they, and the reports of Mounteney's teachers and tutors, brought home to him the inescapable fact that there was no question of his son succeeding him.

If this was a severe blow, which it certainly was, it was concealed from all but his now dwindling number of close friends.

We can now realise that Mounteney's fundamental problem as a child was almost certainly dyslexia, which today would have been recognised and steps taken to remedy his backwardness. With the difficulties of his parents' life together, and then their separation, his slow progress did not become notably serious until 1916. This was not helped at all by the fact that he was jeered at by his fellow schoolboys, who would cry after him 'divorcy, divorcy', divorce then being a rare and scandalous occurrence, and this one in particular having been so prominently publicised. For a lonely backward child, bewildered by events, these derisions could not have helped, nor did they.

Mounteney was devoted to both his parents, and neither neglected him. But the fact was that for much of the time they were distant from him, and if these absences were punctuated with periods when he was with one of them, this was no substitute for having a home, which in his adolescence and young manhood he never had. The doctors, tutors and psychologists whom Wellcome instructed to observe and examine Mounteney presented detailed reports and analyses that revealed that they were baffled why the son of such remarkable parents should have such limited intellect and be so utterly devoid of any ambition. Perhaps they should have looked at the Solomon Wellcome strain more thoughtfully.

This development was a deep disappointment to Wellcome, but it is not altogether a sad story. Other children of famous parents have fared far worse. Mounteney adored his mother and revered his father, and would never hear anything ill said about either of them. As he subsequently said:

> When I was young I had a great deal of admiration for my father and his work and wanted to follow in his footsteps, even though I had no idea what it really entailed, but with my father abroad such a lot I spent most of my time with my tutor, who used to take me into the country – days that I looked forward to. As I got older, I realised that this is what I wanted to do, live in the country and live on a farm. When I told my father he said, 'If that's what you want to do, then go ahead,' and he supported me all the way.

Mounteney was to live a long life of great happiness as a countryman and farmer, and eventually to marry a lady he had long courted and whose interests matched his. And his letters to his father have a certain simple grandeur and total integrity that Wellcome recognised. If he was, quite understandably, saddened that Mounteney could never inherit what he had created, he gradually accepted the situation and did all he could to assist his son to have the life he desired. Syrie also always kept closely in touch with Mounteney and saw much of him, and after their deaths his devotion to the memory of his parents never wavered. There is a curious symmetry that he should have been the last Wellcome, because he had so much in common with all those who had preceded his father.

*

In 1921 a young Canadian, Ada Misner, became Wellcome's personal secretary and assistant. She was young enough to be his daughter and become so close to him that, as in the case of his other friendships with women, it was believed by many that she was his mistress. It was far more likely to have been an affectionate working relationship between a clearly able and attractive young woman and a lonely elderly man disappointed, although not at all embittered, by his son. The fact that he made no special provision for her in his will tends to confirm this and surprised several of his friends, who wrote to her with concern after his death. It may well be that he had made financial provision for her during his lifetime, because she made no complaint. What is true is that she was totally devoted to him, was the guardian of his affairs and arrangements, was never far from his side, and was by far the most important individual in his later life. If she remains something of a mystery, it is because she was totally discreet. Few records of her exist, but the recollections of the employees of the company in the last fifteen years of Wellcome's life emphasise her importance.

*

Although Wellcome was sixty-six years old in 1919 and had his other, often too time-consuming interests, his health and mental alertness were unimpaired, and, with the collapse of his marriage and the sadness over Mounteney, something of the old zest for medical research and the expansion of the Wellcome empire returned. He travelled too much to be in constant touch, but he did rather more than expect results from the institutions he had created and the men he had appointed. He looked forward, as he constantly reiterated, to a new period of expansion and innovation, and was rewarded by a remarkable series of achievements.

At the forefront, as he had planned in 1913, was the Wellcome Bureau of Scientific Research, and the principal figure was Wenyon, who had first experienced Wellcome's pioneering techniques when he had joined the Nile floating laboratory in 1907.

Wenyon had joined the staff of the Bureau in 1914. When he

became Director in 1923, on Balfour's departure, he had become a leading international authority in protozoology and intestinal disorders and diseases, on which his wartime experiences had proved invaluable. Although he was now in effect in charge of the entire Wellcome research operations, it was characteristic of Wellcome that he urged Wenyon to pursue his own research and to write up his findings, which he proceeded to do. In 1926 he published one of the classics of modern medicine, simply entitled *Protozoology*, which was also lavishly illustrated, mainly by Boris Jobling, a refugee from Russia of British descent. Wenyon's election to the Royal Society a year later was exceptionally well merited. By an interesting coincidence one of his most important colleagues at the Bureau was also a refugee from Russia, Cecil Hoare, who, although with a Russian mother and brought up and educated in Russia, had fortunately retained his British citizenship from his father and was accordingly repatriated in 1920. He was brought to Balfour's attention by a mutual friend, who knew of his work with the Russian parasitologist, E. N. Pavlovsky, and joined the Bureau staff. 'Wellcome's philosophy (and Wenyon's protection) allowed Hoare to spend all his time on scientific problems, unhindered by teaching or by pressure to contribute to the business of the Company, a privilege he guarded jealously.'*

This was to prove another superb investment. Hoare's own published work, and especially his later researches in Uganda, further increased the Wellcome reputation and drew other promising young scientists to it, among them W. N. F. Woodland, F. Coutelin and L. J. Bruce-Chwatt. Also, the Wellcome Laboratories now contained outstanding bacteriologists and virologists. But one particularly brave line of research, on yellow fever, resulted in tragedy. Edward Hindle, who had joined the Bureau in 1928 on a five-year Beit Memorial Fellowship, obtained infective tissue from a monkey in Senegal. Hindle produced a vaccine, which caused a major sensation when presented to a meeting of the Royal Society of Tropical Medicine

* L. G. Goodwin and E. Beveridge, typescript history of the WBSR (unpublished).

and Hygiene in January 1929. Tests on human volunteers during an epidemic in Brazil were successful, and the Colonial Office asked for large quantities for clinical trials in West Africa. Wellcome's surprise and mortification were considerable when they were reported to be, in the main, a failure, yet another example of the difficulties in moving from laboratory research to production.

Wellcome had become excited by Wenyon's reports on Hindle's work and had not worried about the large additional expense involved, seeing in it another case of pure research having an immense humanitarian and financial reward, at great profit both to the Wellcome reputation and to the company's finances, a classic Wellcome 'double', like the diphtheria anti-toxin and the isolation of histamine. But now, perturbed by 'the discordant results' of the trials, he began to complain strongly about the expense. Then, his alarm increased considerably when Hindle and two of his laboratory technicians contracted the disease, from which one of the latter died. This was lamentable enough, but what frightened Wellcome (and many others) even more was that there was the potential of an epidemic in London of this dreadful disease, for which the Wellcome Laboratories would be held responsible. Fortunately it did not happen, but on Wellcome's peremptory orders all work on the virus was suspended. Hindle himself left the Bureau shortly afterwards, and later had a distinguished career as Professor of Zoology at Glasgow University, Scientific Director at the London Zoo, and as a founder-member of the Institute of Biology, of which he was the first President. One of the problems was that he was not at all Wellcome's type, being described by a colleague and friend as 'a colourful character and a great clubman'.

Hindle's high-risk work on yellow fever had not been in vain. G. M. Findlay had joined the Laboratories in 1929 to work on chemotherapy, but he was also deeply interested in viral infections and worked closely with Hindle. When the neurotropic strain of yellow fever was isolated in America, Findlay went to the Rockefeller Institute and returned with the vital strain for vaccine preparation.

In conjunction with two other Wellcome scientists, R. D. Mackenzie and F. O. MacCallum, he was able to produce doses of vaccine in large quantities to immunise British servicemen and members of the Colonial Service. This time it was wholly successful, and with one additional unexpected bonus. Sometimes (as Wellcome's biographer can confirm from personal experience) the recipient contracted jaundice, which was unpleasant but not serious. This was to lead to scientific interest in the hepatitis viruses, on which MacCallum, who left Wellcome in 1946 to go to Cambridge, played an important role, although not before his colleague, D. J. Bauer, who had worked with him since 1942 on hepatitis, had been one of the first researchers to discover synthetic chemical compounds with anti-viral activity. This utterly and completely justified Wellcome's lifelong attitude towards pure research and, indeed, to life.

However, his publicly announced suspension of research on the yellow fever vaccine revealed that he was getting old. His interest in the work had been great, as it continued to be on all aspects of Wenyon's activities, but this was evidence of an untypical loss of nerve. It was also significant that Wenyon in effect took little notice and actively encouraged Findlay, Mackenzie and MacCallum to resolve the problem. And Wellcome's loss of confidence in Hindle, not assisted by their very different personalities and outlook, turned out to have been quite unjustified.

But his faith in Findlay proved to be wholly right. His original chemotherapy laboratory, prepared specially for him by Wenyon, became celebrated as early as 1930, when he published his *Recent Advances in Chemotherapy*, whose influence on the practitioners in this new field was incalculable. He received the CBE in 1935 at the age of forty-two and was to be a major consultant to the Allied Forces in the Second World War. His death, at the age of fifty-nine, was a substantial loss for British medical science. By then he had left Wellcome (in 1947), but he, and the history of medicine, had been another beneficiary of the long-term wisdom of Henry Wellcome – and of Wenyon.

One who worked with him for many years has left this engaging portrait of Wenyon:

> As a chief he was admired and respected; he ruled firmly with a light touch and very little escaped him. 'We'll see what happens, what?' meant that he had everything well in hand. He had a lively sense of humour and, in the mood, was a wonderful raconteur and teller of tall stories. One of them concerned the cutaneous nodule on his arm, carefully grown and studied after inoculating himself with *Leishmania* parasites – it was accidentally excised and lost during a game of tennis. There were no regular staff meetings or seminars but all graduate staff members were expected to go for afternoon tea, served on an immense ancient oak table formed by a single plank about 10 foot long, 2 foot six inches wide, and at least six inches thick, by Mrs Brinnand, the Scottish wife of the resident caretaker of the building. . . .
>
> All graduate staff were expected to join the Society [of Tropical Medicine and Hygiene] of which he was secretary for many years, and to attend its evening meetings.
>
> Wenyon also believed in informal and friendly relations with the staffs of other pharmaceutical companies, later to be placed on a more formal basis, to the great benefit of British medical research and science.*

One of the stranger Wellcome appointments was that of Major Humphrey Paget MC to the Chemical Laboratories in 1919, who claimed to be 'not a very good chemist', which was excessively modest, and his research into, and treatment for, hook-worm and round-worm was particularly notable. It is to him that we owe a reminiscence of the King Street laboratories, written in his retirement in 1975:

> It was a most unsuitable building for the purpose, on four floors served by one narrow wooden staircase, panelled with varnished deal, and glass partitions. There was, I think, no fire escape nor special fire precautions though alcohol, petrol and ether were in constant use in large quantities. The basement, the oldest part of the building, accommodated a gas-fired central heating boiler, beyond which, in a

* *Ibid.*, p. 339.

> remote corner liable to flooding after heavy rain, were two tiny lavatories. In two massive alcoves, formerly, I imagine, wine cellars, now fitted with fire-proof doors, a quantity of solvents and chemicals was stored. An ancient domestic ice-box was kept charged with ice blocks by courtesy of the Meat Cold Store.
>
> On the ground floor was the tiny office of the Director, Dr T. A. Henry. . . . Also on the ground floor was a small but comprehensive library of scientific journals and text books, and a number of glass cases displaying in small glass tubes specimens of all substances examined and of all products isolated from them. These were last displayed, I think, in the Wembley Empire Exhibition in 1924. There was no room for any secretarial staff, and these were provided by courtesy of BW & Co.

In this memoir Paget expressed surprise that there had never been a serious accident, when in fact there had been the occasion when the assistant storeman, Leslie Barnett, tripped while carrying flammable solvent near the boiler and was seriously burned.

In spite of these somewhat inadequate premises, there was a new surge of chemical activity and publication of papers under the leadership in the Experimental Department of Dr Sydney Smith, the discoverer of digoxin in 1930, who developed it to commercial production; it was a digitalis derivative and an outstanding cardiac drug.

But the most important single achievement by the company in the immediate post-war period, and one of the most notable up to that time, was the production of insulin.

In 1922, when Dale was Director of the National Institute for Medical Research, he was sent to Toronto by the Medical Research Council to investigate the claims being made for the therapeutic benefits of the newly discovered insulin. Dale returned to Britain with a sample that was to be used as the standard for production. Many years later, in a filmed interview, Dale related how he had to reject an emotional appeal made to him by 'an eminent churchman' to use it for his only child who was dying of diabetes.*

* D. Gordon and E. M. Tansey, *Sir Henry Dale: A Filmed Interview* (Proceedings of the Physiological Society, 19–20 September 1986).

*For the Medical Profession only* **BLOTTER**

## 'WELLCOME' BRAND
## TINCTURE OF DIGITALIS
**U.S.P.** *(Physiologically Standardised)*

Assures reliability and uniform activity. Each bottle bears a time guarantee.

*In bottles of 1, 4, 8 and 16 Imperial fl. oz.*

BURROUGHS WELLCOME & CO. (U.S.A.) INC.
NEW YORK

**EARLIEST EVIDENCE OF KNOWLEDGE OF ANATOMY DRAWN FROM THE ART OF PALEOLITHIC MAN**

**This illustration, reproduced from an Aurignacian cave-painting in Spain, seems to prove that man, during this period, arrived at the knowledge that the heart was a vital spot and the centre of life**

U.S.A. 1266 *Printed in England* *All Rights Reserved* J. 4378

Advertisement for Wellcome tincture of digitalis, 1926

*For the Medical Profession only* **BLOTTER**

*Prescribe for your Patients*

## *'Wellcome' Insulin*

The Insulin of outstanding purity, activity and reliability

TRADE MARK 'WELLCOME' BRAND INSULIN

*Issued in rubber-capped amber-glass phials containing 100 units in 5 c.c. and 200 units in 5 c.c.; also in rubber-capped bottles containing 200 units in 10 c.c.*

Reduced facsimile

WELLCOME INSULIN

BURROUGHS WELLCOME & CO., LONDON (ENG.)
THE WELLCOME FOUNDATION LTD.
[GOVERNING DIRECTOR—HENRY S. WELLCOME ( ) DEPUTY-GOVERNING DIRECTOR—GEO. E. PEARSON]

*Associated Houses:* NEW YORK MONTREAL SYDNEY CAPE TOWN MILAN BOMBAY SHANGHAI BUENOS AIRES

6444 *h/t/s/e/r* *Printed in England* *All Rights Reserved* J. 9559

Advertisement for Wellcome insulin

When it reached Dartford, Richard Fox and his colleagues ordered a freshly slaughtered cow pancreas from Smithfield Market, which they shredded through the mincer in the Dartford canteen kitchen, an operation that Fox later related in a filmed interview for the Wellcome archives with considerable amused relish.

Wellcome was not the only British pharmaceutical company to produce insulin, but it was producing it commercially and successfully, and on a significant scale, within a year, a fact that emphasised again the high quality of Wellcome's scientists and staff. It was not, of course, the cure for diabetes, but it was, and remains, a life-extending drug of exceptional importance.

# 10

# The Last Phase, and Aftermath

Henry Wellcome's relationship with his expanding and prosperous business had been a curious one since 1905, and was even more so after 1910. While he no longer had daily contact with it, and was often abroad, no one in the company had any doubt that he still dominated it – if usually from afar. He would often arrive unannounced at Snow Hill, at the Medical Museum, at Dartford, or at Langley Court, Beckenham, which he had purchased for the Physiological Laboratories in 1921, and his keen interest in the research work of the Bureau remained strong. Although his health remained variable, he was reasonably fit and certainly mentally very alert, and his staff and competitors underestimated him at their peril. If he had become aloof from his business, he was liked and admired by his staff, to whom he was invariably courteous, although to most he had become a remote and somewhat mysterious figure.

What few realised was the sheer scale of his collection-mania, which after the 1914–18 war had assumed even greater proportions, breadth and expense. Those who did know obeyed orders and dispensed cash for his agents in quantities that were alarmingly high. And the Metlakahtlan bill continued to be met every month. Sudlow would have protested strongly at this constant and heavy drain on the company's resources, and would have had an effect; Pearson did question it occasionally, as did the firm's accountants, but somewhat tentatively and with no effect.

In 1924 Wellcome at last removed the final vestiges of Burroughs by creating The Wellcome Foundation Ltd as a private company with a capital of £1 million and himself as sole shareholder. The new company was formally under the authority of a Board consisting of himself as Governing Director, with Pearson as Deputy Governing Director and the chief accountant, G. Leslie Moore, as Company Secretary. But the reality was that Wellcome remained in complete control of every aspect of the company's activities in his seventy-first year, with day-to-day control delegated to Pearson and Moore. One of his frequent sayings was 'never tell anyone what you propose to do until you've done it', and this was to become even more apparent in his last years. It was a formula that had had considerable success, but also had damaging potentialities, as his Trustees were to discover.

One element of his upbringing was a lifelong aversion to financial speculation, somewhat strange in someone who had taken so many other risks. As he wrote to Frank Wellcome in September 1919, presenting him with a hundred $5 shares in the United Cigarette Machine Co., then selling at $8, which he had received in payment of a debt: 'I have made it a rule never to invest in shares or to speculate.' Thus the shares in the Wellcome company after Wellcome's death were to be vested in five Trustees, of whom two would be men of medical eminence, two of business and administrative experience, and one of high standing in the law; all would be in full sympathy with the essential objectives of the Foundation: medical research and the history of medicine.*

The idea of the Foundation came from the Mayo brothers and the Mayo Foundation created in memory of their parents, but Wellcome's was not a 'foundation' in the normal sense of the word and had no charitable status. His Will in 1932, which established a Board of Trustees as shareholders to provide for the continuation of his business, laboratories and museums and to dispose of residual income for medical research after his death, increased the confusion, not

* They were to be Hudson Lyall, Wellcome's solicitor, as Chairman; Henry Dale; T. R. Elliott; L. C. Bullock, another solicitor; and Martin Price, an accountant.

least because after death duties and other expenditure the residual income turned out to be remarkably meagre. This failure to think ahead clearly, and to take good legal advice, was wholly uncharacteristic and showed that Wellcome was becoming old and inattentive to detail, with what could have been disastrous consequences.

For some time there had also been indications that his religious faith, never overwhelmingly strong, had weakened considerably further after the misfortune of his marriage. All the faithful Haggis can claim is that 'there is no doubt that to the end he continued to hold at least the fundamentals of his early Christian teaching', and this muted comment appears to be wholly justified. Nor is it to be wondered at; the doubts of his youth had become confirmed by experience. But it would be wrong to describe him as becoming cynical; what was true was that he was becoming nostalgic. He became increasingly interested in his American roots, and especially in his childhood.

By 1921 the population of Garden City had dwindled to barely two hundred, and Wellcome's friends of his youth had, like him, made fortunes and had long since left Garden City and the Watowan River. Wellcome had always kept in touch with George Palmer, as well as his cousin Frank Wellcome, who had not only become a doctor, but also a highly successful banker and President of the Union Investment Company. All of the ten famous products of the log-cabin school had done well, although Henry Wellcome was the only one who had achieved international fame. As early as 1909 he had been sounding Palmer out on the possibility of building a memorial to his parents in Garden City. Palmer replied that, after discussion with friends and residents of Garden City, a library would be a desirable asset; he had tried to buy the old Wellcome drugstore, but considered the price prohibitive, particularly as it was virtually derelict. He suggested that 'the men who were boys in the old village' should get together to raise funds for the library, which they could easily afford. But Wellcome urged him not to do so, 'nor to talk about it with too much enthusiasm. It is very undesirable that things should be too much stirred up, or it will not be possible to purchase land at a reasonable price.' He asked Palmer to investigate the purchase of plots of land; Palmer was startled by the amount of land Wellcome had in mind, to which Wellcome replied (18 February 1914): 'My idea of taking the whole of this ground is to ensure Garden City sufficient public grounds for public buildings, and suitable common and sports fields.' In 1916 Palmer went ahead and bought land, including the old drugstore; Wellcome then instructed him to buy more, which he did.

In 1920 Palmer wrote to him to tell him that it had been decided to build a new school in Garden City. Wellcome cabled him to buy more land for this purpose, at his expense.

These considerable purchases naturally occasioned comment in Garden City and Mankato, but Palmer refused to disclose who the real purchaser was. A group of local citizens surmised that it could only be Henry Wellcome, whom many remembered, and wrote to him in London. They received no reply, but in July 1921 he suddenly arrived in Garden City with Palmer, who, at Wellcome's request, had organised a dinner at the one remaining hotel for his former schoolfriends. He made an emotional speech about his childhood and his debt to Garden City. He had been told that the land he had bought was not appropriate for a school, but that there was more suitable land, which he would buy and present to the village; his own land he would donate as playgrounds and a park. 'It is to education, more than to all else, that I would like to give,' he declared. He was to make generous provision in his will for the school, but it was to be many years after his death – indeed, not until 1959 – that his wishes could be accomplished. Garden City, Minnesota, is appropriately one of the very few places in the United States where the name of Henry Wellcome is remembered and honoured.

*

Wellcome's last venture into archaeology was considerably more successful than Jebel Moya had been, principally because it was professionally undertaken, and his role was limited to providing much of the funding, in collaboration with Sir Charles Marston, for the work done by J. L. Starkey in Palestine which began in October 1932. Although Wellcome never visited the principal site of Tell ed Duweir, the site of the town of Lachish, he followed its progress closely, and with mounting excitement, particularly the discovery in 1935 of inscribed pottery fragments of the period of Jeremiah that contained contemporary accounts of events mentioned in the Old Testament. This in itself was a find of significant importance, and the delighted Wellcome gave it maximum publicity. Marston, whose relations with Wellcome were distinctly cool, also claimed the credit. To Wellcome this discovery, and the other results of the Lachish diggings, fully justified his large investment; after his death his Trustees were not to take the same view.

While they were contemplating its future, Starkey was murdered by Arab bandits on 10 January 1938. It was decided, so far as the Wellcome involvement was concerned, that it should be abandoned. But the Lachish findings were lavishly published in the style that Wellcome had decreed.

He had deserved this success, although the cost of his archaeological ventures had probably been almost as heavy as that of his collections for his Historical Museum and Library. When the latter was assessed on Wellcome's death in 1936, it contained over 200,000 major exhibits and the same number of books, 10,000 manuscripts and more than 100,000 letters. To these could now be added much material from The Wellcome-Marston Archaeological Research Expedition to the Near East; when Wellcome told the Royal Commission in 1928 that only 'a fraction' of his collections had been on display, this was true even in 1936, in spite of the fact that by then they had acquired a far larger and more imposing home in the Euston Road. Only Wellcome's death and the actions of his Trustees ended the relentless flow of crates to London.

*

Wellcome felt strongly that his services to his adopted country had been ill-recognised, and with good cause. It was not until 1928 that any British university – Edinburgh – gave him an honorary degree.

He had set his heart upon obtaining a knighthood, and among his papers is the official report of 1922 establishing the Honours Scrutiny Committee of the Privy Council after the scandals of the sale of Honours under Lloyd George. There is no evidence whatever that Wellcome had attempted to purchase a knighthood, but he had read and noted the report.* Honours had been given lavishly to people whose contribution during the war had been far less than his or his company's. The fact that he was divorced may well have been one element why successive prime ministers declined to recommend him. As the examples of Stanley, Maxim and Genevieve Ward demonstrated, his American background could not have been an impediment. But the prejudice against divorce was remarkably enduring until the 1950s.

Wellcome made no secret of his desire to be honoured, nor of his ambition to be elected to the Royal Society. This was eventually achieved by Elliott and Dale in 1932, under a special statute honouring people who had made particular contributions to medical science without being scientists themselves. Appropriately, although coincidentally, both Dale and he were knighted on the same day, 26 February 1932, and a month later Wellcome was elected an Honorary Fellow of the Royal College of Surgeons, an exceptional honour for someone who had never had a medical degree. Philadelphia continued to honour him, and in March 1934 the French Government conferred upon him the *Croix de Chevalier de la Légion d'Honneur*. He was promoted to the grade of *Officier* in March 1936. In 1934 he received the Remington Medal, and Wisconsin gave him an honorary degree; he received the Gold Medal of the Royal African Society in 1935 and the Spanish *Ordén de la República* in May 1936.

In contrast, the decision of the Sudan Government to close his

* Although Wellcome carefully kept the company and himself out of British politics, he did make occasional personal contributions to local Conservative funds in London and Dartford; in view of his strong Free Trade opinions, the oddest was a contribution of £100 in 1905 to Joseph Chamberlain's Tariff Reform campaign, although the dominant factor in Wellcome's mind was Chamberlain's imperialistic attitudes.

research laboratories in Khartoum in 1935, without consulting or even informing him, was an act of insensitive ingratitude that hurt Wellcome deeply. Wingate, now in retirement in London, shared his indignation at this gratuitous blow to his old friend and wrote strong letters of protest, which at least resulted in a somewhat grudging apology to Wellcome. The Laboratories had seen their best days, and London was now the acknowledged centre for tropical medicine, but it was the abrupt and discourteous manner of the closure that so distressed Wellcome.

Even now, the Wellcome conglomerate was still Henry Wellcome's fiefdom and personal possession. He had no effective Board of Directors or shareholders to trouble about, or even consult. His personal contacts with his staff, even the most senior, became increasingly remote. The existing detailed records of letters, telegrams, memoranda and telephone calls could give an impression of close attention to the company's affairs, but the reality was different. He had become a lonely autocrat, regarding the company's money as his – not unjustifiably – and spending it as he thought best, or as he desired. Apart from his vast expenditures on his ever-mounting collections, he continued to finance Metlakahtla to the tune of $1,800 a month, and the sums he spent on Lachish – as with Jebel Moya – have never been discovered, but were obviously very substantial, with the consequence that his Trustees were to find that his bequeathed wealth was far less than they had imagined, or than Wellcome himself had believed.

But he spent very little on himself. His London house in Gloucester Gate was leased and was not luxurious, and he spent relatively little time there. He cared very much for those dependent upon him, from Mounteney to the Metlakahtlan Indians and Major Uribe, and looked after them both financially and with kind and considerate letters.

However, he did more for his friends. May Sheldon's impressive financial recovery had been ended by the 1929 Wall Street crash. 'I am now in absolute distress,' she wrote to Wellcome. 'Can and will you help me by giving me something to do, in order to eke out the remnant of my existence? I cannot go to the King of the Belgians!' Wellcome immediately gave her well-paid work at the Historical Museum and also put a car and a driver at her disposal. Her contributions were not notable, but she appeared regularly, 'looking remarkably like Mrs Tiggy-Winkle', as one irreverent young member of the staff later wrote.* She was by then almost the last of his old friends left; of them, only Wingate survived him.

In 1920 Gorgas had died suddenly in London. Such was his eminence that King George v had conferred upon him an honorary knighthood and ordered a state funeral service at St Paul's Cathedral, Wellcome being the chief pallbearer; Gorgas was later buried in Arlington Cemetery.** Moulton died in 1921; Genevieve Ward in 1922; Dorothy Stanley in 1926; and his brother George, who had been blind for several years, in California in 1930. Wellcome cabled: 'Shall take first train. Delay funeral until my arrival. Make suitable and ample provision for funeral.'

Power's death on 30 March 1927 affected Wellcome deeply. In 1921 Wellcome had designed a personal gold medal for Power; the actual presentation, at the Cosmos Club, Washington, was by the joint President of the Smithsonian Institution and of the National Academy of Sciences, Dr Charles D. Walcott. In his speech of thanks, Power said: 'I am grateful for the encouragement and inspiration received from him [Wellcome] on our journey through life, for we have travelled long and far together, but above and beyond all I am grateful for having possessed through so many years so kind, generous and true a friend.' Wellcome happened to be in the United States when Power died, and at once took charge of the funeral arrangements in Washington, for which he insisted on paying. Louise Power later wrote:

* Barbara M. Duncum, letter to J. Symons, June 1982.

** In 1928 Wellcome gave evidence in Washington to the Senate Committee on Foreign Affairs in support of the Gorgas Memorial Laboratory Bill, which was approved by the Senate on 28 April.

> At the close of the short service held there [Washington] the bereaved friend sat alone for a full half hour, with head bowed beside the casket. He later came to Hudson for the church service there, and followed his friend to the grave, where his last tribute was a large wreath of laurel.

In Power's papers was a long-kept present for his wife from Wellcome – a piece of the Roman wall of London, dug up in excavations in 1888, which Wellcome himself had found. Wellcome thought of writing Power's biography and gathered material for it, but he, also, was getting old.

Although he had his large house in Gloucester Gate, he usually preferred to live in hotels. As Leslie Matthews shrewdly commented:

> He lacked friends and he felt it. It drove him to do certain things, for example archaeology in the Sudan and in Palestine. He was highly respected but not very much loved, except by a few women, like Ada Misner. Ladies were acquaintances only – he needed their support. Wellcome was a very good host. People used to congratulate themselves if they had invitations. He gave large dinner parties, mainly at hotels. He had 36 cruets – everyone wondered what they were, but of course everyone had to have their own service.

His financial prodigality, however, was still on what Syrie had called his 'curios', and indeed they became markedly more curious and expensive. As he grew old, he was only intermittently attentive to detail, an emperor who had lost close interest in his empire, while fascinated by its baubles.

As Leslie Matthews recalls:

> He had started as a genuine collector, but it had become a magpie collection. He could not leave anything alone in his field. He lost the medical and historical science theme and would collect anything. He was a cosmopolitan collector. He had no business to be collecting armour and judging by the sales, it was rather bad European armour. I don't know why he ever acquired certain good collections, for example

prehistoric axes, except for the fact that he had advice from a man on the staff* who was an expert on prehistoric matters.

He collected in duplicate and triplicate as Noël Poynter has written:

> Wellcome marked up the auction catalogues himself. He had clear ideas of what he wanted to buy and he took advice from his experts. Most of the books he bought he never saw; they just went straight into the stacks.
>
> If a book was of particular interest to him, perhaps one on David Livingstone, he would ask to see it and then it would come back with notes in the margin in his round Victorian hand.
>
> Because there was no time to catalogue the collection, [we] often bought the same book twice. I'd say, 'I'm sure we've got that book already. I remember buying it.' He'd say, 'Better buy it again to make certain.' There simply wasn't time to make a search and check up.**

'He seemed to work on the principle that anything bought in the 1920s would be of great value and interest a hundred years later,' Mary Cathcart Borer, one of the scientific assistants at the Museum, recorded. 'The sale room managers realised this and a good deal of rubbish was included in the lots for which they were pretty certain he would bid. The most fatuous I remember was "an ivy leaf from the grave of Goethe".'†

Joan Braunholtz, recruited to the Museum in November 1928, disliked Malcolm and loathed the Willesden warehouse,

> in a district unsurpassed for sordidness and desolation; it lay between a tannery and an anchovy essence factory, and there were appalling smells (especially on Fridays). . . . Sir Henry [*sic*] was at that time buying through his agents anything and everything, almost regardless of its connection with the history of medicine – coaches, carriages, perambulators, African spears, skeletons, porcelain, Japanese netsukes – all arrived almost daily in huge consignments. As our ignorance of

* A. D. Lacaille (1894–1975), archaeologist to the Wellcome Museum 1928–59.

** *Foundation News*, November 1973.

† Letter to J. Symons, 22 October 1981.

much of this material was almost total, the cataloguing was largely guess-work.*

George Pearson noticed a marked decline in Wellcome:

> For some years before his death his physical and mental vigour was weakening, although the fundamental character of the man remained as strong as ever. He was gradually losing his powers of concentration, and his memory began to fail him. Before this he had doubtless experienced the feeling that there was hardly any limit to which his powers as the Founder of a monumental Research Institution might be restricted, and the more his ideas in this respect expanded the more difficult it became to express them in the form of concrete proposals. 'My plans exist in my mind like a jigsaw puzzle,' he frequently told me when asked exactly what were his intentions. 'And gradually I shall be able to piece it together.' With his inability to fulfil his intentions came a reluctance to make decisions and a tendency towards procrastination. There is little doubt that at this period the tasks which he had set himself had become too big for him, but the old characteristic of determination to control every detail of the execution of his plans still persisted and prevented him entrusting their development and completion to others so long as he lived – an attitude that often made things extremely difficult for his responsible officials.**

But there were still flashes of the younger Wellcome. In 1935 a competitor began to produce a cheaper brand of insulin; the reaction in some quarters of the company was to emphasise greater economy in production and in the company's publications. Wellcome's immediate minuted retort was that, 'I have had a great experience of these business crises, and I have always found that at such times it pays not to save but to *spend money*.' When he discovered that the firm was sending out sharp letters to doctors who were slow in payment, he stopped the practice, minuting that, 'we need to be very considerate and courteous in formulating our rules and regulations with respect

* Letter to J. Symons, 29 July 1985.

** Notes by A. W. Haggis of conversation with G. E. Pearson, 12 December 1940.

to the firm's dealings with medical men. . . . Above all things we must be forbearing, courteous and diplomatic, and exercise the greatest possible care in correspondence to avoid provocative expressions or implications.' He also continued his love of organising large receptions, particularly at his Historical Medical Museum, as on the centenary of Lister's birth, in April 1927; on the centenary of the death of Henry Hill Hickman, the forgotten Shropshire pioneer of anaesthesia in April 1930; and, in the same year, the tercentenary of the European use of the cinchona bark. But these occasions ceased after the closure of the Museum on its transfer to the Euston Road in 1932.

*

At the beginning of 1932 Wellcome formulated his plans for the future. What was striking for a man of seventy-nine, whose health had always been variable, was that in his talk with colleagues and even junior members of the company the future was the principal topic. His Will was signed on 29 February. Its principal purpose was to nominate his Trustees, define their powers and duties, and set out how much they distributed their funds in support of archaeological, historical and medical research. Although obviously his lawyers were acting on his close instructions, this was essentially a legal document of considerable length and detail. But Wellcome himself wrote a 'Memorandum of my Policy and Aims for the Guidance and Assistance of my Trustees', which he signed on the same day, and which was one of the most revealing of his writings. Indeed, in its style and form it was effectively his personal testament, drawing on his long experience and vision.

The first requirement was that the business should be profitable, that at all levels 'the principle of the selection of the fittest must always prevail', and that anyone who was unfit must go. Characteristically, one test of this fitness was abstinence from alcohol, certainly before the age of twenty-six, and before the evening meal; the Directors and others in position of authority were to set the example and avoid 'beery or vinous muzziness' after lunch. They should not reduce expenditure on publicity or propaganda for the company's products.

Research was essential, with close consultation between the Trustees and the Director of the Bureau of Scientific Research, and the safety of the staff was to be a paramount concern. One of his greatest ambitions was a Model Town and Works in the pattern established by Cadbury's Bournville or Levers' Port Sunlight:

> Among the essentials in selecting the site are healthfulness of locality, freedom from nuisances, practicability for transport and shipment for home or abroad, convenience, expedition and moderate cost of transport within the premises and to and from London and other railway stations and shipping ports, an abundant supply of good pure suitable water from various reliable sources including artesian wells and general cheerfulness of surroundings.

Wellcome's Trustees were to face a considerable problem in deciding what to do with the vast, and largely uncatalogued, collections he had amassed. As in his Model Town, Wellcome had declared his wishes and, as they saw it, left them to his Trustees to work out. The factory in Willesden now stored most of his variegated trophies and acquisitions, and the Trustees were to view them with the same enthusiasm as Syrie had done. Wellcome wanted them properly catalogued and displayed – but how, and where, was not specified. They could see the purpose of the historical library, but not the Museum. In 1941 the exasperated Dale – who had become Chairman of the Trust in 1937 – wrote that 'Wellcome . . . wasted on hobbies and a gigantic advertisement money which ought to have gone to assure the future of his business, and our Trust.' Although this was unfair to Wellcome, the fact remained that he had bequeathed what he believed to be a major treasure to his Trustees and posterity, but which they regarded very differently.

Another view of Wellcome in the late 1920s was given by William Britchford, who started with the company in 1926 as a joiner at the Museum in Wigmore Street:

> I arrived at Wigmore Street to find the museum was undergoing a reorganisation under the direction of Sir Henry [*sic*]. There were

another twelve carpenters and joiners already working on it. I was given a bench and the other joiners were told if they found they could not manage a job they were to bring it to me and I was to do, as you might say, the tricky part of it and then give it back for them to carry on with, but after a month of this work I began to feel that this job was not for me and I let it be known that I would be leaving shortly. The next day one of the office staff came and said Sir Henry wished to see me. I entered his office and he said to me, 'Sit down. I understand you may be leaving us. Why?' I said, 'Before I came here I was a foreman in the building trade and I do not really wish to go back to using the tools all the time.' He then said, 'For some years now I have been looking for someone like you for my museum.' He then began to tell me of his ambitions for the museum, how it would expand and how he hoped one day to have the biggest private museum in the country. He said that if I could stay with him he would assure me of a good position in the museum and so would I think it over in the next weeks. A week after this he sent for me again and asked for my decision. I told him that I would remain for the time being and then . . . I stayed for 42 years. . . . When Sir Henry was collecting exhibits for the museum, much of which was, of course, bought in salerooms, they were stored in different warehouses round London. The man who was in charge of the warehouse we had in Peckham was named Bourne, and one day Sir Henry went to this warehouse and, after looking round, noticed a kind of tray and said to Bourne, 'What's in there?' Bourne replied, 'Only bits and pieces.' 'Let me look,' said Sir Henry. Bourne took the tray down. Wellcome looked at the contents of the tray and said, 'My life's work and you call it bits and pieces. Bourne I'm fed up with you.' Bourne replied, 'Sir, I am fed up with you too.' So Bourne lost his job as warehouse-superintendent but was given another job in the museum.

Britchford continued:

Sir Henry was a perfectionist. . . . At times he would send for me, tell me what he required, and if I said, 'I don't think we could do that', he would put his hand on my shoulder and say, 'You know I think it could be done if we could find the right man,' and then just walk away. After he had gone, I used to put my thinking cap on to see if we could produce what he had asked for and, of course, sometimes I did find the answer to the problem. . . .

One of the things about Sir Henry was that he never thought he would die, he would talk about things he wanted done in five years time and ten years time. I remember a year before he died, instead of opening his house at Gloucester Gate he stayed at the Langham Hotel. He was not really very well then, but I had a call from his secretary who said he would like to see me at 2 o'clock. When I got there, Sir Henry asked me how things were going in the museum, etc., and started to tell me what he was going to do in the future and in five years he would like to do so and so – and he was then 81. Time passed and it got to half-past four, when I said to Sir Henry that I thought there was a little job he wanted done and he said, 'It doesn't matter about that. Come and see me tomorrow at the same time, will you?' I did so and again he talked all of the future. At last when I asked what it was he wanted, his secretary produced a suitcase which had a few scratches which he asked me if I could just cover up as it looked bad, and said bring it back next week. I took it back and he carried on talking and then said if I had any time to spare next week could I come again one afternoon, and then I realised that he was a lonely old man and was asking me there just so that he could talk to somebody. When he was well, and was at his home in Gloucester Gate, Stevens, the auctioneers, would give him the key to their warehouse and he would spend Sunday all alone there looking at the things they would auction during the week.*

There were many of his associates and staff who considered that Wellcome had lost serious interest in the company after 1930, apart from his collections and the Lachish excavations. This was only partly true; he was absorbed by the task of preserving and enhancing the Wellcome inheritance and perpetuating his achievements. The great new Wellcome building in Euston Road was one project to which he devoted much thought and energy; he was as restless as ever, and

* Letter to A. N. Falder, 29 April 1975.

still took considerable interest in new appointments in the Museum, even some quite junior ones. It was his habit often to interview applicants, or to be present at interviews, anonymously. This was regarded as something of a personal eccentricity, but it was in fact an act of sympathy, as he thought that if nervous candidates realised it was Wellcome himself, they would become even more nervous. There was some vanity in this, but his motives were kindly.

Mary Cathcart Borer has related her experience:

> In 1928 I left University College, London, with a degree in Geography and Cultural Anthropology. A few weeks later an advertisement appeared in *The Times* – 'Graduate in archaeology or anthropology, with a knowledge of French and German, wanted for London museum'.
>
> I wrote to the box number and a few days later received a telegram which said: 'Meet advertiser Welbeck Palace Hotel'. I arrived at the appointed hour and showed the telegram to the commissionaire, who said at once: 'If I were you, Miss, I'd go straight home.'
>
> However, I decided to wait in the empty lounge, and a few minutes later an elderly, rather distinguished-looking man walked in, with a younger man who introduced himself as Gordon, and said that his companion was Mr Wilkins.
>
> They asked me a lot of questions about anthropology and the work I had been doing at University College with Dr Perry and Professor Elliot Smith. Then Mr Gordon said: 'Sprechen Sie deutsch?' and I replied 'Ja, ein wenig': and this fairly basic dialogue they seemed to accept as my knowledge of German. They murmured together for a moment and then Mr Gordon said: 'Well, we'll now take you round to the museum.'
>
> It was late afternoon in September and growing dusk. I didn't much fancy the idea and the commissionaire looked even more concerned, as we stepped out of the hotel and disappeared into the gathering gloom. We walked down Welbeck Street and round the corner, past John Bell and Croyden's, and came to the doors of the Wellcome Historical Medical Museum. I said: 'Oh, I know about this place. It's the Burroughs Wellcome Museum, isn't it?' 'This has nothing

whatsoever to do with Burroughs Wellcome,' said Mr Gordon, and ushered me through the door with the brass plate announcing that it *was* the Wellcome Historical Medical Museum, into the dark, deserted, front hall.

Mr Wilkins then departed – and I never spoke to him again during the next seven years – but Gordon turned to me and said: 'Yes – you were right. That was Dr Henry Wellcome and my name is really Malcolm.'

He took me round the place for a few minutes and then said he'd be writing to me.*

Miss Borer was appointed to the job.

The future Professor Theodor Gaster was also interviewed personally by Wellcome at the Welbeck Palace Hotel: 'After asking me whether I read cuneiform, his next question was whether I was now suffering, or had ever suffered, from "loathsome diseases"!' After his appointment, he discovered at Wigmore Street 'a careful card-file of "dirty postcards" systematically arranged by degrees of obscenity. It was eventually explained by [Johnston-] Saint that this was "a scientific record of contemporary humour"!'**

The Museum was Wellcome's principal love, and the Library languished, first in a former stable in Stratford Mews, off Marylebone Lane, and then at 10 Hythe Road, Willesden. Noël Poynter, who was to rise to be Librarian, and eventually Director of the Museum and Library, subsequently in 1961 described his experience on joining as a junior assistant in 1930:

> As a student, I had been accustomed to libraries both large and small, but most of them were ancient, or at least well-matured, with the soft gleam of old leather bindings reflecting the subdued lights, the cathedral hush of scholars at their devotions, the sense of age-old order and perfection. It was a scene which bore no relation whatever to that which confronted me on my first day as a professional librarian. I was led into

* Letter to J. Symons, 22 October 1981.

** Letter to J. Symons, 26 December 1981.

the large but gloomy halls of a former warehouse and there, from floor to rafters, were heaped great mounds of books, brought together from auction-rooms, bookshops and private sales in many countries. Most of them were still tied and labelled just as they had left Sotheby's or Hodgson's years and perhaps decades before. Hundreds of large packing-cases in another hall contained whole collections bought in France or Italy, while others were roughly chalked on the outside, Oriental Manuscripts, Arabic, Persian, Sanskrit, Burmese, Tamil, Chinese, and so on. When the first chill of apprehension at this spectacle had left me and, from somewhere among the rafters, I began to disturb the dust of years, I felt more like stout Cortez. All around and beneath me was a new world of books such as I had never dreamed of. They were not Gutenberg Bibles, it is true, nor First Folios, but there were such splendid books as the anatomical masterpiece of Vesalius, the Mainz Herbal, Gilbert's *De Magnete*, and even the first editions of Newton's *Principia* and Dr Johnson's *Dictionary*, all mixed up with such rubbish as often finds its way into miscellaneous lots at auction-sales. The fever which attacked me then is one from which some never recover; they become chronic bibliomaniacs.

If I may continue a little longer on this personal note, I should like to explain that I was not left very long to this private orgy. I had wondered how it was that so many fine books had evidently accumulated for so long without being sorted out and cared for. On my second day came the answer, as well as my second type of new bibliographical experience. I was instructed to attend the sale-rooms, first merely to list the contents of miscellaneous lots and to examine special items, but later to bid, always pseudonymously, I should add. There, as I looked around the famous room where so many of the world's treasures had changed ownership at the flick of a catalogue or a scarcely perceptible nod, I went through the usual ordeals of the novice until I grew accustomed to the tension in the air. I regarded with awe and respect the internationally famous book dealers who took their chairs round the table with the proprietary air of old hands. I was too late for Rosenbach, alas, who was then braving the Depression at home with all his usual confidence, but I did become familiar with the short, bearded figure of Ben Maggs, and often envied him some of the precious little volumes which he seemed to inspect so casually but carried away so often, some of them, I am happy to say, eventually finding their way to our own shelves.

In those same rooms, I first saw some of the collectors themselves, who came to view but left their bids with dealers. I noticed the loving and almost reverent way they picked up and opened some long-sought item, the few minutes of utter and complete absorption, the far-away look in the eyes as, slowly and reluctantly, the book was returned to its place.

All these impressions, rapidly crowding one upon another in the mind of a young man, left me with an understanding of the bibliomaniac, a respect for the dealer's acumen and knowledge of books, and a deep fellow-feeling for the bibliophile. They also greatly enlarged my own bibliographical horizons.*

In 1964, in his report to the Trustees, Poynter presented a less warm, and very accurate, portrait:

> Between 1928 and Wellcome's death in 1936 other fine material came to the collections from sales at home and abroad, but this was often overlaid at the time by the sheer bulk of books and objects of a non-medical character which were bought in increasing numbers at Wellcome's insistence. From remarks which he made in conversation in his last years it seems that he was thinking of a museum and library of general cultural history as well as the history of medicine. He always managed to convey his vision of 'great things' in the future to his staff, and I think others shared my own view that it was this alone which kept us with him, for the appalling working conditions, the irritation and embarrassments of the anonymity and pseudo-secrecy which was enforced even in our personal relations with professional colleagues in other institutions, together with the apparently unending task of sorting vast and ever-growing quantities of materials, often made our loyalty seem misguided. Wellcome was one of those who find the journey more interesting than the end, and he found collecting more

* F. N. L. Poynter, *Bibliography, some achievements and prospects* (University of California, 1961).

satisfying than the task of organising the collection into a well-planned museum.*

In 1929 Wellcome embarked upon his last ambitious single scheme, the building of the Wellcome Research Institution, in Euston Road, the headquarters of his scientific research organisation, containing the Bureau of Scientific Research, specialising in tropical medicine; the historical Museum; the Chemical Research Laboratories and the Museum of Medical Science, which was primarily a teaching institution; the Physiological and Entomological Laboratories were to remain at Beckenham and Esher. The lease at Wigmore Street was ending, and this may have played some part in Wellcome's decision to build a much larger, more imposing and permanent home for his collection. By this point at the end of the 1920s the Museum had come to be regarded as an institution of real quality as well as rarity, but only a fraction of Wellcome's vast collection could be displayed.

He already owned land in Euston Road, housing the Bureau and Museum of Medical Science, and, after looking at other properties in the area, Wellcome decided to demolish and rebuild. With characteristic care he now looked for an architect to create a building on the same lines he had instructed his family mausoleum to be built in Garden City (although it never was) – 'a strictly classical type of Greek or Ionic order of architecture'. He was driven around London slowly so that he could inspect recently constructed buildings, and was particularly impressed by the remodelling of what became Canada House in Trafalgar Square, the work of Septimus Warwick, much of whose work had been in Canada or for Canadian clients. After meeting Warwick, who had a considerable reputation for the skilful handling of his clients, Wellcome was convinced that he was his man. Indeed, there seems to have been an unusual harmony of purpose between client and architect, Wellcome knowing exactly what he wanted, and Warwick skilfully adapting Wellcome's wishes to his own

* Report, 6 February 1964.

drawings without attracting Wellcome's displeasure. It was sturdily built of Portland stone on a steel frame, and was so conventional in its neo-classical appearance that it was, unjustifiably, criticised as imposing and formidable, but dull. Only the marble used for the floors and walls of the foyer were not from materials supplied by British Empire countries – one of Wellcome's requirements.

Thus, although Snow Hill remained the company's headquarters, Wellcome had by 1932 fulfilled Burroughs's ambition to have 'the best drug Boss House in London', although he would not have relished the reminder. He had eliminated Burroughs's name from the title of the company, which since 1924 henceforth bore only his own. But Burroughs, like Syrie, had long been exorcised, and their names never mentioned. When the Burroughs daughters protested, Wellcome ignored them.

*

Although it had been in Britain that Wellcome had made his fame and fortune, it was also there that he had suffered the two greatest disappointments of his life, and his sense of his American upbringing became stronger in his last years. He not only spent much time in the United States, but, and especially after the death of his brother George in 1930, was increasingly reminded of the happiness of his childhood.

By the end of 1935 Wellcome realised that he was very ill, and he resolved to make one last visit to the places of his childhood and young manhood. He returned to Garden City, where he was admiringly received, and where he could tell fascinated youngsters the stories of the early years, visit the drugstore (then still standing) and his parents' house (also then in existence and inhabited),* and bid farewell to his friends, although he gave no hint of the fact that it was a valedictory visit.

There was one final filial duty to be undertaken. For some time Wellcome had been negotiating with Frank and Lizzie Wood for the purchase of the original Wellcome house and farm at Almond. Land,

* Both were demolished in the 1960s.

particularly in northern Wisconsin, was very cheap early in 1936, but the Woods clearly realised the immense emotional value Wellcome placed in their thirteen-acre property. Wellcome travelled to the area in May and made the Woods an offer of $3,500, which, in the depths of the Depression, was a sum infinitely greater than the farm was worth; indeed, to the Woods, it was a small fortune at that time. It was not until 10 June, when the Indenture was signed and published, that it became known in Almond that the Wellcome Farm had reverted to Henry Wellcome.

There is no record of what Wellcome intended to do with it, and he left no instructions to his Trustees, who thankfully – and some might say, heartlessly – sold it in January 1943 for $1,000 to Herman and Gladys Wittke, of Milwaukee. Although it has changed hands since, it remains virtually unchanged, and the large wooden barn where the young Wellcome had forked hay with his brother survived until the 1980s, when its condition was such that it had to be pulled down and replaced.

Wellcome then went to New York with Ada Misner, to sail back to England on the *Queen Mary*. His last journey to the land of his birth had not been without achievement.

*

Until this final visit to the United States, for someone who had been seriously ill so often, his health appeared good, and one detailed examination in January 1934 in Baltimore revealed 'a history of doing far too much for a man of eighty. Patient should not be under such great strain despite the fact that he feels exceedingly well and vigorous.' He was deemed to be ten pounds overweight, with slight arthritis of the spine, some hardening of the arteries, but with normal blood pressure. Some concern was noted about his prostate, but the conclusion of the examining doctor was that his patient principally needed rest and sunshine. He wrote to Wellcome that,

> I know you have felt that during the past few years avoidance of over-exertion, of tenseness and of pressure was not possible, but from

> now on you owe it to yourself and your friends to live more quietly. I congratulate you, however, upon the excellent condition you are in at this time of life.

The reality was that Wellcome was not at all in an 'excellent condition'. His sinuses continued to cause him much discomfort and severe headaches, but what was far more ominous were his continued intestinal pains and problems, which his medical advisers consistently did not consider serious, although any modern reader of his medical reports from 1934 would consider them thoroughly alarming. It would appear that Wellcome did as well, as he wrote to William Mayo on 2 April 1935 asking for admission to the Mayo Clinic and for the advice of his old friends, which was gladly given.

Wellcome and Ada Misner arrived at the end of May, on the *Aquitania*, the former exhausted and, to some observers, almost in a state of collapse, but 'looking fairly well', according to Dr Waltman Walters. But the prostate was by now alarmingly enlarged and Wellcome was in increasing pain; all the signs were that 'the enlargement is cancerous'. This was confirmed after an operation at the Mayo Clinic on 12 June, when a malignant abdominal growth was removed.

But although the detailed analysis of Wellcome's condition was not hopeful, he responded well to treatment at the Clinic between June and October 1935, his American doctor, A. J. Thompson, reporting that 'He has been very active and seems in first-class physical condition', which reads somewhat oddly in the light of the detailed analysis of his condition. He was well enough to go to Washington in November to see friends, and then to Orlando, Florida, with Ada to convalesce during the winter.

When Wellcome submitted himself again to the Mayo Clinic on 28 April 1936, Thompson declared:

> . . . his condition [has] greatly improved compared to the condition at the time of dismissal of November 6th, 1935. He has gained weight and appears in excellent health for a man of his age. . . . We have advised Sir Henry to refrain from undue exercise and to take mild sedatives as needed to control the mild rheumatic pain which might arise.

However, after Wellcome and Ada returned to Britain, the discomfort became agonising. He was now passing blood and was becoming mentally confused. A new British doctor was summoned, who quickly realised that Wellcome had a massive and incurable bladder cancer. Other advice was sought, including that of Lord Dawson of Penn, but while his doctors consulted about his case, Wellcome suddenly faded. 'He died on July 25th, the final collapse being sudden,' his doctor wrote. 'Although we could not be certain of the cause of death, the rapid onset of respiratory difficulties suggested a pulmonary infarct.'

The Mayo diagnosis had been over-optimistic. The blood transfusions that Wellcome's London doctor had instructed had caused a slight improvement, 'but he ran a temperature for which no explanation could be found'. Unquestionably, the prostate cancer would have killed him, but in fact pneumonia did.

Wellcome's funeral service, after his body had laid briefly in state in the auditorium of the Wellcome Building, was at Golders Green Crematorium. It was not until February 1987 that his ashes were buried in the churchyard of St Paul's Cathedral, and a plaque in his memory placed next to that of Alexander Fleming, the discoverer of penicillin, in the crypt of the Cathedral in the course of an Evensong dedicated to him.

# *Postscript*

# Wellcome after Wellcome

It is so often the case that when the founder of a great enterprise dies, the enterprise itself withers, fades and eventually disappears. Their personal inspiration, imagination and individual fervour have gone, and what is left is an organisation, an institution, but the genius of leadership has vanished.

In the case of Henry Wellcome, for all the feelings of his last years, that particular genius had not totally disappeared, but he had not made sufficient provision for his aftermath. However, he had made better than was subsequently realised or appreciated.

Henry Wellcome's obituaries dwelt not only upon his remarkable life and achievements, but also upon his generous benefactions, and the substantial fortune he had bequeathed to the future of British medical science and research. But his Trustees found themselves in a legal and financial predicament. Dale and his co-Trustees soon realised that The Wellcome Foundation Ltd was not a 'foundation' at all in the usual sense of the word but a company to include the business, the Laboratories and the Museums; it was not a charitable arrangement. The 1932 Will dealt with the estimated large sums that Wellcome would personally leave, which were entrusted to the Trustees for medical and scientific research and the history of medicine. Thus, confusingly, the Wellcome Trust became the real 'foundation', specifically charged with distributing the income, entirely from Wellcome shares, only to legally accepted charitable institutions. This division, between the commercial company (the Wellcome Foundation

Ltd) on the one hand, and the Trust on the other, exists to this day, to the puzzlement of outsiders.

It was even more of a difficulty for the Trustees, who had to appoint a Board of Directors for the Foundation, which until his death had been entirely under Wellcome's personal control. Then the question arose as to which actually owned the collection and the Library. Wellcome wanted them to be the responsibility of the Trustees, but they were assets of the business and, therefore, of the Foundation. The eventual compromise was equally curious. In 1960 the Trustees acquired the collections from the company and took responsibility for their future development.

These problems were much compounded first by the fact that Wellcome's death duties were far higher than had been expected, and then by the outbreak of war in 1939. The famous Will, although immensely long and with clear objectives, had not been well prepared, and contained not only legal ambiguities and confusions, but also proposals that were not feasible, and some that were not even legally binding. Translating this complex document into the kind of action Wellcome had envisaged involved much expenditure on lawyers and legal advice, and even recourse to the courts for necessary alterations – one example being his proposal for the exhuming of the bodies of his parents and brother and their reburial in Garden City, which the courts ruled was an improper provision. Time and again the Trustees asked themselves what had Wellcome really intended: the only possible solution was to have a clear separation between the Foundation (the commercial firm) and the Trust (the charity). But the funds were not adequate for Wellcome's purposes: in the first twenty years of the Trust's existence it disbursed a total of only £1 million.

Wellcome's grandiose plans were, as his Trustees soon realised, quite incapable of being implemented. It appeared that when he died, Henry Wellcome had left a remarkable legacy: the materials for a large unique library and museum to be funded from the profits of a thriving pharmaceutical company, academic research laboratories, and a fund from the profits of a company to be used for the support of medical research and medical history. But in fact, his increasingly eccentric approach to the business during the later years of his life, and his failure to appoint others of high calibre to manage it for him as he grew older, resulted in declining profits and his enormous unlisted, unsorted collections being left with very limited funds to put them in order. Also, no dividends were available to be distributed by his Trustees to support medical research and medical history.

Thus, his Trustees found that they were dependent upon the profits of a company that was beginning to lose its competitive strength, vast unpacked collections in storehouses under the care of the company, and a number of laboratories undertaking medical research, usually of an uncommercial nature. Furthermore, Wellcome had specified that Pearson, who had been his deputy Governor of the company since 1924, should become the Governing Director.

According to Johnston-Saint, who saw Wellcome during his Florida convalescence in 1935, Wellcome had told him that he had decided to retire Pearson and replace him with Thomas Nevin. There is no reference to this in Wellcome's papers, but, even after making allowances for Johnston-Saint's subsequent bitterness about what he considered the betrayal of Wellcome's wishes by his Trustees, there is strong evidence that Wellcome had told Nevin that this was his intention, and that Nevin was extremely disappointed when Pearson was replaced by T. R. G. Bennett, who proved a deeply unfortunate appointment. But nothing was done before Wellcome's death. Considerable sums had to be paid in death duties, which substantially reduced the £3 million Wellcome had left. As a result, some of his wishes – including the large family mausoleum at Garden City and the school – had to be postponed, and in the case of the former abandoned for legal reasons, no doubt to the relief of his Trustees. They stopped the large contributions to the Lachish diggings and began the immense task of dealing with his collections.

The prodigality of his expenditure in his later years on matters wholly unconnected with medical research and the development of new talents, products and drugs now became more evident in a harsher and more sophisticated medical and pharmaceutical climate. These sombre realities prompted some people, then and later, to underestimate severely the extent of Wellcome's extraordinary achievements until the final period of his life.

In themselves, Wellcome's enormous collections posed many problems. The first was that as they did not have charitable status, which Wellcome had omitted to establish, substantial additional death duties had to be paid. And when the Trustees sought information from Johnston-Saint about the items stored in Willesden and Stanmore, their worst fears were fully confirmed. If there were jewels, as there were, there was also much junk. The sheer quantity was bad enough, but it was the dizzying variety that was so stunning. To take only a few examples: the collection included Gordon's Chinese robes, a rose from his garden in Khartoum, and the top of one of the railings surrounding the Mahdi's tomb; there was also Blondin's wheelbarrow, cord and trapeze used in his crossing of Niagara Falls, George IV's 'cradle jig' for his sporting guns, over 80,000 models of patents registered in the US Patent Office that had never been uncrated, tons of military items, 17,000 amulets, fifty-two cases of flints weighing over two tons, and 'a very considerable quantity of metal such as old steel safe doors, obsolete lifting tackle, including chains and blocks, and a large quantity of useless tools and other objects'. The task of deciding what to do with this unwanted inheritance exercised the Trustees for years. Between 1937 and 1939 they authorised a series of sales of a remarkable variety of items, from ship models to model engines and mantraps, and 'Statuary, odd furniture, old trunks, antique bicycles, china, glass and miscellaneous material'. Johnston-Saint also listed 4,000 spears, 600 clubs, 500 paddles and 150 shields – whose financial value he, and many others, seriously underestimated.

Most of the Jebel Moya finds were given to the British Museum in 1945 for first choice (which caused strong resentment elsewhere) and worldwide distribution. The Lachish findings were divided, some going to the British Museum's Department of Western Asiatic Antiquities.* The entire prehistoric collection was also given to the British Museum in 1965, including palaeolithic cave material from France, Gibraltar, India and America; and over fifteen thousand items were given to the University of California in Los Angeles in the same year. The US Patents Models were bought by the Smithsonian for $10,000. In 1977–82 the medical core of the collection was presented to the Science Museum on permanent loan. The sales only partly compensated for the death duties; over six tons of guns, cannon, helmets and shields were given for scrap during the Second World War. But an astonishing amount still remained of the million items he and his agents had gathered.

Pride of place in the new building was given to the Wellcome Historical Medical Museum, which was assigned the first, second and third floors, but, on the removal of the Museum from Wigmore Street in 1932, Wellcome made the disastrous decision that it should remain closed for complete reorganisation under his own supervision. The immensity of the task defeated him; staff morale plummeted and Malcolm proved out of his depth in the new situation. Concrete progress with the new display did not begin until his replacement by Johnston-Saint at the end of 1934.

From then onwards progress was steady until Wellcome's death and the Trustees were content to allow this to continue, although Johnston-Saint was increasingly diverted to work on the elimination of non-medical material from the store at Willesden. The outbreak of the Second World War further delayed the reopening of the Museum. In 1941 some of its space was given up to the Library, which until then had remained at Willesden. Further space was lost

* See Georgina Russell, 'The Wellcome Historical Medical Museum's Disposal of Non-Medical Material, 1936–1983' (*Museums Journal*, vol. 86, Supplement 1986) for a more detailed account. According to Johnston-Saint the proceeds of sales were £21,818 6s between 1937 and 1939; £583 8s to 1942; and £5,321 2s 3d for the sale of armour in 1942. Many of the items, particularly the pictures and portraits, went for absurdly low prices, which was not surprising in the immediate pre-war, and then war, climate.

to the company after the bombing of the Snow Hill head office.

In April 1946 the Library at last admitted its first readers and the reopening of the Museum seemed imminent, but in the autumn of that year it was announced that it was to be evicted and that its space would become the company's new head office.*

*

Wellcome's ambitions would never have been fulfilled, and perhaps the company itself might well not have survived, had it not been for Henry Dale. Although others played important roles, it was above all his persistence, wisdom and shrewdness that gradually made some sense out of the Trustees' complex inheritance, and turned Wellcome's dreams into reality. Indeed, had it not been for Dale, the Wellcome story could well have concluded in sad posthumous anticlimax, which it did not deserve, and for which Wellcome was not responsible.

By 1948 the company was in an unhappy state, as the restrictions on profit-making during the Second World War had prevented any significant recouping of its strength, and finally under T. R. G. Bennett there was a disastrous failure in the production of penicillin which might have saved it, and nearly closed it. Bennett left in 1948 and was succeeded by H. E. Sier, an accountant, appointed to resolve the company's unfortunate condition. He stayed until 1953, when Michael Perrin was appointed.

In spite of Sier's endeavours, by 1952 the condition of the company was, if not exactly parlous, a source of deep concern to Dale. The combination of paying Wellcome's death duties and the effects of the war were serious enough. But far more serious was the fact that

* Johnston-Saint, appalled by what he considered to be the wanton dismantling of his life's work, retired 'in bitter disappointment' in 1947. (John Symons, *The Wellcome Institute for the History of Medicine – A Short History* [The Wellcome Trust, 1993], p. 38.) There is a certain unresolved mystery why Johnston-Saint had remained so long. He claimed that others – notably Wellcome's designated Trustees, whom he held in low regard – had ignored Wellcome's wishes not to let his collections be dispersed. It is not clear, therefore, why he had participated in this process for over ten years, however reluctantly.

Wellcome's policy of ploughing back profits into research for new products had not been followed, with the result that the company was falling badly behind its principal competitors. Another consequence was that the resources available to the Trustees under Wellcome's Will were far less than he or they had envisaged. Although sales were over £10 million annually, it was clear to Dale and others that something approaching a crisis was looming.

There was considerable justice in the fact that it was the United States company that saved the Wellcome empire. In 1925 manufacturing had been moved to Tuckahoe, in New York State, and when the terrible economic depression of the 1930s was at its worst, Wellcome personally inspired and organised the largest, most ambitious and most successful exhibition in the history of the company at the International Exposition in Chicago. It was also a major achievement that during this grim period not a single employee of Burroughs Wellcome Co. in the United States lost his or her job. During the Second World War and the post-war consumer boom the American company prospered under the leadership of Guy S. Dunbar and William N. Creasy.

Peter Williams, later Director of the Trust for twenty-six years, has written that,

> The Board of the company was in London, but the powerhouse of its income was in the United States. The US company ran as a virtually independent entity with its own board, which made as much as 70% of the income of the company as a whole, and paid for its own virtually independent research programme. The remaining 30% hardly made ends meet, and the UK research was very academic in the tradition that Henry Wellcome had created. The researchers believed they were in a special category, and that it was the duty of the Trustees to carry out Wellcome's will and maintain them in a limbo between academia and commerce. A different atmosphere prevailed in the United States. . . . The result was that the US company sustained the whole enterprise through its profits. The US company run by William Creasy, a dictatorial entrepreneur, virtually dictated to the British board.

Creasy also recruited outstanding talent, including George Hitchings and Trudy Elion – future Nobel prizewinners – who produced dramatic new lines of drugs that transformed the world-wide reputation and profits of the company, and for the first time enabled the Trustees to consider seriously how to distribute money as set out in the will. Wisely, they decided to be cautious until the funds had accumulated into a substantial sum.*

The success of Burroughs Wellcome Co. stemmed largely from a range of products marketed under the brandname 'Empirin' (aspirin). 'Empirin' was an analgesic, which 'was in every American woman's handbag'. But also in the United States, and financed by the profits of the US company, was a thriving research activity under the direction of George Hitchings. The research of Hitchings and his colleague, Gertrude Elion, was to produce trimethoprim (an active ingredient combined with a sulphonamide in the anti-bacterial 'Septrin' [co-trimoxazole]); 'Zyloric' (allopurinol), an anti-gout remedy; 'Daraprim' (pyrimethamine), an anti-malarial; and, above all, 'Imuran' (azathioprine), a drug which depressed the immune response and was therefore profoundly significant in organ transplantation. Hitchings and Elion won the Nobel Prize in 1988 for their research. When 'Zyloric' and 'Septrin' came on the market in 1966 and 1968 respectively, the growth in sales in the company was rapid: from £50 million in the late 1960s to £400 million in 1977. The American company thus not only saw Wellcome through a dangerous financial period in the 1940s and 1950s, but also produced the new drugs which took it into a new era.

By 1969 Burroughs Wellcome Co. had outgrown its sixteen-acre site in Tuckahoe, and the decision was made to move to Research Triangle Park in North Carolina. Its successes under Frederick Coe

* Regrettably, Creasy's temperament was such that the main Board in London seized its opportunity when, for the third time, Creasy threatened resignation if he did not get his way, and accepted it. Thus, the man who had perhaps done more than any other individual to restore the Wellcome fortunes left the company.

Jr fully matched the earlier ones of the teams established by Power and Dale, including the pioneering work on immunosuppressant drugs for human transplants by the British surgeon, Professor (later Sir) Roy Calne. Thus, the American subsidiary became highly profitable at the time when the British company was not, and Henry Wellcome's persistence in maintaining it when all commercial sense argued that it should be sold off was fully justified. The question does arise, however, whether it had been Burroughs, and not Wellcome, who had been right in 1887.

In 1952 Dale proposed that Michael Perrin, then forty-seven, should become the Chairman of the Foundation. Perrin had no pharmaceutical experience whatever, although his work at ICI in the development of polythene, and in the war and subsequently on the atomic bomb, had revealed his width of scientific knowledge. His career, however distinguished, did not appear appropriate for the special needs of the ailing Wellcome group in 1952. Perrin thought so, also, when Dale broached the idea to him, but the Board of ICI encouraged him to take up Dale's offer of the Chairmanship of the Foundation, which he did, with many qualms, on 1 January 1953.

Perrin's policy was to return to the principles of Henry Wellcome himself, and to adopt a long-term strategy. He persuaded the Trustees to do so as well, and to agree to reinvest a large proportion of the company's profits into research. In Perrin's opinion they would get far greater dividends in the long run. During his chairmanship some seventy per cent of the company's profits went back into research and development. Perrin was ably supported by a strong Finance Director, Dudley Robinson, and the Managing Director, Denis Wheeler. The company began to thrive once more. The Wellcome Trustees had only received £1 million in dividends between 1936 and 1958, when it published its first report. Between 1958 and 1972, the Trustees allowed the company to retain the majority of its profits to build up its strength. Somewhat to Perrin's surprise these dividends came remarkably quickly. The recovery had begun in earnest.

Nineteen fifty-three was the centenary of Wellcome's birth, and in a style that the founder would have relished, it was decided to celebrate this with as much fanfare and publicity as possible. The name of Wellcome was boosted, as was the morale of the company's staff.

But Wellcome's interests outside Britain and the United States had also stagnated. There were only eight overseas 'houses'; indeed, none had been established since 1912, another example of how Henry Wellcome's energies had flagged, so far as his company was concerned, after the disaster of his marriage and his increasing interest in other matters. Perrin set out, literally, to remedy this, starting in New Zealand in 1954. The most important single participant in this worldwide expansion was Dr Frederick Wrigley, the company's overseas director. Indeed, the team that gradually came together was as remarkable as any that Wellcome himself had assembled, and this time with a much greater commercial attitude, learning from the outstanding achievements of the Americans, who had brilliantly combined high quality original research with their eyes also fixed upon commercial possibilities. And thus the great Wellcome revival occurred, not due so much to individuals as to a team now working to the original Henry Wellcome ethos. By 1970, when Perrin retired as Chairman, Wellcome had fifty-eight subsidiaries located abroad, twenty of which were in Europe. The global ambitions of Silas Burroughs and Henry Wellcome had at long last been largely achieved.

Another emphasis, reflecting the early successes in the 1880s, was put upon consumer products, and notable earners were 'Saxin' and 'Marzine'. The veterinary side of the business was also greatly expanded, partly by the acquisition of the Cooper McDougall & Robertson Group in 1959, which brought in more overseas business. In 1967 the Calmic Group was acquired. The global nature of the company's business was emphasised by the appointment of Regional Managers for all the major regions of the world and of Directors with worldwide responsibilities. A worldwide company house style was introduced in 1969.

The transformation was dramatic. Wellcome started winning

awards again: the Queen's Award to Industry in 1970 for its export achievements and, in 1971, the Queen's Award for Technological Innovation. Perrin was knighted in 1967 – although not solely for his work for Wellcome – and when he retired three years later the company's sales were nearly £86 million. As a result, the Trustees were again able to award grants for medical research – £5,780,268 in the period 1961–70, which could hardly have been a more spectacular improvement. In the entire period between the death of Henry Wellcome and the end of 1956 the *total* sum paid out by the Trust had been only £1,170,000.

Many people had been involved in this renaissance, including Sir John Boyd, a former employee of the Wellcome Company who became a Trustee.

'Zovirax' (acyclovir), the most successful product in the history of the company, was introduced in 1981. It was synthesised by Dr Howard Schaeffer working in the United States, while its anti-viral activity was detected in the Wellcome Laboratories in the United Kingdom. 'Zovirax' went on to win a Queen's Award for Technological Achievement in the UK and the French *Prix Galien* in 1985 – Wellcome's first billion dollar drug.

The company had been restored to the role that Henry Wellcome had planned for it, and the Trust to its position as a major supporter of British medical and scientific research. The contribution of Dr Peter Williams, who served the Trust with unobtrusive quiet distinction for thirty-one years, twenty-six as Director, between 1965 and 1991, by which time the Wellcome Trust was disbursing over £100 million a year, merits particular mention. He worked devotedly and effectively for the Trust and gave it a well-justified reputation for high standards and innovation in the support of medical research. But, as he has emphasised, it was essentially a collective endeavour, first to save the company from extinction, and then to put it once again in the forefront of research and development.

A. A. Gray was Chairman from 1971 to 1977, and in 1977 Alfred Shepperd (later Sir Alfred) took over, having been the Finance

Director for the previous five years – the start of a successful thirteen-year reign. The policy of restricting dividends to the Trust was maintained despite the considerable growth in the profits of the company, with the result that by 1986, the fiftieth anniversary of Wellcome's death, the Trustees were ready to seek permission to take the company public. This happened in February 1986, when they sold twenty-one per cent of their shares.

It has been argued that, without these achievements, scientific as well as commercial, 'Wellcome's legacy would have been of very little importance'. This ignores the fact that Henry Wellcome's legacy had been far greater than financial, and that his company and Trust prospered when they returned to the principles that he had established and pioneered, and which had, once again, been totally vindicated.

*

The story of the first fifty years of the Wellcome Trust has been described in considerable detail in a work that emphasises it was not at all a story of unbroken success, but of skill, resolution and dedication by Trustees and staff to expand its funds and activities to a far greater extent than even Wellcome could have envisaged.*

In 1963 Oliver (later Lord) Franks became Chairman of the Trust and remained so until 1981. Throughout his Chairmanship, Franks strongly believed that most of the profits of the company should be ploughed back in order to strengthen it so that it could compete effectively in the years ahead. Shepperd agreed with this view. In 1981 Franks was succeeded by Sir David Steel.

Until 1986 the Wellcome Foundation was wholly owned by the Trust, but, under Steel's leadership, in February of that year, after the courts had given permission to vary Wellcome's will, the Trust sold some twenty-one per cent of its shares in order to diversify its assets. In the following six years the new holding company for the group, Wellcome plc, prospered greatly, with the result that the sums

* A. R. Hall and B. A. Bembridge, *Physic and Philanthropy: A History of the Wellcome Trust 1936–86* (Cambridge, 1986).

available for research funding increased dramatically, from just under £20 million in 1985 to £100 million in 1992.

On 1 July 1990 Sir Alastair Frame succeeded Sir Alfred Shepperd as Chairman of the company. John Robb was appointed Chief Executive. Over the next three years, under this dynamic leadership, the company made further substantial progress and dividends paid to shareholders increased sharply. After Sir Alastair retired due to ill health, John Robb took over as Chairman and Chief Executive in September 1993.

In 1992 the Governors of the Trust decided to diversify further, as some ninety-five per cent of its assets were represented by its shareholding in Wellcome plc. The resulting international share sale raised over £2.3 billion, enabling the Trust to invest even more heavily in British medical science, to over £200 million in 1994, to the point that its annual expenditure almost matches that of the Medical Research Council; as a result, it is able to provide long-term support as well as a wide variety of short-term grants and training awards. The Professor of Cardiovascular Physiology at Oxford, Denis Noble, perhaps overstated the matter when he claimed that 'The Wellcome Trust has saved medical research in Britain', but the 1992 flotation drew considerable attention to what had been called 'an obscure medical charity in London'. The share sale was masterminded by Roger Gibbs, Steel's successor as Chairman (who was knighted in January 1994) – with stalwart support from the Trust's Finance and Legal Director, Ian Macgregor, and the Trust's newly appointed Director, Dr Bridget Ogilvie. Importantly, it received the wholehearted co-operation of the Board and senior management of the company.

In October 1992 the magnificently renovated and restored Wellcome Building in Euston Road was reoccupied, and part of the founder's collections and especially his unique library were provided with the setting that their richness deserved. It had been vacated by the Wellcome Foundation in 1989, and it was on the urgings of Williams that the Trustees agreed that it should be refashioned and rebuilt not only to house the Library and the staff of the Trust, but also as a suitably magnificent monument to Wellcome himself.

With its greatly increased resources the areas of research covered by the Trust had also expanded, including neuroscience, infection and immunity, pharmacology, molecular and cell biology, tropical disease and the history of medicine. It was suddenly realised outside the biomedical research community how important the Wellcome–Dale legacy had become. Although matters had not turned out quite as Wellcome had intended, his ultimate triumph was complete.

*

Assessments of Henry Wellcome's life and achievements at his death dwelt upon his undeniable achievements and then, after the publication of his Will, praised his generosity towards medical science and research in his adoptive country – few appreciating that he had left relatively little money to fulfil his posthumous ambitions. Private judgments were, however, more variable. With the exception of Wingate, he had outlived all those contemporaries who had really known him, and who had left few records about him. His employees had seen him as a kindly, but remote and formidable man whom few had even met, let alone known. His Trustees found themselves burdened with great commitments and duties and alarmingly few resources with which to honour them. It was to be many years before they could begin to do so, leaving some with the wholly erroneous and inaccurate feeling that Wellcome's real achievements had added up to very little. There are those who have suggested that the Wellcome Trust might be more appropriately called the Henry Dale Trust, so considerable was his personal contribution, and who have claimed that the fabled Wellcome collection was little more than a millionaire's obsession. Dale himself never made the first claim, and the second is belied by the quality of much of Wellcome's collection.

That Dale, his fellow-Trustees, and the skills of the company in America and Britain saved the Wellcome legacy is incontestable, but also is the fact that Wellcome created it. If from time to time Dale – and others – could be dismissive about his benefactor, and complain with some justification about the Will he and his fellow-Trustees had to administer, Dale never lost sight of Wellcome's essential vision, and nor have his successors. The result is not only one of the major international pharmaceutical companies in the world, but also the greatest single private contributor in Britain alone to medical science and research and the history of medicine. The influence of the pharmaceutical company in the development of new drugs, both in Britain and the United States, has been of incalculable value, and its own laboratories, and those financed through the Wellcome Trust, have brought into prominence and achievement the kind of men and women of outstanding quality that Wellcome always sought and paid for.

Here is the point. Having achieved wealth through his own endeavours, Wellcome did not devote it to himself. Perhaps if he had, his marriage might have turned out differently, although, given the disparities of age and personality, this seems unlikely. If he had spent too much on his archaeological expeditions and his collections, these had not been for himself.

*

Syrie long survived him, always an object of controversy, but staunchly supported by her many friends, particularly when she was excoriated by Maugham after her death. She seldom mentioned Wellcome's name; as Rebecca West shrewdly realised, Maugham had been the love of her life and his cruelty to her was a bitter reward. Their daughter Liza, after an unsuccessful first marriage, later married Lord John Hope (later Baron Glendevon), a prominent Conservative Member of Parliament and Foreign Office Minister. Mounteney, happily married, lived a placid country life of great contentment. He died in February 1987.

Admittedly, the width of Henry Wellcome's interests, although attractive and important in the man, had its defects. He had always craved recognition as well as wealth; after he had acquired the latter, the former became almost obsessive, although understandable. His work in the Sudan, in particular, had mixed motives. Part of it was genuinely altruistic; part was genuinely scientific; but part was equally genuinely self-promoting. His desire for official honours, particularly from the British, was in no sense dishonourable, as he had done so much for Britain, but the increasing amount of time he spent in the United States in his later years reveals his ambiguity of nationality. He had done everything he thought necessary to become an English gentleman, and fervently espoused English customs and society, but was never fully accepted as such. Also, in spite of the awards and honours rather belatedly conferred upon him by the medical and scientific worlds, he never really belonged to them either. Archaeologists willingly accepted his money, but never seriously considered him an archaeologist. His fascination for anthropology was lifelong and genuine, and his contribution not inconsiderable, but few modern anthropologists have heard of him. Very unfairly, and very wrongly, his collections have sometimes been regarded in museum circles as a joke. The British Museum and the Science Museum in London, and those who have had the advantage of studying at the Wellcome Institute for the History of Medicine, certainly do not regard them thus. And the investment he made into tropical medicine pays immense human dividends to this day. There was a form of genius in him that was, and is, inadequately appreciated. Indeed, he is virtually forgotten, a fate he would have especially resented.

He should be regarded not simply as a poor young American of ambition and ability who achieved much against formidable odds; nor only as a great entrepreneur and eventual benefactor; but as an exceptional man of vision. He began, as so many of us did, with high hopes and ambitions for which he was prepared to devote himself. Then, although so many were fulfilled triumphantly, others were not. As a result, his personality changed, and gregariousness was replaced by solitude and reclusiveness. But his creation, and his dreams, eventually triumphed. He had won, and of how many individuals can that be said?

## APPENDIX I

# Wellcome's Account of his 1878 Exploration in Ecuador

To reach the Southern portion of the Bosqe Guaranda a small steam launch plies between the city of Guayaquil and Pueblo Nuevo, a small town about 70 miles distant on one of the eastern branches of the Guayaquil River. The trip was an extremely interesting one; hundreds of Indian canoes and balsa rafts were met laden with fish, vegetables and fruit for the market.

We passed innumerable little floating islands covered with exuberant growths of aquatic plants. Loathsome alligators climbed up the river banks to bask in the warm sun; great numbers of white heron flocked along the shore. Here and there little hamlets of bamboo nestle in shady nooks surrounded by groves of oranges, mangoes and bananas.

Occasionally we are startled by the thundering boom of the ever-active volcano, Saugay. To the north, towering far above the clouds, we saw the lofty summit of Chimborazo, 'grand monarch of the Andes', a dazzling pinnacle of everlasting snow, emblematical of the spotless purity that presents a mocking contrast with the people who dwell upon its slopes and call it their Father. . . .

Arriving in Pueblo Nuovo, peons [servants] and beasts are engaged and equipped for the journey on muleback, or, as sometimes facetiously termed, 'On the hurricane deck of a mule'. All travel and transportation must be done on the backs of beasts or Indians as wheeled vehicles are useless for want of roads. In the higher altitudes llamas serve as beasts of burden, and in the valleys of Quito and Rio Bamba I have seen sheep, goats and cattle used for the same purpose.

The trail through the forest is simply a rough bridle path, worn by years of travel, though not improved by use, sometimes leading us through low marshy places of nearly bottomless mire where the beasts were nearly submerged. Proceeding to the interior the forest growths showed greater exuberance; the trees are so netted with vines, creepers and trailing lianas, and the foliage so closely woven together as to present almost impenetrable walls on either side of the way, draped with rich verdure, while leaves of bright and varying tints light up and relieve the sombre shades.

The many beautiful flowers attract and please, but do not so deeply impress and charm one as does the gorgeous foliage in which nature has so lavishly grouped the choicest gems and wrought such perfect harmony in her infinite variety of designs and rich colourings.

Occasionally we find clearings with extensive haciendas of Cacao, coffee, sugar cane, and halted for the night at one of these estates. The huts are constructed of bamboo, and erected on stilts, to prevent the entrance of animals and reptiles, as also for safety in times of floods, which frequently occur during the wet season. The house furnishing is very simple; neither chairs, tables, beds or stoves are found in these huts; fire is used for cooking only and is prepared on a flat rock or on the ground. The fare is quite as meagre; our bill consisted of caldo, locro and roasted plantain. Caldo is their most substantial dish; it is prepared by boiling together, in something like the style of an Irish stew, the tough, rank, meat of a gaunt black pig of the country, with potatoes, onions, garlic and chili peppers. Locro is a peculiar mushy soup, made by boiling potatoes and eggs together with various condiments. Plantains are roasted by burying them in hot coals and ashes before removing the peel. Food is served in a rough carved bowl of wood or calabash; the liquid portion taken with a wooden spoon and the solids fished out with the fingers.

The natives in these forests do not burden themselves with extensive wardrobes. The young, under 15 years of age, often appear in the innocence of perfect nakedness. There is something peculiarly fascinating about the careless simplicity of these people, their procrastinating manner of life and romantic surroundings. In the place of beds we found repose upon the floor; but the nights at the equator are too delightful for sleep; the skies are so clear and transparent that one can seem to peer into the remotest depths of space, and verily, to view the realms of deity. Nothing can surpass the enchanting splendours of the tropical skies; the stars shine out in the great azure dome with a brilliancy unknown in our northern climes, while myriads of more distant luminaries cluster like clouds in the background.

We miss the Dipper of the constellation of the Great Bear, but are amply repaid by a view of the Southern Cross in its stead.

The bright moon and starlight penetrating the foliage of the lofty forest trees produce mystic shadows delineating divers grotesque, unearthly forms, and adding to the weirdness of our surroundings, the lightning beetle flashes out a gleam of greenish yellow light, that, to the brilliancy of a diamond is like contrasting the electric light to a tallow dip.

Balmy, zephyr-like breezes gently fan us into such a dreamy fanciful mood, that we could easily have imagined ourselves transported to a fairyland, were it not for the ravenous onslaughts of cannibalistic fleas and mosquitoes forcibly reminding us that we are yet beings of flesh and blood.

At midnight the temperature fell to about 50 degrees Fahrenheit, and a damp clammy chill came over us making us wrap ourselves more closely in our blankets.

After continuing our journey for some distance into the foothills, we left the regular trail and struck into the newly cleared way to the North, keeping our peons ahead with machetes in hand to cut away the vines which hang in loops that threatened to catch beneath the chin, and jerk one from his beast. Very strong clothing is required for travelling through these forests for the many hooked branches play havoc with one's habit and cut ugly flesh wounds.

In crossing the rivers, a tree felled across from bank to bank served as a footbridge over which we passed while our mules were made to swim; it is not without considerable danger that these crossings are made, and frequently serious accidents occur. . . .

I was greatly disappointed on entering for the first time a tropical forest at midday by the almost oppressive silence that prevailed, and apparent want of animal life. Occasionally we heard the zip of a humming bird, and traced like a flash the glitter of its brilliant plumage in the sunlight as, for a moment, it darted from one flower to another, then, fairy like disappearing in an instant. Great numbers of beautiful butterflies floated silently past waving their banner like wings, resplendent with lustrous hues. Now and then a reptile glided across our pathway, and a gang of monkeys, taking fright at our approach, scrambled away into the tops of the higher trees.

Little else of animal life was seen during the day, but at twilight and in early morning the whole forest seemed to be alive; above all, in the hubbub of unearthly noises could be distinguished the shrill screeches of the macaws, toucans and parrots, and the yelling or howling of monkeys. Little music to be found in all these discordant sounds. It is remarkable that among the many tropical birds of gay plumage there are very few sweet songsters; their notes are nearly always harsh and shrill.

Getting fairly into the mountains the difficulties and dangers increase; zig-zagging up almost vertical cliffs, only to find steep descents, and descending then to climb again. In these mountains it is necessary to trust entirely to the mules. The sagacity of a mule is truly wonderful. They are the only safe animals for travelling in these mountains. Often having to go through narrow passageways between huge boulders, dodging projecting rocks, then winding our way round the mountain sides in narrow grooves, barely wide enough for the beast to get a footing along the verge of frightful precipices of several hundred to a thousand or more feet. In some of the older trails there can be seen in the far depths of the chasms below whitened skeletons of human beings and mules, and now and then ghastly human skulls are found placed in niches cut into the bank along the passage, invariably with a cross above them being tenderly suggestive of lurking dangers.

Words are inadequate to picture the terribly broken and precipitous character of these Andean ranges; on every side traces of ruptured violence is distinctly visible; every rock shows the marks of a tremendous crushing force; the irregular masses of rock and earth heaped together form tortuous ridges and bold craggy spurs, with numerous intersecting fissures, ravines and vast chasms; every physical feature is modelled on magnificence and grandeur. . . . In many places while penetrating the forests, we were obliged to dismount and climb, while our mules were lifted almost bodily up the jagged steeps by the peons; finally we reached a point beyond which it was impossible to take the animals. Leaving them in charge of a peon, we proceeded on foot, picking our way through the blind mazes of dense jungle, clambering over decaying trunks of fallen trees, continually ascending and descending steep places until we gained a point on one of the great spurs, where we saw spread out before us a boundless undulating sea of wilderness, as far as the eye could reach, a gorgeous expanse of matted verdure, illumined by showy blossoms of glowing colours. Here and there tall, slender columns of palms pierced the forest roof and gracefully waved aloft their drooping feathery branches.

The surpassing grandeur of this view was enrapturing beyond expression. On every hand the manifold and varied beauties unfolded themselves with almost bewildering rapidity; but suddenly a huge bank of clouds drifted upon us like a Newfoundland fog, curtailing the scene for a few moments and then quickly passing on.

Our guide soon described some Cinchonas in the distance with glistening leaves, which reflected brightly the vertical rays of the sun.

This characteristic reflex of the foliage, together with the bright roseate tints of the flowers, afford the means of discovering the Cinchonas amongst the mass of forest giants. In prospecting by the appearance of the leaves alone, a novice is easily misled by the India Rubber tree, which has a glossy leaf very like the magnolias of our southern states and when seen in the distance in the bright sunlight is easily mistaken for the Cinchona.

Our guide led us down a steep, slippering bank, formed of a reddish yellow clay which yielded like grease beneath our feet; we were obliged to cling to vines and limbs for support, as every few steps rocks would detach and fly crashing through the thickets below, finally reaching the bottom of the ravine we followed the sinuous course of a small stream, until suddenly our guide shouted 'Cascarilla!' (Spanish word for bark) and we were gladdened by the sight of several fair-sized trees of Cinchona on the slope nearby.

The older Cinchona trees as found, in the virgin forest, are really very grand and handsome. They appear to seek the most secluded and inaccessible depths of the forest for their habitation. They are rarely grouped in large numbers or close together, but are distinguished in more or less irregular, scattering patches; sometimes single trees are found widely separated from any others of its family, variety and diversity are notable features of tropical forests.

The Cinchona Succiruba ranges from forty to eighty feet in height, trunks straight and branches regular; leaves opposite, evergreen, broadly oval, six to ten inches in length, of a rich, dark green colour, sometimes tinged with crimson, the upper surface of an almost waxy lustre, pubescent beneath, finely veined, mid-rib decided and strong.

The flowers have a five-toothed superior calyx and tubular corolla, are arranged in terminal pinacles of bright rose tint and diffuse a pleasing fragrance.

The capsules are ovoid and contain thirty or forty flattened seeds, winged all around by a broad membrane, irregularly toothed and lacerated at the margin. The bark of the large tree is usually completely covered and fringed with mosses of the most delicate, lace-like texture, interspersed with lustrous lichens and prettily marked diminutive trailing ferns. Air plants and vines in profusion entwine themselves among the branches and hang in graceful festoons, forming hammocks in which cluster an abundance of parasitic growths, particularly of the orchid family; these plants cling to every limb and vine flourishing in their fullest splendour, exhibiting many remarkable phenomena in their curious mimicry of insect and animal forms. Vegetable growths develop with wonderful luxuriance beneath the almost dismal shades of the closely interlacing branches which permit but the faintest rays of sunlight to ever filter through their rich leafy drapery; everything saturated and dripping with moisture, the very air we breathed seemed a clammy vapour. In these forests the atmospheric changes are continuous and very abrupt; drifting banks of gloomy clouds are followed by glaring sunshine and then tempestuous showers all in rapid succession.

[Wellcome's paper then describes in some detail the techniques for stripping the bark and conveying it to ports; he was shocked by the extremely low pay that the workers received, and the hazards that they faced.] The malaria in some of the forest valleys is simply fearful, and owing to great exposure and want of nutritious food the Indians yield very quickly to its influence. I was told by a bark merchant that during a severe malarial season, as many as 25% of the Indians employed in one district died from fevers before the harvest was completed. Malarial fevers are regarded with great terror by the Indians, and it is only by extreme poverty, or obligation as peons, that they are induced to enter the bark forest to encounter the dangers for the meagre pittance of 10 to 25 cents per day.

As regards the prospects of further supplies of Cinchona barks from the native forests of South America, the outlook is exceedingly discouraging, the greatly increased use of Cinchona alkaloids during the past few years, with the consequent demand for larger supplies of bark, has caused a very thorough working of the old forests and energetic seeking for new ones. The discoveries of paying forests are becoming more and more rare every year, and the new forests are found at greater distances from the shipping ports and more difficult of access.

The track of country yielding the Cinchona is not so unlimited as some writers would give us to believe, nor is the supply inexhaustible; it is a fact recognised by natives and dealers, who are well informed about the extent and resources of the Cinchona bearing districts, that if the present ruinous system of destroying the trees is continued, and no effort made to propagate new growths, they will before many years be exterminated from their native soil.

# APPENDIX 2

# Glossary of Selected Wellcome Institutions

Wellcome was a prolific founder of institutions. The following is a glossary of those founded by him and those which grew out of them. For the sake of brevity the history of each institution is presented in simplified form.

Institutions which have their own entry in the glossary are in *italics*.

**Burroughs Wellcome & Co.** A partnership established in London in 1880 by Silas M. Burroughs and Henry S. Wellcome. The precursor company to the *Wellcome Foundation Ltd.* The head office was in Snow Hill, Holborn, and the principal factory at Dartford, Kent.

**Burroughs Wellcome Co.** The subsidiary of *Wellcome plc* concerned with commercial pharmaceutical activities in the United States of America.

**The Wellcome Building** 183–93 Euston Road, London NW1. Originally called the *Wellcome Research Institution*, renamed the Wellcome Building in 1955.

**Wellcome Bureau of Scientific Research** Set up by Henry Wellcome in 1913. From 1924 a unit of the *Wellcome Foundation Ltd.* It carried out research in tropical medicine. Administratively it included as affiliated bodies Wellcome's other UK museums and laboratories. In 1946 its research laboratories became the *Wellcome Laboratories of Tropical Medicine*.

**Wellcome Chemical Research Laboratories** Established by Henry Wellcome in 1896 at 6 King Street, London EC1, with F. B. Power as Director. From 1913 affiliated to the *Wellcome Bureau of Scientific Research*.

From 1924 part of the *Wellcome Foundation Ltd.* In 1932 moved to the *Wellcome Research Institution.* In the 1940s the name Wellcome Chemical Research Laboratories was taken over by a chemistry laboratory at Beckenham, Kent, which in 1946 combined with the *Wellcome Physiological Research Laboratories* to form the *Wellcome Research Laboratories.*

**Wellcome Entomological Field Laboratory** Established by Henry Wellcome in 1920. Joined the *Wellcome Laboratories of Tropical Medicine* *c.* 1948.

**The Wellcome Foundation Ltd** A private limited company set up in 1924 to unite all of Henry Wellcome's commercial and non-commercial activities. After Wellcome's death the non-commercial activities were gradually transferred to the *Wellcome Trust.* From 1986 a subsidiary of *Wellcome plc.* In Wellcome's lifetime its head office was in Snow Hill, Holborn.

**Wellcome Historical Medical Library** The collection of books and other documents built up by Sir Henry Wellcome between about 1898 and his death in 1936. From 1913 a part of the *Wellcome Historical Medical Museum.* In 1968 it became the Library of the *Wellcome Institute for the History of Medicine.*

**Wellcome Historical Medical Museum** The collection of antiquities built up by Sir Henry Wellcome from about 1898 and under his personal direction until his death in 1936. Formally established in 1913 and affiliated to the *Wellcome Bureau of Scientific Research.* From 1924 one of the non-commercial units of the *Wellcome Foundation Ltd.* From 1961 a part of the *Wellcome Trust.* Located in various buildings in London, principally at 54a Wigmore Street (1911–32) and the *Wellcome Building* on Euston Road (1932–47, 1954–68). In 1968 became the Museum of the *Wellcome Institute for the History of Medicine.*

**Wellcome Institute for the History of Medicine** A body established by the *Wellcome Trust* in 1968 in the *Wellcome Building* on Euston Road, London. It comprises Sir Henry Wellcome's Library (with subsequent new accessions) and an Academic Unit active in research and teaching in the history of medicine and related subjects, and affiliated to University College London. Until 1977 the Institute also included the former *Wellcome Historical Medical Museum*, which then moved to the Science Museum, South Kensington, and became the *Wellcome Museum of the History of Medicine*.

**Wellcome Laboratories of Tropical Medicine** From 1946, took over the research functions of the *Wellcome Bureau of Scientific Research* in the *Wellcome Research Institution*. In 1965 moved to Beckenham, Kent, and joined the *Wellcome Research Laboratories*.

**Wellcome Museum of the History of Medicine** The successor organisation to the Museum of the *Wellcome Institute for the History of Medicine*, consisting of antiquities of medical history and related subjects collected by Sir Henry Wellcome (enlarged by subsequent new accessions). A part of the Science Museum, South Kensington, to which it was transferred on indefinite loan from the *Wellcome Trust* in 1977–82.

**Wellcome Museum of Medical Science** The successor organisation to the *Wellcome Museum of Tropical Medicine and Hygiene*. A teaching museum, it was in the *Wellcome Research Institution* (later *Wellcome Building*) from 1932 to 1939 and from 1945 to 1985. Succeeded by the *Wellcome Tropical Institute*.

**Wellcome Museum of Tropical Medicine and Hygiene** Established in 1914 as part of the *Wellcome Bureau of Scientific Research*. Succeeded in 1926 by the *Wellcome Museum of Medical Science*.

**Wellcome Physiological Research Laboratories** Established by Henry Wellcome at Brockwell Hall, south London, in 1899, the laboratories took over from an earlier laboratory set up by Burroughs Wellcome & Co. in 1894 for production of anti-toxins. The laboratories carried out both commercial work (e.g. quality control) and important scientific research. From 1913 affiliated to the *Wellcome Bureau of Scientific Research*. In 1922 moved to Beckenham, Kent. From 1924 part of the *Wellcome Foundation Ltd*. In 1946 combined with the *Wellcome Chemical Research Laboratories* to form the *Wellcome Research Laboratories*.

**Wellcome plc** A commercial pharmaceutical company registered in 1986 and quoted on the London Stock Exchange. The parent company to the Wellcome group of companies.

**Wellcome Research Institution** The collective name of the research museums and laboratories originally housed in the building constructed by Sir Henry Wellcome in 1931–2 at 183–93 Euston Road, London NW1. In 1955 the building was named the *Wellcome Building*.

**Wellcome Research Laboratories** The UK laboratories of the *Wellcome Foundation Ltd*, in Beckenham, Kent. The successor organisation to the *Wellcome Physiological Research Laboratories*, the *Wellcome Chemical Research Laboratories*, and the *Wellcome Laboratories of Tropical Medicine*.

**Wellcome Tropical Institute** Established by the *Wellcome Trust* from 1985 to 1988 to take over the functions of the *Wellcome Museum of Medical Science* in facilitating the teaching of tropical medicine. Succeeded by the *Wellcome Tropical Resource*.

**Wellcome Tropical Research Laboratories** Founded by Henry Wellcome in 1903 at Gordon Memorial College, Khartoum. Under the control of the Sudan Government since 1913.

**Wellcome Tropical Resource** From 1993 a unit of the *Wellcome Trust* concerned with producing teaching aids in tropical medicine. Successor to the *Wellcome Tropical Institute*.

**The Wellcome Trust** A British registered charity established by the Will of Sir Henry Wellcome upon his death in 1936. On his death the ownership of 100 per cent of the shares of the Wellcome pharmaceutical company passed to the Wellcome Trust. The Trust retained this holding until 1986, after which, by sale of shares in 1986 and 1992, it reduced its holding to about 40 per cent of *Wellcome plc* in order to diversify its assets. In accordance with Wellcome's will, the Wellcome Trust supports research in medicine and its history.

In addition other institutions have buildings called Wellcome Laboratory, Wellcome Library, Wellcome Museum, Wellcome Gallery, Wellcome Unit, etc., so named because they were constructed or equipped with the aid of a grant or other support from the *Wellcome Trust*.

# Index

## A



## B

## C



## D

E

## H



## I/J

# M

## N



## O/P/Q

# R

## Y/Z